FIGHTING CROSS-BORDER CARTELS

This book is the first detailed treatment of the approaches taken to enforce competition laws against cross-border cartels (CBCs) from the perspective of young and small competition authorities (more than 70% of the total number of authorities worldwide). No other legal or inter-disciplinary scholarship exists in the market that deals with the issue of a taxonomy of CBCs combined with young/small competition authorities' problems.

The book looks at the extent of the harms caused by CBCs and issues associated with tackling them at a transnational level. It explains why past solutions to problems with cooperation have failed and proposes novel ideas on how to improve cooperation and coordination in certain types of CBC investigations (transnational and regional CBCs). The proposals are based on primary-source information and observations made by the author as part of his work in the UN, and interviews with leading enforcers from young, small, old and large jurisdictions.

Young/small competition authorities, competition lawyers and economists, scholars and students within the fields of competition law and international law, and those interested in international cooperation and coordination in the area of cartel enforcement in emerging markets will greatly benefit from this book. It is clearly structured and extensively referenced, providing a valuable guide to the topic.

Volume 25 in the series Hart Studies in Competition Law

Hart Studies in Competition Law

Media Ownership and Control: Law, Economics and Policy in an Indian and International Context
Suzanne Rab and Alison Sprague

The Interface between Competition and the Internal Market: Market Separation under Article 102 TFEU
Vasiliki Brisimi

Anti-Cartel Enforcement in a Contemporary Age: Leniency Religion
Edited by Caron Beaton-Wells and Christopher Tran

Public Procurement and the EU Competition Rules
Albert Sánchez Graells

The Concept of Abuse in EU Competition Law: Law and Economic Approaches
Pınar Akman

The Competitive Effects of Minority Shareholdings: Legal and Economic Issues
Panagiotis Fotis and Nikolaos Zevgolis

The More Economic Approach to EU Antitrust Law
Anne C Witt

Private Power, Online Information Flows and EU Law
Angela Daly

The Role of Competitors in the Enforcement of State Aid Law
Fernando Pastor-Merchante

The Legality of Bailouts and Buy Nationals: International Trade Law in a Crisis
Kamala Dawar

A Critical Account of Article 106(2) TFEU: Government Failure in Public Service Provision
Jarleth Burke

Dawn Raids Under Challenge
Helene Andersson

A Framework for European Competition Law: Co-ordinated Diversity
Christopher Townley

Evidence Standards in EU Competition Enforcement: The EU Approach
Andriani Kalintiri

The Metaphysics of Market Power: The Zero-sum Competition and Market Manipulation Model
George Raitt

Competition Law's Innovation Factor: The Relevant Market in Dynamic Contexts in the EU and US
Viktoria H.S.E. Robertson

Competition, Effects and Predictability: Rule of Law and the Economic Approach to Competition
Bruce Wardhaugh

Fighting Cross-Border Cartels

The Perspective of the Young and Small Competition Authorities

Pierre Horna

•HART•

OXFORD • LONDON • NEW YORK • NEW DELHI • SYDNEY

HART PUBLISHING
Bloomsbury Publishing Plc
Kemp House, Chawley Park, Cumnor Hill, Oxford, OX2 9PH, UK
1385 Broadway, New York, NY 10018, USA

HART PUBLISHING, the Hart/Stag logo, BLOOMSBURY and the Diana logo are trademarks of Bloomsbury Publishing Plc

First published in Great Britain 2020

A catalogue record for this book is available from the British Library.

Library of Congress Cataloging-in-Publication data

Names: Horna, Pierre, 1978- author.

Title: Fighting cross-border cartels : the perspective of the young and small competition authorities / Pierre Horna.

Description: Oxford ; New York : Hart, 2020. | Series: Hart studies in competition law ; vol 25 | Based on author's thesis (doctoral – Graduate Institute of International and Development Studies (Geneva, Switzerland), 2018) issued under title: Cartels in Latin America : a cross-border competition assessment.

Identifiers: LCCN 2019052345 (print) | LCCN 2019052346 (ebook) | ISBN 9781509933686 (hardcover) | ISBN 9781509933693 (Epub)

Subjects: LCSH: Cartels—Developing countries.

Classification: LCC K3854 .H67 2020 (print) | LCC K3854 (ebook) | DDC 364.10609172/4—dc23

LC record available at https://lccn.loc.gov/2019052345

LC ebook record available at https://lccn.loc.gov/2019052346

ISBN: HB: 978-1-50993-368-6
ePDF: 978-1-50993-370-9
ePub: 978-1-50993-369-3

Typeset by Compuscript Ltd, Shannon
Printed and bound in Great Britain by CPI Group (UK) Ltd, Croydon CR0 4YY

MIX
Paper from responsible sources
FSC® C013604
www.fsc.org

To find out more about our authors and books visit www.hartpublishing.co.uk. Here you will find extracts, author information, details of forthcoming events and the option to sign up for our newsletters.

To Melanie

FOREWORD

Rapid technological developments in transport, communication, and information, along with the rise of the Internet of Things and the spread of market fundamentalism across huge swathes of economies, have profoundly changed the global landscape of trade and commerce. These developments have substantially reduced transaction costs, greatly facilitating people's mobility and expanding opportunities for trade of goods, services, and innovations between and within economies. With globalisation, economies have become more integrated and interconnected; many of them, particularly those in Asia, have succeeded in growing many times over in the past 50 years.

To be sure, the benefits of globalisation have been uneven across and within economies. The evidence suggests that globalisation is a powerful force for economic growth and poverty reduction in developing economies if, to begin with, their domestic policies and institutions, including regulatory regimes, promote efficient resource allocation, trade and investment, and innovation. An effective competition policy that allows markets to work well for the long-term benefits of consumers is part of this favourable condition for globalization to achieve inclusive development.

Cross-border cartels can reduce the benefits of globalisation to developing economies. Cartelisation has been facilitated partly by the high levels of concentration for certain commodities, products, and services at either the global or regional level. With the rise of the Internet of Things technologies, cross-border cartels have become a more pressing and pervasive issue now than at any other period in modern economic history. These technologies that have allowed consumers and societies to enjoy the benefits of expanded trade, on one hand, may enhance the incentive and ability for cross-border collusive conduct, on the other, whether through price fixing or market allocation arrangements. For developing economies, the effects of such conduct is particularly egregious to consumers if the product or service accounts for a relatively high proportion of their incomes (eg, food or pharmaceutical products), or represents an important factor of production for their economic activities (eg, fuel or fertilizer). Even if the conduct results in small price changes only, the cumulative effects could be detrimental to society, particularly the poor. In these economies, the overwhelming majority of the population have low levels of per capita income; enforcement institutions are weak; and there is limited bureaucratic capacity to address the most binding constraints to development. Predictably, they are technological laggards and must rely on the inflow of foreign investments and trade to access more advanced technologies and products.

Hence, consumers in small developing economies are critically handicapped in the face of cross-border cartels: anticompetitive conduct (which is likely to go undetected, given weak institutional capacity) reduces the already meager disposable incomes of the poor. Multinational companies looking to invest in developing economies may find themselves facing high or prohibitive input costs because of these acts of collusion. Such situation may lead them to defer or shift their operations elsewhere. As a result, the economy is deprived of much needed technological upgrading and job growth, so that it is kept at low income levels. The increasing evidence demonstrating how the concentration of market power and growing political influence are intertwined lends further weight to the concern that the issue of cross-border collusion is not receiving the attention it deserves.

It is imperative that policymakers in developing economies address key issues that hound market competition, including those that explicitly prevent the forces of competition from significantly increasing economic welfare and contributing to social objectives such as poverty reduction.

This book, *Fighting Cross-Border Cartels: The Perspective of the Young and Small Competition Authorities*, is both timely and relevant, especially to young or small competition authorities in developing economies who continue to get their bearings and situate antitrust policy within their economies' development strategies. Drawing from his extensive experience in antitrust implementation and international cooperation, Pierre Horna explores the characteristics and issues surrounding cases of cross-border cartel behaviour and proposes approaches to analysing and tackling them. New competition agencies will find the frameworks offered by the author to be definitively path-breaking and useful, as international networks for coordination of enforcement activities become part of the norm for competition authorities. The exposition makes prudent use of the lessons of history, as it draws on the experiences of other jurisdictions involving several of the most widely recognized cases of cross-border cartels.

The volume has placed cross-border cartel analysis some notches higher. It is a must-read for antitrust enforcers, private-sector practitioners, policymakers, development agencies, academics, and students of competition law and policy, especially in developing economies.

Professor Arsenio M. Balisacan
Chairman
Philippine Competition Commission
31 August 2019

ACKNOWLEDGEMENTS

In writing this book, I have benefited greatly from the counsel and comments of a number of people who helped develop and refine my analysis and arguments. In the early stage of drafting this manuscript, between 2010 and 2012, numerous enforcers were interviewed, in particular from Central America. In 2013, I was able to participate in the most important regional cooperation scheme in Latin America, and this owed much to openness, cooperation and commitment of three heads of competition authorities at the time: Felipe Irarrázabal (Chile), German Bacca (Colombia) and Hebert Tassano (Peru).

During the period from 2013 until 2016, I had the valuable opportunity of expanding my research to the South East Asia region. In this connection, I am particularly grateful for the conversations and insights about cross-border cartels in emerging markets provided by Dr Nawir Messi, the then-Chairman of the competition authority of Indonesia.

Embarking then on the final stage of drafting my manuscript in 2017, I was able to build on conversations and observations from additional competition enforcers and academics from around the world. My special thanks go to Scott Hammond, David Anderson and Russel Damtoft (USA), Marisa Tierno (Spain), Paulo Burnier Da Silveira and Fernando Furlan (Brazil), Antonio Capobianco (OECD), Luis Guzmán (Nicaragua), Saadaki Suwasono (Japan) and Anna Pozdnyakova (Russia). Furthermore, I am indebted to the 22 enforcers interviewed at the annual conference of the International Competition Network (ICN), held in Portugal in May 2017. Many of their inputs and insights contributed to the practical proposals made in chapters eight and nine of the book.

Let me also acknowledge the extensive support by the Centre for Competition Law and Policy at the University of Oxford, and Professor Ariel Ezrachi, Professor of Competition Law in Oxford and Director of the Centre. It was an honour for me to complete my manuscript between January and June 2017 in Oxford. Several other academics commented on specific chapters of my manuscript during that period, notably Professors Mihail Danov, Julian Nowag and Maurice Stucke. Moreover, Leonila Papa provided me with substantive and editorial support. Finally, I would like to thank Sita Zimpel for her critical eye in reviewing an updated version of my manuscript that would eventually be published as this book.

Last but definitely not least, throughout the years since 2009, two critical persons have always supported me in this academic adventure: my thesis supervisor, Professor Joost Pauwelyn, and my wife, Melanie. My eternal thanks go to them both, as it is their trust and confidence that has kept me committed to this work, in the knowledge that it will constitute value added to the discourse on international cooperation, cross-border cartels and competition policy. May this book be useful in promoting the subject, and providing guidance, particularly to young and small competition authorities in the developing countries.

Geneva,
15 August 2019

CONTENTS

PART II
CHALLENGES OF CROSS-BORDER COOPERATION IN MULTIJURISDICTIONAL CARTEL ENFORCEMENT

PART III
NOVEL PROPOSALS TO TARGET SELECTED TYPES OF CROSS-BORDER CARTELS

Introduction

> It was a criminal case unlike any in the history of law enforcement. For years, a top executive with one of America's most politically powerful companies worked as a cooperating government witness, providing evidence of a vast international conspiracy. With little obvious incentives, Mark Whitacre secretly recorded colleagues and competitors as they illegally divided world markets among themselves, setting far higher prices for their products than free competition would allow.[1]

The unprecedented true story of the lysine cartel that affected American, Japanese and many other consumers around the world was discovered thanks to the unusual cooperation of a whistle-blower, Mr Whitacre, during the 1990s. The FBI's investigation of the lysine cartel forms an important junction in the history of cartel enforcement, triggering several changes in international cooperation mechanisms across many jurisdictions throughout the world. Businesses in the US are now much more mindful about the impact of fixing prices with competitors. Even current influential world leaders who once were businessmen said that 'cartel … it's a total illegal monopoly – [which] if businesses ever formed … everybody would be put in jail'.[2]

Did the case herald a shift in the global community's ability to curtail cartel activities? Perhaps, but unfortunately, the reality has proven to be rather challenging. While the lysine cartel case is considered a success story in cartel investigation, the fight against cartels is on-going and becoming more difficult than ever. Between 2000 and 2016, 75 new multinational cartels were uncovered each year.[3] However, the sad fact is that despite all the extraordinary efforts by lead jurisdictions such as the US, the EU and Japan, among other large or mature jurisdictions throughout the world, it is believed that a great number of cartels remain undetected.

More than 100,000 companies (7,200 named) were found liable for international price-fixing, with gross overcharges exceeding $1.5 trillion, 60 per cent of which are attributed to cartels.[4] Cartels, as a result, can make substantial profits worldwide, and in some cases, the deterrence provoked by heavier sanctions in

[1] Eichenwald (2009: 7).

[2] In 2008, Donald J Trump, the current US President said: 'Every time they lower interest rates the cartel, because I call it a cartel, the illegal monopoly, raises oil prices. So the monopoly, because that is all it is, it's a total illegal monopoly – if businesses ever formed OPEC, everybody would be put in jail – here they are, and every time a country hits oil, they are invited into the cartel. It's a disgrace.' CNBC, 'Donald Trump Revealed His Plan for Squeezing OPEC in 2008'.

[3] Connor, 'International Cartel Stats'.

[4] ibid.

mature or large jurisdictions might be insufficient to successfully deter the occurrence of these cartels across other jurisdictions with weaker enforcement records.[5]

In addition, evidence shows that these large-scale international unlawful business activities have severely impacted not only consumer welfare in developing and developed countries, but also producers' welfare, notably in the developing world and countries in transition.

In fact, these cartels have caused tremendous damage to economies, especially emerging markets, as they limit the benefits from international trade[6] and access to global supply chains. The effects on developing countries are particularly pronounced, with these countries heavily reliant on imports of goods from industries involved in price-fixing conspiracies.[7] These imports represented 6.7 per cent of all imports and 1.2 per cent of gross domestic product in developing countries. For the poorest developing countries, cartels represent an even larger percentage of trade, namely 8.8 per cent of all imports. The actual effect on developing countries may even be more profound, considering that the foregoing figures suffer from a downward bias, as they pertain only to discovered cartels, and cover the effects of only that one anti-competitive practice.[8]

Catching the Uncatchable

The difficulty in detecting cartels is attributable to a number of reasons, one of which is that many of the cartels detected involve intermediate goods[9] that are not well-known or interesting to the general public, particularly those in jurisdictions which have relatively young competition regimes. It does not help that the term 'cartel' has been associated with drug cartels. Indeed, the industries involved in cartels are so alien to the public that these cartels remain relatively obscure and interest only a select group of individuals, such as public policy-makers, competition authorities, and practitioners. The lysine, liquid oxygen and cement cartels, which have impacted Latin American markets for years, remain unfamiliar to many. 'For most people, international cartels bring to mind collusion in drug, oil and diamond, certainly not in vitamins or bromine, or seamless steel tubes'.[10]

One type of cartel, the cross-border cartel (CBC), is of special concern because of its massive effect on consumers in different jurisdictions.[11] An example of a

[5] Michaels (2016: 236).

[6] The relationship between international cartels as obstacles to international trade has been well studied since 1944. See Edwards (1944).

[7] Evenett, Levenstein and Suslow f(2001).

[8] Noonan (2008: 59–68).

[9] LeClair (2011).

[10] Yu, (2003: 3).

[11] The term 'Cross-Border Cartel' is extensively discussed in ch 1.

CBC is the international aluminium cartel, which ran undetected for almost 100 years from 1901. It is only in recent decades that the enforcement of competition rules became robust in the developed world and some emerging economies, resulting in an unprecedented number of detected and sanctioned CBCs, such as those involving citric acid (1991–95), ferrosilicon (1989–91), graphite electrodes (1992–97), lysine (1992–95), shipping (Far East) (1991–94), shipping (North Atlantic), sodium gluconate (1993–95), sorbates (1979–96) and vitamins (1990–99).[12]

In the elusive quest to enhance enforcement efforts, the role of cooperation amongst mature and large jurisdictions is noteworthy, as their concerted action can significantly increase the deterrence of these activities across the world.

The pressing need for international cooperation to restrain the harmful effects of CBCs has prompted policy-makers from different jurisdictions to execute cooperation agreements between competition authorities.[13] There has also been an increased enactment of competition laws and establishment of competition authorities in the emerging economies as well as countries in transition across continents. By 2019, competition laws and authorities were in place in 141 jurisdictions.[14] With more and more competition authorities coming in, mature competition authorities and international organisations[15] have taken the lead in shaping the path of international cooperation. The dynamics of cooperation between different jurisdictions can be classified as follows: mature or large, to young or small competition authorities on the one hand, and young or large, to young or small competition authorities on the other.

Despite the advances made by the competition community, significant barriers remain that hamper attempts to unleash the full potential of international cooperation in CBC enforcement. A number of recurrent issues are often cited by competition authorities as to why cooperation fails, particularly in the relations between mature or large to young or small competition authorities, as well as young or large to young or small competition authorities.[16]

[12] Levenstein and Suslow (2003: 807–11).

[13] Beyond the attempts to include an international authority to deal with competition matters worldwide such as in the Havana Charter in 1948 and then in the WTO in 1996.

[14] Federal Trade Commission (2019).

[15] There are likewise important efforts on international cooperation at the multilateral level between international organisations, such as the Organization for Economic Cooperation and Development (OECD), the United Nations Conference on Trade and Development (UNCTAD), and successful international networks of competition agencies, such as the International Competition Network (ICN). These international actors have played an unprecedented role in providing assistance, advisory services and valuable reflections on improving international cooperation amidst the enactment of competition laws across the globe. In practice, however, these efforts have not always translated into effective collaboration, especially when small economies and agencies are involved. OECD, ICN and UNCTAD can be regarded as the main international networks that work at the global basis for further coordination and technical assistance activities.

[16] The difference between 'young or small' and 'mature or larger' competition authorities is discussed in ch 2.

Pathways to Cooperation in Cartel Enforcement

This research sets out to explore the complex and sometimes inconsistent enforcement landscape relating to CBCs, and the range of incentives at stake. Its aim is to offer avenues to empower young and small competition authorities and improve their capacity to cope with cartel activity at the international level. At this, experimental solutions from an inter-disciplinary approach are provided for young and small competition authorities, particularly those located in the Latin American region.

For young or small competition authorities, the most notable challenge lies in interacting with their larger or more mature peers when initating investigations of CBCs. Before discussing this problem in-depth, it is necessary to differentiate between five distinct categories of CBCs: export, import, multinational, transnational, and regional CBCs.

A case study described in chapter seven forms the basis for the novel solutions proposed. There are a number for reasons why the jurisdictions in Latin America are a showcase for effectively addressing CBCs. First, they possess a wealth of enforcement experience:

1. the majority of the competition authorities in Latin America are young or small, but some countries such as Brazil and Mexico are considered young but large jurisdictions, thus necessitating regional cooperation between large/young authorities and small/young authorities;
2. the competition authorities of Latin America have a workable experience in the domestic enforcement of anti-cartel laws with respect to investigating inter-linked regionally connected sectors due to intraregional trade; and
3. Latin America can provide valuable insights into the organisation of sub-regional supranational competition authorities and the lessons learned for other sub-regional groupings across the region and elsewhere. This particularly concerns the experiences of some member states of the Andean Community (Bolivia, Colombia, Ecuador and Peru) that reactivated a sub-regional supranational authority during 2016, an example that could be replicated in other sub-regions, both within Latin America and beyond.

Secondly, the Latin American experience poses an interesting and viable model for young competition authorities, as the region's efforts are generally considered above average compared to other young or small competition authorities.[17]

[17] For instance, in the ASEAN region, the enforcement of anti-cartel laws is asymmetric, ie Singapore, Indonesia, Vietnam with better and longer enforcement records than the rest of the countries of the ASEAN community where competition laws were only enacted in the past four years since 2015. As a result, regional cooperation schemes are only at a nascent stage with the implementation of the ASEAN Regional Cooperation Framework. Similarly, in the African, CIS, Balkan regions, efforts to implement anti-cartel laws at the domestic level are also underway, but enforcement at the regional level is still scant. Some regional groupings (notably in Africa and CIS) have set up regional competition authorities, for example SADC and COMESA as well as WAEMU and the Eurasian Economic Union in the CIS region.

Lastly, bilateral, trilateral, regional cooperation[18] between Latin American countries, while still focused on selected countries and/or sub-regions, is evolving rapidly thanks to the revitalisation of old regional competition schemes (such as the Andean Community of Nations) and the creation of new ones (notably the Central American Network of Competition Authorities), along with the establishment of informal cooperation agreements (e.g. the 'Lima Declaration' between Colombia, Chile and Peru launched in September 2013 and the 'Strategic Alliance' between Argentina, Brazil, Chile and Mexico launched in April 2017).

Dismantling Perceptions about CBCs in the Developing World

This research strives to inevitably dismantle the following six (mis)perceptions about CBCs.

Perception 1: Younger or Smaller Competition Authorities Should Prioritise Going after Domestic Cartels before Investigating Complex CBCs

A number of general factors facilitate the successful prosecution of a cartel by newer or smaller competition authorities, whether international or domestic. Many newer or smaller competition authorities, however, mistakenly assume that domestic cartel investigations are low-hanging fruit and should therefore take precedence over international cartel enforcement. In reality, evidence points to the fact that many newer jurisdictions have found more success in prosecuting a CBC compared to cracking domestic cartels as the latter are often affected by capture and other local dynamics.

[18] The available tools for cooperation between competition authorities in the fight against international cartels are abundant. These include bilateral cooperation agreements which can be formal (eg, memoranda of understanding and competition provisions in regional trade agreements) or informal (eg, the 'Lima Declaration'). Indeed, a substantial number of bilateral cooperation agreements between competition authorities have been signed in recent years, not only involving major jurisdictions but also emerging economies such as Russia and China. Geopolitics has played a crucial role in deciding which major jurisdictions are willing to sign MOUs with emerging jurisdictions, and it is expected that the latter will be intensified in the years to come. More advanced competition authorities have also found ways to cooperate in investigations in worldwide cartel investigations. Many countries that have entered into trade agreements have introduced competition provisions, such as in the South-South and North-South RTAs. While some of these agreements have a good level of detail in the type of conduct that would be considered anti-competitive, and some of them even create a regional authority to investigate and issue binding resolutions, there is still a long way to go in order to reach full implementation of these agreements in terms of cases dealt at the regional level.

Perception 2: Cross-Border Cartels are All the Same, and there are One-Size-Fits-All Solutions

For more mature and larger competition authorities, CBCs are all the same. However, from the perspective of younger and smaller competition authorities, it matters whether a cartel is multinational, transnational, regional, or export, or import in scope. They need to be more selective and thus to understand the nature, formation and potential impact of different types of CBCs in order to determine an effective investigative approach, not least in light of limited resources (and capacities) at their disposal.

Therefore, a distinction should be made between multinational and transnational CBCs. Multinational CBCs are those international conspiracies where the world market is considerably affected. Transnational CBCs are also international conspiracies but with a more limited effect because the conspiracy relates to selected key markets, including emerging markets or small-sized markets. This distinction is important for newer and smaller competition authorities as they are under greater pressure to prioritise their enforcement actions in light of limited resources. They might therefore opt for investigating a transnational CBC for its potential deterrent effect and considering the limited jurisdiction affected by the CBC. In other words, compared to a multinational CBC, a transnational CBC might be more manageable for a younger competition authority.

Perception 3: Regional CBCs can only be Successfully Targeted by Effective Regional Competition Authorities

Ideally, the establishment of regional competition authorities is the best solution to target regional CBCs. However, in the absence of a regional authority, it is still possible for national competition authorities to investigate regional CBCs through effectively coordinated actions, even in cases where their procedural rules vary. In this regard, novel ideas and solutions to deal with regional CBCs will be shown for national competition authorities at different stages of maturity.

Perception 4: Anti-Cartel Laws in Emerging Markets are Still in their Infancy

According to conventional wisdom, anti-cartel enforcement records are limited in emerging markets where newer or smaller competition authorities exist. Contrary to that view, emerging jurisdictions, such as key BRICS member countries as well as selected larger jurisdictions in different other economic groupings have already developed a significant track record of anti-cartel enforcement within a relatively short period of time. At this, developments in emerging economies, such as Latin

America and the ASEAN region, can hardly be underestimated or overlooked in the discussion of CBC enforcement.

Perception 5: Trust is the First Issue to Look at when Dealing with Younger Jurisdictions

While trust is indeed a general concern in international cooperation on CBC investigations, there are already well-established mechanisms between more mature competition authorities, based on intensive and repeated engagement which has been facilitated by both endogenous and exogenous factors. This is also acknowledged and trusted by international or multinational companies as well as law firms. However, for newer and smaller competition authorities, the question of trust arises on two levels: between competition authorities, as well as between authorities and companies in the case of leniency applications. It is therefore important to note that the involvement of younger competition authorities can affect the level of trust and the dynamics of its growth.

Perception 6: In Cartel Enforcement, All Information Exchanged by Competition Authorities is Confidential

Competition officials from more mature competition authorities are often cautious when sharing information with their younger counterparts. This is typically due to the perception that everything they deal with should be confidential. In reality, as the research examines, not all information exchanged between authorities is confidential, depending on the domestic laws in the respective jurisdictions. Such recognition prevents the 'knee-jerk' application of confidentiality to all information provided by the parties. In fact, investigations would benefit from competition authorities differentiating the types of information to be shared and establishing a benchmark for sharable information, with a more nuanced approach to confidentiality.

Turning a Paper Tiger into an Effective Hunter

The research puts forward novel proposals for effective cooperation, primarily in regard to investigating and prosecuting transnational and regional CBCs. This is in consideration of the optimal level of deterrence of multinational CBCs as well as the political ramifications of export and import CBCs. In this regard, chapter eight presents three building blocks for solving the puzzle of cooperation between mature or large and young or small competition authorities. Reasons are also given as to why young or small competition authorities should rather refrain from targeting multinational CBCs.

The building blocks for effective cooperation in transnational CBC investigations are as follows:

1. Creating trust and mutual understanding between mature and young competition authorities, taking into account and building on cooperation efforts and exchanges, including technical assistance (section 8.1).
2. Dealing with confidential information and establishing an international benchmark of 'non-confidential information' or 'sharable' information to be exchanged (section 8.2).
3. Maximising and streamlining the instruments for international cooperation provided by the International Competition Network (ICN) and the United Nations Set on Principles on Competition. An amalgamation of these two instruments is proposed with a feature that could be triggered by any member of the United Nations., including those that are not members of the ICN (section 8.3).

The research concludes with the proposal of a two-tier approach to foster regional cooperation between young but large authorities, as well as young and small competition authorities. Taking the example of Latin America as a reference point, this is the foundation of a novel solution described in chapter nine that covers the following aspects:

1. Creating a more in-depth trust (or knowledge-based trust) amongst young or relatively advanced competition authorities and younger ones in Latin America, taking into account the sub-regional efforts made in recent years (section 9.1).
2. Solving the coordination problem faced by young competition authorities wishing to work together against regional CBCs, beyond sub-regional efforts such as the Andean Community of Nations (section 9.2).

The research concludes with an outlook and a number of forward-looking suggestions for the benefit of young or small competition authorities that wish to work with mature or larger ones against a common enemy: CBCs. The proposed measures will allow more top executives, such as Mark Whitacre, to cooperate with competition authorities in the future, thereby exposing CBCs from within.

Methodology and Exposure

The research applies an interdisciplinary approach, combining insights from international relations, politics, as well as legal analysis. The methodological framework is founded on reviews of international CBC cases handled in mature, large, young and some small competition authorities. In addition, a great variety of reports from major international organisations dealing with this topic is included, along with relevant academic literature on international cooperation in cartel enforcement, including monographs, journal articles, and theses in different languages (English, Spanish and French).

A number of presentations on the subject matter provided by enforcers in several conferences and events throughout the world were also reviewed. Last but not least, the research provides experimental solutions for better addressing the effects of transnational and regional CBCs, based on two hypotheses which are presented in chapters eight and nine. Both hypotheses were contrasted with interviews carried out at the International Competition Network (ICN) Annual Conference held in Portugal during May 2017, along with other ad-hoc interviews held in January and June 2017.[19]

Last but certainly not least, the author relies on observations from his work at the UNCTAD Secretariat in assisting developing countries for over 15 years, most recently as lead coordinator of the UNCTAD Discussion Group on International Cooperation.[20] Composed of 55 member states (including young and small competition regimes), this Discussion Group serves to negotiate guiding principles and procedures for a better implementation of section F of the UN Set related to international measures. While many insights from the Discussion Group are still confidential due to the ongoing process of deliberations among member states, some general inputs have been accommodated.

[19] The enforcers interviewed came from 21 jurisdictions including mature, large, young and small competition authorities, as well as Latin American competition authority officials. See the bibliography.

[20] The Discussion Group was established in 2017 for an extension of two years until July 2019. See 'Report of the Discussion Group on International Cooperation'.

PART I

Cross Border Cartels

Part I sets the frame for discussing the core problem of this research and is formed of three chapters.

Chapter one defines cross-border cartels, or CBCs, providing a review of the economic literature regarding the harmful effects of these cartels to the economy. It further highlights the different institutional frameworks of competition authorities of different sizes and maturity. It finally reviews the interrelations between CBCs and algorithms, in light of potential international cartelisation which is facilitated by digitalisation and ultimately impacts both developing countries and economies in transition.

Chapter two proposes a classification of CBCs based on trade volumes, the country of origin of the cartelists, and the geographical coverage, among others. This classification is instrumental in assessing the specific measures which young and small competition authorities can apply when addressing CBCs.

Chapter three is divided into five sections, discussing the theoretical and practical tenets of international cooperation in CBC enforcement. The first section deals with the underlying reasons for and the benefits arising from the cooperation of competition authorities, including different phases for cooperation as well as the role and implications of geopolitics. The second section is devoted to a discussion of the various forms and tools of international cooperation, through both formal or informal arrangements. Finally, the last section covers the role of international organisations involved in cooperation, such as the OECD, UNCTAD and ICN, in promoting 'soft law' developments.

1

Conceptual Framework

In 1982, when the head of the Department of Justice Antitrust Division met in Paris with his European counterpart to the pending transatlantic IBM investigations, no one realised that the world of international competition was about to change.[1] And indeed an intensified cross-border activity emerged to tackle internationalisation of cartel activity worldwide.

1.1. Definition of Cross-Border Cartels

Cross-border cartels – CBCs – have been the subject of extensive scholarship by John M Connor.[2] CBCs generally fall within the legal meaning of international price-fixing agreements provided by the Antitrust Division of the US Department of Justice (DOJ). In addition, the term can be covered by the definition provided by EC competition law provisions under article 101 of the Lisbon Treaty (TFEU).[3] The definition and common forms of cartels are explored below, with special consideration for which features are particularly important from the point of view of young and small competition agencies.

1.1.1. Cartels as Horizontal Agreements between Competitors

This section deals with the workable definition of cartels. The historical facts that led to their vast expansion in the 1930s[4] will not be addressed in this section[5]

[1] First (2003: 23).

[2] Connor, 'Cartels & Antitrust Portrayed'; Connor, 'Effectiveness of Antitrust Sanctions'; Connor, 'Global Antitrust Prosecutions'; Connor, 'Global Antitrust Prosecutions'; Connor, 'International Cartel Stats'; Connor, 'Optimal Deterrence and Private International Cartels'; Connor, 'Private International Cartels: A Concise Introduction'; Connor, 'Private International Cartels: Effectiveness, Welfare, and Anti-cartel Enforcement'; Connor, 'Recidivism Revealed'; Connor, 'The Private International Cartels (CBC) Data Set'; Connor, 'The Rise of Anti-Cartel Enforcement in Africa, Asia, and Latin America'; Connor and Helmers (2007); Connor and Lande (2012); Zimmerman and Connor (2005).

[3] Connor, 'International Cartel Stats' p 3.

[4] For a comprehensive insight on how a cartel worked for almost 100 years, see Bertilorenzi (2016).

[5] See Connor, *Global Price Fixing*, p 46.

because that would go beyond the scope of the present research. Nevertheless, contextual facts for each of the modern cartels will be discussed in chapter two below.

A 'cartel'[6] has been described as 'a group of two or more independent sellers who agree to fix or control prices or output in a given market'.[7] The term 'hard-core cartels' arises as the worldwide uniform definition of price-fixing, market division or bid-rigging business adopted by all existing competition laws[8] prohibit this conduct.[9] In this regard, there is no need to assess the effects of these unlawful practices in the market, it is sufficient to prove its occurrence in order to infringe the competition. As such, the so-called 'objective box' under EC competition law[10] and its jurisprudence[11] would mean that without regarding the market power of the participants, motives or business justifications.[12] The practice should be deemed as a violation of competition laws. Under US antitrust law the interpretation of hard-core cartels is considered as 'per se' rule practice, as opposed to the 'rule of reason' approach.[13] Major world institutions such as the EU Commission or the US Supreme Court have described cartels as 'cancers on the open market economy or the supreme evil of antitrust'.[14]

The former Working Group on Trade and Competition Policy of the World Trade Organisation (WTO) used the term 'hard-core' cartel to '[underscore] the harm caused by [cartel] arrangements and [distinguish] them from joint ventures or other inter-firm arrangements that involve active collaboration among firms and potentially enhance social welfare'.[15]

It is a fundamental principle of any competition system that companies within the same industry should not communicate with each other. If they do, they may be engaging in cartel activities; evidence that companies have explicitly talked to each other is a 'smoking gun' in competition procedures and it is usually condemned as a per se violation.[16] This is in the sense of the terms 'explicit', 'plain' or 'overt' collusion in the following discussion.

Collusion has been defined as follows: 'an agreement among a group of firms, called a cartel, designed to limit competition among the participants. If all firms in the cartel follow the agreement, buyers will face higher prices, giving the cartel members profits above the normal competitive level'.[17] In this sense, when

[6] The term originates from the German word *Kartell*, later anglicised as 'cartel'. Cartels also operate under various names: trusts, combines, comptoirs, syndicates, pools and ententes: 'The International Cartel Movement' (*CQ Researcher by CQ Press*).

[7] Connor, 'Global Antitrust Prosecutions', p, 240.

[8] To date, 139 countries have enacted competition laws. See Fox (2016).

[9] Whish and Bailey (2015: 546).

[10] *cf* The criticisms made of the 'object box' by Saskia King in her PhD dissertation. See King (2015).

[11] *GlaxoSmithKline Services v Commission* 2969 (ECR II).

[12] Noonan (2008: 60).

[13] See US Sherman Antitrust Act 1890.

[14] Citing the speech of Commissioner Mario Monti and the US case *Verizon Communications v Law Offices of Curtis*. See Whish and Bailey (2015: 547).

[15] See para 3, WTO (2002: 2).

[16] Fonseca and Normann (2012: 1759).

[17] Bajari and Summers (2002: 143).

companies agree not to compete, in order to increase the combined profits of the whole group, while reducing output, competition will be substantially restrained and no productive efficiency advantage (such as a better use of resources, or costs saving) will occur.[18] This is why horizontal collusive practices are one of the main focuses of competition (or antitrust) law around the world.[19] There are commonly three major types of collusive practice: price-fixing agreements, quantity-fixing agreements, and market allocation,[20] whereby the cartelists maximise their profits directly at the expense of consumer welfare.[21]

1. **Price-fixing agreements** take place between competitors, whether explicitly or implicitly, when they jointly set the prices at which they market their products.[22] Such arrangements can take place through uniform pricing among competitors or through the determination of maximum or minimum prices that these companies must respect when buying or selling goods or services.[23] A special case of this practice is bid-rigging or collusive tendering,[24] in which potential competitors coordinate the offers they will present to a call for bids, and agree on who will win each of the coordinated bids. Within this category we also find bonus-fixing, rebates, commissions, and other practices that determine the price of a particular product. For any price-fixing agreement, a horizontal agreement on output production (a quantity-fixing agreement) is generally necessary; otherwise members of the cartel might increase production to gain a greater market share at the cartel price and, if left with unsold product, would be tempted to undercut the cartel price to unload it. Thus, like price-fixing, horizontal agreements to restrict output are typically regarded as per se illegal under US and EU law.[25]

2. **Quantitative fixing agreements** refer to conduct the effects of which can be similar to that of price-fixing, but which instead involve setting a quantity or quota. Through these a number of companies operating in the same market convene to limit their output to certain agreed quantities or to split the market according to certain fixed shares[26] without producing any compensating benefits.[27]

3. **Market allocation** describes horizontal agreements between unrelated rivals to divide a market, and these also are *per se* illegal. Such market divisions

[18] For a comprehensive assessment on why collusion is profitable and how it is implemented in practice see Marshall and Marx (2012).

[19] See more at Clarke and Evenett (2003).

[20] It seems that in the EU, the 'object box' is being expanded to additional restrictions of competition besides the three most obvious. See the discussion in: Whish and Bailey (2015: 125).

[21] *cf* Lande and Marvel (2000).

[22] Ezrachi (2016: 159–61).

[23] See a comprehensive assessment of price-fixing in Kaplow (2013).

[24] Ezrachi (2016: 166).

[25] See more in Jones and Sufrin (2016).

[26] According to EU case law, quotas have been very numerous in recent years. See Whish and Bailey (2015: 570, fn 244).

[27] Indeed, there are some agreements that could be beneficial to competition, such as joint production, R&D agreements, standardisation. Whish and Bailey (2015: 569).

generally involve territorial divisions, where each company agrees to limit itself to a geographic area demarcated from the other firm. This can also refer to dividing customers, such as having one rival sell to commercial users and another to regular consumers. As mentioned above, this practice is commonly used for bid-rigging cases where competitors coordinate efforts for providing certain product at a certain price depending on the regions set up in the bid call.[28]

In principle, agreements explicitly involving fixing prices, quantities or market allocation should be easy to identify. In practice, however, it is common that the elements of these agreements are veiled.[29] Veiled practices include, inter alia, enterprises agreeing to use a common sales representative, business associations negotiating terms of purchase or sale on behalf of their affiliates, or competitors exchanging information on prices. In some circumstances, these practices have no impact on competition, in others, the effects may be anti-competitive.

1.1.2. Overt (Explicit) vs Covert (Tacit) Collusion

Another distinction that applies to cases of collusion, often found in competition laws and case law, is between cases of 'overt' or 'explicit' collusion, and cases of 'covert' or 'tacit' collusion. Overt or explicit collusion refers to situations wherein there is a specific agreement to collude and there is direct evidence of communications between the enterprises agreeing to not compete. Conversely, tacit collusion is a market equilibrium reached when several competitors behave 'as if agreeing with each other', but without displaying direct communication between them.[30] It occurs when the agreement to collude cannot be proved directly, but rather through indirect evidence, including, among others, communications between employees of the same company making reference to agreements with competitors, and parallel conduct that cannot be reasonably explained without an explicit agreement among competitors. The collusive outcome in this case arises simply from the fact that each company individually chooses to set prices, or quantities, or to target a certain group of customers, and that decision is analogous with the one that a cartel would take in order to maximise joint profits.

In economic theory, however, whether the communication has been overt/explicit or covert/tacit does not matter, as the incentives to adhere to collusive agreements are the same with or without communication.[31] In other words, the issue as to whether collusion is tacit or explicit is not relevant for economists, who are only concerned about the effects of collusion in the market.[32] In this regard, it

[28] See 'Market Sharing and Non-compete Agreements' in Ezrachi (2016: 168).
[29] Bajari and Summers (2002); Marshall and Marx (2012).
[30] Tacit collusion will mean to competitors enjoying the benefits of a particular market structure without actually entering into an agreement to do so. Whish and Bailey (2015: 597).
[31] Fonseca and Normann (2012: 1759).
[32] Whish and Bailey (2015: 597).

has been argued that 'there is gap between antitrust practice which distinguishes between explicit and tacit collusion and economic theory which (generally) does not'.[33]

To avoid the opprobrious word 'collusion', lawyers have instead gravitated to the concept of 'conscious parallelism'.[34] Conscious parallelism implies the existence of a parallel conduct of competitors in a market, regarding their pricing or output decisions or their access to certain markets, which is consistent with a hypothetical covert collusion.[35] According to EU jurisprudence, conscious parallelism may be crystallised in tight oligopolistic markets when three requisites are met: (1) there is transparency of markets and monitoring by other competitors; (2) companies are capable of punishing deviators from tacit agreement; and (3) competitive constraints do not jeopardise the implementation of the common strategy.[36] Furthermore, conscious parallelism is generally regarded as an important piece of evidence in cases of covert collusion, especially when it appears in conjunction with other factors that reinforce their interpretation as evidence of collusive behaviour (for example, ancillary restraints, communication between competitors, documents relating to the existence of explicit agreements, etc.).[37]

Since the last decade of the twentieth century, many countries have intensified their competition policies that seek to prove the existence of covert collusion through obtaining additional direct evidence.[38] The most important of these policies is undoubtedly the 'leniency programme',[39] which consists of giving incentives to enterprises to plead guilty of engaging in collusive behaviour, and to provide evidence to directly prove the occurrence of the conduct in question, thus incriminating other enterprises in the cartel.[40] These incentives generally include immunity for the denouncing enterprise, or substantially reduced sanctions, in relation to the conduct in question. Usually, these programmes are only available to the first company in the cartel to confess its guilt and, sometimes, only when it relates to cartels that are not already being investigated by antitrust authorities.[41]

Another issue of relevance to the legal framing of collusion is the conduct of chambers of commerce and of business or professional associations. These institutions, whose main mandate is to represent a group in its claims and negotiations

[33] Fonseca and Normann (2012: 1760).

[34] Lawyers prefer to avoid the opprobrious word 'collusion' and be replaced by 'conscious parallelism'. Seeibid.

[35] Ezrachi (2016: 317).

[36] ibid, 317.

[37] For other dimensions of Tacit Collusion see Decker (2009: 224).

[38] For a comprehensive assessment of competition instruments to combat cartels, see Kovacic '(2006).

[39] Blair and Sokol (2015: 424); see more in Spagnolo (2000).

[40] See Motta and Polo (1999).

[41] Free competition on markets is a major concern in competition policy. The cartelisation of firms is a threat to free competition. Leniency programmes, as a device for cartel detection and cartel destabilisation, have been implemented, or reformed, across countries since the early 1990s (USA 1993, European Union 1996). See more in Klein (2010).

with government and labour unions, as well as to foster their members' activities, are usually the most effective instrument, and indeed are sometimes indispensable, in carrying out collusive practices. Agreements on prices and quantities or certain market allocation arrangements may be struck within these institutions, thus enabling them to act as 'cartel watchdogs' which can detect and punish violations of the established agreement. Associations can also take a less active role, though equally important, by facilitating communication and disseminating agreements between enterprises in a market. The use of chambers and associations to conduct collusive agreements has the effect of turning veiled collusive practices into overt collusion. This generates many cases of collusion involving chambers of commerce and business associations, so considerable antitrust agency resources are devoted to monitoring such institutions. The institutionalising of collusion through chambers and associations has historically entailed a certain legalisation of collusion, since it is common for this type of entity to enjoy protection through specific norms, issued by organs of the state, allowing them to set minimum fees, zoning, establishing artificial barriers to market entry and conduct other activities that may indirectly limit competition, such as strikes, lockouts or boycotts.

1.1.3. Private vs Public Cartels

Another salient distinction for cartels lies in their private or public nature, as distinguished by Connor. Public cartels, he explains, are those which are protected by national sovereignty.[42] An example of a public cartel is the Organisation of Petroleum Exporting Countries (OPEC) established in 1960, composed of oil-producing states which have formed a trans-government cartel to fix oil prices internationally.[43] The story of OPEC is mostly about politics, as the organisation is based on diplomatic recognition and ambassadorial representation from other countries. From an economic perspective, it has very limited influence in setting prices of oil in the global oil market.[44] The state doctrine principle exempts state-promoted international cartels from the application of competition laws,[45] since this principle covers an 'act of state' that includes not only an executive or administrative exercise of sovereign power, but also legislative and administrative acts, such as a statute, decree, or order.[46] Conversely, private cartels are considered such when the economic activities undertaken by the cartelists are not acts of the state.[47]

[42] Connor, 'Private International Cartels: A Concise Introduction'.

[43] See Tourk, 'Opec Cartel'.

[44] Colgan (2014: 601).

[45] See for instance the *Spectrum* case whereby US companies brought a suit against OPEC, which US courts dismissed. Matsushita and others (2015: 811).

[46] Zander (1959: 826).

[47] Acts of the state are different from acts sponsored by the state. This is discussed more extensively in the Vitamin C export cartel.

Further to this distinction, another important concept is that of competitive neutrality. This refers to the application of competition laws to public companies as they would be applied to private companies. The premise behind this principle is that there should be a level playing field for public entities or state-owned enterprises (SOEs) and for private companies. Pursuant to the foregoing, private cartels can also cover government activities that support specific price-fixing arrangements.[48]

1.1.4. International vs Domestic Cartels

International cartels imply that companies based in multiple nations fix prices across multiple jurisdictions, with a global geographical coverage.[49] The profits from these cartels spill over into other countries, and the consequent overcharges paid by the affected markets are enough to offset possible fines and penalties that may be imposed against the cartelists. On the other hand, domestic cartels imply that companies, whether or not they are based in multiple jurisdictions, fix prices that affect one jurisdiction only. According to Ariel Ezrachi, domestic cartels involve the transfer of wealth from consumers to producers involved in anticompetitive conduct, while international cartels involve the 'transfer of wealth from the domestic market to foreign market, and vice versa'.[50]

For example, an international cartel in vitamins was formed by multinational firms based in Canada, Germany, Japan, Switzerland and the US. The global vitamins cartel is considered to be one of the most pervasive and harmful criminal antitrust conspiracies ever uncovered, in which the firms colluded to fix prices, rig bids, and allocate global market shares in the sale of vitamin products. The international cartel operated from 1990 to 1999.[51] According to the former EC Competition Commissioner, Mario Monti, international cartels intend to divide the world market between the conspirators:

> At their core, international cartels have essentially the same purpose – to increase profits among the conspirators by carving up world markets – and they operate pursuant to the same methods – fixing prices, rigging bids, allocating territories and customers, and allocating sales volumes among the conspirator firms on a worldwide basis.[52]

1.1.5. CBCs and CAPs

According to Brendan Sweeney, CBCs are different in nature from other cross-border anti-competitive practices (CAPs), such as private commercial barriers,

[48] See more in Capobianco and Christiansen (2011).
[49] Connor, 'Private International Cartels: A Concise Introduction', p 1.
[50] Ezrachi (2012).
[51] For a complete survey of the vitamin cartel, see Clarke and Evenett (2003).
[52] Monti and others (2001: 38).

unilateral conduct, export cartels, and merger transactions. CAPs are related to any type of anticompetitive practice that presents a cross-border nature. The assessment provided by Sweeny below reflects the underlying evidence and challenges surrounding each conduct. As can be seen below, the link between trade and competition issues arises because there are a number of cross-border practices that impede not only international trade of goods or services but also it impacts competition at the international level. Table 1.1 provides an initial classification of CAPs according to Sweeney, the evidence and its respective challenges.

Table 1.1 Five different types of CAPs

Conduct	Evidence	Challenges
1. **Private commercial barriers** by economic agents that affect the agreed commercial commitments through agreements of free trade.	Evidence of the effects of these practices is likely to become obvious in the future. Import barriers will be an important issue.	There is no effective enforcement of competition rules against private commercial barriers for three reasons: (i) the conduct is not illegal, (ii) the limited capacity of national competition authorities, and (iii) protectionist measures of the governments on import barriers from their own economic agents.
2. Export cartels.[53]	The evidence of the damaging effects of export cartels is not well-known.	The standards of national competition do not affect domestic markets.
3. Private international cartels or cross-border cartels (CBCs).	Abundant evidence of the damage of this conduct is seen in economies, principally in emerging countries.	There are problems in prosecuting CBCs, because of the lack of strengthened cooperation, in: (i) confidential information, (ii) seeking extra-judicial evidence, (iii) application of the law by judges.
4.- Mergers or international concentrations or CBCs.	Will be a potentially significant problem.	Global action is needed for this type of behaviour. However, domestically the rules differ from one jurisdiction to another.
5. Unilateral conduct of a firm internationally.	Presently this is not significant but there is a growing tendency for firms and commercial operations to act in this way.	There is a need for global action for this type of conduct. However, at a domestic level, the rules differ between each jurisdiction.

Source: SWEENEY, Brendan. *The Internationalization of Competition Rules.* (Routledge Research in Competition Law, 2010) p 354.

[53] Notably, Sweeney mentions the 'export cartel' as a type of CAP (contrary to the proposal in the present research that it is a type of CBC. It is submitted that this mentions export cartels as a type of CAP. Note that this is a classification that does not go beyond the specific.

1.1.6. Harmful Effects of Cross-Border Cartels

Measuring the true impact of CBCs on developing countries is difficult because of the unquantifiable nature of many of the factors at play, such as the loss suffered by developing country producers beyond the economic concept of consumer loss.[54] As it is sometimes difficult to access information on how major competition authorities have calculated cartel overcharges and the impact to consumers, 'economists have used proxy company sales using international trade date where imports of goods by developing countries for countries that hosted the cartel producers are used to estimate the cartels' sales to developing countries'.[55]

CBCs are considered the most harmful practice, having been labelled the 'dark side of globalisation'.[56] Recent statistics estimate that for the period 1990–2016, 75 new CBCs were uncovered each year. After the CBCs were investigated, 96 per cent resulted in a conviction whereby 533 individuals were sanctioned with charges of international price-fixing.[57] Indeed, due to the serious harmful effects to the competitive process itself, CBCs are now illegal in nearly every corner of the world. According to Richard Whish, '[a]t both a moral and a practical level there is not a great deal of difference between price fixing and theft',[58] and in consequence will find a rare example of global harmonisation of legal-economic policies.[59]

1.2. Implications of the Size and Maturity of Competition Regimes for CBC Enforcement

The classification of young vs more mature competition authorities is made on the basis of exogenous and endogenous factors which shape authorities worldwide and contribute to their overall effectiveness and evolution over time. Exogenous factors surround the work of the authority and are connected to the local dynamics of the jurisdiction and markets in which it operates. According to Ezrachi, 'the effects of the domestic environment are an integral part of competition law and are echoed in the properties of the law'.[60] Endogenous factors, on the other hand, refer to internal factors that shape the functioning of the authority, such as the internal structure of competition authorities, and the skills and expertise of their staff.

The following summarises the two main factors:

1. **Years of enforcement:** There is presently no internationally recognised standard for classifying competition authorities as 'young' or 'mature'.

[54] Yu (2003: 8).
[55] ibid.
[56] Connor, 'Private International Cartels'.
[57] Connor, 'International Cartel Stats',p 2.
[58] Whish and Bailey (2015: 547).
[59] Connor, 'Private International Cartels' p 1.
[60] Ezrachi (2017: 33).

In a 2009 survey, the OECD used 1990 as the cut-off year and considered authorities that 'began enforcing competition laws since 1990' as young. 1990 was considered the start of the 'modern era' of competition policy in the international context, as it was during this time there was rapid expansion in the number of countries implementing new competition policies, and '[c]entral economic planning in Central and Eastern Europe and Central Asia had ended.'[61] However, it is also important to factor in the maturity of the market in which competition authorities operate: for example, the Hong Kong Competition Commission, the Competition and Consumer Commission of Singapore, and the Korean Fair Trade Commission are relatively new competition authorities, founded only in 2014, 2004 and 1980, respectively, but they may be regarded as 'mature' due to the highly advanced markets in which they operate.

2. Independence and accountability: The independence and accountability of competition authorities constitute important factors. While functional or budgetary independence may not be an option in many developing countries and emerging economies (e.g. due to limited resources or other political constraints), independence with respect to their operations and enforcement decisions can substantiate the effectiveness of the authorities, also vis-à-vis other sector regulators and stakeholders in the government, as well as the broader public.[62]

Of the 141 competition authorities currently in existence worldwide, the majority are either young or small authorities and can generally be found in developing countries and countries with economies in transition. These jurisdictions typically face common challenges,[63] among others human resources and financial constraints[64] which can be felt at various levels and ultimately reduce the overall effectiveness of competition regimes. Human and financial resources are critical factors in international cases, in particular when dealing with different jurisdictions across multiple continents. In this regard, larger jurisdictions such as the EU and Japan have more than 400 officers attached to their competition authorities. In emerging markets and countries in transition, there are also some large authorities such as the Russian Federal Antimonopoly Service, which has more than 1,000 officers within the authority; however, this authority is an umbrella agency that deals with issues beyond competition law.[65] Similarly, Peru's authority (INDECOPI) has more than 1,000 officers and deals with eight different areas, one of which is competition, with roughly 50 dedicated officers.[66] That said, however,

[61] OECD, n 5 above.

[62] According to South African and Australian enforcers, a critical benchmark for competition authorities to trust others is how accountable and independent they are vis-a-vis the central governement. See Bezzi (2017); Interview with Ratshisusu, (2017).

[63] UNCTAD, Secretariat Note on 'Challenges in the Design of a Merger Control Regime for Young and Small Competition Authorities' 14.

[64] When referring in this case to consumer protection authorities. OECD Secretariat, 'Consumer Protection Enforcement in a Global Digital Marketplace', p 6.

[65] FAS (2005).

[66] 'Estructura Organizacional – Indecopi'.

one should be mindful about the different geographical and population sizes of jurisdictions when comparing their financial and personnel resources.

On a political level, priorities for basic service delivery or investment promotion often take precedence over allocating sufficient budget to competition authorities.[67] On a practical level, this then translates into limited buy-in for the competition agenda, and by extension, limited funds. Competition policy is often not perceived or acknowledged as a key economic tool to foster economic development by governments and policymakers, and thus not included in major political campaigns.[68] Adding to this may be weak democratic institutions, little interagency coordination, lengthy bureaucratic loops and a lack of legal certainty that further impede the effective enforcement of competition policies.

Because there is insufficient trust in the enforcement authorities, not only have they to operate with limited staff but may also be unable to train them. In fact, in jurisdictions where no competition regime previously existed, expertise in competition law and economics may still be limited. A 2009 survey by the OECD revealed that each younger agency surveyed faced the issue of insufficient expertise among its professional staff.[69] Even competition authorities that have managed to train their staff still may not be able to retain them, especially if they cannot match the salaries offered by the private sector.[70] Without sufficient expertise in competition law and economics, it will be difficult to create sophisticated models for the analysis of complicated anti-competitive transactions.[71] Gal and Fox warn that transplanting the application of complex analytical rules used in developed jurisdictions to jurisdictions with limited ability to perform them will significantly increase errors in the analysis.[72]

Aside from the need to build technical or enforcement capacities, it should also be cautioned that in many developing countries where competition policies are newly introduced or implemented, the basic understanding of the tenets of a market economy and market-based institutions may still be lacking. In countries whose economies are in transition, the private sector associations and civil society organisations are still forming, and there is a need to delineate the respective roles and responsibilities vis-à-vis the government. Misconceptions about the government having to regulate and set prices – instead of allowing market forces to

[67] Kunene, 'Challenges Faced' 6.

[68] Mario Umana, Lead Comp. Specialist, Inter-American Dev. Bank, Promoting Competition Advocacy with Limited Resources; OECD Directorate for Financial and Enterprise Affairs, 'Small and Developing Competition Agencies – UMANA – IDB – December 20 …' (16:03:24 UTC), www.slideshare.net/OECD-DAF/small-and-developing-competition-agencies-umana-idb-december-2017-oecd-discussion, accessed 28 May 2018.

[69] 'OECD Global Forum on Competition, 'Challenges Faced by Young Competition Authorities', www.oecd.org/daf/competition/GFC2009-Challenges-faced-by-young-competition-authorities.pdf, accessed 23 May 2018.

[70] ibid.

[71] 'Competition Law & Policy in Developing Countries: Explaining Variation' by Umut Aydin and Tim Büthe, https://scholarship.law.duke.edu/lcp/vol79/iss4/1/, accessed 20 May 2018.

[72] Gal and Fox, 'Drafting Competition Law for Developing Jurisdictions' 69.

operate – can have a detrimental effect on competition in the markets, and subsequently, cause harm to consumers.

Another issue concerns the poor quality of data and lack of research to underpin evidence-based policymaking. Rodriguez and Menon state that as the statistics collated by the developing countries' national statistics authorities are 'for most part, useless for antitrust practice'.[73]

These factors, both exogenous and endogenous, together determine whether a competition authority is considered to be older, large, young or small; ultimately, they also determine the competition authority's ability to deal with multinational, transnational, regional, export and import CBCs. It is important to remember, however, that all competition authorities have undergone a process of evolution, including older authorities.[74] Therefore, it is safe to say that maturity is a process whereby an institutional development cycle evolves through many small steps.[75]

Table 1.2 displays a two-by-two matrix of examples for each combination of young, small, mature and large competition authorities. This is only a reference and it should be considered as such for the purposes of the present research.

Table 1.2 Classification of Competition Authorities

	Mature	Young
Large	The EU (1958), the US (1890), Japan (1947), South Korea (1980).	China (2007), Russia (1990), Brazil (1994), India (2002), and South Africa (1998).
Small	Australia (1974), Singapore (2004), Hong Kong (2014), and some EU national authorities (e.g. Austria).	Nicaragua (2008), Mauritius (2007), and the Philippines (2015).

With the above in mind, the question arises as to the viable avenues for action for younger competition authorities if there are indeed so many different challenges that they need to tackle simultaneously. Resource constraints and enforcement records are closely interlinked, as from the former follows a limited scope of action, and quite possibly, limited opportunities to build capacities in order to adequately address not only domestic competition issues, but CBCs and algorithmic collusion. Limited enforcement in turn affects political support domestically and can also hamper international cooperation. Under significant pressure to prioritise their

[73] Rodriguez and Coate, 'Competition Policy in Transition Economies'.

[74] Even mature competition authorities need to adapt to the evolution of change. For example, business change because of the algorithm economy. See Interview with Qaqaya, Hassan, 'Interview with the Former Head of the Competition and Consumer Policies Branch of the United Nations Conference on Trade and Development (UNCTAD)' (30 May 2017).

[75] Sometimes a cycle can be going backwards and forwards, depending on the political situation of the country. In Latin America, there are two cases: Argentina and Venezuela. See Interview with Coloma, Germán, 'Interview with the Director of Economic Studies of the Argentinean Competition Commission' (1 June 2017).

enforcement actions, younger competition authorities need to carefully discern the costs and benefits of addressing certain competition concerns and cases.

In view of the intrinsic challenges faced by young or small competition regimes, cartel enforcement is often recommended as a priority in young and small competition authorities. Cartel detection is arguably less complex when it comes to the skills and steps required. While the procedures in cartel cases are comparatively straightforward, investigating abuses of dominance or anti-competitive mergers requires more advanced economic analysis for which the capacities in young authorities and developing countries are often still limited. Moreover, it has been found that competition authorities can generate considerable benefits and impact for the economy and vulnerable consumers if they prosecute cartels (and other types of anticompetitive agreements), particularly in sectors that affect the poor.

Contrary to common perceptions, cartel enforcement against local companies is sometimes more challenging than going against international cartels. As mentioned in an interview with an enforcer from a relatively advanced competition authority in Latin America, it might be more effective in some instances to prosecute an international rather than a domestic cartel.[76] This is for the simple reason that domestic cartels are often subject to regulatory capture and other local dynamics, notably if business and politics are closely intertwined.

1.3. CBCs and Algorithms[77]

Nowadays, algorithms can be encountered in virtually every aspect of life: from booking air tickets through dynamic-pricing comparison websites, to using online applications to navigate traffic jams, and even delegating certain routine tasks to home assistant systems (eg Amazon's Alexa or Apple's Siri).[78] Moreover, technological advances have made it possible for computers to process huge data sets according to specific procedures or instructions, thus facilitating choices that consumers would otherwise have to make more consciously and autonomously.[79] While overall, this has contributed to much efficiency, it also poses critical ethical questions about the transformation of consumer interactions and transactions, as well as the impact on market dynamics and power.[80]

[76] Interview with Irrarazabal, Felipe, 'Interview at the ICN Annual Conference in Porto (10–12 May 2017) with the National Economic Prosecutor of Chile (FNE)' (10 May 2017).

[77] Section based on an UNCTAD Research Paper authored by P Horna entitled 'Implications of Algorithmic Decision-Making for Consumer and Competition Policies: Challenges and Opportunities for Young Enforcement Authorities' United Nations, 2019.

[78] In some places, autonomous cars (eg driverless Google cars) are permitted to circulate on public roads.

[79] Gal (2017).

[80] European Consumer Consultative Group (2018: 8).

In the context of the digital or algorithm economy, many of the traditional information asymmetries between businesses and consumers are reduced. At the same time, consumers are exposed to new forms of harm that are unique to the internet: while they have more choices and quicker access to global markets without having to rely on intermediaries, they can also more easily fall victim to fraudulent online business practices (eg misleading advertisement). Furthermore, they may face greater difficulties in obtaining refunds or redress than when dealing with 'bricks-and-mortar' businesses. Finally, there are crucial concerns about data mining and privacy. Protecting 'digital consumers' therefore becomes an urgent priority for policymakers, as well as consumer protection and competition authorities alike.[81]

When it comes to the effects of the digital economy on businesses, the ensuing greater opportunities for expansion and innovation first come to mind. However, the benefits of fair competition are also increasingly called into question. In 2014, Peter Thiel, co-founder of PayPal, declared that '[c]ompetition is for losers'.[82] His argument was that competition places too much internal strain on companies as it forces them to only think about being or becoming better than their rivals, instead of considering workers, products and their 'impact on the wider world'.

Moreover, Thiel argued that concerns about the costs of a monopoly for consumers, and ultimately for society, would be dissipated by the dynamism that characterises ADM processes. In other words, innovation frequently leads to the creation of new products and the emergence of new markets, thus potentially outweighing traditional notions about the problems of excessive market power. Similarly, Mina Salib, Chief Executive Officer of Usspire, said that '[the] true losers are not those who embrace and surround themselves with competition, but rather those who cannot, or do not, collaborate with the competition'.[83]

In any case, the advent of algorithms, artificial intelligence and big data has made it possible for machines to understand human speech, compete in strategic game systems, drive cars autonomously, or even independently interpret complex data in stock markets. Innovations, such as online platforms and portals, are significantly changing trade and other forms of commercial transactions, leaving an impact on market structures while also affecting consumer choice and privacy. Hence, this section looks at the implications of algorithms to the formation of CBCs.

It is worth noting that the European Commission recently investigated a number of consumer electronics manufacturers, in part for using ADM processes that automatically adapt retail prices to match those of their leading competitors.[84]

[81] OECD Secretariat (2018: 8).
[82] Thiel (2014).
[83] 'Blog' (*Mina Salib*), www.minasalib.com/blog/, accessed 29 May 2018.
[84] EU Commission 'Press Release – Antitrust: Commission Fines Four Consumer Electronics Manufacturers for Fixing Online Resale Prices'.

The question arises whether the mere adoption of such algorithms is an indication of cartel-like behaviour, namely a conscious commitment to the common objective of aligned prices. As such, price-matching algorithms carry inherent risks, in particular if authorities assess whether competition rules apply to price-signalling behaviour.[85]

The latter raises a number of issues concerning the fact that perhaps in the algorithm economy, intent is becoming less central in competition enforcement due to an increasing dependence on computer pricing and high-tech approaches to business decisions, many of which lie beyond any lay person's understanding. It can be argued that intent remains relevant, although it might change from an intention to fix prices directly to intent to adopt an algorithm.[86] In this vein, arguments have arisen regarding whether the concept of an agreement should be revisited in order to equivocate 'a meeting of algorithms' and 'a meeting of minds' when they are both essentially reached with the assistance of algorithms.[87]

Taking a bird's-eye view to competition enforcement in the digital era, the core question arises as to whether competition authorities have the adequate tools to address emerging issues. In 2017, an article in the *Financial Times* discussed how digital cartels could be policed, in light of the potential (ab)use of AI and powerful algorithms for collusion. The article found that technological advances have indeed helped create and consolidate durable pricing cartels that are difficult to combat with traditional competition enforcement tools. Therefore, the potential advantages of the digital economy – namely greater innovation, lower informational and transactional costs, greater market contestability – are overshadowed by the possibilities that data-driven algorithms open up for collusion, market eviction and monopolisation. In this vein, it has been argued that the strategies of international e-commerce firms may be inherently prone to facilitating digital cross-border cartels.[88]

Algorithms could eventually lead to oligopolistic cross-border collusion scenarios that distort competition. Indeed, with the emergence of the digital economy, problems are also compounded by algorithmic collusion. Ezrachi and Stucke have already warned enforcers about the 'digitised hand', which is fast replacing Adam Smith's 'invisible hand' in the shaping of the economy and harbours new threats to competition. One of the most pressing concerns is that as companies gather increasing amounts of data, this valuable information could be used to

[85] 'Price Signalling and Global Antitrust Enforcement: Practical Counselling Tips | Insight | Baker McKenzie'.

[86] Although there is conceivably a world where quantum computing becomes so advanced as to allow algorithms to collude with each other without specific instruction to do so, that day is not here, not on the horizon, and unlikely to arrive in our lifetimes. This thesis should be confronted with Synced (2017).

[87] OECD, 'Algorithms and Collusion' pp 36–37.

[88] David J Lynch, 'Policing the Digital Cartels' (*Financial Times*, 8 January 2017), www.ft.com/content/9de9fb80-cd23-11e6-864f-20dcb35cede2, accessed 5 February 2017.

restrict competition. Data-driven algorithms have the potential to be employed to monitor the pricing strategies of competitors, thus facilitating collusion. In addition, a dominant company in possession of valuable data to which their competitors do not have access might be able to use this information for exclusionary purposes. Therefore, the seemingly beneficial increased transparency may, ironically, result in harming both competition and consumers.[89]

Ezrachi and Stucke considered four scenarios in which ADM processes can promote collusion: the Messenger, Hub and Spoke, the Predictable Agent, and the Digital Eye.[90]

In the Messenger scenario, companies agree to collude by using computers that execute their will. This scenario is similar to what happened in the US case of *Topkins*.[91] There are no examples of such cases in emerging economies, although it is possible that companies in some BRICS countries may have agreed to collude through computers.[92] The OECD classified this type of algorithmic collusion as parallel algorithms in which colluding companies automatise their decision processes so that prices react simultaneously to any changes in market conditions, thereby replicating a scenario of conscious parallelism.[93]

The Hub and Spoke scenario refers to the coordination between competitors using the same 'hub' in developing their pricing algorithms. In this scenario, the companies end up relying on the same algorithms, or very close versions of them, to develop their pricing strategies.[94] This is illustrated by Uber, which (after acquiring relevant market power as a platform) was able to create vertically collusive agreements where the algorithm developer helped orchestrate the industry-wide collusion, leading to higher prices.[95] In some emerging economies, notably India and South Africa, while cases (primarily initiated by local taxi companies) have been brought against Uber on grounds of predatory pricing,[96] these were not related to the Hub and Spoke scenarios as described above.

The Predictable Agent scenario, on the other hand, involves 'algorithm-enhanced conscious parallelism[97] 'or 'monitoring algorithms', according to

[89] Ezrachi and Stucke (2016).

[90] Stucke and Ezrachi (2016).

[91] David Topkins and his co-conspirators agreed to fix the prices for specific posters sold online. They adopted specific pricing algorithms that collected competitors' pricing information. They also wrote computer code that instructed their algorithm-based software to set the posters' prices in conformity with their illegal agreement. Under this scenario, humans collude. They use computers to assist in creating, monitoring, and policing a cartel. Mehra (2016).

[92] Although algorithmic pricing is not illegal and is a common practice in many industries, it was the existence of an agreement to jointly implement the algorithm that made the case for the DOJ. OECD, 'Algorithms and Collusion', p 27.

[93] ibid p 26.

[94] ibid p 27.

[95] Stucke and Ezrachi (2016).

[96] See Ghuman, 'Analysis of Competition Cases Against Uber'.

[97] This more complex depiction of reality involves algorithmic tacit collusion (conscious parallelism) where the same anticompetitive outcome is achieved (namely higher prices) without rivals having agreed to tamper with prices. Ezrachi and Stucke (2017).

the OECD's definition.[98] In this scenario, the algorithms collect and process information from other competitors (but not necessarily because of the direct will of the companies), and in some cases they automatically adjust pricing as well as punish deviations.[99] Of course this scenario leads to ADM processes whereby no prior agreement among competitors exists as each company unilaterally adopts its pricing algorithm, which sets its own price.[100] The example provided by the OECD is the computer vision algorithms when monitoring fuel prices in the petrol industry.[101] A case in Chile's retail-petrol industry illustrates how monitoring algorithms work in emerging companies through government websites.[102]

Lastly, 'Self-Learning Algorithms' or 'the Digital Eye'[103] involve algorithms with mechanisms (notably machine learning and deep learning) that could maximise profits while recognising mutual interdependency and readapting behaviour to the actions of the other market actors. In these scenarios, tacit collusion schemes appear as a result of creating a new level of stability and scope of the collusion, going beyond price, oligopolistic markets, and easy detection.[104] Ezrachi and Stucke attribute this evolution to two factors: first, the computers' ability to process high volumes of data in real time (a God-like view of the marketplace); and second, the autonomous-decision-making-and-learning-through-experience algorithms.[105]

1.4. Summary

In the past decades, CBCs have become a common phenomenon in many parts of the world and present serious problems to the economies that they target. Historically, multinational CBCs have been difficult to uncover. For example, the international aluminium cartel that started in 1901 was only detected and prosecuted in the mid-1980s. Modern multinational CBCs, however, are often uncovered. During the period 2000–16, 75 new multinational CBCs were uncovered each year

[98] OECD, 'Algorithms and Collusion'.
[99] ibid p 24.
[100] Stucke and Ezrachi (2016).
[101] OECD, 'Algorithms and Collusion', p 25.
[102] In February 2012, petrol stations had to post their fuel prices on a government website and to keep prices updated as they changed at the pump. An economic study found that this Chilean regulation softened, rather than increased, competition. The petrol stations' margins increased by 10% on average following the prices being posted on the government website. The softening of competition was common across brands, and was not limited to a single Chilean city. Interestingly, although the stations' margins increased across Chile, the effect was not uniform: the petrol station margins 'increased the most in areas with low or non-existent consumer search (low-income areas), while they increased the least, and even decreased, in areas with high search intensity (high income areas)'. Ezrachi and Stucke (2017: 7).
[103] Stucke and Ezrachi (2015).
[104] OECD, 'Algorithms and Collusion', 30.
[105] Stucke and Ezrachi (2015).

and more than 100,000 companies (7,200 named) were found liable for international price-fixing whereby gross cartel overcharges exceed US$1.5 trillion, 60 per cent by multinational CBCs.

The documented CBCs have significantly damaged economies, particularly those in emerging markets. The effects on developing countries are particularly pronounced, with such countries importing billions in goods from industries engaged in price-fixing conspiracies. Despite the staggering number of discoveries, experts agree that a great number of CBCs remain undetected and undeterred.

2

Classification of Cross-Border Cartels

In 2001, *Evenett et al* classified CBCs into three different types: hard-core cartels, private export cartels, and state-run export cartels.[1] Connor classifies CBCs or private international cartels as global, EU-type and national.[2] Further, the Competition Action Plan adopted by the Association of South East Asian Nations (ASEAN) for the period 2016–25 classifies CBCs into international private and export/import cartels.[3]

Indeed, there are several ways to classify CBCs depending on the benchmark criteria one should apply. As *Evenett et al* said: 'There are a wide variety of organisations that could plausibly be described as international cartels …'[4]

Hence, for the purposes of the present research, however, having a general distinction between hard-core international cartels, private export cartels and state export cartels as well as global, regional and national does not necessarily satisfy the level of assessment that will be carried out in the following chapters.

In this connection, from the specific angle and perspective of young and small competition authorities, a different classification of CBCs would shed light as to the likelihood of prosecuting and sanction specific types of CBCs[5] and allocate the scarce resources they have so as to focus their enforcement efforts into the most harmful practices. An important aspect that one should take into account in younger agencies is to assess the ability to counteract the effects of these CBCs into their domestic markets. Let us now present the classification and its rationale.

2.1. Rationale for the Classification of CBCs

Younger and small competition jurisdictions have limited financial and human resources to effectively enforce anti-cartel laws. As such, it is recommended that before investigating complicated international cartel activity elsewhere, they should be able to effectively prosecute domestic cartels and trigger their leniency programmes, if any. Given the present research's focus on Latin America and as can

[1] Evenett, Levenstein and Suslow (2001: 1222).
[2] Connor, 'International Cartel Stats', p 4.
[3] ASEAN Experts Group on Competition (2016).
[4] Evenett, Levenstein and Suslow (2001: 1222).
[5] A similar classification and assessment was carried out by Noonan and specific solutions for each cross-border anticompetitive practices were proposed. See Noonan (2008).

be seen in Chapter 1 related to the positive developments of anti-cartel enforcement records in key Latin American jurisdictions, one should be able to suggest that some of these jurisdictions are ready to move forward to investigate, prosecute and sanction international activity impacting in their own markets.

Therefore, in the attempt to classify CBCs and trigger ad-hoc international cooperation in cartel cases by young and small competition authorities wishing to counteract the adverse effects of these practices, one should look at the following first-level criteria:

i. **The number of jurisdictions involved in the CBC investigation, prosecution and sanctioning:** This criterion takes into account the impact of these CBCs on the market(s) from the perspective of the national competition authority's relevant market wishing to participate in the cooperation.[6] The harm to consumers is essential here as an overall prerequisite to investigate any type of cartel. This criterion is essential for young and small competition authorities to ascertain how many jurisdictions are currently looking into the CBC investigation. At the procedural level, if a young or small competition authority wishes to investigate a given CBC, it would be essential for the strategic organisation of the investigation to know how many jurisdictions (mature, large) have been investigating or even sanctioning the same CBC.[7]

ii. **The geographical coverage of the CBC:** This criterion refers to the relevant markets affected by the cartel (ie, product market and geographical market considerations). While available evidence would ascertain whether a cartel had a geographical reach of global, transnational, regional or even domestic scope,[8] it is not always possible to calculate all the effects and geographical coverage of a cartel, given the scarcity of data in many jurisdictions where competition laws and authorities are new or do not exist. As an alternative way to counteract this limitation would be to measure the trade volume through the level of sales targeting different markets across jurisdictions. Where regional trade agreements are in place to reduce or eliminate tariff barriers, regional cartel activities can take place because of the increased level of trade between the regional groupings. This criterion can also include the production and consumer sides and the number of countries affected by the cartel.

iii. **The country of origin of the cartelists:** This criterion refers to the specialisation and multimarket contacts[9] and which companies are members of the cartel (cartel international membership). By knowing the country of origin of the cartelists, it would be possible to look at the different domestic constituencies involved in the legal, political and socio-economic context of the cartelists'

[6] Interview with Bezzi.

[7] Interview with Ragazzo (11 May 2017).

[8] From a sample of 532 PICs, only 64 cartels had a global reach, cross-national cartels reached 109, local subnational 114 and single nation 425. See Connor, 'Price-Fixing Overcharges', p 32, Table 2.

[9] Budzinski (2008: 16).

country of origin.[10] Common business cultures and environments, interrelated value chains, strategic alliances, joint research and development, and common cooperation and networks with foreign institutions facilitate transnational cartelisation.[11] This criterion is relevant to understand the factors that led to the formation of the cartel and whether the cartel was formed as a response to fierce foreign competition.[12] It would also be useful to understand how the cartelists would base their operations once the cartel is formed.[13] Notably, cartelists will not only set the price or allocate markets, but also monitor their agreements with respect to price and sales, agree on punishment methods for enforcing the cartel, use of buy-backs to compensate cartel members, impose methods for responding to external disruptions from non-cartel suppliers and handling over-zealous sales representatives, and use operational procedures in terms of the frequency of meetings and the cartel's organisational structure.[14]

Other second-level criteria that could be useful to differentiate amongst CBCs are:

1. The *margin of profits* that a cartelist would typically get depending on the particular type of CBC. The margin of profits is calculated based on the price overcharges that resulted from the increase of joint profits of the cartel's members.[15] As the core objective of the cartel conspiracy is to raise prices above the competitive level, that difference between the cartelised price and the competitive price would be the most relevant attraction for cartelists to join the conspiracy.[16]
2. The *typical duration* or lifespan of the cartel, which is a result of the structural and organisational conditions within which a cartel would operate and maintain the loyalty of its membership.[17] The economic rationale for cartelists (ie, profitability)[18] will have effects on the typical duration of the cartel.[19] The estimates provided in the present research are based on the data available for multinational/global as well as transnational cartels. In the area of regional,

[10] See for instance the political context of the longest international cartel in history. Bertilorenzi (2016).

[11] Budzinski (2008: 17).

[12] See below, the case of a Chinese export cartel targeting US vitamin A market. Breed, Bernick and Emch, 'Deferring to Chinese Government'.

[13] See Harrington and Skrzypacz (2011).

[14] See Harrington Jr (2006).

[15] Connor, 'International Cartel Stats', p 15.

[16] In the PIC data set there are two methods of calculating of the overcharge rate. The columns headed 'OVERCHARGE/AFFECTED SALES %' simply divide dollar overcharges by affected sales in the appropriate national or regional market. Conventionally, this is the way in which overcharge rates are reported by lawyers, judges, or in the press. However, in the columns to the right headed 'OVERCHARGE /COMPETITIVE SALES %,' the denominator is 'competitive sales' rather than all sales during the cartel's life. That is, 'competitive sales' is affected sales minus the dollar overcharge. For effective sellers' cartels, competitive sales are smaller than affected sales and the computed overcharge rate will be larger. From an economic perspective, the latter overcharge rate is the more appropriate measure of a cartel's power over price. Connor, 'International Cartel Stats', p 16.

[17] Based on Connor, 'International Cartel Stats'.

[18] Marshall and Marx (2012).

[19] See Bertilorenzi (2016).

import and export cartels, the data for the benchmarking of typical cartel duration is not conclusive.

3. The *likelihood of prosecution and deterrence* is linked to the probability of detection by competition watchdogs particularly in mature and large jurisdictions. The fear of detection, imprisonment, and the possible monetary fines to be faced in multiple jurisdictions have a deterrent effect on cartelists.

2.2. Types of CBCs

Based on the criteria presented above, the present research puts forward the following classification of CBCs: export, import, regional, multinational and transnational, summarised in Table 2.1.

Table 2.1 Proposed Classification of the Types of Cross-Border Cartels

	Number of jurisdictions investigating	**Country of origin of the cartelists**	**Geographical coverage**	**Likelihood of prosecution & deterrence**
Export CBCs	Two jurisdictions: exporting and importing jurisdictions.	Companies are solely exporters within one country. 'Pure export cartels' (political-industrial considerations).	Only foreign market.	Difficult to prosecute by foreign competition authorities. Extraterritoriality principle may apply in some cases.
Import CBCs	One jurisdiction: the importing country.	Only domestic importing companies with clear incentives to restrict import foreign competition.	Only domestic market.	Easy to prosecute but politically is supported by the importing country's competition authority.
Regional CBCs	National jurisdictions comprise within a regional economic grouping.	EU-type cartel companies operate within a region (supply capacity cannot go beyond regional borders).	One region only	Supranational (sub) regional authorities (EU Commission, Andean Community, CARICOM).

(continued)

Table 2.1 ***(Continued)***

	Number of jurisdictions investigating	Country of origin of the cartelists	Geographical coverage	Likelihood of prosecution & deterrence
Multinational CBCs	A multiple number of 'usual suspects' (large/older jurisdictions).	Large multinational companies (global market share). A leader to deal with dissimilar business cultures and environments.	Global or quasi-global effects (little choice for consumers to opt for a substitute in other regions).	Only larger jurisdictions create a meaningful deterrent effect. Instability of the cartel is high.
Transnational CBCs	Selected jurisdictions.	Selected number of countries where there are interrelated business links.	Selected foreign relevant markets.	Emerging jurisdictions to prosecute (relevant deterrent effect). Instability of cartel is very high.

Source: own compilation

These five types of CBCs would present different challenges to young and small competition authorities, as presented in Part II of the present research. Key solutions to these challenges which are relevant and feasible for young and small competition authorities are discussed in Part III.

2.2.1. Export Cross-Border Cartels

Export cartels occur when the companies involved in a cartel are solely exporters within one country. Exporters may collude explicitly and even supported by their own governments, to enter joint production and/or joint marketing, price fixing and market allocation.[20] According to *Victor*, export cartels can be pure, mixed, national or international depending upon their scope and constituency.[21] As such, whereas *pure* export cartels would involve restraints that are directly targeting foreign markets, *mixed* export cartels show restraints in both domestic and foreign markets.

[20] Historically, export cartels have been promoted by governments. For instance, in 1944, Mason said that international cartels (referring to export cartels) have been negotiated by governments. Mason (1944: 605).

[21] Victor (1991).

Victor also describes *national* export cartels, which are exporters from one country alone, and *international* export cartels whereby exporters are from different countries.[22] Nonetheless, for the purposes of the present research, the concept of 'export cartels' will only cover national export cartels which are of the pure export cartel type. Based on practice, all export cartels that are not pure export cartels should fall within the definition of *transnational* cartels in section 2.1.1.5.

When export cartels promote the formation and stability of CBCs, with the encouragement or tolerance given by exporting states, there could be a link between export and transnational cartels. However, the distinction remains clear. Transnational cartels would refer to member firms which are based in different states, while undertakings engaged in export cartels are exporters from one exporting state to another country.

Compared to *multinational* cartels, on the other hand, export cartels are often driven by domestic considerations rather than more diverse considerations coming from multinational firms that had incentives to collude in certain markets. Countries may have fewer incentives to tolerate multinational or transnational cartels in comparison with export or import cartels that may protect specific domestic circumstances and even industrial policy arguments, when the cartel conduct takes place in the exporting country, but the adverse effects are felt exclusively or mainly in the importing country.[23]

To enable competition authorities outside of the jurisdiction of the export cartelists to go after the foregoing, the extraterritoriality principle must be resorted to. This is seen in the case of China promoting export cartels in the vitamins industry after the collapse of the worldwide vitamins cartel dismantled during 2001.[24]

The Chinese vitamin C export cartel targeted US markets[25] and was prosecuted in 2013 by US courts.[26] The Chinese government supported the export cartel on the grounds of the state doctrine principle and participated in the case

[22] ibid.

[23] Export cartels also have been defined as 'mercantilist trade political tools' which benefit home countries at the expense of others. Jensen-Eriksen (2007: 7).

[24] First (2000).

[25] Chinese exporters were found guilty of manipulating prices and limiting production during the period from December 2001 to June 2006. The jury found that the plaintiffs had sustained damages of $54.1 million, which was trebled under US antitrust law, for a total award of $162.3 million. In this law suit, a group of Chinese firms were sued by a class of vitamin C purchasers led by a small distributor. Prior to the jury's verdict, three of the original five defendants reached a settlement with the plaintiffs, with two of them reportedly agreeing to pay the plaintiffs $22.5 million. North China and Hebei Welcome Pharmaceutical Co remained in the case at the time of the verdict. Hence, the alleged collusion was of an export cartel operated by exporters from the same state – China. Under American law, in some circumstances companies may avoid antitrust liability if a court finds that a foreign government compelled the companies to engage in anticompetitive behavior. The defendants filed a motion to dismiss, and argued they were acting under the direction of regulators. See 'China Vitamin C Price-Fixing Verdict Scrutinized by Court'.

[26] *US Vitamin C Export Cartel* [2011] US District Court New York Case 1:06-md-01738-BMC-JO, Document 440.

via *amicus curiae*,[27] the first time that a Chinese institution had addressed US courts.[28] The US District Court of NY sanctioned the case on the grounds that the export cartels, while encouraged explicitly by the Chinese government, involved the private conduct of the Chinese exporters, which violated US antitrust laws.[29]

The Chinese government unequivocally criticised the judgment as unfair, saying that the judge had refused to respect China's own interpretation of Chinese law. In the US, however, this case was regarded as a significant victory for private antitrust enforcement against an export cartel. However, later in September 2016, the US Second Circuit Court of Appeals overturned the judgment on the ground that the companies were compelled to fix price and output by Chinese law, and therefore, their conduct was outside the antitrust jurisdiction of US federal courts.[30] As Kovacic said in an interview:

> The fact that they [the three Chinese competition authorities] were all there, arm's joined, providing a common view was a signal to the court 'we are serious about this'. We are serious about the arguments we are making and we are in effect giving you a seminar on how our government functions but also if you reject our views it will offend us. At first they had not made their case so clear. But then they did.[31]

It is worth noting that later in 2018, the US Supreme Court again reversed the ruling of the District Court, saying that a foreign government's interpretation of its own law is not binding on US courts.[32]

Beyond the back and forth in US legal instances, this case shows how the enforcement of competition rules in the US can adversely affect implementation of China's trade policy, while other importing countries prohibit export cartels effectively.[33] These cartels affect the trading relations between countries, and hence it has been claimed that 'it is not enough to simply consider them in light of existing competition law regulations but a more nuanced approach encompassing trade law [would be] therefore required …'.[34] Consensus on the detriment of export cartels is growing but a potential conflict between exporting and importing countries in this issue remains unavoidable.[35]

[27] An amicus brief also had been submitted to the court by the Chinese Ministry of Commerce (MOFCOM), informing the court that the plaintiffs challenged 'a regulatory pricing regime mandated by the government of China'. Therefore, it seems that this export cartel was compelled or at least encouraged by the exporting state. Exporting states' encouragement and tolerance is a common aspect of some export cartels, which also represents the greatest challenge for the realisation of an optimal regulation on them. 'China Vitamin C Price-Fixing Verdict Scrutinized by Court'.

[28] Breed, Bernick and Emch(nd).

[29] *US Vitamin C Export Cartel.*

[30] Breed, Bernick and Emch (nd).

[31] Interview with Kovacic.

[32] *16-1220 Animal Science Products, Inc v Hebei Welcome Pharmaceutical Co* (06/14/2018) 15.

[33] For a comphensive assessment of the new antitrust case law emerging in the US involving Chinese export cartels, see Martyniszyn, 'A Comparative Look on Foreign State Compulsion as a Defence in Antitrust Litigation'.

[34] Kwok (2013).

[35] See the proposal to advocate for mandatory notification and transparency of export cartels by the WTO. Daniel Sokol (2008: 980).

2.2.2. Import Cross-Border Cartels

In line with *Matsushita et al*, the definition of import cartels suggests the existence of agreements (explicit or tacit) between a group of importing companies to control prices, quantity, and market allocation.[36] Importers may collectively limit the aggregate amount of specified goods entering into the market, or sources of supply for such imports being specifically chosen (tendering requirements)[37] and/or fix the prices and terms of purchase the cartel members will pay for such imports.[38]

By its nature, companies involved in import cartels are only domestic importing companies with incentives to restrict foreign competition from entering the domestic jurisdiction. Consequently, the geographical coverage of an import cartel's impact is limited to the domestic market of the importing jurisdiction. Moreover, only the competition authority in the importing jurisdiction is involved in the investigation of the same.

Import cartels can be triggered as a response to foreign aggressive measures in the form of suppliers' 'natural' monopolies. Hence, competition laws in many countries recognise the legitimacy of import cartels 'even where domestic importers establish an import cartel for the purpose of boycotting the import of foreign goods'.[39] For instance, the so-called 'New Deal Sugar Cartel'[40] in the US was a 'legal' cartel[41] that restrained the import sales quotas of sugar into the US markets, thereby limiting sugar sales and raising its price. There is sufficient evidence that this import cartel substantially lessened the production in each sugar factory.[42] Another example took place in 1983 where Japanese importers restricted soda ash imports from the US.[43] Interestingly, in this case, the US government approached the Japanese Competition Authority and they reached a conclusion that an import cartel was in violation of the Japanese Competition Law and ordered the immediate dissolution of the import cartel accordingly. The key question was whether the import cartel was authorised by the Japanese government or was registered in the Transaction Law.[44]

In the examples above, the aggressive measures aimed at limiting sugar or soda ash imports to protect domestic producers from import competition were later

[36] Matsushita and others (2015: 812).

[37] Consider the case of tendering requirements in the market of lab equipment being imported by Spain from China. See Oficina Económica y Comercial (2002: 15).

[38] 'Import Cartels', The Encyclopedia of World Problems.

[39] Guzmán (2011: 133).

[40] 'New Deal cartels' refers to those agreements formed under the auspices of the National Recovery Administration during the Great Depression in 1930. See Bridgman and others (2009: 6–10).

[41] Although it was a legal cartel created and supervised by the Government, the Supreme Court ruled that these cartels were unconstitutional. Despite that, these cartels lasted for 40 years. See Bridgman and others (2009).

[42] For a historical view of these facts, see Folsom (2009).

[43] Matsushita (1991: 188).

[44] ibid: 189.

considered unlawful by the judiciary in the US, and the Competition Authority in Japan. Import cartels are often concluded to counterbalance a foreign state trading agency but assessing this type of cross-border anti-competitive practice from a domestic point of view might lead to distorted conclusions.

There is a blurry situation in the Banana Cartel (2011), prosecuted and sanctioned by the EU Commission to two main importers and sellers of bananas,from ACP countries.[45] Even though the cartel members were two importers that sold bananas within the EU, due to its duty-free quota with ACP countries, the EU considered this cartel a regional type of cartel.[46] Pacific Fruit and Chiquita, during the period July 2004–April 2005, fixed weekly sales prices and exchanged price information in relation to their respective brands, thereby directly harming consumers in the EU countries.[47]

Given the reasons above, and for the purposes of our definition, these importing companies could be in only in one country but not in different countries, otherwise the category would fall into the type of mere transnational CBCs involving agreements concluded among competing firms in one or several countries. Finally, it should be noted that both import and export cartels are trade restrictive measures at the international level. However, there is an important distinction between the two. The effects of the import cartels are immediately reflected in the country wherein the cartel activities occur. Hence, import cartels should be regarded as unlawful activities.[48]

2.2.3. Regional Cross-Border Cartels

For the purposes of the present research, regional cartels involve cartelists whose supply capacity and economies of scale cannot go beyond regional and neighbouring countries.[49] Factors such as transportation costs, homogeneity of the product, inelasticity of demand and high entry costs have facilitated regional collusion between companies[50] and made it profitable. Special features of regional cartels can also be absence of language barriers, similar business culture and a certain level of trust. Connor has named this type of cartel the 'EU cartel' because these cartels operate within a regional economic setting, such as a customs union or a single market, and may even have a supranational competition regime.[51] An example is 'the Chemical Cartel', where seven companies were sanctioned in 2006 for having

[45] EU Commission, 'Press Release – Antitrust: Commission Imposes €8.9 Million Fine in Banana Cartel'.

[46] Interview with Mehta.

[47] EU Commission, 'Press Release – Antitrust: Commission Imposes €8.9 Million Fine in Banana Cartel'.

[48] Sweeney (2009: 57).

[49] Consider the voluntary regional cartels that were established in the late 1920s in Europe. See part 1 of Henley (1988).

[50] Harrington and others (2015: 111).

[51] Connor, 'Private International Cartels', 4.

fixed prices of the market in hydrogen peroxide.[52] The regional cartel carved-up the chemical market across Europe and the fine imposed was £275 million.[53]

Regional cartels, which occur beyond the EU throughout different regional groupings worldwide, are difficult to uncover due to the lack of robust regional competition law. For instance, in the SACU/SADC region, South African local cartels (in fertiliser, bread, steel, mining-supply, cement, construction) have been prosecuted at the domestic level.[54] This fact does not evidently preclude the same unlawful practices occurring elsewhere in SACU/SADC countries, considering the close business ties trends in trade and investment in the region and therefore, the chances are self-evidently higher that a cartel in South Africa is most likely taking place or has taken place in other SACU/SADC countries, leading to the existence of SACU/SADC regional cartels.[55] A particular exmple is the cement cartel in Southern and East Africa, where most economies are relatively small in size and domestic markets do not provide the economies of scale for the companies operating therein.[56]

It is worth noting the distinction between regional cartels and domestic cartels that have an international dimension, or even a 'transnational' dimension in the meaning provided by this research. Connor has called this type of regional small cartel a *domestic international cartel*, because they have a limited scope (in the geographic sense) and have international representation. but are operated solely within a single national border.[57] Classical examples of these cartels are the cement cartel cases[58] in Argentina,[59] South Africa,[60] India[61] and Germany.[62]

2.2.4. Multinational Cross-Border Cartels

Multinational CBCs are those involving international price fixing arrangements where companies from different jurisdictions conspire to affect global or quasi-global markets. According to Connor, the frequency of global cartel prosecution has increased, but the world-wide deterrent effect is still low. Consider the following quote below:

> Global cartels are the worst of the worse: bigger in sales size, covering more territory and jurisdictions, and causing greater injuries to their customers. Although moving in

[52] This chemical is an agent for bleaching textiles and an ingredient in many domestic soap powders. See Economics Online (2006).

[53] ibid.

[54] Kaira (2015: 2–6), Section 3: Cartel Enforcement in South Africa.

[55] ibid: 6.

[56] Vilakazi, 'Regional Cartels and a Review of Developments in the Cement Industry'.

[57] Connor, 'Private International Cartels' 4.

[58] Cement cartels in Austria, Germany, Norway and Poland are also interesting cases where some countries 'legalised' them. See Fink and Frübing (nd: 6).

[59] 'Argentina's Supreme Court Rejects Cartel Arguments'.

[60] Donnelly, 'Competition Authorities' Cartel-Busting Pays off for SA' (*The M&G Online*).

[61] 'The Curious Case of the Cement Cartel'.

[62] Harrington and others (2015).

> the right direction, global schemes are penalized less severely on average by antitrust authorities than their greater injuriousness would warrant.[63]

As these cartels conglomerate a number of jurisdictions having different business cultural environments, members of the cartel will struggle to maintain the stability of the cartel by establishing three main stages: (1) market allocation according to market shares prior to cartel formation, (2) frustration in attempts to increase sales when they have expanded capacity, and (3) incongruity between a cartel member's allocated quota and its desired output. As such, breaking up a multinational CBC by mature or large competition authorities may depend on how the cartel members managed the natural instability of these cartels.[64] Failure to do so would mean that any member of the cartel could be unhappy and might like to withdraw from the cartel and even whistleblow to the relevant authority to find leniency and immunity.

Historically, multinational CBCs have been difficult to uncover, such as the international aluminium cartel that started in 1901[65] but was only detected and prosecuted in the mid-1980s.[66] Modern multinational CBCs, however, are often uncovered. During the period 2000–16, 75 global cartels were uncovered each year and more than 100,000 companies (7,200 named) were found liable for international price fixing, whereby gross cartels overcharged in excess of US$1.5 trillion, 60 per cent of this by multinational or global cartels.[67] Despite the staggering number of discoveries, it is believed that a great number of global cartels remain undetected. Those cartels that are documented have brought about tremendous damage to economies, particularly to emerging markets. The effects on developing countries are particularly pronounced, with these countries importing huge amounts of goods from industries that had seen price-fixing conspiracies.[68]

These imports represented 6.7 per cent of imports and 1.2 per cent of gross domestic product (GDP) in developing countries. For the poorest developing countries, they represented even larger proportions of trade, namely 8.8 per cent of imports, thereby limiting those countries' benefits from international trade and access to global supply chains. The full effect on developing countries may be more profound, considering that the foregoing figures suffer from a downward bias as they pertain only to discovered international cartels, and cover the effects of only that one anti-competitive practice.[69] Multinational CBCs can make substantial

[63] Connor, 'International Cartel Stats' 33–34.

[64] Cartel instability can be summarised in three stages: (1) market allocation according to market shares prior to cartel formation, (2) frustation to adjust grow sales when they have expanded capacity, and (3) incongruity between a cartel member's allocated quota and its desired output. Harrington and others (2015: 107).

[65] According to Connor, seven cartel eras can be distinguished : the years prior to 1890, 1890–1919, 1920–45, 1946–73, 1974–89, 1990–99, and 2000–13. These periods differ from each other with respect to the level of overcharges. Connor, 'International Cartel Stats' 40.

[66] Bertilorenzi (2016).

[67] Connor, 'International Cartel Stats'.

[68] Evenett, Levenstein and Suslow (2001).

[69] Noonan (2008: 59–68).

profits worldwide even if they are sanctioned and punished by mature jurisdictions; thereby the deterrent effect of bigger fines would be insufficient.[70] Cartelists are normally large multinational companies whereby market share can only be measured at the global level.[71]

In 2004, a sample of 'contemporary' multinational CBCs affecting nine international markets was identified: citric acid (1991–95); ferrosilicon (1989–91), graphite electrodes (1992–97), lysine (1992–95), shipping (Far East) (1991–94), shipping (North Atlantic), sodium gluconate (1993–95), sorbates (1979–96) and vitamins (1990–99).[72] The seamless steel tubes cartel (1990–95) was part also of this trend, its economic significance similar to the vitamins cartel.[73]

Looking more closely at the cartels, a first observation is that in all cases either the US Department of Justice or the EU Commission acted as prosecutor.[74] A second observation relates to the country of origin of the indicted firms. While in all cartels (with one exception) the indicted firms were from the US; in only one cartel (shipping Far East) were the indicted firms located also in developing emerging countries such as Malaysia.[75] Of these multinational cartels, two of them merit particular attention due to the fact that the impact of these multinational CBCs was also assessed in Latin American markets, in particular by Brazil and Mexico. These were the lysine and vitamins cartels.[76]

2.2.4.1. The Lysine Cartel (1992–95)

Lysine, an amino acid that speeds the development of lean muscle tissue in humans and animals, was first commercially produced in Japan by Ajinomoto Company based on scientific discoveries in 1956.[77] In the 1960s, early production of Lysine began at Ajinomoto's plant. Ajinomoto's rival, Kyowa Hakko also commenced Lysine production at the same time. During the mid-1970s, Japanese exports of Lysine to the US targeted mainly US manufactures of feeds for swine and poultry.[78] Ajinomoto expanded more rapidly (building plants in France, Thailand and the

[70] Michaels (2016: 236).

[71] According to Mehta, there is no global cartel that can cover global demand. Even in the case of the vitamins cartel, India has its own national companies and they blocked importation of vitamins from Switzerland through high tariffs. See Interview with Mehta.

[72] Levenstein and Suslow (2003: 807–11).

[73] For a comprehensive analysis of the seamless steel tubes cartel, see Yu (2003: 17–49).

[74] Levenstein and Suslow (2003: 807–11).

[75] ibid: 809.

[76] According to the US Department of Justice, in the lysine cartel, prices increased by 70% in the first six months and doubled over the course of the conspiracy; the defendants agreed to pay US customers more than $45 million in damages in March 2001. In the citric acid cartel, prices increased by over 30% during the course of the conspiracy. In the graphite electrodes cartel, prices increased by over 60% during theconspiracy; and finally, in the vitamins cartel, the defendants agreed to pay US customers more than $1 billion in damages. Griffin (2001).

[77] Connor, 'Our Customers Are Our Enemies' 6.

[78] ibid.

US) than its rival Kyowa, dominating the world market for three decades.[79] By the late 1980s, two more companies entered the lysine market: ADM (US) and Cheil Jedang (South Korea).[80] ADM's aggressive large-scale entry triggered the formation of the lysine cartel in 1992 in Mexico City,[81] through the organisation of the 'World Lysine Association', which met on a regular basis to collect and distribute production and market-share information.[82]

Global sales of $913 million dollars were calculated over four years of the cartel's duration whereby 95 per cent of the global market share was controlled by the cartel members.[83] As a result of this global domination, developing countries imported $470 million worth of Lysine, given exclusivity to selected developing country producers until the dismantling of the cartel in 1995 and foreclosing other producers and importers.[84]

The lysine cartel is a landmark case because it clearly illustrates how the formation of a global cartel was triggered by a necessity to 'survive' in a global market that was being rapidly eaten up by fierce competitors (ADM), and how domestic conditions of one company (ADM) forced it to approach Ajinomoto and the other rivals in Japan.[85] The lysine cartel case is also special as it was the first time that US enforcers entered the 'electronic age', and recorded all cartel activity since its formation until it ended.[86] Despite the prosecution of this global cartel being highly publicised,[87] '… just four years later a cartel of even greater scope would be uncovered in the bulk vitamins business.'[88]

2.2.4.2. *The Vitamins Cartel (1990–99)*

Vitamins are organic substances of natural components of foods that function as the stabiliser of cell membranes and promoter of a number of biological activities. Vitamins are considered commodities and homogenous products, where

[79] Up to the present time, Asia Pacific companies have been dominant in the lysine market. Andrew, 'Asia Pacific to Continue Hold Dominance in Global L-Lysine Market'.

[80] Connor, 'Our Customers Are Our Enemies' 7.

[81] These discussions led to the 23 June 1992 meeting in Mexico, which constitutes the beginning of ADM's collusion with the members of the Asian/European cartel *EU Case COMP/36545/F3 – Amino Acids* 2001/418/EC EUR-Lex-32001D0418-EN-EUR-Lex Para. 71.

[82] Indeed, Ajinomoto developed a strategy to cope with ADM's entry in 1990 so as to avoid ADM global dominance, but it did not work. In 1992, ADM had caused big losses to Ajinomoto's plant in the US and that made Ajinomoto urgently fix prices with its Japanese traditional rival.

[83] The calculation was based on the aggregated exports from the US, Japan and Korea, including the production plan of one of the cartelists which was located in Brazil. Yu (2003: 15).

[84] As a result of price discriminations across regions, the cartel blocked entry by potential developing country producers, as two of the Cartel's members were Korean producers. ibid: 15–16.

[85] Connor argues that ADM's real reason to form a cartel was due to the considerable loss on its lysine operations due to the strategy to reduce prices against import competition. There was also another reason, which was the contamination of its lysine fermentor. Connor, 'Our Customers Are Our Enemies' 9.

[86] ibid: 19.

[87] See two books published about the lysine cartel: Lieber (2000) and Eichenwald (2009).

[88] LeClair (2011: 112).

little or no differentiation exists across producers.[89] Hoffmann-La Roche, a Swiss drug company, was the first company to synthesise vitamins and pro-vitamins, leading to its first commercial success: synthetic vitamin C (ascorbic acid), introduced in 1934. By 1938, Roche had mastered the research and bulk manufacture of key vitamins A, B1, B2, B5, B6, C, D, E and K1 through synthetic chemistry, which was Roche's major source of sales.[90] Vitamin production was followed rapidly by Merck and Co (US) and Takeda Chemical Industries (Japan). In the 1980s, US pharmaceutical companies were closed or sold off to the 'big three' leading European firms (Roche, Badische Anilin und Soda Fabrik – BASF and Rhône-Poulenc – RP).

In the 1990s, various small Chinese manufacturers[91] made China the fourth location for vitamin production.[92] As a reaction to this development, 21 manufacturers joined one or more of the 16 conspiratorial groups, each of which met regularly to set quotas and target prices, exchange internal sales records, and monitor implementation of the quotas.[93] Roche, the industry leader, organised 14 of the 16 cartels, with BASF as its main partner in crime (12 cartels), followed by Takeda (five cartels) and RP (three cartels). Hoffmann-La Roche was fined by the EU Commission for its involvement in the multinational vitamin cartel,[94] which led the allocation of sales quotas and global price fixing with its counterparts from Germany (BASF and Merck), France (Aventis), Netherlands (Solvay) and Japan (Daichi and Eisai).[95] Annual global sales of the cartel amounted to $1.34 billion as prices rose by 35 per cent during the time of the cartel.[96] While the value of vitamin importation is small relative to developing countries' imports of seamless steel tubes and pipelines, the impact on direct consumers importing vitamin-enriched foods for human and animal consumption was staggering, amounting to as much as $1.7 billion.[97]

[89] Igami and Sugaya (2016: 13).

[90] Connor, 'The Great Global Vitamins Conspiracy' 16.

[91] 'The major significance of these suggestions about technological barriers in understanding the evolution of vitamin price fixing is the fact that the Chinese exporters were spoilers for the cartels. The Chinese vitamin companies were too small, too numerous, and too inclined to be aggressive about exporting – all characteristics that made them unsuitable candidates to recruit to the vitamins cartels. Whenever Chinese chemical companies could adopt production methods that made their vitamin production price-competitive (assisted by Chinese government export subsidies), they aggressively captured U.S. market shares that in some cases were so large that the cartels affected were unable to sustain their conspiracies. This certainly happened in the case of vitamin C around 1995. Chinese incursion into the U.S. market was also one factor for the early demise of the cartels established in vitamins B1, B2, B6, B12, and folic acid.' ibid: 29.

[92] ibid: 18.

[93] According to Mr Mehta, the real reason of the formation of that multinational CBC was to foreclose Chinese exports. Interview with Mehta.

[94] First (2000).

[95] EU Commission, 'Press Release – Commission Imposes Fines on Vitamin Cartels'.

[96] Yu (2003: 11).

[97] The calculation is an underestimation of the welfare loss from collusion in the vitamins industry. ibid.

An important feature of these multinational CBCs (lysine and bulk vitamins) is that the products are intermediate products and not being sold directly to consumers, which leads to prices easily able to be concealed by the different intermediate agents part of the global value added chain.[98] These two cartels were also prosecuted by two Latin American competition authorities considering the direct impact on their domestic markets. In both cases, international cooperation between mature and young competition authorities was incipient, despite some efforts made by the younger authorities to reach out to their more mature peers.

2.2.4.3. The Marine Hoses Cartel and the Air Cargo Cartel

The trade of multinational CBCs, such as the marine hoses cartel (1986–2007) and the air cargo cartel (2000–06), have led to more international cooperation among mature competition regimes particularly, partly thanks to cooperation agreements and MOUs signed to move forward on specific cooperation issues. The details of these instruments will be assessed in chapter three. Let us briefly review the two cases below.

The **marine hoses cartel** involved a specialised market for the production and supply of marine hoses, which are used to transfer oil and petroleum products into and out of tankers.[99] It was formed to allocate tenders, fix prices, quotas, sales conditions, share the market geographically, and exchange sensitive information on prices, sales volumes and procurement tenders.[100] Revealed as having been operational since 1986, the marine hose cartel, was a textbook example of the use of a 'coordinator', who in this case was an ex-employee of one of the cartel companies.

This coordinator regularly communicated by fax, e-mail and, sometimes, telephone for each new tender.[101] 'The coordinator gave members market share reports, market development reports and specific instructions on their bids. In addition, the coordinator selected a "champion" for each contract. This "champion" would win the tender, while other members of the cartel would submit "cover bids" so as not to give away the cartel ….'[102] In May 2007, a closely coordinated action involving the US Department of Justice, the EU Commission and the Office for Fair Trading of the United Kingdom arrested eight producers of marine hoses in Houston, Texas, while they were attending an industry conference. Raids were carried out at various premises in the US, France, Italy, and the UK, where, according to the UK authority, they conducted their first search of a home address as part of a cartel investigation.[103]

[98] LeClair (2011: 113–14).
[99] 'The Marine Hose Cartel: A New Era In International Co-operation'.
[100] Pino (2009).
[101] ibid: 53–54.
[102] ibid: 54.
[103] 'The Marine Hose Cartel: A New Era In International Co-operation'.

Another multinational CBC was discovered thanks to the confession of Lufthansa that triggered leniency under the so-called whistle-blower government programmes, in the **air cargo cartel.**[104] In a very transparent market, which was traditionally developed through national airlines across the world, the routes and pricing were initially heavily regulated by treaties that gave reciprocal rights to the nation's airlines. Deregulation and privatisation took place in the 1990s, removing regulation and the requirement of government approval for pricing.[105] This led some air carriers to collude on the price of fuel surcharges in early 2000.

Over time, the other air carriers joined the conspiracy, growing the geographical coverage of the cartel exponentially. As a result, Lufthansa and around 20 competition authorities worked together to explore the potential application of the different competition laws (EU, US, South Africa, Australia) to the case.[106] Extraordinary coordination took place between major jurisdictions regarding the timing of the dawn-raids that were conducted worldwide.

2.2.5. Transnational Cross-Border Cartels

In a transnational CBC, limited jurisdictions are involved because of the limited relevant market of the CBC, which is localised through cross-border specific product markets. A transnational CBC investigation would involve at least three jurisdictions, one of which would be a young or small competition regime. In multinational CBCs, the assumption is that young or small competition regimes are unable to participate in the investigations as they would need to invest more resources in order to understand the complexity and variety of jurisdictions involved in the CBC.

As for the size of the market affected, prima facie, at least two different jurisdictions across continents would need to be affected by a transnational CBC. Compared to a multinational CBC which eliminates all possible alternatives for consumers (ie, all the competitors which have global impact are involved in the cartel[107]), transnational cartels would leave consumers with substitute choices as competition is only distorted in affected transnational relevant markets.

Furthermore, in transnational CBCs, the companies' country of origin would be limited jurisdictions from different continents or regions. Often, the member companies would have a 'regional' dominant position in their respective regions. These companies would typically compete at the international level. Their incentive to collude is to maintain their dominance in their respective regions and

[104] Bergman and Sokol, 'The Air Cargo Cartel'.
[105] ibid: 3–4.
[106] ibid: 10.
[107] *cf* with the assumption that even multinational CBCs with global coverage will not cover the whole world. See the case of the vitamins CBC, whereby Indian vitamin companies were protected by high-tariff schedules. Interview with Mehta.

foreclose the entrance of other foreign competitors, which would be difficult to do if they were acting separately.

While there are a number of strategies to maintain intra-cartel communication[108] in a transnational cartel, the typical duration or lifespan of this cartel would be limited because of the failure to adjust organisationally to changing external market definitions,[109] particularly the economic conditions.[110] Despite the foregoing, the profitability of the cartel would be as high as 40 per cent above the competitive price. The examples of the major transnational cartels are divided into two waves, below.

2.2.5.1. *First Wave of Transnational Cartels*

The first wave of transnational cartels took place in the 1990s and has been characterised as 'brief'. The main examples of transnational cartels of this first wave are the aluminium phosphide cartel (January 1990 to November 1990), where companies from Brazil, India, the US and Germany fixed prices for almost a year, affecting the US market, and the carbon cathode block (February 1996 to December 1997), where companies from Germany, Japan and the US agreed to hit US and other markets, also for a short period.[111] Other brief international cartels took place in markets such as explosives (1988–92), fine arts (April 1993–Dec 1999) and thermal fax paper (1992–92). In these cartels, US and other European or Asian companies colluded to affect specific domestic markets, mainly the US.[112]

2.2.5.2. *Second Wave of Transnational Cartels*

This second wave, characterised as more sophisticated, occurred from 2000 onwards and features landmark international cases, such as specific international schemes from the auto-parts multinational cartel, including the auto lighting products aftermarket (2001–08) whereby US and Canadian markets were affected, the auto refrigerants cartel impacting the EU single market, and the auto parts sheet metal aftermarket which targeted the US market.[113]

More recently in the area of financial services, a number of cartel investigations have been conducted by the US,[114] Switzerland, the EU, South Korea, Singapore,

[108] Spagnolo (2000).

[109] Connor, 'Private International Cartels' 3.

[110] See Levenstein and Suslow (2006).

[111] See Levenstein and Suslow (2003: 807), Table 1: Recent International Cartels Investigated by the US and EU authorities.

[112] ibid: 808–11.

[113] Indeed, in 2013, Connor listed 34 recent alleged auto-parts cartels, of which only four had two-single nation geographical coverage. Connor, 'Is Auto Parts Evolving into a Supercartel?'.

[114] The far-reaching Libor investigations continued in 2016, involving US and Swiss authorities working together to sanction (separately) banks such as Credit Suisse, JP Morgan, RBS, UBS for rigging-related activities. See the Libor Case in Gibson Dunn (2017: 13).

among others, to prosecute and sanction a number of banks which formed a series of transnational cartels aiming at rigging two global interest rate benchmarks.[115]

In the ocean shipping/roll-on, roll-off cargo cartel,[116] US, EU, Japanese, Australian[117] and Chinese[118] enforcers investigated an alleged conspiracy to fix prices, allocate customers and rig bids of international ocean shipping services for roll-on, roll-off cargo used in the international shipment of cars, trucks, and buses, and eventually sanctioned Norwegian and Japanese companies. Younger competition authorities such as Brazil,[119] Chile and recently Peru[120] have also investigated and in some cases sanctioned the transnational case. In the capacitors case, authorities from Asia, South America, Europe and US investigated the capacitors' manufacturers. In the posters case, US and UK authorities sanctioned a US company for having used a price-fixing algorithm.[121]

Other transnational cartels that can be mentioned are as follows:

1. **The Asia fine paper cartel**: A typical transnational cartel model whereby two foreign companies (in Singapore and Indonesia[122]) targeted Australian markets in the paper and pulp sector.[123] Between 2000 and 2004 the two companies agreed to supply to Australian costumers uncoated wood free folio and cut-size paper (UWF paper) with the purpose and effect of fixing, controlling or maintaining the average price per metric tonne at which they would supply UWF paper to customers in Australia thereby contravening the Australian Competition and Consumer Act.[124]

[115] Four of the banks are accused of colluding to set interest rate derivatives for the euro (Euribor). Six of them colluded to fix the rates for the Japanese yen (Libor). Both decisions were adopted under the Commission's cartel settlement procedure after a two-year investigation. Fines were reduced by 10% because the banks agreed to settle. European Voice (2013).

[116] Note that this CBC is considered transnational because the shipping companies colluded in certain jurisdictions. Even though it was investigated and prosecuted by various jurisdictions, including young and small in Latin America (Brazil, Chile and recently Peru), one cannot ascertain fully that the global supply of ocean shipping routes was all cartelised. There was still a possibility for substitution of ocean routes at the international level, and no 'global foreclosure' took place.

[117] The action essentially piggybacks on the work of the US, Japanese and European Commission regulators but in order to conduct its case, the ACCC had to find evidence of the behaviour on the Australian routes: 'ACCC in Cartel Case Contest'.

[118] In 2015, China fined seven shipping companies a total of 407 million yuan ($65 million) for price-fixing in what appears to be the same cartel. The National Development and Reform Commission (NDRC) oversees the pricing restrictions of the antimonopoly law. The agency said that for four years the companies had colluded to raise rates on shipments of cars, trucks, and construction machinery across five shipping routes, including between China and North America, Latin America and Europe. The cartel targeted 'roll-on, roll-off' shipping rates for cars, trucks and construction equipment. These are specialised cargo ships that can carry hundreds of vehicles. 'China Fines 7 Shipping Companies $65 Million'.

[119] CADE, 'Superintendence Investigates International Cartel of Maritime Transportation of Automobiles – '.

[120] 'Indecopi Inicia Procedimiento Contra Seis Líneas Navieras Por Presuntas Prácticas Colusorias En El Servicio de Transporte Marítimo Internacional de Carga Rodante – Inicio – Indecopi'.

[121] Gibson Dunn (2017: 17).

[122] Asia Pulp & Paper Company Ltd (Singapore) and PT Indah Kiat Pulp and Paper Tbk (Indonesia).

[123] Australia Competition Law Org (2011).

[124] ibid.

2. **The automotive bearings cartel**: A transnational price fixing agreement that took place between targeted jurisdictions (US, Canada, Europe and Australia) whereby a number of subsidiaries in Australian bearing companies would regularly met and discuss market trends and performance of the companies, including historical sales figures, at a 'Southern Cross Association–SCA', between 1999 and 2011.[125] Indeed, according to the EU proceedings, these multilateral meetings (also called by some participants 'steel' or 'club' meetings) would have as an objective to coordinate the passing-on to automotive customers of increases in the steel price.[126]

3. **The gas-insulated switchgear cartel**: Over the period 1988–2004, gas-insulated switchgear[127] suppliers in Europe and Japan[128] conspired to inform each other of calls for tender to coordinate their bids,[129] hitting their own costumers which were the public utilities companies that typically select switchgear producers based on 'calls for tender.' The riggers would take turns placing the best bid according to previously agreed quotas.[130] This transnational CBC did not impact US markets because the US market uses a different type of 'air-insulated' technology in the generation of power.[131]

As a separate note, the case of two CBCs can be blurry because of the state-run intervention. First, the consortium cartel (1977), whereby the US Department of Justice did not take action against a number of US and European petroleum companies that had formed an import cartel, a so-called consortium to deal with the harsh and oppressive policies of the Libyan government towards the operating facilities in oil wells, including confiscating production facilities.[132] Second, the

[125] See Bezzi (2014: slide 6).

[126] '... In that context, the participants exchanged information on: • which customers had (not yet) accepted a price increase due to the steel price increase, • the amount of the requested or accepted increase, • the timing of the increase, as accepted by the OEMs, and • the status of the negotiations with their respective automotive customers, if still pending.' *EU Case Bearing Automative Cartel* [2014] 12.

[127] Gas-insulated switchgear (GIS) is used to control energy flow in electricity grids. It is heavy electrical equipment, used as a major component for turnkey power substations. *EU Case COMP/F/38899 Gas Insultated Switchgear* [2007] 9.

[128] The companies were: Siemens AG, ABB Ltd, ALSTOM (Société Anonyme), AREVA T&D SA, Fuji Electric Holdings Co Ltd, Hitachi Ltd, Schneider Electric SA, Siemens Transmission & Distribution Ltd and Japan AE Power Systems. See Shearman & Sterling LLP, 'Gas Insulated Switchgear'.

[129] Indeed, the EU found the following violations of competition law: (a) the sharing of markets; (b) the allocation of quotas and maintenance of respective market shares; (c) the allocation of individual GIS projects to designated producers and manipulation of the bidding procedure for those projects (bid-rigging) in order to ensure that the assigned producers were awarded the contract in question; (d) the fixing of prices by means of complex price arrangements for projects which were not allocated; (e) the termination of licence agreements with non cartel members; (f) the exchange of sensitive market information. See *EU Case COMP/F/38.899 Gas Insultated Switchgear* [2007] 8.

[130] '... In addition to bid-rigging, suppliers also allocated business by geographic market and used code names for companies and individuals in their communications to maintain secrecy ....' Shearman & Sterling LLP, 'Gas Insulated Switchgear'.

[131] Interview with Mehta.

[132] Matsushita and others (2015: 813).

ASEAN rice cartel (2008) whereby the Thai government wished to create a cartel of rice-producing countries in partnership with Vietnam, Cambodia, Myanmar and Laos, similar to the OPEC-model oil cartel.[133] Fortunately, the plan was abandoned and instead Thailand met with top Asian exporters including India, China, Vietnam, Myanmar, Cambodia and Pakistan to improve productivity.[134]

2.2.5.3. *The Auto-Parts Cartels*

Some may argue that the auto-parts cartels cases (2000–10) involved multinational CBCs, rather than transnational cartels under the classification presented above, as the US Department of Justice has stated that it has been the largest investigation that it 'has ever pursued, both in terms of its scope and the potential volume of commerce affected by the alleged illegal conduct'.[135]

However, following the criteria provided in this research, the auto-parts cartels would fit in the transnational CBC category because of the following considerations: first, despite having multi-jurisdictional investigations[136] that led to the discovery of 34 auto-parts cartels worldwide,[137] these interrelated cartels operated relatively small and target-oriented bidding processes for specific auto part supplies in selected car manufacturer's assembly plants.[138] Second, even though the aggregate coverage of taking all these cartels as a whole could be regarded as multinational, competition at the global level was not essentially affected.

From the data available, it seems that the scope of the auto parts cartels was not global but transnational targeted markets of auto-parts supply to a number of automaker companies in certain jurisdictions. Hence, the auto parts cartels would more appropriately be classified as a transnational cartel. Third, the cartel members rigged their bids to distort competition. On some occasions, the auto-parts suppliers were vertically integrated to the automaker company, and they colluded to impose extra manufacturing costs on a rival automaker brand, such as in the Japanese case on the small electric motor auto systems cartel.[139]

Heretofore, more and more cartels related to the auto parts case are being discovered, and are subject of a continuing investigation. As of December 2016,[140]

[133] Post Publishing PCL, 'Thailand & Neighbors Join Together on Rice'.

[134] 'Thailand Abandons Plan for Southeast Asian Rice Cartel' (CBC News).

[135] 'Acting Assistant Attorney General Sharis A. Pozen Speaks'.

[136] The US coordinated efforts with Japan, EU, Canada, Korea, Mexico and Australia. See Shepard and Keyte (2014).

[137] Connor, Is Auto Parts Evolving into a Supercartel?' 12.

[138] Indeed, the auto-parts supply market is a highly concentrated market, with few suppliers geographically clustered in assembly plants and high barriers to entry due to the automakers' policies of running qualification programmes for supplies. Ibid: 3.

[139] ibid: 3.

[140] According to the US Department of Justice, the investigation is not complete, and more investigation activities were expected during 2017, punishing companies and executives that sought to maximise their profits through anticompetitive means. See Gibson Dunn (2017: 15).

enforcers from the US[141] and other major competition authorities worldwide[142] had prosecuted and indicted 47 companies and imprisoned 65 executives, with the 66th executive being prosecuted in February 2017.[143] As a matter of fact, the storm of investigations in the auto parts cartels investigation changed significantly the way the so-called 'prototypical global industry'[144] operated and triggered full-fledged compliance programmes for the Japanese companies.[145]

The difference between multinational and transnational CBCs may not be crucial to mature and large competition authorities, which can readily prosecute a CBC if it impacts their domestic markets.[146] However, from the perspective of young or small competition authorities with limited resources, this difference matters. Knowing the kind of CBC involved is strategic to a young or small competition authority as it gives an idea as to the number of jurisdictions that it needs to interact with as well as the resources and risks they would face in a possible investigation.[147]

2.3. Summary

As can be seen, CBCs are a reality throughout the world. They have been a core feature of international business activities for more than a century. With the rise of competition enforcers gradually across the world together with a detailed account of CBC activity by prominent scholars, one can now estimate the effects of these CBCs on different markets, identify the country of origin of the companies involved in the cartel as well as the reasons as to how the cartel was formed. The objective of chapter two was to provide a 'workable' classification that could be used in the following chapters, particularly in assessing the Latin American region's dynamic markets and the way CBCs have impacted the region. In the classification provided in this chapter, the reader must be aware of some limitations. Considering the lack of available data on the effects on regional cartels, it may be argued that a number of companies operating in those regional markets can also have a transnational or even global effect. Since evidence is not available to prove otherwise, it is preferable to avoid speculative assumptions that might hamper the seriousness of the present research.

[141] From September 2011 to February 2015, the US Department of Justice had been prosecuting the auto parts case. See US Department of Justice press release, 'Auto Parts Investigation 2015'.
[142] 'Global Cartel Fines Reach New High in 2014'.
[143] 'Auto Parts Industry Executive Pleads Guilty to Obstruction of Justice'.
[144] The sourcing methods in this global industry are identical across the auto-assembly plants across the world. Connor, 'Is Auto Parts Evolving into a Supercartel?' 3.
[145] 'Traditionally, Japanese companies have been tolerant towards holding meetings with competitors and provide no education to employees about the risks associated with this type of activities'. 'Cartels: EU Car Parts' 63.
[146] Interview with Bezzi.
[147] Interview with Ragazzo.

3

Theory and Practice of International Cooperation

Chapters one and two explored the intense CBC activity at the global, transnational and regional levels, which reflects the trend of business patterns that interconnect across countries through a global supply chain of goods and services. This globalisation of business patterns and economic activity has led to two different and perhaps competing tendencies that may provide a challenge for policymakers and regulators. Globalisation means that industries reduce their business activities in certain regions and differentiate across them more as they localise their production chains throughout jurisdictions worldwide; at the same time, there is a second tendency wherein certain companies prefer to localise their production patterns and supply chains in a particular region, which partly explains the proliferation of regional development policies based on local clusters of firms and industries.[1]

Competition agencies that know the apparently paradoxical tendencies of globalisation vs localisation would need to be attentive to ways and means of establishing cooperation mechanisms either when dealing with strictly regional CBCs (as defined in chapter two), or when dealing with the harmful effects of transnational, multinational CBCs.[2] In all of these cross-border transactions, the transfer of wealth from consumers to producers distorts domestic competition enforcement considerations, as they will warp the concept of consumer welfare as its main domestic goal.[3] The fact is that consumers are always left behind when regional business cartelists conspire with other competitors under any other form of CBC.

Fostering international cooperation is especially important in respect to both the trends of globalisation and the unduly negative impact on local consumers. Chapter three therefore provides a theoretical and practical discussion on the international cooperation that is needed to effectively address CBCs. The present chapter has five sections. The first will deal with the underlying reasons why competition authorities need to cooperate and the benefits arising from it.

[1] See more in Enright (2000).

[2] In the current trend of political uncertainty (Brexit, Trump), with tariffs and walls, it seems that the 'local' is superseding the 'global'. See more in Livesey (2017).

[3] Ezrachi (2012).

The second section will address the barriers and incentives to cooperate at the general and case-specific levels. The third topic to be discussed is the role of politics in the area of international cooperation. The fourth section will explore the forms and tools of international cooperation whether formal or informal arrangements are in place. A last section will cover the role of the international organisations in the area of cooperation.

3.1. Rationale for Cooperation

By January 2019, there are about 141 national competition authorities in the world, alongside more than five regional competition authorities.[4] Some years ago, in 2016, there were about 138 competition authorities worldwide.[5] This translates to an increasing proliferation of young and small competition authorities wishing to acquire the most relevant international practices in order to enforce competition laws in their respective jurisdictions. The ensuing complexity highlights the importance of international cooperation in the fight against CBCs, where less experienced authorities can benefit from the experience of other relatively more advanced or mature competition authorities.[6] These competition authorities/jurisdictions can benefit from the information and reasoning given by other, more experienced jurisdictions that have investigated or ruled on the case.[7] This case-specific cooperation is generally carried out through formal or informal consultations and remains a crucial aspect of cooperation in competition law enforcement[8] that has important implications for the work of the competition authority at the domestic level. Consider the following quotation from a young but important competition authority in the ASEAN region, Indonesia:

> Enforcement by other authorities can help with domestic criticism on a particular case or attempts to restrain their powers or scope of enforcement, in a way that we can say to our domestic partners (like ministry, parliament, practitioners, or scholars) that our enforcement was in line with the international standards or practices that has been tested by other competition authorities.[9]

Failure to cooperate can lead to less informed decision-making, the quality of which can consequently be lower.[10] It can also harm the attempt to promote convergence between neighbouring partners, both in the analysis of specific or general cases;

[4] Federal Trade Commission (2019).
[5] Fox (2016).
[6] One aspect of cooperation is related to law enforcement but other aspects where cooperation can play a role are related to competition advocacy or the proper design of competition laws and institutions. Jenny (2003: 974).
[7] Setiawan, (2015: slide 2).
[8] Jenny (2003: 974).
[9] Setiawan (2015: slide 2).
[10] See ch Guzmán (2011: 217).

and finally it can lead to 'unfamiliarity between agencies and mutual understanding of their enforcement processes, which in turn may help affect future cooperation and trust'.[11]

With the great number of competition laws worldwide, the chances for duplication or multiplication of proceedings, misunderstanding of laws and regulations affecting common markets and the diversity of criteria applied by anti-cartel laws are greater than formerly, when there were very few competition authorities in the world. Hence, it is clear that strategic and methodical cooperation is a challenge, but one that is of great value to young and small competition authorities.

Despite the seemingly clear logic behind cooperation, it does not happen naturally. Spontaneous cooperation is restrained by the lack of common enforcement interests between mature and young competition authorities, an effect of the so-called 'distributional conflict' explained by economists through game theory.[12] This is when mature competition authorities' interests in dealing with multinational CBCs differ markedly from those coming of younger authorities (amongst younger authorities, interests might be less asymmetric), which, as a result, aggravates coordination. Mature authorities do not have incentives to assist young authorities in, for instance, gathering the foreign evidence that they need to open their investigations, under the guise of an inability to cooperate in specific cartel matters due to differences in the legal standing in cartel offences.[13] Consequently, while a small or young competition authority may be interested in investigating the effects of a multinational CBC in its own jurisdiction, there is no common enforcement interest for the mature competition authority. The solutions to address the lack of incentives for cooperation are discussed in depth in chapter five.

3.1.1. Phases of International Cooperation in Cartel Investigations

International cooperation in cartel investigations can take place during the different stages of an investigation, whether it is purely administrative in nature, quasi-judicial or judicial. Normally, in an open cartel investigation, whether domestic or international, there will be a **pre-investigatory phase** where the preliminary information-gathering takes place and competition authorities can cooperate

[11] Setiawan (2015: slide 3).

[12] The 'distributional conflict' is explained by economists as a problem of coordination games whereby international coordination might be difficult to achieve because the different payoffs between mature and young competition agencies and unwillingness to depart from the dominant strategies. As such, the attempts to coordinate cartel investigations internationally 'can be assumed to involve a genuine willingness to coordinate regulatory policies across jurisdictions rather than an incentive to engage in non-cooperative strategies and cheating …': Bradford (2007: 415).

[13] In an interview with an anonymous referee, it was mentioned that for US enforcers the fact that the evidence is located in Germany creates difficulties, given the difference in the 'administrative vs criminal' legal standing between these jurisdictions.

formally or informally regarding the markets to be investigated, companies to be targeted, the location of evidence, and avoidance of destruction of evidence'.[14] This includes the 'publicly available information'[15] as well as the 'agency internal information'.[16]

Examples of competition authorities sharing information at the pre-investigatory phase can be seen in the marine hose cartel and the air cargo cartel, described in chapter two. At the **investigatory phase**, competition authorities have formally opened an investigation. In this phase, evidence is gathered and analysed, and the case against the cartel violators is constructed. Authorities will determine at this stage whether the information provided by the parties is deemed 'privileged'[17] or 'confidential information'.[18] As such, these types of information can be provided either voluntarily (via leniency applications) or compulsorily (via inspection and subpoena). Finally, at the **post-investigatory phase,** competition authorities find themselves either in the adjudication phase (if the authority has an administrative tribunal) or prosecution phase (if criminal investigation should be prompted).[19] In this particular phase, competition authorities may exchange information and evidence through case discussions between the investigators.

In these three phases, there are four types of information that authorities usually handle:

(1) **Public information**: 'In this case, one agency simply helps another agency to gain time by providing information which is already in the public domain (perhaps a hard-to-find market report, or information about the market arising from studies carried out by the agency.'[20]

(2) **Agency information**: 'This is information which is not necessarily in the public domain, but which is generated within the agency itself, rather than provided by parties to the investigation (although it may be based on information supplied by the parties). Such "agency information" may concern for example the stage which the investigation has reached, the planned timing of further steps, the

[14] ICN (ed), 'Co-operation between Competition Agencies in Cartel Investigations', p 9.

[15] ibid 9; information that is already in the public domain. In this case, one authority would simply help another to gain time by providing information that is perhaps a hard-to-find market report, or information about the market arising from studies carried out by the agency. See ICN, 'Anti-Cartel Enforcement Manual Chapter 9'.

[16] Information that competition authorities are permitted to exchange. This information is not necessarily in the public domain but is generated by the authority itself. Examples: the nature or status of their investigations, their investigation theories, their preliminary conclusions. ICN, 'Anti-Cartel Enforcement Manual Chapter 9', p 9.

[17] Information that is subject to a legal right to keep some very limited kinds of communications confidential and exempt from disclosure in civil and criminal law proceedings. The definition is general and each jurisdiction may provide a different definition depending on the legal systems at stake. ibid 9.

[18] Information defined as such by national law. For instance, confidential information could be defined as business secrets of a company whereby its disclosure could prejudice the commercial interests of the company. See ibid 4.

[19] ICN, 'Co-operation between Competition Agencies in Cartel Investigations', p 9.

[20] ibid 7.

provisional orientation of the investigation, conclusions reached about the nature of the market and so forth.'[21]

(3) **Information from the parties already in possession of one agency**: 'This kind of material can be evidence of an infringement or background information on the market or the activities of the parties (such as turnover figures). The information may have been provided voluntarily (by an immunity/amnesty applicant, for example) or under compulsion (in an inspection, under subpoena, and so forth.'[22]

(4) **Information obtained from the parties at the request of another agency**: 'Where two agencies have a highly developed cooperative relationship, it may be possible for one of them to request the other to obtain information from parties in its jurisdiction, which is not already in its possession. This could involve carrying out surprise searches, raids or inspections, issuing subpoenas, interviewing witnesses, and so forth.'[23]

Domestic laws govern how these types of information can be exchanged in accordance with the different requirements that competition authorities are bound such as procedural safeguards and due process considerations.[24]

3.1.2. The Role of Politics in International Cooperation

Historically, politics has been a consideration in the design of competition policies and laws.[25] While competition policies are government policies and laws intended to 'ensure that competition in the marketplace is not restricted in such a way as to reduce economic welfare',[26] public policymakers and politicians tend to employ these policies for other public policy goals distinct from the pure competition goals stated in the laws.

For example, the role of domestic politics decided the extent and scope of the first US-EU bilateral cooperation agreement in 1991.[27] Both EU and US regulators chose the crafting of a soft bilateral agreement that would not require ratification from their national constituencies but rather lay under their discretionary authority.[28] In this manner, the transatlantic cooperation framework brought

[21] ibid.
[22] ibid.
[23] ibid.
[24] Zanettin (2002).
[25] For instance, competition law has occupied 'a place in the corpus of English law for many centuries'. See for a comprehensive assessment of the evolution of competition law and policy in the UK Scott, 'The Evolution of Competition Law and Policy in the United Kingdom'.
[26] Motta (2004: xvii).
[27] See US & EU Governments, 'Agreement between US and EU on the Application of Their Competition Laws'.
[28] Damro (2006: 183).

about a non-treaty international agreement which relied largely on the regulators' discretionary prerogatives. These regulators, in some instances, were, of course, constrained by their domestic institutions' dynamics, despite the fact having formed a transnational government network between these two jurisdictions.[29] The role of politics is essential in the enactment of cooperation agreements, and additional allegations point to cooperation agreements between major jurisdictions and emerging ones which may have been the result of the geopolitical context in which the countries exist. The relationship between the US and China as of 2005 is a case in point.[30]

Informal cooperation between American and Chinese competition officials dated back more than 12 years before the enactment of China's Anti-Monopoly Law in 2008. In 2010, China became the second largest economy in the world, surpassing Japan.[31]

In 2011, the first and only memorandum of understanding (MOU) between the American and Chinese competition authorities was signed.[32] At that point, President Obama's foreign policy strategy with China had been steady during his two terms in office (2008–16). Obama said that 'the relationship between the United States and China is the most important bilateral relationship of the twenty-first century' and this was realised in the form of unprecedentedly close ties between the two countries, with high degrees of cooperation.[33] Hence the 2011 MOU formalised an informal system of cooperation between the two countries wherein the US had many opportunities to assist the drafting process of the Chinese competition law.[34] It is clear that geopolitics[35] in this respect played an

[29] Paraphrasing Slaughter's ideas, the proliferation of government networks shows common functions with the purpose: (i) to expand regulatory reach, allowing governments to close the gaps between their jurisdictions; (ii) to build trust and establish relationships among their participants, conditions which are essential for long-term cooperation; (iii) to exchange information regularly and develop databases of best practice; and (iv) to offer technical assistance and professional socialisation to members from less developed nations. Anderson and Slaughter (2005: 1271); A comprehensive and detailed analysis was presented by Anne-Marie Slaughter in her book entitled *A New World Order*. This influential book baptised the regulators as new diplomats, defining vividly the concept of disaggregated state A (Slaughter, 1997); scholars in global governance have done research on the rising phenomenon called transnational or trans-governmental regulatory networks as defined by Verdier (2009: 114).

[30] By 2005, China had become the third largest economy in the world and convergence toward deepening cooperation, stability, and peace were some of the key aspects of US-China relations. Also the other path could be the deterioration that leads to increasingly open competition and perhaps even war. The answers to these questions are of enormous importance for global geopolitics. Most analysts who write on US-China relations deploy arguments derived from the three main camps in contemporary international relations theorising: realism, liberalism, and constructivism. See more in Friedberg (2005).

[31] Barboza (2010).

[32] US & Chinese Governments (2011).

[33] Li (2016).

[34] Winston & Strawn LLP, 'US, China Sign Memorandum of Understanding'.

[35] Global geopolitics between US and China also led to misunderstanding and tense moments during the Obama Administration. For instance, '... on the trade front, the TPP began as a neutral trade agreement but later evolved into a counterweight to China's expanding regional influence. When China established the Asian Infrastructure Investment Bank in early 2016, the Obama administration saw

important role in the consolidation of relations in the area of competition law and policy between the two largest economies in the world.[36]

After the change of the US administration in January 2017, again geopolitics facilitated the resurgence of populist protectionist rhetoric. The US President, Donald J. Trump, blames globalisation for the loss of jobs and rising economic insecurity in US.[37] It is no surprise that, in January 2017, the US issued a formal notice formally withdrawing from the Transpacific Partnership discussions.[38] In March 2017, the Trump administration released a Trade Policy Agenda premised on the American people's supposed frustration with old trade policies of the US government, and their failure to see clear benefits from international trade agreements.

The Agenda espoused a new approach of expanding trade 'in a way that is freer and fairer for all Americans,'[39] including the use of 'all possible sources of leverage to encourage other countries to open their markets to U.S. exports of goods and services', negotiating better trade deals, such as the North American Free Trade Agreement (NAFTA), and withdrawing from the same if such renegotiations were unsuccessful.[40] In the US–China Summit held in April 2017, the then US Secretary of State Rex W. Tillerson emphasised that the 'chief goal of [US] trade policies is the prosperity of the American worker. To that end, [the US] will pursue economic engagement with China that prioritises the economic well-being of the American people.'[41]

Populist protectionism has likewise been blamed for the United Kingdom's impending withdrawal from the European Union.[42] Consequently, the United Kingdom's 2018 trade policy indicated 'widespread concern about the benefits of free trade and how evenly these are spread across the whole of the UK.'[43]

it as an attempt to rewrite the global rules of engagement and therefore accelerated TPP negotiations. Obama hopes to make the TPP a late-term policy achievement, and no doubt he will strive to promote it for as long as he is in office'. Li (2016).

[36] '... At the official level, (2008–16) US-China relations have brought an impressive degree of constructive cooperation. From an economic standpoint, post-crisis developments such as China's massive purchase of U.S. Treasury bonds, the expansion of the U.S.-China Economic and Strategic Dialogue, and the ongoing negotiation of the U.S.-China bilateral investment treaty (BIT) have induced an unprecedented level of economic integration. Culturally speaking, people-to-people exchange programs – like U.S.-China Strong's Hundred Thousand Strong Initiative and One Million Strong Initiative, as well as the countries' agreement to offer reciprocal 10-year tourist visas – continue to expand and deepen. Likewise, China and the United States not only have refrained from directly airing ideological differences, but they also have avoided dwelling on politically sensitive events like the Wang Lijun scandal and the Edward Snowden disclosures ...' Li (2016).

[37] See the full transcript of Donald Trump's jobs plan speech: www.politico.com/story/2016/06/full-transcript-trump-job-plan-speech-224891.

[38] 'The United States Officially Withdraws from the Trans-Pacific Partnership'.

[39] Office of the United States Trade Representative, '2017 Trade Policy Agenda and 2016 Annual Report'.

[40] ibid.

[41] US Department of State, Remarks on the China Summit.

[42] 'Airbus Condemns Brexit, Trump as Double Protectionist Threat – Bloomberg'.

[43] 'Preparing for Our Future UK Trade Policy – GOV.UK'.

3.2. Tools for International Cooperation and Information-Sharing

Competition authorities and international organisations have devised a spectrum of tools designed to foster international cooperation and information-sharing in the area of cartel enforcement. These tools are classified into formal and informal arrangements, and this section shall explore the composition and consequences of each method.

3.2.1. Formal Cooperation

> Generally speaking, when competition agencies wish to exchange more sensitive information, or wish to use information formally in their proceedings, they must exchange such information through formal avenues.[44]

When the incentives to cooperate are met, formal cooperation schemes have been precisely designed to exchange information that would not normally be shared in informal settings.[45] The quotation above presupposes willingness to enter into formal arrangements.[46] Yet, surprisingly, there have been some occasions when formal cooperation agreements have been used as 'break-the-ice strategies', where two competition agencies do not necessarily want to cooperate but where they are obliged to do so.[47]

Due to the increasing number of competition authorities and laws worldwide, different types of formal arrangement have proliferated over the last decade. There are state-to-state cooperation agreements (agreements), agency-to-agency cooperation arrangements (arrangements), mutual legal assistance treaties (MLATs), free trade agreements (FTAs), economic partnership agreements (EPAs), regional

[44] ICN, 'Anti-Cartel Enforcement Manual Chapter 9: International Cooperation and Information Sharing' 9.

[45] See for example the international cooperation agreement signed between the US and EU in 1991 whereby both authorities agreed a more formalised approach of 'rapid' consultations procedures and dispute avoidance mechanism in competition matters. See Ham (1993: 571).

[46] International cooperation in cartel enforcement presents specific features different from other anticompetitive practices such as mergers or unilateral conducts at the international level. There is sufficient evidence of the harmful effects of hard-core cross-border cartels to developing countries and countries in transition since the detection and sanctioning of international cartels in the 1990s. Due to the intrinsic international nature of cartels, key domestic tools provided by domestic laws such as dawn raids and leniency programmes are insufficient to target cross-border cartels. Classic international instruments such as formal cooperation agreements have proven to be under-used due to the diverse legal standing of anti-cartel laws (administrative vs criminal offences) and the inability of legal treaties to overcome these difficulties. See Cowen and Sutter (1999).

[47] Consider the case of China's competition law. The Antimonopoly Law (AML) is a product of compromise based on existing political and economic realities and 'pragmatism'. The law was drafted short and abstract, so its future implementation will prove to be a trial-and-error process. See Huang (2008: 131).

trade agreements (RTAs), memoranda of understanding (MOUs) and domestic provisions. Each of these formal tools provides competition agencies with unique ways to share information with their foreign counterparts.[48]

Of these methods of formal cooperation, the following section reviews some of the most common forms of bilateral cooperation: memoranda of understanding vs agreements, and competition chapters, which are part of regional trade agreements. In many different ways, these tools have provided alternative approaches. They enable effective cooperation on the basis of publicly available or non-confidential information; waivers of confidentiality; cooperative relationship building; and deferral to partners in appropriate cases.[49] All of these differ from informal cooperation in their transparent and approved procedures.

3.2.1.1. Memoranda of Understanding vs Agreements: The Legal Principle of Comity

There is a long-standing tradition[50] of application of the legal principle of comity in international public law;[51] competition law is no exception to this principle. In this regard, international cooperation in this field presents two types of comity: negative[52] and positive[53] comity. The latter type appears to be the best strategy to ensure reciprocal understanding of laws and procedures, hence the exponential number of cooperation agreements and memoranda of understanding signed the recent decade. Examples from 2011 include major jurisdictions (the US and EU) signing agreements and memoranda of understanding with emerging jurisdictions such as China and Russia.[54]

In the area of mergers, China has been the focus of more international cooperation recently, such as with the agreement signed between DG Competition and the Ministry of Commerce of the People's Republic of China (MOFCOM) in 2015.[55]

[48] ICN, 'Anti-Cartel Enforcement Manual Chapter 9' 10.

[49] = Damtoft (2014: slide 11).

[50] 'Comity is the legal principle whereby a country should take other countries' important interests into account while conducting its law enforcement activities, in return for their doing the same … Comity is therefore a horizontal, sovereign state -to-sovereign state concept, as laid down by the United States Supreme Court in *Hilton v Guyot* in 1895. 2 It is not the abdication of jurisdiction; instead, it is the exercise of jurisdiction with an accompanying understanding of the impact that the exercise of jurisdiction may have on the law enforcement activities of other countries.' OECD, 'International Cooperation in Competition Law Enforcement' 20.

[51] For a complete overview of comity in international law see: Paul (1991).

[52] Negative or traditional comity involves a country's consideration of how to prevent its laws and law enforcement actions from harming another country's important interests. OECD, 'Improving International Co-operation in Cartel Investigations' 20.

[53] Positive comity involves a request by one country that another country undertake enforcement activities in order to remedy allegedly anti-competitive conduct that is substantially and adversely affecting the interests of the referring country; ibid: 21.

[54] EU & Russian Governments, 'MoU on Cooperation between the Directorate-General for Competition of the EU Commission and the Russian Federal Antimonopoly Service'; US & Chinese Governments.

[55] See Slaughter and May, 'EU Competition & Regulatory'.

The positive comity provisions aim to enable the country which was adversely affected by an anticompetitive practice that originated in another signatory country to enforce competition rules accordingly.[56] Unfortunately, despite the potential benefits of positive comity, the instrument has been used only infrequently. This is because the principle is not enshrined in any national law, and remains a discretionary prerogative, the scope of which may be substantially limited in competition authorities with scarce resources.[57] Ideally, if these agreements are used more often, there would be real and meaningful cooperation, through which the exchange of non-confidential information, the synchronisation of investigations and the coordination of enforcement activities could take place, which would be especially useful in the case of international cartels.[58] This was the case of the bilateral agreement signed between the US and EU in 1991[59] and renewed in 1998,[60] which also embedded a notification alert in the agreement whereby each party would notify its partner when a case was likely to affect important interests of the other party.

3.2.1.2. Competition Chapters in Regional or Multilateral Trade Agreements

According to the database of the World Trade Organisation (WTO), there are 287 RTAs that have been officially notified. The last RTA to have been notified at the time of writing was in November 2016.[61] By 2012, almost 100 RTAs contained competition provisions.[62] RTAs that have created a supranational competition authority are the EU, the Common Market for Eastern and Southern Africa (COMESA), the West Africa Economic and Monetary Union (WAEMU), the Caribbean Community (CARICOM) and the Andean Community of Nations. Other RTAs such as the Association of Southeast Asian Nations (ASEAN), the North American Free Trade Agreement (NAFTA) and the *Mercado Comun del Sur* (MERCOSUR) have some competition provisions in force but have not created a supranational authority that can deal with competition matters at the regional level.

The implementation of competition provisions in RTAs was assessed in 2005 and 2007 and the evidence at that time was that there was a weak implementation record, which 'was partly explained by the fact that RTAs with Competition Related Provisions (CRPs) are a relatively new phenomenon [and] the history of

[56] Although these provisions have rarely been formally activated, they are an inspiration for daily cooperation. An important exception to this observation is the so-called Nordic Cooperation, where positive comity provisions are often activated. See Nordic Cartel Network (2012: 34).

[57] OECD, 'Improving International Co-Operation in Cartel Investigations' 23.

[58] Djelic and Kleiner (2006: 10).

[59] US & EU Governments, 'Agreement between US and EU on the Application of Positive Comity'.

[60] ibid.

[61] WTO official database.

[62] OECD, 'Improving International Co-Operation in Cartel Investigations' 31.

regional integration has shown that "deep integration" rules, such as competition provisions, need time to fully materialise, particularly in RTAs involving developing countries'.[63]

From 2005 to 2016, the number of RTAs has continued to grow but the competition provisions in these RTAs lacked details on the implementation. The factors identified in 2007 remain valid: 'cooperation is too costly to be pursued, as the agreements [were] ill-designed in a way that the burdens for cooperation tend to be higher that the perceived benefits arising from it … [and] there [was] no real interest in spending the resources required to push such cooperation'.[64] The latter was exacerbated by the lack of national coordination between competition authorities on the one hand and trade negotiators on the other.[65] However, progress in this regard has taken place, which has also been accompanied by the strengthening of the capacity of developing and transitioning RTA member countries. This has been achieved in part by the reinforced commitment from developed countries to effectively address the main competition policy concerns of their trading partners.

3.2.2. Informal Cooperation

Whether it is a mature or young competition authority, informal cooperation has proven to be a tool that can produce tangible results.[66] There are two types of informal arrangements that can be found in practice: general and case-specific informal cooperation experiences. On the first concept, it refers to what competition officials do when they meet in international events around the world. The following quote summarises the meaning of general informal cooperation:

> General informal cooperation can take place in conferences, bilateral meetings and other forms of exchange of knowledge and information that can be shared between competition experts in the course of their deliberations. Also, capacity-building and technical assistance cooperation may provide the platform where beneficiary countries can get together and promote common objectives. In this regard, UNCTAD, OECD and ICN are engaged in this type of informal cooperation through their contributions to multilateral, regional and bilateral meetings.[67]

In turn, the second type of informal cooperation refers to case-specific type of cooperation, whose definition is:

> Case-specific informal cooperation could include discussion of investigation strategies, market information and witness evaluations. It would also entail sharing leads and

[63] Cernat (2005: 34).
[64] Rosenberg (2007: 7).
[65] Horna and Kayali (2007: 55).
[66] For a further analysis of the exchange of information and evidence between competition authorities, particularly the case of the Polish Competition Authority, see Błachucki and Jóźwiak (2012).
[67] UNCTAD, 'Informal Cooperation among Competition Authorities in Specific Cases' 6.

> comparing authority approaches to common cases. This form of cooperation can help young competition authorities in particular to streamline an investigative strategy and focus an investigation.[68]

With either form of cooperation, there is a wide consensus that informal cooperation is an integral part of the work of competition authorities when they interact internationally.[69] However, case-specific information represents the exception to the rule, in particular when mature and young competition authorities interact with each other. Thus, to unleash the full potential of informal cooperation in the case-specific context and at all the three stages of investigations, competition authorities need to appreciate the utility of sharing non-confidential information, such as public and agency information(see above).[70] For case-specific informal cooperation, the usual interaction is when various competition authorities engage in CBC investigations together.[71] An important case study in Latin America regarding informal cooperation is discussed in chapter four.

3.3. International Organisations

International soft-law institutions in the area of competition law and policy have been instrumental in facilitating the convergence of best international practices in the enactment of competition laws across jurisdictions worldwide and have led to the formation of transnational government networks in the meaning provided by Slaughter. At the international level, there are three main institutions that have been advocating the role of competition law and policy in economic development and enforcement practices. First, the Organisation for Economic Cooperation Development (OECD), which was established in 1960.[72] Second, the United Nations

[68] Case-specific informal cooperation could include discussion of investigation strategies, market information and witness evaluations. It would also entail sharing leads and comparing authority approaches to common cases. This form of cooperation can help young competition authorities in particular to streamline an investigative strategy and focus an investigation. Ibid.

[69] Informal information sharing is an important tool that many competition authorities utilise as an enforcement strategy.

[70] Mature authorities currently exchange information on a variety of issues such as background information of the industry, sharing of case theories or the disclosure of investigative or analytical findings. Bilateral meetings at the management level generally involve high-level discussions of common cases, including the status of the investigation and other case-related information. In addition, bilateral meetings are also a good forum to discuss policy issues, or to seek guidance from another competition agency on a specific issue or concern. All these informal cooperation settings can take a number of forms including in-person meetings, e-mail exchanges, and telephone calls between individuals or case teams.

[71] This form of contact normally occurs when multiple competition agencies are investigating the same or similar conduct in their respective jurisdictions. The contact can occur through in-person meetings, by e-mail, or by telephone. However, in-person meetings are rare due to logistical difficulties with arranging these meetings between several competition agencies. Multilateral contacts typically include discussions of investigative and analytical findings, the sharing of case theories and the coordination of formal powers. ICN, above n 44 at p 9.

[72] In Paris, on 14 December 1960, the governments of the Republic of Austria, the Kingdom of Belgium, Canada, the Kingdom of Denmark, the French Republic, the Federal Republic of Germany,

Conference on Trade and Development (UNCTAD), which was established by the United Nations General Assembly in 1964 as a permanent intergovernmental body,[73] an offshoot of the work on competition which the United Nations had started as early as 1946.[74] The third and most recently established institution is the International Competition Network (ICN) which was set up in 2002 by national competition authorities.[75]

3.3.1. The Work of the Organisation for Economic Cooperation and Development (OECD)[76]

The OECD,[77] whose origins are found in the Organisation for European Economic Co-operation (OEEC), was formed pursuant to the Marshall Plan in order to reconstruct Europe after World War II.[78] The OECD has been working on international cooperation between its member states since the establishment of its Working Party No 3 (WP3) on Enforcement in 1964, in accordance with its mandate which is concerned with the 'effectiveness of competition law enforcement, through measures that include the development of best practices and the promotion of co-operation among competition authorities of member countries'.[79] In 1998, the OECD issued a recommendation on hard-core cartels.

During the period 2012–14, the OECD worked extensively on international cooperation, eventually amending the 1995 recommendations on international cooperation and adopting new recommendations in September 2014.[80] Two key

the Kingdom of Greece, the Republic of Iceland, Ireland, the Italian Republic, the Grand Duchy of Luxembourg, the Kingdom of the Netherlands, the Kingdom of Norway, the Portuguese Republic, Spain, the Kingdom of Sweden, the Swiss Confederation, the Turkish Republic, the United Kingdom of Great Britain and Northern Ireland, and the United States of America formed the OECD. OECD, 'Convention on the Organisation for Economic Co-Operation and Development – OECD'.

[73] '... In the early 1960s, growing concerns about the place of developing countries in international trade led many of these countries to call for the convening of a full-fledged conference specifically devoted to tackling these problems and identifying appropriate international actions. As such UNCTAD was held in Geneva in 1964. Given the magnitude of the problems at stake and the need to address them, the conference was institutionalized to meet every four years, with intergovernmental bodies meeting between sessions and a permanent secretariat providing the necessary substantive and logistical support. Simultaneously, the developing countries established the Group of 77 to voice their concerns. (Today, the G77 has 131 members.)' See UNCTAD, 'Unctad.Org | History'.

[74] In February 1946, key member States of the United Nations established Committee III on Restrictive Business Practices (RBPs) at the first session of the preparatory committee of the United Nations Conference on Trade and Employment (UNCTAE) in Church House, Dean's Yard, London. See Horna (2016).

[75] Budzinski (2004).

[76] This section has been enriched by talks with OECD officers. See Interview with Capobianco.

[77] For a comprehensive history and evolution of the OECD and its principal functions in the global economy, see Woodward (2004).

[78] OECD, 'History of the OECD'.

[79] OECD, 'Challenges of International Co-Operation in Competition Law Enforcement'55, fn 6.

[80] See OECD, 'Recommendation of the OECD Council Concerning International Co-Operation on Competition Investigations and Proceedings'.

reports related to international cooperation in cartels were prepared by the OECD in this process: *Improving International Co-operation in Cartel Investigations* (2012)[81] and *Challenges of International Cooperation in Competition Law Enforcement* (2014).[82] A joint survey OECD/ICN on international cooperation enforcement will be reviewed in the section on ICN work.

The assessment provided in the 2012 OECD report identified the challenges encountered in attempts at cooperation: that the implementation of OECD instruments in the area of cartels were sub-optimal and not available for all jurisdictions, that informal cooperation appears to be more frequently used than formal arrangements, that political commitment, legislative change and innovation are needed to make progress in this area, that developing and emerging economies face additional challenges related to lack of expertise and resources, and that solutions to cross-border cartel enforcement could be found in other policy areas.[83]

Similarly, the report of 2014 revealed that 'many, if not most, competition authorities where the law has been violated, have either not investigated in their own jurisdictions or did not have access to sufficient evidence to impose fines'.[84] This alarming statement is worsened by the fact that cartel victims are deprived from claiming damages in many jurisdictions partly as a result of the limited ability of competition authorities to enforce their domestic law. The 2014 report added that this ability is 'clearly hindered by the lack of effective information sharing [which undermines any] successful prosecution [that] would require gathering evidence from other jurisdictions and [where] there is relatively little experience with small jurisdictions successfully obtaining, receiving or communicating such information across borders … A gap in governance appears to exist with respect to international cooperation for … cartel investigations'.[85]

Another remark concerning international cooperation in cartel enforcement referred to an increase of competition authorities prosecuting international cartels rather than domestic ones, given the upward trend of international trade flows. The 2014 OECD report predicted that the cooperation complexity index would increase by 92 per cent to 162 per cent by 2030, as a result of cross-border enforcement cartel increasing in line with world trade predictions.[86]

In July 2019, the OECD Council adopted a recommendation regarding the fight against hard-core cartels.[87] The Recommendation updates and replaces the 1998 Recommendation Concerning Effective Action against Hard Core Cartels. While still valid, the OECD Competition Committee concluded that the 1998

[81] OECD, 'Improving International Co-Operation in Cartel Investigations'.

[82] OECD, 'Challenges of International Co-Operation in Competition Law Enforcement'.

[83] OECD, 'Improving International Co-Operation in Cartel Investigations' 20.

[84] OECD, 'Recommendation of the OECD Council Concerning International Co-Operation on Competition Investigations and Proceedings' 49.

[85] OECD, 'Improving International Co-Operation in Cartel Investigations' 49–50.

[86] OECD, 'Recommendation of the OECD Council Concerning International Co-Operation on Competition Investigations and Proceedings' 52.

[87] OECD Council, 'Recommendation of the Council Concerning Effective Action against Hard Core Cartels'.

Recommendation lacked some of the significant developments in anti-cartel policy and enforcement practice of the last 20 years, in particular in the area of leniency programmes and their effectiveness.

3.3.2. The Work of the United Nations Conference on Trade and Development (UNCTAD)[88]

As indicated above, the UN system has worked in the area of international cooperation on cartel enforcement from one year after the UN was created in 1945.[89] From 1946 until the establishment of UNCTAD in 1964, the United Nations worked under the framework of the Economic and Social Council (ECOSOC) setting up an ad-hoc committee on Restrictive Business Practices (RBPs) that produced reports over a number of years, particularly in the 1950s.[90]

In 1946, when the US delegation prepared the initial blueprint on RBPs within the framework of Committee III on Restrictive Business Practices at the first session of the preparatory committee of the UN Conference on Trade and Employment (UNCTAE), they informed them of the US antitrust experience in dealing with RBPs which were restraining trade within the Federal Union. Thus, it was no surprise when the brief statement given by Mr Wilcox, head of the US delegation, highlighted the reasons as to why a chapter on RBPs should be included in a world trade charter known as the Havana Charter. He said:

> goods can move from one country into another, surmounting the tariff wall, if they pay the duty, but when you have a *cartel* agreement between enterprises in two countries whereby each of them agrees as to the part of the world's territory that he is so to share and the part that the other one is to have, there you have a clear agreement of division of markets, the goods do not move at all. You have not a moderate tariff or a high tariff; you have an absolute embargo.[91]

[88] This section has been greatly enriched by an interview with the former head of UNCTAD's Competition Branch. Interview with Qaqaya.

[89] The founding members of the United Nations considered it essential that '… cooperative economic measures be supplemented by further international measures dealing directly with trade barriers and discriminations which stood in the ways of an extension of multilateral trade' Official Archive of the United Nations, 'Report of the 1st Session of the Preparatatory Committee of the UN Conference on Trade and Employment) 15 Oct to 26 Nov 1946' (United Nations Secretariat 1946) E/PC/T/33.

[90] The founding members of this Ad-hoc Committee were 10 states (Belgium, Canada, France, India, Mexico, Pakistan, Sweden, UK, US and Uruguay) and were entrusted to prepare and submit to ECOSOC, no later than March 1953, proposals on methods to be adopted by international agreement for implementing the recommendation on how to control RBPs. On 26 May 1955, ECOSOC resolution 568(XIX) reaffirmed its continuing concern with the existence in international trade of RBPs which have harmful effects; urged governments to continue the examination of RBPs with a view to the adoption of laws, measures and policies which will counteract such effects; and recommended member States to continue to communicate to the Secretary General information concerning laws, measures and policies adopted by them in respect of such RBPs.

[91] Emphasis by author. Statement provided in the afternoon session of 23 October 1946. See Official Archive of the United Nations, 'Verbatim Report of the Second Meeting of Committee III'.

In 1976 at the UNCTAD IV Ministerial Conference in Nairobi, UNCTAD received a more ambitious mandate that reinvigorated the application of the Havana Charter at the international level. UNCTAD member states decided to start negotiations 'with the objective of formulating a set of multilaterally agreed equitable principles and rules for the control of RBPs having adverse effects of international trade [the Set] … [and] to convene further meetings of the ad hoc intergovernmental group of experts (IGE) on RBPs which, taking into account the work of the Second Ad-hoc Group of Experts on RBPs'.[92]

Despite the divergence of views between developed and developing countries members of the United Nations on the subject of controlling RBPs, a committee of experts resolved the preliminary technical issues based on a mandate given in Nairobi. In 1978, the UN General Assembly decided to convene a conference on RBPs. In two sessions, held in November-December 1979 and April 1980 under the auspices of UNCTAD, the remaining issues were resolved.[93] The resulting United Nations Conference on Restrictive Business Practices (UNCRBP)[94] was concluded on 22 April 1980, with the adoption of a resolution that approved a 'Set of Multilaterally Agreed Equitable Principles and Rules for the Control of Restrictive Business Practices'.[95] The US delegation in this UNCRBP said the following:

> Experts of western and other developed nations have believed, based on their own OECD experience that one-time, international agreements with hard and fast rules are not at present a feasible method of dealing with restrictive business practices in all their contexts. Rather, it is believed that a gradual exchange of information and experience, comparison of legislation and enforcement, and development of common norms based on majority approaches will, over time, serve an educational role, develop personal contacts between antitrust experts in different countries, facilitate bilateral cooperation and consultation, and create bases for further work, particularly at the regional level.[96]

This quotation summarises what UNCTAD has been doing since the adoption of these rules up to the present. The Set has been valid for over 35 years, with seven review conferences organised every five years. The UNCTAD has been able to assist developing countries and economies in transition in the implementation of competition policies and law through its three pillars: (1) the Intergovernmental Group of Experts (IGE) on Competition Law and Policy and its Model Law on Competition; (2) research and analysis; and (3) technical assistance and capacity

[92] Official Archive of the United Nations, 'Proceedings of the UNCTAD. Fourth Session A' 13.

[93] Official Archive of the United Nations, 'United Nations General Assembly Resolution 33/153'.

[94] The UNCRBP deserves particular attention because it is the first global negotiation to produce a compact on the control of restrictive business practices since formal international discussions on the issue began in 1946. Moreover, the UNCRBP participants compounded their surprise by producing a lengthy and intricate text despite their strikingly diverse political philosophies coming from different regional groupings, developed, developing countries as well as the socialist bloc. See Oesterle (1981).

[95] The United Nations Set Of Principles And Rules On Competition.

[96] Oesterle (1981: 54).

building work, all of which are vital in building these laws and policies. Major ministerial conferences of UNCTAD since 1980 and review conferences of the UN Set on Competition have consistently endorsed the UN Set.

In the area of international cooperation in cartel enforcement, the UNCTAD Secretariat received a mandate from its member states to further intensify efforts to fight against cross-border anticompetitive practices at the international level. To this end, secretariat reports discussed at the 2012, 2013, 2014 IGEs have focused on the following topics: cross-border anticompetitive practices and the challenges for developing countries and economies in transition;[97] modalities and procedures for international cooperation in competition cases involving more than one country;[98] the impact of cartels on the poor;[99] and informal cooperation among competition authorities in specific cases.[100]

At the 16th session of the IGE in July 2017, the UNCTAD Secretariat prepared a background note on enhancing international cooperation in the investigation of competition cross-border cases.[101] During that session, member states requested the UNCTAD Secretariat to facilitate the establishment of a discussion group on international cooperation, open to member states participation on a voluntary basis, with the objective to pursue the exchange and debate on the modalities for facilitating cooperation under Section F of the Set of Multilaterally Agreed Equitable Principles and Rules for the Control of Restrictive Business Practices and report to the 17th session of the Intergovernmental Group of Experts in July 2018.[102]

By mid-2018, the Discussion Group released a report of its activities, including the preparation of a survey report entitled 'obstacles to international cooperation', a survey to which more than 50 agencies worldwide provided their inputs.[103] The UNCTAD survey report has three main parts: the first part deals with providing a pre-assessment of the responding authority with respect to the willingness to cooperate with foreign peers as well as the factors surrounding international cooperation. The second part assesses critical factors that a competition agency faces when engaged in international cooperation activities. The survey classified three types of factors: awareness, as well as legal and practical aspects that facilitate a quicker response from competition authorities. The third part looked at the future of cooperation and suggestions that each member of the group could put forward.[104]

[97] UNCTAD, 'Cross-Border Anticompetitive Practices: The Challenges for Developing Countries andEconomies in Transition'.

[98] UNCTAD, 'Modalities and Procedures for International Cooperation in Competition Cases Involving More than One Country'.

[99] UNCTAD, 'The Impact of Cartels on the Poor'.

[100] UNCTAD, 'Informal Cooperation among Competition Agencies in Specific Cases'.

[101] UNCTAD, 'Enhancing International Cooperation in the Investigation of Cross-Border Competition Cases: Tools and Procedures'.

[102] See para 9 of the Agreed Conclusions. UNCTAD, 'Report of the Intergovernmental Group of Experts on Competition Law and Policy on Its Sixteenth Session'.

[103] 'Report of the Discussion Group on International Cooperation'.

[104] ibid p 3 of the Survey at annex 2.

Another section was included to request participating competition authorities to provide ideas on what they see as a way forward on this issue at the global level while considering the specific needs of younger and smaller agencies. Based on that, member states decided to renew the mandate of the Discussion Group until July 2019.[105] At the first meeting of the Discussion Group in October 2018, members decided to set up a drafting committee composed by 10 member states to propose a consolidated text that was discussed at the 18th session of the IGE in July 2019. By June 2019, the Drafting Committee finalised a document entitled 'Guiding Policies and Procedures under Section F of the UN Set on Competition' (hereinafter GPPSF).[106]

The GPPSF was the result of intensive consultations and both virtual as well as direct meetings among various UN member states between October 2018 and June 2019. In April 2019, the UN Secretariat organised an Ad Hoc Expert Group Meeting in Geneva, Switzerland, under the header 'International Cooperation in Competition Law Enforcement: Challenges and Opportunities for Younger and Smaller Agencies in Developing Countries and Countries with Economies in Transition'.[107] The meeting proved essential in advancing the negotiation of the text of the GPPSF. The supporting work of countries, such as Japan, the United States, the Russian Federation, Austria and Italy was instrumental in reaching a consensus on the different provisions covered by the GPPSF.[108]

The GPPSF, as they stand now, outline important guiding principles for cooperation in competition cases, including benefits of such a cooperation, which would be based on mutual trust and founded on an ability of participating agencies to effectively and credibly ensure that shared information will be kept confidentially and used for permitted purposes only. While there is agreement on the need and urgency to provide guidance, particularly to younger agencies in the developing countries, the GPPSF accord flexibility as to the way the cooperation would be realised. This would be in due consideration of prevalent domestic laws and policies, as well as per mutual agreement and understanding. Depending on these, the prospective cooperation could entail, among others: (a) initial contacts; (b) further communication among agencies; (c) timing alignment; (d) exchange of information, confidentiality, and waivers of confidentiality; as well as (e) discussions on substance and case resolution.

As concerns the role of the UNCTAD Secretariat itself, the GPPSF foresee potential assistance in developing confidentiality provisions and in promoting mutual trust towards a more effective cooperation. In line with its mandate, the

[105] UNCTAD Secretariat, 'Report of the Intergovernmental Group of Experts on Competition Law and Policy on Its Seventeenth Session'.

[106] UNCTAD Drafting Committee, 'Guiding Policies and Procedures under Section F of the UN Set on Competition'.

[107] UNCTAD Secretariat, 'Unctad.Org | Ad Hoc Expert Group Meeting on Competition Law and Policy'.

[108] UNCTAD Secretariat, 'Report of the Meeting of the UNCTAD Ad Hoc Expert Meeting on Competition International Cooperation'.

UNCTAD Secretariat would furthermore assist in the provision of publicly available legal texts and guidelines that are of relevance to the cooperation, such as rules on confidentiality, investigations, or data protection as they exist in different jurisdictions. Finally, the UNCTAD Secretariat would maintain a list of contact persons at the authorities in each of the member states in order to facilitate cooperation, also on specific types of conduct (e.g. mergers, cartels etc.).

With specific reference to consultations under Section F of the UN Set, the requesting agencies may receive support from the UNCTAD Secretariat regarding the following: (a) preparing the request for consultation; (b) advice on procedural matters within the scope of the consultation; (c) provision of mutually agreed conference facilities by the Secretary-General of UNCTAD, if needed; (d) guidance, especially for agencies from developing countries and countries with economies in transition, concerning confidentiality assurances and any use of information shared in the course of such consultation, if necessary; (e) interpretation of the UN Set provisions; as well as (f) direct participation in the consultation itself, upon specific request and consent by the participating agencies.

3.3.3. The Work of the International Competition Network (ICN)

The creation of the ICN was prompted by the contradictory transatlantic assessments of a global merger in the GE/Honeywell case in 2001.[109] The ICN, which was envisaged to promote best global practices for mergers, was officially invoked on 25 October 2001, when high-level officials from 13 countries and the EU announced the creation of the network. It was observed that 'the ICN has undeniably had a promising and rapid start, with concrete steps taken and already some positive outcomes. In particular, the promotion of global "best practices" around certain issues, like mergers, has been seen as a clear success and revealing the strength of a flexible network'.[110]

The ICN's Working Group on Cartels produced, on a chapter-by-chapter basis, a detailed manual on anti-cartel enforcement to be applied at domestic and regional levels by its members. The ICN developed 10 independent but coordinated chapters on anti-cartel enforcement dealing with key practical issues such as how to conduct an inspection (chapter 1);[111] how to draft and implement an effective leniency policy, in particular to the newly set up competition authorities (see chapter 2).[112] Chapter 3 discusses a critical point for many competition

[109] Djelic and Kleiner (2006: 16).
[110] ibid: 18.
[111] ICN, 'Anti-Cartel Enforcement Manual Chapter 1: Searches Raids and Inspections'.
[112] ICN, 'Anti-Cartel Enforcement Manual Chapter 2: Drafting and Implementing an Effective Leniency Policy'.

authorities; how to gather digital evidence;[113] as well as key aspects in the areas of cartel initiation.[114]

Many ICN members have praised the best practices included in chapter 5 as the carrying out of an investigative strategy remains critical for many young and small competition authorities and relevant for technical assistance purposes.[115] Other chapters, such as the one dealing with 'Interviewing Techniques',[116] 'Cartel Case Resolution'[117] and 'Cartel Awareness, Outreach & Compliance' (2012)[118] remain important to specific authorities wishing to gain public support in the fight against cartels. An important chapter for the purposes of this research is chapter 9 which discusses the topic of 'International Cooperation and Information Sharing'.[119] This chapter is mentioned several times throughout the research. Finally, there is a chapter 10 that deals with the relationships between Competition Authorities & Public Procurement Bodies (2015).[120] As can be seen, the ICN Manual provides the most relevant best practices and techniques employed by mature agencies at various stages of anti-cartel enforcement, which have been proven effective and successful in practice. Particularly pertinent for this research is the chapter on 'International Cooperation and Information Sharing' which reviews the main trends and practices of competition agencies. It covers types of information, the ability to share information, tools for international cooperation, methods of information sharing (informal, formal, as well as international organisations and technical assistance work), uses of information, prospective challenges and finally examples of cooperation.[121]

Another important product that the ICN produced, this time in collaboration with the OECD, was a survey that assessed international cooperation in competition cases. Indeed, this survey, in 2013, revealed that, within the period 2007–12, and out of 57 participating countries that took part in the survey (of which 31 were OECD members), a majority of non-OECD countries had little experience in international cooperation cases.[122] Notably, more than half of the respondents of the survey were from Europe, while Africa accounted for 7 per cent, Asia 13 per cent, and Americas 16 per cent. This fact reflected, first, lower participation of non-OECD countries in the survey and that would lead to seeing the problem

[113] ICN, 'Anti-Cartel Enforcement Manual Chapter 3: Digital Evidence Gathering'.
[114] ICN, 'Anti-Cartel Enforcement Manual Chapter 4: Cartel Case Initiation'.
[115] ICN, 'Anti-Cartel Enforcement Manual Chapter 5: Investigative Strategy and Interviewing'.
[116] ICN, 'Anti-Cartel Enforcement Manual Chapter 6: Interviewing Techniques'.
[117] ICN, 'Anti-Cartel Enforcement Manual Chapter 7: Case Resolution'.
[118] ICN, 'Anti-Cartel Enforcement Manual Chapter 8: Cartel Awareness, Outreach and Compliance'.
[119] ICN, 'Anti-Cartel Enforcement Manual Chapter 9: International Cooperation and Information Sharing'.
[120] ICN, 'Anti-Cartel Enforcement Manual Chapter 10: Relationships between Competition Agencies and Public Procurement Bodies'.
[121] ICN, 'Anti-Cartel Enforcement Manual Chapter 9: International Cooperation and Information Sharing' 9.
[122] OECD & ICN (2013: 9).

of cooperation from a partial view since the vast majority of young and small competition agencies remain in Africa, the Americas, and Asia.[123]

In 2015, an important ICN member, the Japan Fair Trade Commission (JFTC), the third competition authority to be established (it was created in 1947), became concerned that the vast majority of ICN respondents in the OECD/ICN survey reported that no cooperation had been achieved so far. In response, Japan sought to explore alternative methods for cooperation that would be able to reach young and small competition regimes worldwide. They submitted a proposal to the ICN to strengthen information-sharing amongst ICN members. The proposal, entitled 'Proposal for establishing the ICN Framework for promotion of sharing non-confidential information for Cartel Enforcement' (ICN Framework),[124] came after 12 years of the existence of the Cartel Working Group, but cooperation is still scarce amongst the increasing number of competition authorities in the world. It is therefore of crucial importance to search for more ways to enhance cooperation and realise these important objectives of the ICN.[125]

The idea behind the ICN Framework is to enable competition agencies to initiate an investigation of an international cartel case within their own jurisdictions, based on the exchange of information that the initiating agency could get from a peer agency that has already investigated the same cartel case in its own jurisdiction.[126] In the ICN Framework, participating competition authorities can register and then put forward liaison officers to coordinate requests for cooperation. This facilitates cooperation between the case team officers of the requesting competition authority and its peer authority as they can communicate directly without unnecessary intermediaries and reduce bureaucracy at the cross-border level. Overall, the ICN Framework underscores the importance of information-sharing between competition agencies which fosters coordination in cross-border enforcement and avoids parallel proceedings. These points are picked up again in chapter 10, where proposals on stronger cooperative between competition authorities is examined in detail.

Finally, the ICN has produced further reports to foster convergence in national practices such as the compilation of 'Good Practices' from the Anti-Cartel Enforcement Manual of the ICN Cartel Working Group, Anti-Cartel Templates,[127] Leniency Waiver Templates and an accompanying Explanatory Note.[128] Other ICN publications on cartel enforcement are 'Defining hard core cartel conduct: effective institutions, effective penalties',[129] 'Cooperation between Competition

[123] Fox (2016).

[124] ICN, 'Proposal for Establishing the ICN Framework for Promotion of Sharing Non-Confidential Information for Cartel Enforcement'.

[125] Djelic and Kleiner (2006: 10).

[126] Nambu (2014).

[127] ICN, 'Compilation of "Good Practices" from the Anti-Cartel Enforcement Manual of the ICN Cartel Working Group'.

[128] ICN, 'Waivers of Confidentiality in Cartel Investigations – Explanatory Note'.

[129] ICN (ed), *Defining Hard Core Cartel Conduct: Effective Institutions, Effective Penalties*.

Authorities in Cartel Investigations',[130] 'Cartel Settlements Report',[131] '2010 Trends and Developments in Cartel Enforcement',[132] as well as the online compilation of cartel awareness materials[133] and the worldwide Leniency Programme links.[134]

3.4. Summary

Cooperation is a multi-faceted phenomenon where international and regional organisations and networks all play a fundamental role in allowing competition authorities to initiate or continue the process of convergence of substantive competition standards.[135] Chapter 3 therefore attempts to provide an overall framework on international cooperation for this research. It explores the abundant tools for cooperation between competition authorities in the fight against CBCs; these include cooperation agreements which can be formal (ie MOUs and competition provisions in RTAs) or informal. Indeed, a substantial amount of bilateral cooperation agreements between competition authorities have been signed in recent years, not only between mature jurisdictions but also involving emerging economies such as Russia and China.

Geopolitics in this respect has played a major role for mature jurisdictions wishing to sign MOUs with emerging jurisdictions and will continue to do so in the years to come. The international soft-law institutions, such as the OECD, UNCTAD and ICN, have played an unprecedented role in providing assistance, advisory services and valuable reflections on improving international cooperation amidst the enactment of competition laws across the globe.

While CBCs continue to be detected, prosecuted and sanctioned by mature and emerging jurisdictions worldwide (particular examples of which are given in chapter two), the question remains whether international cooperation efforts are sufficient when addressing the increasing complexity that the proliferation of both competition laws and authorities poses.

The current work of UNCTAD in the area of international cooperation merits further development throughout this research as currently member states of the UN are discussing ways and means to address the obstacles of international cooperation.

[130] ICN, *Co-Operation between Competition Agencies in Cartel Investigations.*
[131] ICN, 'Cartel Settlements. Report to the ICN Annual Conference Kyoto, Japan'.
[132] ICN, 'Trends and Developments in Cartel Enforcement'.
[133] ICN, 'Cartel Awareness & Outreach'.
[134] ICN, 'Leniency Materials. Country/Organization + Link(s) to Leniency Program Materials'.
[135] OECD, 'Challenges of International Co-Operation in Competition Law Enforcement' 17.

PART II

Challenges of Cross-Border Cooperation in Multijurisdictional Cartel Enforcement

As the focus of the present research is on how young or small competition authorities interact with mature or large authorities (as per the definitions discussed in chapter one), Part II of the research focuses on the specific hurdles faced by young or small competition authorities in investigating mainly two of the five types of CBCs, in accordance with the typology introduced in chapter two.

Indeed, there are three types of CBCs that the present research does not provide specific solutions for: multinational, export and import CBCs. The reasons are as follows:

1. As far as multinational CBC investigations are concerned, and due to the global impact of these CBCs, it seems that only mature and large competition authorities with long-standing functioning cooperation mechanisms have the optimal deterrent effect. Young or small competition authorities, on the other hand, could only deter multinational cartels by 'piggy-backing' on the effects of investigations carried out by more mature and large authorities. It is therefore more pressing for younger and smaller jurisdictions to concentrate their efforts and resources on CBCs where they might achieve greater impact and a higher level of deterrence.
2. As far as export CBC investigations are concerned, the solutions proposed in chapter five regarding *amicus curiae* submissions might have potential in the future. This is true, in particular when young but large competition authorities develop their expertise, provided that the export cartels are not state-sponsored.[1] In addition, an alternative for addressing export cartels has been through the imposition of antidumping duties. This may prove sufficient in certain cases,[2] provided that it does not violate other obligations, such as

[1] See more about the Chinese way in Huang (2011).

[2] This refers to the figure of 'predatory pricing of exports being caught by antidumping rules' to foreclose international competitors. Of course, this will be the case if the exporters are engaged in predation in their export market and not in their domestic market. As such, in the unlikely event that the exporter is predating in both markets, antidumping can still be used if the constructed cost definition of dumping is employed. See Bhattacharjea (2005). An important caveat should be discussed here: applying antitrust principles to dumping has been strongly opposed by EU and US in the WTO Working Group on Trade and Competition. See also 2000 WTO DSU decision on the United States Antidumping Act

the obligations imposed by the multilateral trade system through the World Trade Organization. Hence, there does not seem to be an immediate urgency for young and small competition authorities to address export CBCs.

3. In relation to import CBC investigations, the solution is a question of incentives for the relevant competition authority to investigate and sanction import cartelists. Chapter five refers to cooperation between large but young competition authorities and their younger and smaller peers wishing to obtain foreign evidence, which requires the willingness of the foreign competition authority to be successful. In this relationship, if the competition authority is not a young one, technical assistance or capacity building can be an alternative method of triggering cooperation at a later stage, as the younger authority will become a beneficiary of development cooperation aid. The latter acts as an incentive for cooperation on the part of the young and small competition authority.

Based on the interviews carried out at the ICN Annual Conference in Porto in 2017, there are two types of CBC that have a significant impact on juridisctions with young competition authorities: transnational and regional CBCs. This is because specific transnational and regional CBCs impact directly their own domestic markets, creating an urgent need to act upon these unlawful practices. For mature or large jurisdictions, on the other hand, there might be fewer incentives to tackle these types of CBC, as their own markets are not directly impacted.

Bearing in mind the foregoing, the discussion about cooperation on transnational and regional CBC investigations centres around the following:

Chapter four looks at why smaller and young competition authorities do not necessarily consider trust, business culture and optimal deterrence as practical hurdles in transnational CBC investigations. Subsequently, specific issues that emerged in targeting transnational CBCs are assessed, in particular when cooperation is needed between mature or large competition authorities and younger or smaller ones. In this connection, concerns such as leniency, confidentiality and the importance of the physical presence of the transnational companies are highlighted.

Chapter five reviews the main challenges arising in regional CBC investigations, with a focus on the lack of coherence and compatibility of competition laws across regional economic groupings. This covers substantive differences in legal standing as per cartel offences, as well as differences with respect to the powers of investigation and adjudication techniques. All of these factors can undermine proceedings and present challenges to young and small jurisdictions, both in Latin America and elsewhere. Chapter five also discusses the problems of investigating export and import CBCs by young or small competition authorities. In this regard, the

of 1916, according to which anti-dumping procedures were the only way in which members could deal with predatory pricing by foreign exporters.

lack of incentives and willingness to cooperate are discussed, along with legal issues to gather information abroad.

In each of these chapters, the following observations about young and small competition authorities form the basis for discussion:

1. **Technical assistance and capacity building**: young or small competition authorities face a variety of interlinked issues that depend on how the competition regime has developed over time. The alleged lack of expertise of competition officials in young and small competition authorities is one such issue, which makes dealing with multijurisdictional cartel cases particularly difficult and complex. As a result, the discussion of technical assistance as an instrument to strengthen capacities to better understand and deal with CBCs comes into play.

More highly trained officials in young or small competition authorities would have a more comprehensive capacity to deal with the great amount of technical assistance provided by mature competition authorities through international networks such as the ICN and others, as well as international organisations that work for developing countries in this field, such as UNCTAD and the World Bank. This lack of expertise is a structural problem that underpins the ability of young and small competition authorities to deal with the harmful effects of CBCs of all types. The following chapters address the issues that these authorities face in a disaggregated manner.

2. **Substantive and procedural issues:** this research avoids drawing a line between substantive and procedural issues for the purposes of the discussion. In fact, there is a blurry differentiation between substantive and procedural issues in competition law analysis because of the complicated processes that emerge. As indicated by Terhechte, the 'adjective and substantive law not only shows its existence in the procedure, but in many cases comes into existence because of it'.[3] In other words, competition rules can have multifaceted dimensions that touch upon the 'antitrust' substantive analysis as well as the administrative procedural law. As a result, in many instances both dimensions are an indivisible unity and can be considered as *two sides of the same coin*.

Finally, the analysis assumes two further important premises, namely that:

(a) Joint investigation and cooperation are needed to further strengthen and streamline the work of young competition authorities at large; and
(b) Investigations need to involve the cooperation of two or more competition authorities.

[3] Terhechte, 'International Competition Enforcement Law Between Cooperation and Convergence'.

4

Multinational vs Transnational CBCs

This chapter constitutes the core analysis of the research as it argues the merits and demerits of the critical challenges that multinational and transnational CBCs present, particularly to young or small competition authorities. In the following, the various dynamics in cross-border cartel investigations are explored. This forms the backdrop to assessing and arguing for concrete entry points for younger authorities to utilise international cooperation mechanisms when investigating and prosecuting CBCs.

It may be said that transnational and multinational CBCs can be treated in the same manner, as they both can be investigated by several jurisdictions, and both mature or large as well as young or small jurisdictions. However, it becomes clear that a distinction between these two types of CBCs is warranted when looking at certain factors, such as incentives for the mature authority to cooperate with its peer, or implications for optimal deterrence, resource allocation and priority-setting on the part of the younger competition regime.

In the case of a multinational CBC, multiple authorities launch an investigation of international or global scale. In doing so, they need to overcome challenges related to **overall trust, culture and optimal deterrence** across jurisdictions. In the case of transnational CBCs, on the other hand, a limited number of juridisctions are concerned; the issues at hand tend to be more localised.

In fact, enforcement practices and 'cultures' may be similar, but the degree of enforcement may still vary. Based on the interviews carried out for this research,[4] as well as the author's own observations, the most important recurrent issues for transnational CBCs concern the lack of incentives to cooperate, hurdles related to leniency, and finally, the lack of a consensus on what constitutes confidential information. Table 4.1 below illustrates these crucial points.

Table 4.1 Drawing the Line between Multinational and Transnational CBCs

Multinational CBCs	Transnational CBCs
Lack of trust between competition authorities.	Lack of effective implementation of leniency programmes in young competition authorities.
Legal culture barriers to cooperation.	Lack of incentives to cooperate.

(continued)

[4] See the list of all interviews in the Bibliography.

Table 4.1 ***(Continued)***

Difficulties in achieving comparable sanctions and remedies to cartel infringements.	Lack of trust by the leniency applicants in providing a confidentiality waiver to young competition authorities and lack of specific cooperation arrangements of mutual recognition in leniency and immunity issues.
–	Lack of an international definition of confidential information.
–	Lack of physical presence of the international cartelist companies in the young competition authority's territory.

Source: own work.

4.1. Challenges in Multinational CBC Enforcement

Multinational CBCs increasingly are being targeted because of the greater cooperation between mature authorities and some young competition authorities with large jurisdictions, such as the BRICS. However, for the remaining group of authorities, notably young and small ones, they would still face challenges in trying to prosecute multinational CBCs. In many instances, these challenges might overwhelm them in such a manner that it would be better to adopt a 'wait and see approach' and 'piggyback' on the effective multijurisdictional work of mature agencies worldwide.

4.1.1. Overall Trust

During the annual conference of the International Competition Network held in Portugal from 10 to 12 May 2017,[5] a sample of mature and young competition enforcers were interviewed[6] to gather information on the recurrent issues faced by competition authorities in multinational CBC investigations.

In all interviews, the term 'trust' was repeatedly mentioned as one of the most critical factors in establishing relationships between mature and young competition authorities, particularly if multiple jurisdictions are affected by a global or multinational cartel. As of 2018, more and more young and mature authorities

[5] 'ICN 2017 Annual Conference'.

[6] Several interviews were conducted during the period of 10–12 May 2017 at the margin of the ICN Annual Conference in Porto, Portugal. Representatives from the Andean Community, Australia, Brazil, CARICOM, Chile, Honduras, Nicaragua, Panama, Peru, Singapore, South Africa, US academia and private practitioner were interviewed.

had started to effectively communicate and cooperate with each other, which is a positive trend and likely to continue in the future.[7] One interviewee described trust as 'the lubricant that oils the machine of international cooperation'.[8] Trust is necessary in dealing with the other issues such legal culture barriers to cooperation, and even the methods of information exchange between jurisdictions.

The likelihood of young competition authorities involved in multinational CBC investigations for the first time being willing to cooperate with their mature counterparts is higher. This is because of the multiplicity of jurisdictions and the ways in which multinational companies operate at the global level. An initial lack of trust between mature and young competition authorities is plainly noticeable, whereby mature authorities look at the reputation of the new authority from the perspective of its particular nation. In addition, legal culture barriers to cooperation could also be an issue, together with the fact that achieving comparable sanctions and remedies at the global level would require greater cooperation from the affected jurisdictions. That task becomes almost impossible when taking into account the diversity of rules and procedures on competition law across continents. In addition, as discussed in chapter three, the lack of common interests between mature and young competition authorities restrains cooperation between them.

The starting assumption is that there is no prior interaction between mature and young authorities. The OECD notes that, where there is lack of prior interaction, trust poses a particular problem:

> Lack of prior interaction between agencies and lack of trust, for example, affect the willingness of enforcers to co-operate with each other, and limit effective co-operative relationships to a small group of agencies which regularly engage in cooperation.[9]

Trust, taken as an institutional phenomenon, presupposes a combination of individual and institutional trust which develops differently. The former might develop through 'repeated interactions with others and is based on familiarity, interdependence, and continuity in relationships',[10] which are developed between people rather than institutions.[11] The latter develop when 'individuals must generalize their personal trust to large organizations made up of individuals with whom they have low familiarity, low interdependence, and low continuity of interaction'.[12] Undoubtedly, if mutual understanding, trust and interaction are achieved in the relations between competition authorities, cooperation is much facilitated and yields tangible results in any stage of a cartel investigation whether one or multiple

[7] Linklaters (2018: 4).
[8] Interview at the ICN Annual Conference in Porto (10–12 May 2017); interview with Bezzi.
[9] OECD & ICN (2013: 18).
[10] Lewicki and Bunker. (1995: 137).
[11] For a comprehensive study on the nature and functioning of relationships of interpersonal trust, see McAllister (1995).
[12] Lewicki and Bunker (1995: 137).

jurisdictions are involved.[13] However, trust and mutual understanding take a lot of time to build and are both easier to destroy than to construct.[14]

In order to understand how to develop trust between authorities, one question must be resolved: why do some competition authorities lack trust in each other? One possible explanation is the difficulty of predicting how an authority will act. The principle of 'knowledge-based trust',[15] which is grounded on information and predictability, propounds that: 'the better we know the other [authority], the more accurately we can predict what [the authority] will do; as long as the other remains predictable (that is, confirming our knowledge and acting consistently with that knowledge), trust will endure'.[16] In other words, authorities will trust in each other if information contributes to the predictability of the other's actions and if that information is consistent over repeated interactions. For instance, in regional groupings, trust among competition authorities can be developed on the basis of their common business and cultural backgrounds and languages, such as the case of Latin American Spanish-speaking competition authorities.[17]

In the interests of exploring the issue of trust in more depth, the causes of a lack of trust between competition authorities will be examined below (vis-à-vis the types of CBCs presented in chapter two).

4.1.1.1. Lack of Repeated Personal Interaction can be Found at the Global Level

The lack of repeated personal interaction of members of mature and young competition authorities in multi-faceted activities at the international level could be an issue when younger authorities do not have the necessary means to participate in these fora. For instance, attendance by young competition authorities at worldwide annual meetings organised by the ICN, OECD or UNCTAD represents a significant financial burden if development cooperation partners do not fund their participation to these events. In interviews conducted at the Annual Conference of the ICN in May 2017, interviewees said that the ICN provides the platform to get to know other competition enforcers that otherwise would not be possible.[18]

[13] Indeed, trust is the essential condition for successful international cooperation in all stages of the investigation of cartels, including the exchange of information, coordination of dawn raids, and discussion on general investigative strategy and aiming at investigating cross-border anticompetitive practices.

[14] For a comprehensive analysis of why trust is easier to destroy that it is to build, see Lewicki and Bunker (1995: 415).

[15] Lewicki and Bunker identified three different types of trust: calculus-based, knowledge-based and identification-based. These three types of trust are related to each other in some manner as the development of trust should proceed through these three stages. Ibid: 153.

[16] ibid: 149.

[17] *Cf* whereby two Latin American competition authorities have not been able to 'trust' each other due to a number of reasons related to the lack of personal contacts between the enforcers. See the case study in Botta (2009).

[18] See for instance the interview at the ICN Annual Conference in Porto with Alberto Lozano (2017).

However, even if interaction occurs through this sort of platform, it is not necessarily the case that these interactions would be repeated over time as many of these young competition authorities might seldom participate in these events and the likelihood of establishing a steady and consistent interaction with mature competition enforcers is unlikely.

It is more probable that young competition authorities meet with mature ones only where a cross-regional link already exists or is set up; this could take the form of shared conferences, workshops, or established bilateral cooperation agreements and consequent technical assistance between the two. For instance, relations between Australia and the Philippines competition authorities could be established through the Australian development projects that have been instigated with the ASEAN countries in the area of competition law and policy. As such, the likelihood that the US and Mauritius competition authorities would establish a repeated interaction might be low, as there is no specific link between the authorities, nor any platform that can facilitate the interaction of their officers, unless a capacity-building project is put in place by the mature or large competition authority.

4.1.1.2. Lack of Shared Interests and Values

Putting together mature and young competition authorities can also give rise to other issues that might undermine the development of trust such as the lack of shared interests and values. Often the lack of shared interests and values is prompted by the difference of economic, social and political environment in which competition authorities operate. This issue has already been discussed, in chapter one, when classifying competition authorities worldwide. Consider the case of Canada and Vietnam's competition authorities, where a potential lack of shared interests in enforcing competition law fully at the domestic level as well as a divergence of values towards implementing competition policies was evident.[19]

As a result, the lack of collective identity that could be reached amongst mature competition authorities is undermined by the lack of common interests. In the case of Australia and Chile, trade relations between these two countries and their workable degree of interdependence and commonality can play a pivotal role developing trust in the long run.

4.1.1.3. Lack of Understanding

Often in the interactions between young and mature competition authorities there is a lack of understanding for the respective needs of their counterparts, as well as for each jurisdiction's separate laws and regulations. A young competition

[19] There is indeed an interest of the Canadian Competition Bureau to assist Vietnam Competition Authority in their current reform of their competition laws.

authority seeking cooperation from a mature one would also mean a certain amount of exposure for the former, when questions are raised as per the effectiveness of their legal framework and whether their legal system's procedure is seen as sufficiently transparent abroad, and whether there are adequate safeguards for due process. In particular, this means that even if the young competition authority's legal framework is adequate and transparent as well as respecting due process, the mature competition authority nevertheless may perceive the young authority as untrustworthy. This sort of perception derives from a lack of understanding of the laws and regulations of the young competition authority; any unfavourable perceptions formed in this way could be very harmful if they were leaked to non-legitimate parties in such as a way that would undermine the whole cross-border investigation.

In the Americas, interaction between the mature northern competition authorities (Canada and the US) and the younger southern competition authorities (the Latin American countries) is mostly concentrated between the mature regimes, but still occurs with young competition regimes such as Brazil, Chile and Mexico. As a result, a workable knowledge and understanding of each other's laws and regulations between the mature and younger authorities has been possible over time, leading to a slight convergence between them. For instance, the three younger jurisdictions have criminalised key aspects of their cartel laws under dual systems (both administrative and criminal), which helps the northern mature competition authorities to share information on the basis of increased trust and similarity between their competition systems. Conversely, the remainder of the younger competition authorities, such as the Central American, Andean and Caribbean competition authorities, might be left behind in this process, leading to a complete lack of mutual understanding of their laws and regulations (they are all civil law jurisdictions, with the exception of CARICOM countries). That would be a considerable barrier to cooperation.

4.1.1.4. Lack of Joint Activities

A lack of trust between authorities also stems from a lack of joint activities such as transnational competition studies between the jurisdictions. BRICS countries signed an MOU in 2016 whereby a number of joint activities could be envisaged in the shortcoming future. If joint competition studies occur on a transnational platform, then there would be more possibilities to overcome trust issues amongst BRICS countries if a transnational CBC investigation arises.

The question is whether this experience can be extrapolated to other situations, in particular in the relationship between mature and young competition authorities. Apart from ICN working groups wherein young and mature competition authorities can contribute to the drafting of common ICN products such as the Anti-cartel Manual (see chapter three), there is little hope that truly joint activities can happen elsewhere in the international arena. Little incentives from the part of mature competition authorities to engage in joint substantive activities with their younger peers might be also a problem because they might think that there is little value to be gained from the experience, apart from perhaps in the case of a relatively advanced young competition authority which has already gained the respect and deference of its mature peers.

In sum, when investigating multinational CBCs, dissimilar competition authorities across continents may need to interact for the first time. As such, other than the incentive of the requesting-information authority to get useful information at the pre-investigatory phase, the lack of repeated personal interaction, shared values and interests, degree of interdependence, and degree of understanding of each other's competition laws all caused by the lack of trust between the agencies would most probably lead to a complete standstill in terms of cooperation arrangements in any of their forms. That notwithstanding, thanks to the efforts of the development cooperation as well as the work of the ICN, OECD and UNCTAD, many of these hurdles are being addressed and therefore it might not be the real issue at stake when assessing the concrete obstacles to cooperation in transnational CBCs.

4.1.2. Legal Culture[20] Barriers

In a multinational CBC investigation, the number of competition authorities belonging to different legal systems can be considerable and one could expect to come across basic but critical issues, such as legal culture barriers. These barriers relate to the administrative law principle of legality that normally governs domestic competition law proceedings in jurisdictions, where cartel law is usually an administrative offence only. Even though mature or large competition authorities' willingness to cooperate – within the limits of their confidentiality legislation – has increased in today's globalised economy, cooperation remains markedly hampered by legal and cultural obstacles related to the administrative principle of legality that governs domestic competition law proceedings.[21]

Commonly, in civil law jurisdictions, the principle of legality provides that civil servants shall assume that 'anything that is not expressly permitted is prohibited.'[22] As such, unless they are 'expressly' authorised to do so by law, competition officers will not carry out any informal cooperation activity with their foreign counterparts. To address this, changes are needed that would mandate the officers to reach out to their foreign counterparts in order to share information on similar cases being treated abroad. Of course, this has not happened.[23]

[20] For a definition of Legal Culture, see Nelken (2004).
[21] Interview with Damtoft.
[22] See Dyzenhaus, Hunt and Taggart (2001).
[23] Interview with Damtoft.

The second barrier concerns the potential for criticism by peers in a given competition authority. If a case handler is not going to be criticised for failing to reach out to a foreign counterpart, but risks criticism if he or she does, it is easy to understand their choice in this situation.

A third barrier is psychological. Consider a new case handler in a young agency who is not willing to contact mature competition authorities as there is a natural human barrier to be overcome, due to the lack of trust and lack of confidence in presenting a sound request for information. In this sense, intangible and often personal incentives might be decisive for a pick-up-the-phone relationship or simply for reaching out to foreign counterparts. Reaching out to more mature competition authorities could be encouraged if it is endorsed at the organisational level within the mature or smaller agency.[24]

Consider the 1998 lysine cartel case in Mexico (see chapter seven).[25] The US had a criminal system wherein criminal law procedure applied to this anticompetitive practice, while Mexico's competition regime, at that time, was purely based on administrative law. The marked difference between legal culture in Mexico and in the US prevented the sharing of information. This happened despite the fact that the US and Mexico had the NAFTA, a regional trade agreement between the two nations which mentioned competition. To remedy the situation, the Mexican Competition Authority relied on publicly available information from the US, and on the basis of one piece of evidence, the ADM annual financial report, the case went forward.[26] Perhaps that was one of the reasons why Mexico and the US signed a more detailed cooperation agreement on competition issues in 2000, two years after the conclusion of the first Latin American investigation of a multinational CBC.[27]

For mature competition agencies, administrative law in terms of sharing information relating to competition investigations is relatively developed. For young competition agencies, however, administrative law in relation to competition law is in its infancy.[28] Thus, civil servants tend to stick to what they know – that they have limited freedom to go beyond what their domestic laws expressly permit them to do. Officials of young competition agencies might fear getting into trouble for alleged misconduct. Despite the initial willingness of the young competition authority to reach out, this fear will be a barrier against establishing a pick-up-the-phone relationship between the young and mature competition agencies. The young agency might consequently pay more in costs to get access to the same information that they could have secured simply by calling more mature agencies.

Another argument that must be taken into account is the fact that in younger jurisdictions there is a preference for a legal interpretation of the facts in

[24] See Clark and Wilson (1961).
[25] 'Cartel in the Lysine Market in Mexico'.
[26] 'Amino-Acids Cartel'.
[27] See US & Mexican Governments, 'Agreement between US and Mexico Regarding the Application of Their Competition Laws'.
[28] Dyzenhaus, Hunt and Taggart (2001).

competition cases rather than the economic analysis of them, and this might be an issue when interacting with mature jurisdictions, where the opposite is normally the case. As such, sensitivity to differences in legal culture and preferred methods must be displayed so as to ascertain the best approach towards a competition case.[29] In this particular case, economic experts might not have practical knowledge of the differences of legal culture between jurisdictions and that could lead to cases where economic reasoning is not heard, which is particularly damaging for cartel cases that may rely on particular economic evidence. As such, failure to express the economic evidence in practical terms (with a backup of theoretical study if needed) would completely dissuade those responsible for deciding the outcome of competition cases.[30]

4.1.3. Diverging Sanctions vs Optimal Deterrence

Young and mature competition regimes wishing to cooperate at the post-investigation phase would have a complicated situation when they want to achieve some level of comparable sanctions and remedies in an anti-CBC proceeding. Further, this complicated scenario could get even more difficult if other jurisdictions that are being affected by the cartel would also like to take into account the views of other competition authorities before fixing the type and level of sanction most appropriate to the case.[31] In any event, looking for a convergence of comparable sanctions is an ambitious quest, as even the possibility of agreeing on a principle of effectiveness of sanctions imposed in parallel cartel investigations would mean that each national system would need to have 'at its disposal a comparable arsenal of penalties enabling the competition authority effectively to achieve punishment and deterrence equivalent to the sanction imposed by other authorities.'[32]

Competition authorities that want to coordinate their own sanctions and remedies in a multijurisdictional cartel case need to consider a gamut of factors: the appropriate level of sanctions; prison sentences and disqualification of directors; double jeopardy; sanctions that can lead to mergers and acquisitions, joint ventures or strategic alliances thereby potentially reducing competition; duplication of competition authorities' efforts; leniency programmes and limitation periods; court action following sanctions; exceptions for cartels in different jurisdictions; and assets and persons available within the jurisdiction.[33]

The optimal deterrence of cartel infringements depends heavily on the level of fines and the nature of the remedies. Fines and remedies which do not sufficiently counteract the harmful effects of CBCs allow these unlawful business activities to

[29] Malashevich and Kobe (2016: 134).
[30] ibid: 133.
[31] Schoneveld (2003: 2).
[32] Cauffman and Hao (2016: 218).
[33] Schoneveld (2003: 7–12).

proliferate undeterred. The problem of insufficient sanctions was seen in the lysine multinational CBC (discussed in chapter two), where the heavy fine imposed on ADM by major competition jurisdictions did not reduce ADM's ability to acquire other companies active in the same market sectors that were affected by the same multinational cartel.[34] Hence, it would be beneficial for competition authorities to share some information regarding the activities of the companies that have been subject of cartel sanctions in their home jurisdiction. This information would be useful to avoid possible anticompetitive activity in the future in the same markets.

4.2. Challenges in Transnational CBC Enforcement

As pointed out earlier in the assessment of transnational CBC investigations, young and small competition authorities have better chances to address these types of CBCs effectively and deter their harmful effects if they can identify with clarity and strategic vision the challenges they are facing. In the following, a detailed account is given of the different hurdles that may obstruct cooperation in transnational CBCs.

4.2.1. Lack of Incentives for Cooperation[35]

Incentives can be an important part of cooperation between mature or large competition authorities and young or small ones. The following quotation provides a concise summary:

> Co-operation implies agreement by two or more organizations on a set of rules that will govern their behaviour vis-a-vis one another in such a way that the autonomy of each is respected, an allocation of potential incentives is agreed upon, and the rewards of observing the rules are held to be greater than the rewards of breaking them.[36]

Generally, cooperation between competition authorities is viewed as being driven by the professional incentives available to the individuals making up such authorities.[37] On some occasions, incentives may be linked to egotistical motives of self-preservation or self-gratification.[38] Beyond purely internal consideration, companies and competition authorities, as organisations, have their own system of incentives and rewards when it comes to cross-border cooperation. However, those incentives may differ when it comes to international cartel or merger transactions.

[34] In 2002, the EU Commission approved ADM's acquisition of a controlling stake in the ACTI companies involved in international trading of agricultural markets. ibid: 8.

[35] This section is based on Horna, 'David & Goliath'.

[36] Clark and Wilson (1961).

[37] See Terhechte (2011).

[38] See Clark and Wilson (1961: 129) citing Chester Bernard Harvard.

Indeed, cooperation in cartel investigation differs from investigations in international merger cases as parties are incentivised to cooperate so mergers are recognised in as many jurisdictions as possible. The merging companies need to have legal certainty from major jurisdictions, so as to avoid nullifying their merger operations in different markets.[39] Conversely, the parties being investigated for having conspired in international cartel activities have no incentive to cooperate with other jurisdictions as they fear being incriminated and fined in multiple jurisdictions.[40]

The incentives under which cooperation can occur vary in detail from jurisdiction to jurisdiction. Incentives for cooperation at the level of cross-border investigations can materialise in a number of coordination mechanisms carried out mostly by mature or large competition law enforcers. For instance, in the air cargo cartel, international cooperation at the enforcement stage took place in the form of coordinated international dawn raids by key mature competition authorities worldwide,[41] among which similar powers of investigation, systems of internal rewards and even convergent anti-cartel legislation exists. Comparable incentives can sometimes produce dissimilar results in different contexts as it can be from the different perspectives below: mature, young and practitioners' incentives to cooperate.

The level of maturity of a country's competition culture, as discussed in chapter one, can likewise affect the applicable incentive system.[42] In particular, countries that have recently adopted competition rules, have young competition authorities, or have a very limited competition culture will be unable to take part in multinational CBCs investigations such as the air-cargo cartel (see chapter two) because of their limited ability to investigate multinational CBCs and counteract the deterrent effects of these business activities. To illustrate, in relation to the ICN Framework discussed below, information solicited from mature jurisdictions by young or small competition authorities was apparently unutilised. In some cases, mature but small competition authorities (Singapore or Switzerland) have failed to initiate their own domestic cartel investigations due to lack of response to their requests for information from the world's leading competition enforcers.[43] Based on the foregoing, there is a need to identify the applicable incentives for all the

[39] See Jenny (2003).

[40] '... there is more co-operation between competition authorities in merger review than cartel investigations because the nature of the proceedings is different. Unlike a cartel case, where parties are investigated for alleged infringements of the law, merger review is an authorisation process. In the latter, the parties have all the incentives to co-operate with the reviewing authorities and to ensure consistent outcomes through effective co-operation between the authorities involved. Conversely, in cartel cases the investigated parties have no interest in the authorities co-operating, which may only result in multiple sanctions, unless they are in leniency/amnesty programmes. Therefore, creating the incentives for co-operation in cartel investigations rests largely with competition authorities ...' OECD, 'Improving International Co-Operation in Cartel Investigations' 19.

[41] Bergman and Sokol (2014).

[42] Clark and Wilson (1961: 162).

[43] Interview with Anderson; Interview with Han Li Toh.

stakeholders to cooperate in cartel investigations. Let us examine the main actors' interests and seek ways to induce cooperation.

4.2.1.1. *For Mature or Large Competition Authorities*

> The [US] Antitrust Division, like competition authorities around the world, strongly supports improving the ability of governments to share information in the investigation of hard-core cartels. Consumer groups and even some members of the private antitrust bar take a similar position. On the other hand, many business groups, although by no means all, take a different view. They advocate a more cautious approach that creates unreasonable barriers to information sharing in cartel cases; barriers that do not exist when governments exchange information to investigate other financial offenses, such as fraud, tax, or securities violations.[44]

On a practical level, individuals in more mature authorities may be willing to help their peers because of agenda-driven considerations, but those in case teams are normally too overloaded with work to respond to numerous requests from small or young jurisdictions.[45] Mature or large authorities would be incentivised to respond to requests for information if they feel and trust that the information shared with the foreign agency would not be misused or leaked to third parties. As more and more small or young competition authorities are set up, the concern becomes how mature competition authorities would handle a proliferation of case-specific requests.

To address the foregoing concern, UNCTAD posed a question to its member states as to how general information cooperation can turn into case-specific informal cooperation,[46] a challenge that remains today.[47] Of course, 'good will, trust, and a desire to work together ... [as well as an] understanding of each others' needs and confidentiality restrictions [are] the best instruments for cooperation via telephone or e-mail'.[48] Obviously, that is not as simple as it seems; otherwise, all competition authorities could have already done it. It is evident that other factors must be taken into account.[49] Popular myths such as 'lack of a formal cooperation mechanism prevents effective cooperation' or 'cooperation requires

[44] Hammond (2004).

[45] Jensen (1994).

[46] Case-specific informal cooperation can be possible, if a number of potentially sharable non-confidential information can be exchanged between agencies. These categories of information could be: (1) existence of investigation; (2) theories about harm, markets, or remedies; and (3) industry background. See Damtoft (2014: slide 11).

[47] UNCTAD, 'Informal Cooperation among Competition Agencies'.

[48] Damtoft (2014: slide 14).

[49] In interviews with heads of young and small agencies, it transpired that cooperation with other agencies faces legal barriers that arise from the distinction between common law and civil law systems, as well as top-down policies whereby civil servants might be sanctioned if communications with foreign colleagues are concerned in the cases handled, especially if these cases are related to cartel enforcement. The primary source here is anonymous at the request of the interviewees.

an enforcement mechanism to make it work' or that 'cooperation only takes place among developed countries'[50] can be contrasted against the reality where 'effective cooperation happens every day, with and without a formal mechanism' and where 'cooperation requires mutual trust and strong relationships' as well as the fact that 'cooperation takes place wherever there are enforcement interests in common'.[51] It must be noted, however, that enforcement interests of a mature or large and a young or small competition authority are not often the same, as was the case in the auto parts investigation undertaken by the Colombian Authority in 2012 (as discussed in chapter two).[52]

4.2.1.2. For Young or Small Authorities

Although the incentives for young or small authorities are straightforward in terms of gaining privileged agency information and intelligence from more mature competition authorities,[53] nevertheless, their representatives often do not feel comfortable picking up the phone and reaching out to their counterparts abroad.[54] In some cases, language barriers and cultural differences become limitations.[55] In most of the cases, however, it is just a matter of lack of willingness, trust, and understanding vis-à-vis their counterparts. Furthermore, if they eventually decide to cooperate, younger and smaller competition authorities tend to have very broad and vague requests for information which the counterpart agency may find difficult to process, due to, in a number of cases, heavy workload and other priorities.[56]

In addition, the prosecution of certain types of CBCs by younger or small competition authorities might have a limited deterrent effect, in particular when it comes to multinational CBCs as per the meaning provided in chapter two. Hence, other types of CBCs such as regional ones operating among younger competition authorities' jurisdictions may be the priority for these young or small authorities rather than multinational CBCs.

A possible explanation is that international investigations by mature competition authorities that would break up a CBC would evidently benefit developing countries as well, so it would be more efficient for the young or small competition

[50] Damtoft (2014: slide 18).

[51] ibid.

[52] In this investigation, SIC had requested information from these US authorities at the initial stage of investigation so as to effectively get the evidence from the international case. Unfortunately, due to the SIC not being able to build a close cooperative relationship with the US authority, the case was archived because of the lack of sufficient access to evidence under the legal requirements of Colombian law. See Interview with a SIC Case Handler, Ms Maria Claudia Martinez Beltran in 2013 on the issue 'International Cartel Investigations in the SIC: Investigation Limitations and Possible Future Solutions'.

[53] See Ramakrishnan and Thakor (1991).

[54] Interviews with anonymous referees carried out in January 2017.

[55] Clark and Wilson (1961).

[56] Interviews with anonymous referees carried out in January 2017.

authorities to put their lesser resources into tackling domestic cartels,[57] where there would be no possibility of free-riding.[58] In those cases, the need for cooperation would exist only if there was some reason that the developing country would need to have a separate remedy. In this particular case, pure regional cartels as in the meaning provided in chapter two would be the main target of these young competition authorities. As will be indicated in the introduction of Part III below, the latter is considered as one of the main reasons why this research does not provide solutions to multinational CBCs for young competition authorities.

4.2.1.3. For the Parties, Companies and Lawyers

There is a common perception that parties would be more in favour of inter-agency information-sharing in international merger cases compared to cartel cases.[59] Incentives for the parties might not be clear to young or small competition authorities, but reality shows that parties, including international law firms involved in open cartel investigations worldwide, would be happier in many cases if young or small competition authorities could be briefed by mature competition authorities on the general information of the case (without the need to have waivers).[60] This situation is considered more efficient compared to the international law firm undertaking the briefing itself. The briefing that mature competition authorities could provide to younger competition authorities would simplify procedures and reduce transaction costs, considering that the complexity of procedures for a young agency's interaction with law firms in its local jurisdiction may lead to unnecessary additional hurdles, such as questions on the exact information to be submitted, local formalities, and of course, additional legal fees. As a result, parties should be, in principle, in favour cooperation whereby non-confidential information could be shared efficiently between mature and young or small competition authorities.[61]

Presumably, the incentive for competition authorities and parties would be to have legal certainty and coherence in the parallel investigations launched by both the mature and young or small authorities. Of course, willingness to cooperate and trust in the system are prerequisites for all of these to work effectively.

[57] Interview with Toh; Interview with Lozano.

[58] See also more in: Schoneveld (2003).

[59] Already by 2003, there was an impressive list of documented cases of cooperation in mergers (Jenny, 2003: 993); see also Zanettin (2002).

[60] Parties in neighbouring countries whereby trade and commercial ties are high, the fact that both authorities can discuss the cases will benefit the companies dealing with both jurisdictions. See for instance the Second Generation Agreement between Switzerland and the EU : EU & Swiss Governments, 'Agreement between the EU and the Swiss Confederation concerning Cooperation on the Application of their Competition Laws', http://eur-lex.europa.eu/legal-content/EN/TXT/PDF/?uri=CELEX:22014A1203(01)&from=EN, accessed 22 February 2017.

[61] Interviews with anonymous referees carried out in January 2017.

4.2.2. Diverging Leniency Regimes

Generally, in more mature competition regimes, there is a common practice of executing waivers when sharing confidential information in connection with cross-border leniency applications. This may not necessarily be the case with younger competition authorities where an international leniency applicant might not be able to trust the authorities concerned because they either do not possess a leniency programme, or it is not perceived to be sufficiently robust.

In fact, mature authorities would expect a functioning and effective leniency programme to be in place across all involved jurisdictions so that they can share information and considers waivers for the leniency applicants. For many young and small competition authorities, however, getting information at the investigatory phase of a transnational CBC can already be a dead-end due to the structural problem of ill-designed leniency programmes in their own jurisdiction, or their non-existence in other jurisdictions. If evidence is found in multiple jurisdictions, the lack of availability of leniency programmes, or lack of trust towards them, would make it difficult to obtain said evidence. This not only adds to the complexities of cross-border cooperation but also significantly hampers transnational CBC investigations.[62]

4.2.2.1. Lack of Effective Implementation of Leniency Programmes in Young Competition Authorities

The main problem in many younger jurisdictions, and indeed even in mature ones, is the lack of successful implementation of leniency programmes at the domestic level. This can be due to a number of factors, such as 'State dominance of the economy at least until the 1980s and continued State monopolies, higher variability in development among sectors, and different socio-economic and political factors'.[63] These factors have conceivably influenced the effectiveness of leniency programmes in jurisdictions that strive to actively fight cartels.

In Latin America (see chapter seven), leniency programmes remain a critical challenge, with the exceptions of Brazil, Chile and Mexico. In 2016, while Argentina, Bolivia, Costa Rica, Paraguay and Venezuela did not have formal leniency programmes established by law, Ecuador, Panama, Peru and Uruguay did have formal leniency programmes, but no leniency cases so far.[64] In an interview in 2017, the head of the Authority of Panama claimed that the main reason as to

[62] In accordance to an interview conducted with the head of the Competition Commission of Singapore, leniency is critical for the development of good trust relations between mature and young competition authorities. If leniency is not well developed in younger jurisdictions, there is little chance for successful cooperation between these authorities. See Han Li, 'International Cooperation in Cartel Enforcement: The Singaporean Experience' (2017).

[63] UNCTAD, 'The Use of Leniency Programmes as a Tool for the Enforcement of Competition Law'.

[64] Young Council Latin American Regional Forum (2016: 5–6).

why Panama had no leniency cases after 10 years of implementation was that the majority of cases that the Panamanian Competition Authority (ACODECO) has been investigating are related to bid-rigging activity in public procurement bids whereby there is a criminal dimension and ACODECO cannot guarantee immunity to the whistle-blower.[65]

An additional problem associated with the lack of implementation is that any leniency application in Panama will not pre-empt private damage actions triggered by cartel victims.[66] In the example provided above, legal reform should follow to reinforce the leniency programmes in younger and smaller jurisdictions.

4.2.2.2. Lack of Trust by the Leniency Applicants in Providing a Confidentiality Waiver to Young Competition Authorities

As a consequence of the lack of effective leniency programmes or in the absence of those in younger jurisdictions, leniency applicants are in a difficult position to grant confidentiality waivers to exchange leniency information among the authorities' jurisdictions where the company operates due to risks of leaking the information to unintended parties.[67] In addition, even if the leniency programme is in place in the younger jurisdiction, there is always the question of trust for the leniency applicants as to how much the confidential information shared by the mature competition authorities can actually be kept in confidentiality in the younger jurisdiction.[68] In other words, the whole system would not work unless leniency applicants have confidence in the confidentiality practices of younger competition authorities.[69]

Another problem that causes leniency applicants to distrust younger jurisdictions' leniency programmes pertains to the lack of clear formulation as to what exactly the terms of the waiver should be, whether a full or procedural waiver should be disclosed.[70] In fact, despite efforts carried out by the ICN in the formulation of template waivers in cross-border leniency applications,[71] many young competition authorities have no clear view as to how a waiver should limit the

[65] Interview with Cardoze.

[66] Although in Panama, civil damage actions have not been successful at all. See ibid.

[67] Interview with Bezzi.

[68] Indeed, it has occurred in practice that when confidential information is being exchanged between a mature and a younger competition authority, the information has been leaked to public domain the very next day after the information exchanged. See Interview at the ICN Annual Conference in Porto. Interview with Toh.

[69] UNCTAD, 'Enhancing International Cooperation in the Investigation of Cross-Border Competition Cases: Tools and Procedures' 5.

[70] Whereas the purpose of the procedural waiver is the coordination of key investigative steps between competition authorities, a full waiver would contain beside the procedural aspects, the exchange of information between authorities on the substance of the leniency applicant's submission. See ICN, 'Waivers of Confidentiality in Cartel Investigations' 4.

[71] See ICN, 'Waivers of Confidentiality in Cartel Investigations'.

consent of a leniency applicant in accordance with domestic confidentiality rules.[72] In a transnational CBC investigation, a waiver of confidentiality provided by the parties could elicit confidential information that had been submitted in the context of the CBC investigation by another competition authority (younger) dealing with the same CBC. However, the decision of a leniency applicant to waive the right to confidentiality protection is voluntary and therefore it would rely entirely on trust, which unfortunately is not yet there in many younger jurisdictions.[73]

For a young competition authority wishing to request information from their mature counterparts, two-way trust needs to be in place in order to smooth cooperation between the two authorities. For instance, when the Colombian Competition Authority opened an investigation into the transnational auto-parts cartel (see chapter seven), it had little or no trust in its counterparts in Japan and the US. As such, although the Colombian Competition Authority recognised that the involvement of the US Department of Justice (DOJ) at the initial stage of investigation could help establish the case by providing information on which firms had already pleaded guilty, it had difficulty doing so as there was no previous cooperative relationship between the Colombian Competition Authority and the US-DOJ.[74] In this particular case, there were indeed better communications between young (India, China, Singapore, Brazil, among others) and mature (Japan, South Korea, Germany, EU, Canada and the US) jurisdictions.[75] It is worth noting that the young authorities involved were quite large and already relatively advanced, thus they were in a better position to counteract the effects of these cartels.

4.2.2.3. Lack of Specific Cooperation Arrangements of Mutual Recognition in Leniency

As discussed in chapter three, leniency programmes are increasingly being used by young and small competition authorities to gain access to information about cartels. The implementation of these leniency programmes, however, is hampered

[72] In the ASEAN region, younger competition authorities would need to always interact with mature ones (Australia) in order to get the best international practice as to how a waiver should be prepared. Australia can always refer to the ICN template and that has been effective to avoid different levels of confidentiality being disclosed. See Interview with Bezzi.

[73] A clear distinction can be found among mature competition authorities whereby parties and leniency applicants would trust that the information provided can actually be treated with caution and no leak of information would occur. For instance in the transnational CBC of the bearing automotive cartel discussed in ch 2, the international leniency application submitted to US, Canada and Europe was incorporated at a later stage by the Australian Competition Commission. The ACCC received a notification of the bearing automotive cartel thanks to a waiver submitted to US and Canada whereby it allowed discussions on the case. This actually led to a different outcome of the case in Australia, as the Australian-based conduct was different to the allegations made in counterpart jurisdictions and there was no need to follow-up with a document exchanged request. See Bezzi (2014: slide 9).

[74] *Colombia Autoparts cartel – Closing the investigation* [2015] Superintendencia de Industria y Comercio Resolution No 37523.

[75] Linklaters (2018: 4).

by the lack of agreement between jurisdictions regarding access to foreign evidence. This comes not only from a leniency application but also from the lack of coordination between civil, administrative and criminal proceedings in the affected jurisdictions.[76] However, at the stage where competition authorities are seeking pieces of information, evidence, and public but not immediately accessible information to open their formal cartel investigations, the fact of not having coordination mechanisms that cover evidence gathered from leniency applications considerably harms the information transfer.

As discussed below, failure to agree on a definition of confidential information hampers the way that information from leniency can flow between competition authorities. It is well established that 'the protection of the confidentiality of leniency applicant statements against disclosure in Court is commonly seen as a cornerstone of leniency regimes'.[77] The name of the leniency applicant and its unlawful practices in a given jurisdiction has been considered confidential information and kept as such by major jurisdictions such as the US, where the US's DOJ Antitrust Division has had to deal with this problem by plea agreements in open courts.[78]

Another key issue is the young competition authorities' lack of trust in sharing leniency information with competition authorities in other jurisdictions, even if such information resulted from its knowledge of the market and the intelligence that it gathered during the pre-investigatory cartel investigation phase. This problem was illustrated in the countries neighbouring South Africa. There, even if the legal treatment of cartels is the same (all the countries use criminal law to prosecute cartels), cartel leniency confessions and settlements in South Africa have not resulted in similar confessions in the Southern African Customs Union (SACU) and the Southern African Development Community (SADC) countries (Botswana, Namibia, Swaziland, Zambia and Zimbabwe), even those with functional competition authorities. The asymmetry between South Africa and the rest of the SACU/SADC competition agencies means that the uncovering and punishment of regional CBCs in key sectors such as fertilisers, petroleum and cement are of relevance primarily to South African domestic markets.[79]

[76] See more in Hansen, Crocco and Kennedy (2012).

[77] ibid: 2.

[78] Since 1993, with the adoption of the DOJ Antitrust Division's Corporate Leniency Policy, a bedrock principle of the leniency programme in the United States has been the ironclad assurance of confidentiality for all leniency applicants. In 2008, the DOJ reiterated this principle and stated that: '[t]he Division holds the identity of leniency applicants and the information they provide in strict confidence, much like the treatment afforded to confidential informants. Therefore, the Division does not publicly disclose the identity of a leniency applicant or information provided by the applicant, absent prior disclosure by, or agreement with, the applicant, unless required to do so by court order in connection with litigation.' The Division also adopted a 'policy of not disclosing to foreign antitrust agencies information obtained from a leniency applicant unless the leniency applicant agrees first to the disclosure.' The Division has been able to dutifully abide by these confidentiality guarantees in most cases and most, if not all, of the information supplied by leniency applicants has been kept confidential and out of the public domain. Ibid: 13.

[79] See more Kaira (2015).

4.2.3. Lack of an International Definition of Confidential Information

In an OECD/ICN survey of 2013, the OECD and non-OECD member countries claimed that:

> there is no commonly agreed definition at the international level concerning what information is 'confidential' in competition matters. Some responses also indicate that there may be different definitions within the same jurisdiction ... These definitions of 'confidential information' are not necessarily included in legal statutes, but may instead be developed by practices of the enforcement agencies and of the courts.[80]

A standard international approach to determine what is confidential has been difficult to achieve as the standards and methods for such determination differ across countries and legal systems.[81] Indeed, the said OECD/ICN survey mentions that jurisdictions could use one or more of the following criteria to define confidential information: the nature and type of information, the way in which the information is collected, the purpose to which it was collected or submitted, and the way in which the parties define it. These will be explored in more detail below.

1. **By the nature and type of the information**: this pertains to whether, if the information is disclosed, it would harm the commercial interests of the source that trusted the authority. In the OECD/ICN survey, the majority of respondents considered business secrets to be confidential, but other authorities differed from that particular benchmark.[82] For instance, under US law, a definition of confidential information can be extracted from Article 1905 of the US Code, which proscribes confidential information being regarded as 'information [that] concerns or relates to the trade secrets, processes, operations, style of work, or apparatus, or to the identity, confidential statistical data, amount or source of any income, profits, losses, or expenditures of any person, firm, partnership, corporation, or association; or permits any income return or copy thereof or any book containing any abstract or particulars thereof'.[83]

In addition, in EU laws and regulations, confidential information is linked to the term 'professional secrecy', which every EU official must observe and which covers all kinds of information related to companies (undertakings in the meaning provided under EU competition law), their business relations or their cost components.[84] By this definition the term, 'business secrets' covers technical or financial information relating to an 'undertaking's know-how, methods of assessing costs, production secrets and processes, supply sources, quantities

[80] OECD & ICN (2013: 127).
[81] Shan (2008: 58).
[82] Other survey respondents considered confidential any information which is prejudicial to the commercial position of the subject matter. OECD & ICN (2013: 128).
[83] '18 U.S. Code § 1905 – Disclosure of Confidential Information Generally'.
[84] 'Contribution from the European Union – Discussion on How to Define Confidential Information' 2–3.

produced and sold, market shares, customer and distributor lists, marketing plans, cost and price structure and sales strategy'.[85]

Further, the notion of confidential information under EU laws includes other types of confidential information such as 'information that would enable the parties to identify complainants or other third parties where those have a justified wish to remain anonymous. The category of other confidential information also includes military secrets.'[86] Finally, in China, confidential information is associated with the term 'trade secret' and is often referred as information 'unknown to the public [which means] that the information is unknown to, and is difficult to be obtained by, the relevant personnel in the relevant field'.[87] Interestingly, according to China's Supreme People's Court, there are exceptions to the definition of trade secrets which are enumerated expressly in the jurisprudence.[88]

As can be seen above, there are many similarities and differences between the definitions of confidential information in the EU, the US and China. While there are some similarities between the definitions of 'trade secret' as part of the definition of confidential information between US and EU,[89] differences remain as to the scope of the term 'confidential information' amongst Chinese, US and EU laws. For instance, China's definition of 'trade secret' is blurry as its real meaning is left to be determined by the jurisprudence of courts. Another difference between China and the EU pertains to the level of protection of trade secrets: while trade secrets need to be protected in accordance with unfair competition laws in China, in the EU, trade secret protection is protected differently in each EU member state.[90] In the US, trade secrets are mainly protected from misappropriation by state laws and the Uniform Trade Secrets Act (UTSA), which codifies the basic principles of common law trade secret protection, adopted by the majority of the states in the US.[91]

2. **By the way in which the information is collected:** the majority of OECD/ICN respondents said that they would 'consider confidential any information obtained

[85] ibid: 3.

[86] ibid: 3.

[87] Foley and others, 'Trade Secret Protection in China: A Perspective from China and Hong Kong'.

[88] The information is common sense or common industrial practice for the personnel in the relevant technical or economic field. The information only involves a simple combination of dimensions, structures, materials, and parts of products, and can be directly obtained through the observation of products by the relevant public after the products enter the market. The information has been publicly disclosed in any publication or any other mass medium. The information has been publicised through reports or exhibits. The information can be obtained through other public channels. The information can be easily obtained at little or no cost. Ibid.

[89] 1. The owner or person lawfully in control of the information must have taken reasonable steps to maintain its secrecy; 2. The information must be secret in the sense that it is neither generally known to nor readily ascertainable by another person; and 3. The information must derive economic or commercial value from its secrecy. Ankenbrandt and Vormann (2016: 5.

[90] For example, in Italy, trade secrets are protected under intellectual property law. In France and Germany, they are protected under unfair competition laws, in the Netherlands under tort law, and in the UK and Ireland under breach of confidence rules. See China IPR SME Helpdesk (2015: 7).

[91] Yeh (2016).

by the competition authority in the course of performance of its official duties and functions'.[92] This view has recently been endorsed at the latest ICN Annual Conference, whereby a few interviewees coming from young competition jurisdictions highlighted that any information that is gathered by the authority should be deemed as confidential, particularly that information that has been provided by the parties in an open investigation, regardless of the nature, type, or purpose.[93]

3. **By the purpose for which the information was collected or submitted:** if the information is submitted for a pre-merger notification, it would need to be considered confidential and to not cross-fertilise other proceedings that the authority is undertaking, such as a cartel investigation.[94] This definition of confidential information is restricted and reflects the level of caution exercised in the course of an investigation. In some cases, this high level of protection can be considered to be excessive, and when employed by young competition authorities it can reflect their inexperience; in these cases the authorities would consider that everything that the parties have said and documents provided need to be treated as confidential, otherwise companies would simply deny the existence of the information or do not cooperate if they deem that the information is being exchanged with foreign institutions without their permission.[95]

4. **By the way the parties define it:** in the course of an open investigation, the parties can and probably will consider that all information provided needs to be treated as confidential. In other words, 'any information that the source has defined as such is considered confidential'.[96] That consideration would need to be automatically endorsed by the authority. Fortunately, only eight respondents of 55 authorities surveyed in the OECD/ICN report said that they would choose this option.[97]

As we can see from the foregoing, there are important differences amongst jurisdictions as per the definition of confidential information. Indeed, these differences and the lack of a workable international definition of confidential information hamper the exchange of information between competition authorities because of the failure to draw a line between information that cannot be shared with other authorities in the absence of waivers, and information that can be shared with others. This limitation is more pronounced in cartel investigations whereby the use of waivers of confidentiality is less used than it is in the case of merger cases.[98]

[92] OECD & ICN (2013: 128).
[93] Irrarazabal (2017) and Interview with Lozano.
[94] OECD & ICN (2013: 128).
[95] As Nicaragua is considered a young competition authority, the lack of a robust competition culture in the business sector is still a problem. This is also reflected when the authority investigates cartels: if they do not consider the information provided by the parties to be 'confidential', the parties would simply decline to cooperate and provide the information. Interview with Guzman.
[96] OECD & ICN (2013: 128).
[97] ibid.
[98] OECD, 'National and international provisions for the exchange of confidential information' 2.

OECD countries have failed to agree on an international benchmark on the definition of confidential information in order to differentiate it from the areas where 'sharable' information can be exchanged in the three stages of a cartel investigation. As such, chapter three defined four types of information (public, agency, party information and information obtained from the parties at the request of other parties), and there is no common agreement as to what information should be protected under domestic rules on confidentiality and what information should not, as each jurisdiction has its own rules regarding confidentiality. A particularly contested area is that of rules related to the rights of the investigation parties and the public to access information in the agencies' files.[99]

As a result, in many instances requesting competition authorities would need to 'engage in a time-consuming coordination process to avoid possible accusations from the firms or individuals that provided the information to the authority receiving the request'.[100] This would only take place provided that a mature competition authority had the necessary incentives to cooperate and share information with a young one. As explained in chapter three, incentives to cooperate are always a constraint and therefore it would only be possible if there were common enforcement interests between a mature and a young competition authority.

In sum, the lack of an international definition of confidential information is a problem for the exchange of information in an international cooperation. As seen above, different views, approaches and interpretations at the domestic jurisdiction have created a number of incompatible legal definitions of confidential information, as in the examples of US, EU and Chinese laws. This is exacerbated by the fact that the confidentiality test that competition authorities undertake when the information is received at the investigatory phase differs from jurisdiction to jurisdiction. Part III of this research deals with this particular problem and provides solutions to further consolidate an international benchmark of what is 'sharable' information as opposed to attempting to define the term 'confidential'.

4.2.4. Lack of Physical Presence

The lack of physical presence of the international cartelist companies in the young competition authority's territory can cause further problems when dealing with multinational and transnational cross-border cartels. One important requirement for the competition authority to commence an investigation of a cartel is to

[99] For example, Turkey's Competition Authority recently published a communiqué on the right to access a file and the protection of trade secrets; the agency is required to balance the need to use evidence to prove its case against legitimate confidentiality claims. Chile's Transparency Act allows any person to request any specific document or more general information from the FNE, but provides justifications for FNE to deny such requests in order to protect the confidentiality of business secrets. OECD, 'Procedural Fairness and Transparency' 17.

[100] UNCTAD, 'Enhancing International Cooperation in the Investigation of Cross-Border Competition Cases: Tools and Procedures' 5.

have jurisdiction over the alleged cartelist. In this connection, legal domicile of the cartelist must be determined. Due process considerations and constitutional rights for defence dictate that the alleged cartelist be validly notified of the official opening of a cartel investigation.

The issue of notification becomes complicated when the investigation involves international companies which operate, but do not necessarily have a physical presence, in the jurisdictions of many young and small competition regimes' territories. This lack of physical presence renders getting evidence from dawn raids, interrogations, or requests for written statements extremely difficult,[101] if not impossible.

This issue was demonstrated in Colombia in 2012 when the Colombian competition authority opened a formal cartel investigation against the transnational auto-parts CBC. However, the investigation, which lasted for three years, was closed due to the lack of physical presence of the transnational cartelists in the domestic jurisdiction of Colombia.

The alleged cartelists were notified by email on the basis of evidence appearing in non-official documents that were plea agreements written in a foreign language and produced by a foreign competition authority. They were used by the Colombian competition authority without the foreign competition authority's express consent and endorsement as to their veracity.[102] Mr German Bacca, the former Head of Investigations of SIC in Colombia, provided this statement regarding the dismissal of the investigation:

> The truth of the matter is that the [auto-part investigation] was a clear example of what we should not do when it comes to structure a trans-border investigation. We did not carry out a preliminary investigation of the exact locations of the investigated companies, we did not contact the competition authorities of the originating country of the companies under investigation in order to get ex-ante collaboration prior to the formal opening of the case; and the infringement was based on non-official documents in foreign language that allowed the defence lawyer to counteract this administrative act with void and flagrant violation of the right of defence.[103]

This issue is not so relevant to emerging competition regimes with large economies, such as the BRICs countries, as the physical presence of multinational companies in their own territories means that they have better chance to deal with this problem. This was the case for Brazil when the Brazilian Competition Authority investigated and sanctioned the multinational CBC in the vitamin cartel case in 2007; see chapter seven.[104]

[101] Even the presence of a branch or subsidiary in developing countries does not necessarily guarantee effective investigations. International cartels are normally organised by head offices located abroad, and thus branches or subsidiaries located in developing countries may have no knowledge or documents directly relevant to the formation or operation of the cartel. UNCTAD, 'Cross-Border Anticompetitive Practices: The Challenges for Developing Countries and Economies in Transition' 6.

[102] *Colombia Autoparts cartel – Closing the investigation.*

[103] Translation from Spanish oral interview made by author. Interview with Bacca.

[104] Secretariat of Economic Law (2009).

4.3. Summary

Multiple interviews[105] and surveys carried out for this research and the practical experience of the author reveal that many competition agencies attribute the lack of trust as 'the problem' to explain why authorities tend to be unwilling to cooperate in multinational CBC investigations. However, this underlying issue is not founded on a lack of exchange and interaction between the authorities. Rather, it is related to a lack of trust of the more mature authority in the leniency programme of its younger counterpart. Ultimately, this prevents them from fostering trust vis-à-vis international leniency applicants who wish to report multinational or transnational CBCs.

Aside from overall trust, it is often argued that differences in legal culture between the mature and younger authorities constitute barriers to cooperation.[106] Beyond overall trust and legal business cultures, the issue of optimal deterrence of multinational CBCs constitutes an important consideration that small and young authorities should bear in mind as their ability to deter multinational CBCs is limited to a number of factors, including the size of the markets in their respective jurisdictions.

Finally, competition authorities need to consider the costs of cooperation and possible incentives or motivating factors. In the case of transnational CBC investigations, a mixture of young and mature jurisdictions might be involved irrespective of the fact that the cartelists' country of origin might be in any of these jurisdictions. In such a situation, the enforcement interests between the two competition authorities might converge because of the need to get the necessary evidence to formally open an investigation.

An interesting example is the aluminium phosphide cartel case that could have triggered common enforcement interests in Brazil, India, the US and Germany since companies from these jurisdictions had fixed prices to affect the US market. However, from the analysis of these transnational cartels in Chapter 2, it seems that only mature or young competition authorities in larger jurisdictions (e.g. Brazil and India) cooperated where their own companies or markets were at stake.

As detailed in Chapter 2, the ocean shipping or roll-on/roll-off cargo cartel involved the usual suspects of multinational cooperation such as EU, US, Japanese, Australian and even the Chinese. In this transnational CBC investigation, Australia had to piggy-back on the work of the US, EU, and Japanese authorities to bring the case to court.[107] The solution of reducing the distributional and information related problems of the authorities cooperating internationally also requires a high level of trust between the authorities.

[105] Interview with Bacca; Competition Policy International (2016); interview with Damtoft.
[106] Interview with Damtoft.
[107] 'ACCC in Cartel Case Contest'.

5

Specific Issues for Young or Small Competition Authorities in Investigating Regional Cross-Border Cartels

The focus for chapter five is on young or small competition authorities that deal with regional, export or import CBC investigations. This research aims to look beyond the interaction between generally mature competition authorities, for example the EU regional competition law enforcement experience, and instead to pay attention to the issues facing the developing authorities in young or small jurisdictions. The experience of the EU as a supranational competition authority dealing with EU regional cartels is well documented. This experience is not the focus of the research, but rather the regional economic groupings beyond the EU whereby a number of challenges are faced in order to successfully implement regional competition rules, as in the case of the EU.

As a matter of fact, Dabbah provides a number of observations as to why regional competition law and policy outside the EU has developed slowly in different regional groupings around the world: (1) the high number of initiatives, (2) problems in harmonisation; (3) difficulty in competition advocacy; (4) division in competence; (5) overlap in membership; (6) relentlessly copying EU experience without fully accounting for the local dynamics; (7) lack of clear direction; (8) capacity constraints; (9) issues of sub-regional cooperation; and (10) issues of bilateral cooperation.[1]

The effect of these factors has been varied, depending on the region involved. For instance, in the regional competition law system of the West Africa Economic Monetary Union (WAEMU), the issue of division in competence may be the most critical one, as relations between the regional and national authorities need to be further improved in terms of their cooperation. Other regional groupings present different recurrent problems such as the Association of South East Asian Nations (ASEAN) region, where a centralised regional secretariat (ASEAN Secretariat, or ASEC) needs to be empowered by the member countries in order to deal with regional issues.

[1] Dabbah (2010: 409–15).

As a result, CBC investigations have to deal with the different dynamics of how young competition authorities interact. For instance, the question of trust, discussed in chapter four, may be less relevant in regional CBC investigations because trust can be built up more easily in these areas. This is due to shared interests and values, and other interlinked factors such as interdependence and commonality of goals and objectives as well as being the result of frequent interaction amongst young competition enforcer peers, as in the case for the Latin American region.

Of course, there is always room for improvement when it comes to trust in regional CBC investigations amongst young competition authorities, but the focus has recently shifted to legal constraints rather than solely behavioural attitudes based on lack of trust, as in the case of multinational CBCs discussed in chapter four. An example of this was the domestic liquid oxygen cartel cases in Latin America, whereby parallel proceedings took place due to a lack of trust between key competition authorities, despite the existence of bilateral cooperation agreements and other instruments.[2] Lack of continual communication stymied the exchange of information between enforcers, and exacerbated the situation.[3] Shared values and interests amongst Latin American competition authorities can be jeopardised when there is too much diversity between their national competition laws and institutions[4] as well as a low deterrence-based trust[5] due to the lack of mechanisms to allow communication.[6] In any case, one should be aware that young competition authorities may address the question of trust in a different manner to mature competition authorities.[7] This is because of the modest level of competition culture in the young jurisdiction or the level of technical expertise on competition law analysis on the part of the competition enforcers. Relatively advanced but still young competition authorities may contribute to improving the capacity of their peers and provide technical assistance, which could become the first stage of trust development. Chapter nine will cover these aspects in more detail.

In addition, young competition authorities may face different constraints when they go through the stages of CBC proceedings where cooperation might be required.[8] In the pre-investigatory stage, a young competition authority willing to investigate a cartel infringement with an international dimension should be able to access crucial information, such as the notification of an investigation that has commenced abroad, the names of the companies involved in a parallel

[2] Horna (2017).
[3] Lewicki and Bunker (1995: 150).
[4] See ch 3.
[5] Low deterrence-based trust will be discussed in ch 10 when addressing the problem of trust development between competition authorities.
[6] See the case between Brazil and Argentina. Botta (2009).
[7] See the conceptual framework of trust development in ch 10.
[8] ICN, 'Anti-Cartel Enforcement Manual Chapter 9: International Cooperation and Information Sharing' 12.

investigation abroad, the location of the evidence, the theories of harm, and the effects of the alleged cartel conduct in their territory, if any.[9] Furthermore, if a regional CBC is involved, and cross-border cooperation is seen as a solution, then the young or small competition authority may want to know if there is a regional supranational competition authority, any cooperation agreement with its neighbouring competition authorities, and the scope of these agreements if so, and whether the physical presence of the alleged regional cartelists exists in the territory of the competition authority.

A regional CBC investigation may involve practical problems if, for instance, the region in which the cartel operates lacks the institutional framework to deal with this anti-competitive practice. Therefore, the first problem would be whether the regional economic group possesses a regional competition authority or not. Next, since neighbouring countries becoming aware of the absence of regional competition law enforcement might wish to cooperate, they would face another problem in terms of the potential differences of legal standing regarding cartel offences. The latter will have different implications as to how cooperation can proceed and whether evidence can be shared on the basis of what the domestic legal frameworks permit. The following section reviews the problems that can occur at any stage of a CBC investigation between young competition authorities. These include ineffective regional competition authorities, different legal standings as per cartel offences and the associated problems causes by those inconsistencies, and other differences such as diverse rules on powers of investigation and diverse adjudication techniques.

5.1. Lack of Effective Regional Competition Authorities

Regional CBCs are more likely to proliferate in areas where there are no competition authorities with proper investigative and sanctioning powers. If there is no prohibition on cartels at the regional level, and no regional body to enforce it, regional CBCs are lawful, and only national laws and institutions can attempt to remedy cartels affecting their domestic markets, and parallel proceedings will be necessary. Therefore, collective measures are not possible at the regional level unless coordinated domestic efforts are focusing in one regional CBC.[10] For example, in Central America, national competition authorities, all young and small, were set up at the domestic level in recent years and have dedicated their efforts to prosecute parallel domestic cartels in critical sectors such as agricultural markets and banking services, and that can lead to regional CBCs being tackled much more effectively.[11]

[9] ibid: 9.

[10] Ch 9 proposes a solution to the problem of coordination in young and small competition regimes, focusing on Latin America.

[11] See Odio-Rohrmoser (2016).

The lack of a supranational authority that deals with competition issues in the region may lead to the proliferation of regional CBCs, as key Central American sectors are highly concentrated and often belong to family business groups.[12] Indeed, if Central American competition authorities want to sanction regional cartels, they would have to be empowered to cooperate effectively at the pre-investigatory phase,[13] which is the critical phase for the framing of the entire CBC proceedings. In this period, a competition authority needs to gather the potentially limited information in order to start a formal cartel investigation and to frame the approach for the case by establishing the theory of harm as well as the actual and potential effects of the cartel conduct, in accordance with the applicable law.

Despite the importance of this stage, many competition authorities exert less effort at this stage compared to the investigatory stage. For instance, when the SIC in Colombia opened an investigation to assess the impact of the transnational auto-parts cartel during 2012 and 2013[14] (as discussed in chapter two), it decided to open a formal investigation based on previous investigations in the US without going through a comprehensive checklist of pending issues that the pre-investigatory phase demands (as outlined in chapter two). The investigation had to be terminated due to several procedural errors that could have been avoided had the SIC properly assessed the checklist outlined in the pre-investigatory phase.[15] In light of this, what follows is a review of the main issues that could arise when competition authorities, particularly those young or small competition authorities that do not have a culture of cooperation, require information from other competition authorities to successfully open the investigation against a CBC.

At the pre-investigatory phase, young competition agencies in Central America which only have access to information within their respective jurisdictions find it difficult to gather the information needed to open an investigation into a regional CBC. Even if the young competition authority manages to open an investigation, its domestic tools may be insufficiently deterrent to counteract the harmful effects of these CBCs. As indicated in chapter four, the efforts of the Central American regional network (RECAC) have been jeopardised by the fact that agency information cannot be easily exchanged at the initial phase of cartel proceedings, due to the lack of a workable definition or international benchmark of what constitutes confidential information.

The creation of a regional competition authority in Central America has not been successful partly due to the lack of a common political and social vision of regional economic integration. Despite commitments agreed with the EU when

[12] A Central American study revealed that about 28 groups or business conglomerates controlled key Central American markets at the regional level such as soft drinks, banking, agro-industry, supermarkets, construction, dairy products, stock markets, air transport, leisure activities, among others. See Segovia (2005: 62–70.

[13] See ch 3 for the definition of pre-investigatory phase.

[14] *Colombia Auto parts Cartel – Opening the investigation.*

[15] *Colombia Autoparts cartel – Closing the investigation.*

Central American countries signed an association agreement[16] and the compromise of the last country in the Spanish-speaking region (Guatemala) that needed to enact its domestic competition law,[17] heavy lobbying from business conglomerates in Central America prevented the ratification of a regional competition law. As a result of all these hurdles, the Central American competition authorities do not discuss case-sensitive information when they meet regularly under the framework of RECAC. Their meetings are more about strengthening the capacities and institutions of their domestic legal frameworks, which they achieve by organising workshops and jointly preparing the proposal for a regional competition framework.[18]

In the absence of a supranational authority in such concentrated regional markets, a robust system of informal regional cooperation to share information at this particular phase of the investigation is important. The Lima Declaration, discussed in chapter four, fulfils this role in the Latin American countries.

5.2. Different Legal Standings Regarding Cartel Offences

Legal standing with respect to criminalisation of cartels differs from jurisdiction to jurisdiction.[19] These differences have been regarded as a major impediment to cooperation in all stages of multijurisdictional cartel investigations. The different nature of the proceedings means having either a criminal or an administrative standing to investigate and sanction cartel offences. The resulting distinguishing characteristics of criminal law (eg, burden of proof and legal presumptions, among others) would be different from the classic approach of administrative proceedings which has normally been adopted by young competition regimes to enforce cartel laws.[20] In addition, beyond the economic harmfulness of CBCs discussed in chapter one, there is an ongoing debate at the international level as to whether cartels should be criminalised, which encompasses issues of both moral and social acceptance.[21]

Indeed, when there are commonalities in the legal standing, there will be more incentives to cooperate. Unfortunately, the tendency to criminalise cartels has developed asymmetrically worldwide.[22] For instance at the level of the EU member

[16] 'EU-Central America Association Agreement – Trade – European Commission'.

[17] See more in Odio-Rohrmoser (2016).

[18] Barillas (2015).

[19] For a comprehensive assessment of the legal and economic implications of criminalising cartel laws, see Cseres and others (2006).

[20] The characteristics are related to criminal penalties, criminal intent, moral condemnation, less strict relationship between penalty and harm, criminal rights of defence. See Wils, 'Is Criminalization of EU Competition Law the Answer?'.

[21] Beaton-Wells and Ezrachi (2012: 289).

[22] Ezrachi and Kindl (2011: 421).

states, some countries such as France, the Netherlands, Austria and Luxembourg have decriminalised their enforcement of competition laws, while others such as Ireland and the United Kingdom have criminalised their competition laws.[23] It should also be noted that the US anti-trust laws have been clearly influenced by those jurisdictions that share the same common law tradition, rather than the more continental tradition of civil law systems as exemplified by the German and French jurisdictions.[24]

On the whole, diversity in the legal standing of anti-competitive practices has many important implications when it comes to international cartel investigations, and they shall be examined below, before returning to the exploration of other differences between competition authorities that make cooperation difficult.

5.2.1. Dual Criminality

In countries where cartel offences are criminal in nature, competition agencies rely on extradition to prosecute foreign cartelists worldwide.[25] Hence, examining the impact of extradition rules in multinational cartel investigations would mean reviewing the universal principle recognised by the majority of states across the world: the duality of offences or the threshold requirement of 'double criminality' that is a basic precept in extradition law and is reflected in extradition statutes and bilateral treaties.[26] The double criminality principle suggests that a criminal offence must be considered punitive in both states, reflecting the paramount principle of criminal law, *nulla poena sine lege,* which must be observed in both jurisdictions.[27] In multijurisdictional cartel investigations, there is a risk of having two or more legal systems that fundamentally differ in terms of how dual criminality is treated. Even in countries that share the same legal tradition, such as Canada,

[23] Wils, 'Is Criminalization of EU Competition Law the Answer?' 23–25.

[24] Common law and civil law systems are approaches on how law should be applied and the usual distinction between the two systems is referred as follows: whereas common law system tends to be case-centred and hence judge-centred, allowing scope for a discretionary, ad-hoc pragmatic approach, the civil law system tends to be a codified body of general abstract principles which control the exercise of judicial discretion. However, in practice both systems have a moderate level of judicial discretion whereby a convergence of interpretation of law between civil law and common law principles can take place. For instance, the European Court of Justice, being a civil-law based court, is increasingly recognising the benefits of establishing a body of case law or *stare decisis*. Slapper and Kelly (1999: 3).

[25] '... Many indicted foreign executives have assessed the risk of extradition and made a calculated decision to give themselves up, and the US has so far criminally charged more than 60 foreign nationals.' Thomas and De Stefano (2016: 3).

[26] Williams (1991: 582).

[27] '... The dual criminality requirement has undergone a tremendous change in the last 100 years. In the late nineteenth century the requirement was intended to force a requested State to justify its denial of an extradition request in order to protect the individual facing extradition from unjust prosecution. However, in this century dual criminality has become an unwanted barrier to extradition to both requesting and requested States ...' See more in: Hafen (1992).

the US and the UK, there are differences in approach in their interpretations of extradition treaties and statutes, and in particular how they should be interpreted under international law or domestic law considerations.[28] Definitions of cartels in different jurisdictions[29] might also have an impact on how courts assess how analogous the crime is across two jurisdictions.[30]

Even if the principle of dual criminality is satisfied, several jurisdictions have laws that prevent the extradition of their own citizens.[31] In the multinational marine hoses CBC (discussed in chapter two), Mr Romano Pisciotti, a former senior executive of Parker ITR, a marine hose manufacturer based in Italy, was arrested in Germany based on an extradition request made by US authorities with the support of Interpol, and was extradited to a US prison in 2014.[32] The extradition of Mr Pisciotti was an outright violation of the non discrimination principle prescribed by Article 18 of the Treaty of the Functioning of the European Union (TFEU), under which there shall be no discrimination between EU citizens and nationalities within the union. This principle was not observed when Mr Pisciotti was extradited to the US, since he was an Italian but not a German citizen.

The critical issue that we can see here is that extradition is not an easy task in multijurisdictional cartel investigations. Without the same legal standing between competition regimes regarding cartel offences, it becomes impossible. If two competition authorities are willing to cooperate, a checklist of specific issues should be observed to successfully extradite foreign national in international competition cases: (1) there must exist an extradition treaty between the countries at stake; (2) the alleged cartel offence must be considered punishable under criminal laws of both jurisdictions; (3) the nationality of the defendant must not prevent extradition as countries protect their own citizens from extradition; (4) other legal and procedural specific requirements must be fulfilled depending on each jurisdiction's laws.[33]

[28] For a comprehensive and comparative analysis of how treaties and statutes should be interpreted under English, US and Canadian Laws, see Williams (1991).

[29] Between the US and Canada, cartel offences differ from being rule of reason approach in Canada and per se rule in US. See Canadian Competition Act 1985; US Sherman Antitrust Act.

[30] For example, in *Wright v Henkel*, the British government requested the extradition of a man who had committed a fraud and fled to US. The question of this extradition was whether the dual requirement was satisfied and whether the slightly difference of definitions between English and US laws can be 'substantially analogous' despite differences in the wording. Hafen (1992: 200).

[31] The Law Library of US Congress has published a chart containing information on the terms that apply to the extradition of citizens in 157 jurisdictions around the globe. The statistics are available at: www.loc.gov/law/help/extradition-of-citizens/chart. php/?locr=bloglaw. Of the countries surveyed, 60 were found to have laws that prevent the extradition of their own citizens. Other requirements may apply in different countries, or they may have a provision that simply allows a government minister to refuse the extradition of a citizen. Thomas and De Stefano (2016: fn 14).

[32] ibid: 2.

[33] ibid: 3–4.

5.2.2. Implementation of Mutual Legal Assistance Treaties (MLATs)

In connection with the dual criminality aspect discussed above, Mutual Legal Assistance Treaties (MLATs) have been instrumental in channelling cooperation and assistance amongst their signatory countries, as they generally allow for the exchange of evidence and information in criminal and related matters. For instance, in areas beyond competition law enforcement, such as money laundering cases, MLATs are extremely useful in obtaining banking and other financial records from abroad.[34] In the area of competition enforcement, competition authorities such as the US often use MLATs to gather evidence abroad[35] based on the US International Antitrust Enforcement Assistance Act (IAEAA) of 1994.[36] Nonetheless, not all MLATs can be used for competition matters due to explicit exclusion (as in the case of the US-Swiss MLAT or the Canada-Germany MLAT), or because there is the requirement of criminal status 'equivalence' (in both jurisdictions).[37] It is worth noting that in some MLATs the requirement of dual criminality is theoretically not applicable, such as the case of US-Spain and US-Italy.[38] However, these MLATs have not been used in practice in the area of competition matters. The reason may be that Italy and Spain are part of the EU, whereby the normal interlocutor with the US would be the EU Commission.

Another problem with MLATs, besides the issue of being only applicable to criminal cartel cases in both jurisdictions seeking assistance, is that the provisions of the MLATs 'do not necessarily override domestic rules governing confidentiality, therefore not all competition authorities may be able to share information obtained through their own enforcement measures'.[39] In response, the IAEAA in America attempted to overcome this limitation, but since its creation in 1994 up to today, only one agreement has been signed, between the US and Australia in 1999.[40] The application of IAEAA received strong criticism because

[34] For example, the US has signed a great number of narcotics MLATs such as with Antigua & Barbuda, Argentina, Australia, Austria, the Bahamas, Barbados, Belgium, Belize, Brazil, Canada, Cyprus, Czech Republic, Dominica, Egypt, Estonia, France, Germany, Greece, Grenada, Hong Kong, Hungary, India, Ireland, Israel, Italy, Jamaica, Japan, Latvia, Liechtenstein, Lithuania, Luxembourg, Malaysia, Mexico, Morocco, the Kingdom of the Netherlands (including Aruba, Bonaire, Curacao, Saba, St Eustatius and St Maarten), Nigeria, Panama, Philippines, Poland, Romania, Russia, St Lucia, St Kitts & Nevis, St Vincent & the Grenadines, South Africa, South Korea, Spain, Sweden, Switzerland, Thailand, Trinidad & Tobago, Turkey, Ukraine, United Kingdom (including the Isle of Man, Cayman Islands, Anguilla, British Virgin Islands, Montserrat and Turks and Caicos), Uruguay, and Venezuela. Bureau Of International Narcotics And Law Enforcement Affairs, 'Treaties and Agreements'.

[35] US Department of Justice and Federal Trade Commission, 'Antitrust Guidelines for International Enforcement and Cooperation' 49.

[36] '[USC07] 15 USC Ch. 88: International Antitrust Enforcement Assistance'.

[37] ICN, 'Co-Operation between Competition Agencies in Cartel Investigations' 15.

[38] ibid.

[39] Martyniszyn (2012: 39).

[40] US & Autralian Governments, 'Agreement Between The Government Of The United States Of America And The Government Of Australia On Mutual Antitrust Enforcement Assistance'.

of the fear of entering into an agreement with a jurisdiction that has far-reaching extraterritorial jurisdiction over foreign states.[41] As indicated in chapter nine, the question of extraterritoriality has been understood as an intrusion to the national interests of the foreign state.

5.2.3. Limitations on the Use of Information

Another problem that arises when cartels have different legal standings in different jurisdictions is the treatment of information gathered from a dawn raid considering that the purposes and goals of criminal vis-à-vis administrative investigations differ markedly. For instance, under EU administrative proceedings and pursuant to Article 12(2) of Regulation 1/2003: '[I]nformation exchanged shall only be used in evidence for the purpose of applying Article 81 or Article 82 of the Treaty and in respect of the subject-matter for which it was collected by the transmitting authority'.[42] Thus, when gathering data secured from inspections in competition cases, the inspectors would only be allowed to take copies of the documents relevant to the purpose of their investigation. They cannot take other documents that may be incriminating in other jurisdictions but which fall outside the scope of the administrative investigation under EU competition rules.[43]

For instance, in 2004, pursuant to Article 28 of Regulation 1/2003, the EU responded negatively to a request for information submitted by the Turkish Competition Authority in relation to the evidence collected in a cartel investigation on the electrical equipment market.[44] The party information provided in the foregoing formal investigation was considered protected and could not be shared with third parties unless waivers were secured.

5.2.4. Different Levels of Protection of Due Process Rights

Even in the most integrated and sophisticated regional cooperation network of national competition authorities, the European Competition Network (ECN), procedural rules across national member states differ. Stucke observes that the 'notion of level of due process rights is inherently ambiguous'.[45] A domestic competition authority which secures evidence from outside its jurisdiction would need to know if such evidence was gathered in accordance with the due process rules

[41] Martyniszyn (2012: 41).
[42] Council Regulation (EC) No 1/2003 of 16 December 2002 on the implementation of the rules on competition laid down in Articles 81 and 82 of the Treaty 2003 p 11.
[43] The limitation seeks to ensure that the functioning of the European Competition Network will not empty of their substance the procedural guarantees concerning the limitation on use of the evidence. See Hawk (2005: 527).
[44] Dabbah (2010) and Martyniszyn (2012: 35).
[45] Stucke (2012: 378).

that are applicable in each member state.[46] The diversity of procedural rules in the different phases of investigation would heavily impact the outcome of the cooperation because competition authorities need to provide safeguards that should be equivalent between each other, and that is not necessarily the case between mature and young competition authorities. The business community has been very vocal in stressing that competition authorities must protect and respect due process rights, especially in light of recent technological developments which make the capture of great quantities of data possible.[47]

5.2.5. Diverging Goals of Competition Policy and Law

While there is a worldwide consensus on the conceptualisation of hard-core cartels, the political, economic, and social situation of the jurisdiction wherein the cartel activity takes place can also influence and shape the domestic contextualisation of such a definition.

This domestic contextualisation happens in two different ways. First, through the adoption of 'competition plus objectives', or objectives that may go beyond the promotion of competition, consumer welfare, and dynamic efficient, competitive process. This includes the protection of small and medium-sized enterprises that may be relevant to traditional community economies, national economic development considerations or industrial policy goals.[48] Second, even when there is no explicit reference in the competition law to other objectives, competition policy can be 'polluted' with social, ethical and moral concerns that can be attributed to the association with national champion considerations that countries decide to protect their infant industries, regulation and rent-seeking activities.[49]

5.3. Diverse Set of Rules Concerning the Powers of Investigation

An essential part of any competition authority's enforcement capacity is its ability to conduct effective investigations. Many competition authorities across the world

[46] Interview with Mehta.

[47] Business and Industry Advisory Committee to the OECD (BIAC) (2013: 2).

[48] 'Competition laws and regulations in some jurisdictions such as China, Hungary, Poland and South Africa specifically mention that public interest is an important element to be considered, especially in assessing the competitive impact of mergers. For example, when a merger is considered, section 12 A (1) of the South Africa Competition Act, 1999, requires the Competition Commission or Competition Tribunal to initially determine both the competitive and public interest impacts of the merger. In this regard, though there may be cases where a merger is likely to substantially prevent or lessen competition, it may be approved on substantial public interest grounds. In other instances, despite substantial potential impacts on competition, a merger may not be approved on public interest grounds'. UNCTAD, 'Model Law on Competition (2015) – Revised Chapter I'.

[49] Ezrachi, 'Sponge' 50.

invest in getting technical assistance from mature competition authorities in order to learn the best international practices in investigation. Despite efforts made by the international community to recommend best practices for the conduct of investigations,[50] rules on powers of investigation in the majority of young competition authorities across jurisdictions, from the inspection of business premises up to seizing and gathering evidence, remain diverse.[51] Notably, when the EU and Switzerland decided to move forward from their original traditional competition cooperation agreement to a second generation of competition agreements, one of the matters addressed was the harmonisation of their rules concerning powers of investigation.

5.4. Diverse Adjudication Techniques

Assuming that a young competition agency successfully reaches the post-investigatory phase after the foreign evidence has been gathered, assessed, and ultimately admitted under their own domestic legal system (being part of the file – cartel proceedings), the next challenge that it faces is the adjudication of the case against the cartelists and the imposition of sanctions and remedies.

Adjudication techniques are affected by factors that shape the choice of a model for competition laws, such as economic, legal and political views.[52] The phrase 'politics of law and economics' is applicable here and signals that that adjudicating competition cases involve not only economics but an intricate puzzle of domestic laws and politics.[53]

For instance, Canadian competition policy has gone through a 'pure political accountability' model, whereby the authority was part of a Ministry, to an 'independent agency' model and later to a 'judicialised tribunal' model.[54] The UNCTAD Model Law on Competition has classified the choices for the structuring of competition authorities into three institutional models: the bifurcated judicial

[50] See ICN, 'Investigative Tools Report'.

[51] For instance, in the Balkan region where the majority of competition authorities are young or small, including two EU competition authorities (Croatia and Bulgaria), the efforts to converge investigation rules on inspections have been relatively successful. '… All Balkan competition authorities are authorized to carry out inspections at the premises of any legal entities and natural persons performing economic activities. Under almost all Balkan competition regimes the formal authorization has to specify the legal basis and the purpose of the inspection as well as the addressees and objects of the inspection. Only under half of the Balkan competition regimes the timeframe to carry out an inspection on spot is determined in the authorization decision and the persons empowered to conduct the inspection are specifically designated. The main differences are related to the power to inspect non-business premises as well as to the art of the inspection authorization.' Sofia Competition Forum (2015: 9).

[52] Tyhurst, 'The Adjudication of Competition Law Issues in Theory and Practice' 9.

[53] See more in Fox (1986).

[54] See ch II of the Master Research: Tyhurst, 'The Adjudication of Competition Law Issues in Theory and Practice'.

model, the bifurcated agency model and the integrated agency model.[55] UNCTAD observations suggest that most of the competition authorities are granted as much administrative independence as possible, so as to avoid political interference in particular in developing countries and countries in transition.[56]

Having different institutional structures for adjudication also influences the exchange of information between competition authorities because of the different criteria that adjudicators have in handling the information. For example, within Latin America, the Costa Rican Competition Commission is composed of commissioners who are not civil servants and whose activities are not precisely regulated by government administrative rules.[57] On the other hand, the members of the Chilean Competition Tribunal, being part of the judicial branch, are bound by the administrative rules of the Supreme Court of Chile.[58] The different rules governing the conduct of the adjudicators in Chile and Costa Rica yield different responsibilities in handling the agency information, and would be a barrier against the free exchange of information between these two adjudicatory bodies. Presumably, the stricter administrative rules of the Supreme Court of Chile would cause its staff to be more careful in sharing information with their counterparts in Costa Rica.

5.5. Issues Related to Export and Import Cross-Border Cartel Investigations

This section deals with export and import CBC investigations from the perspective of young and small competition authorities. Even though the assessment provided here differentiates the treatment of export and import CBCs, the issue of the political willingness of competition authorities to cooperate is a common denominator between the two. Nevertheless, a separate assessment of each is provided below because of the nature of these practices and the cause of political unwillingness to cooperate. In fact, export cartels have been exempted from the scope of competition laws and therefore there was no need to cooperate with others when the

[55] '… (i) The bifurcated judicial model – the Authority is empowered to be investigative, and must bring enforcement actions before courts of general jurisdiction, with rights of appeal to general appellate courts. (ii) The bifurcated agency model – the Authority is empowered to be investigative, and must bring enforcement actions before specialized competition adjudicative authorities, with rights of appeal to further specialized appellate bodies or to general appellate courts. (iii) The integrated agency model – the Authority is empowered with both investigative and adjudicative functions, with rights of appeal to general or specialized appellate bodies ….' UNCTAD, 'Model Law on Competition (2010) – Chapter IX' 2.

[56] See ibid: 4, para. 8.

[57] See Art22 Costa Rica, Ley 7472 1995.pdf.

[58] See Chile New Competition Act 1973.

conduct is lawful, and effects of that cartel are overseas. In turn, the decision to prosecute import cartels is heavily reliant on political considerations.

5.5.1. Export CBC Investigations

The main issue that young or small competition authorities need to deal with when it comes to export CBCs is that in many jurisdictions, some forms of cartelisation are lawful. As a result, the importing country would first need to establish whether the export CBC is in violation of its own competition law and if so, they would need to establish where the evidence is and how to obtain it.[59]

In fact, export cartels not only are legal but in many instances are promoted by their own governments. For example, the US lists the export cartels that are exempted from its anti-trust laws in accordance with the Webb-Pomerene Act of 1918,[60] and Japan with the Transaction Law 299 of 1952[61] has done something similar. However, while some competition laws have either implicitly or explicitly exempted export cartels from the scope of their application,[62] export cartel exemptions are being discussed internationally in order to change the status of legal cartels because they are detrimental to trade and development.[63]

5.5.1.1. *Lack of Incentives and Willingness to Investigate Export Cross-Border Cartels*

As explained in chapter two, export CBCs are pure export cartels wherein export producers within a specific jurisdiction collude to target a precise foreign market. In this type of CBC, the exporting country is the birthplace of the collusion and will most probably be the location of evidence against the cartel. The competition authority in the targeted jurisdiction therefore needs information on the location of the evidence. It would also benefit from knowing if the competition authority in the originating jurisdiction is willing to cooperate and provide further information.

As export CBCs are generally exempted from the application of competition rules in the originating jurisdiction due to the lack of effects in their own territories as well as due to industrial policy considerations,[64] the competition authority in

[59] Interview with Mehta.

[60] US Department of Justice and Federal Trade Commission, 'Antitrust Guidelines for International Enforcement and Cooperation' 12.

[61] Matsushita (1979: 104), n 8.

[62] Jenny (2012: 107) argues that almost all countries have an implicit exemption from domestic law for export cartels.

[63] See Levenstein and Suslow (2004: 785).

[64] Consider the Finnish pulp industry where national export cartels have been crucial for the Finnish industry because most of the individual Finnish companies were so small that they could not have competed independently with much larger foreign competitors. See Jensen-Eriksen (2007).

the originating jurisdiction would normally have no incentive to provide evidence to prosecute and punish export cartels in the targeted jurisdiction.

The issue is compounded if the targeted jurisdiction has a young or small competition agency. Access to evidence on the alleged export CBC is more difficult for young and small competition authorities compared to mature competition agencies. For young competition agencies, access to most basic agency information at the pre-investigatory phase would require the support of the other competition authority, and without compelling arguments to convince their peer, it is unlikely that this will happen. Also, a young competition agency in the originating jurisdiction will not have an incentive to share information about export cartels unless the targeted jurisdiction has leverage against the originating jurisdiction. For instance, in the vitamin C export cartel, the competition authority in the targeted jurisdiction, the US, started its pre-investigation phase without the prior support of the Chinese competition authorities. Perhaps due to the pressure exerted by the US, Chinese authorities later sent an *amicus curiae* to the US courts to plead in favour of the export cartels, arguing that they were formed in accordance with Chinese laws.[65]

5.5.1.2. Lack of a Compulsory Agreement to Gather Information

Another issue that relates to the legal standing of cartel offences is the lack of compulsory agreements to gather information on behalf of other competition authorities. This issue exists despite the Hague Convention on Taking Evidence Abroad in Civil or Commercial Matters (Hague Evidence Convention).[66] The Hague Evidence Convention failed to result in compulsory agreements to gather information on behalf of a requesting competition authority due to the reasons detailed below.

1. **The mandatory or non-mandatory character of the Convention**: when the Hague Convention was being negotiated, it was unclear if it was mandatory or not. No provision in the Convention expressly addressed this issue. However, the founders of the Convention, particularly those states with common law jurisdictions,[67] were of the belief that the convention was not mandatory. This issue was settled in *Aerospatiale*, wherein the US Supreme Court held that the Hague Convention does not have a mandatory character.[68,69] After the US judgment,

[65] *US Vitamin C Export Cartel.*

[66] Hague Conference on Private International Law, 'Hague Convention on Taking of Evidence Abroad in Civil or Commercial Matters'.

[67] In turn, states with civil law traditions were convinced that the Convention had a mandatory character.

[68] *US Societe Nationale Industrielle Aerospatiale And Societe De Construction D'avions De Tourisme, Petitioners v United States District Court For The Southern District Of Iowa, Etc* (United States District Court For The Southern District Of Iowa).

[69] Martyniszyn, 'Discovery and Evidence in Transnational Antitrust Cases' 13.

comity considerations and common sense would suggest that the Convention deserves initial use. Unfortunately in private anti-trust actions in the US, courts favour the use of domestic discovery rules rather than the Convention.[70]

2. **The failure to define 'civil and commercial matters' in the Convention**: the legal definition and scope of the term 'civil and commercial matters' has also caused problems in the implementation of the Hague Convention. While common law jurisdictions are of the view that the Convention covers all proceedings except those which are criminal in nature, civil law jurisdictions claim that the Convention cannot apply to tax and administrative matters.[71] As a result, mature competition authorities such as the US and the EU have never relied on the Hague Convention when enforcing their laws. The limited use of the Hague Convention in countries where cartel laws are criminalised has made it inadequate for international assistance in the field of anti-trust enforcement.[72]

3. **Unfamiliarity amongst legal practitioners and courts**: Probably because of the two reasons above, in the US, few legal practitioners and courts know about the Convention. Those who are unfamiliar with it feel that it is not an effective tool of obtaining foreign-based evidence.[73] Despite this fact, in the EU, efforts to promote private enforcement have led to the 'rediscovery' of the Convention, which could ultimately make a great contribution to transnational competition law litigation, unless the trend of criminalisation of competition rules undermines the usefulness of the Convention.[74]

5.5.2. Import CBC Investigations

The problems facing import CBC investigation are similar to those for export CBC investigations. There is the lack of willingness to investigate import CBCs and the legal limitations derived from the lack of compulsory agreements to admit foreign evidence when provided by affected exporters. These issues will be explored in turn below.

5.5.2.1. Lack of Incentives and Willingness to Investigate Import Cross-Border Cartels

Young or small competition authorities might find it difficult to secure critical information to start the investigation of import CBCs, much as was the case in export CBC investigations, due to the nature of import CBCs and the way that

[70] ibid: 15.
[71] ibid: 16.
[72] Zanettin (2002: 148).
[73] Martyniszyn, 'Discovery and Evidence in Transnational Antitrust Cases' 17.
[74] ibid: 18.

they are understood in other jurisdictions. In the citric acid cartel (1991-1995),[75] US and EU companies fixed prices and output levels so as to form a homogenous oligopoly with evident foreclosure effects to the imports coming from China, as the fierce Chinese import competition was hampering the local industries in the US and EU.[76] Indeed, by 1995, when the cartel was still operational, US producers lobbied to impose anti-dumping duties on Chinese imports.[77] As a result, 'Chinese imports of citric acid fell substantially allowing the cartel another year's lease of life'.[78] A similar outcome had happened in the 1980s, in the EC chemical cases.[79]

While technically it would be a transnational CBC in the sense provided in chapter two (as there are companies from different jurisdictions colluding to stop imports from foreign suppliers in China), the example is still relevant in this discussion because the US, Canada, and EU authorities did investigate the cartel and even sanctioned it. They did not consider the cartel to be an import CBC but a multinational CBC that allocated sales in the global acid market.[80] Indeed, the economic rationale for this cartel was to raise prices of citric acid by up to 24 per cent, as it did in the US market,[81] and to impede Chinese citric acid from entering the US markets.

When an import CBC occurs, it is difficult for the competition authority in the import country to find the necessary incentives to prosecute it. Import cartels often are a response to aggressive foreign measures, such as the consortium import cartel formed by US and EU authorities in response to Libyan oil. In both jurisdictions, no domestic action was made by these authorities to investigate the import cartels, as it would have been against their own national interests. This is in contrast to the citric acid case where no national interests were at stake. Once again, politics plays an important role in the operation of competition authorities. For example, chapter two also addressed an import cartel in the US, where domestic competition authorities turned a blind eye toward the so-called New Deal sugar cartel, although they were aware that limiting import quotas in the US market substantially lessened the production in each factory.

[75] Citric acid, being a class of additives, is used for sterilisation, bacteriological stabilisation and flavour enhancement, among other purposes. Citric acid is a component of almost two-thirds of all synthetic or biotech acidulents, which are added to food and beverages and detergents. Citric acid production started in the 19th century in Europe, and was a monopoly in Italy in the early 20th century, and later evolved to become a business of many small-scale Asian factories in the 1970s. In the 1980s, citric acid was produced in the US by a duopoly composed by Pfizer, Inc and Miles Laboratories (the latter was eventually acquired by Bayer AG of Basel Switzerland). After a series of acquisitions in the late 1980s, by December 1990, the US citric acid industry had three domestic producers: ADM, Cargill, and Bayer, which were dominant producers in Europe as well. Around the same time, the low-tech and affordable methods of Chinese citric acid suppliers caused the Chinese companies' world market share in citric acid production to rise from 17% by 1989 to 28% in 1996. 'The Global Citric Acid Conspiracy: Legal-Economic Lessons' 2–4.

[76] ibid: 7.

[77] Yu (2003: 12).

[78] ibid: 8.

[79] See Messerlin (1990).

[80] Yu (2003: 12).

[81] ibid.

The import country's lack of incentives and willingness to cooperate can only be overturned when two mature competition agencies have conflicting interests, as in the case of the soda ash import cartel which was based in Japan and which affected the US market. US authorities requested the Japanese competition authority to prosecute and sanction the import cartel as a violation of Japanese competition laws.[82] The US, being a mature foreign authority with considerable economic and political leverage, negotiated with Japan, another mature competition agency, and managed to offset the disincentives to investigate these cartels within Japan. Unfortunately, young competition agencies would have little leverage to do so unless specific incentives are in order. This will be discussed subsequently.

The lesson to be drawn from the citric acid cartel is that both mature jurisdictions (the US and the EU) decided to prosecute and sanction this import cartel because of its adverse economic impact on both US and EU markets, unlike the CBC import consortium which did not produce any economic consequences for both countries, and where political considerations had more influence in the final decision not to prosecute the CBC.

5.5.2.2. Limitations on the Admissibility of Foreign Evidence

Limitations on the admissibility of foreign evidence resulting from the information exchanged by competition authorities remains a critical issue in import CBC investigations because of the many necessary legal considerations. This issue is exacerbated by the fact that general cooperation agreements do not cover these types of specific evidence-gathering cooperation because of the lack of international legal binding instruments. This leads to young competition agencies being unable to use foreign evidence as it would be negatively considered by courts due to failure to sustain a similar analogy in the jurisdiction at stake.[83]

In the liquid oxygen cartel case investigations in Latin America presented in chapter three, the Chilean Competition Authority (the Tribunal) and the Chilean Supreme Court disagreed as to the value of information submitted by a foreign competition authority (Argentina) in relation to the same case brought before courts earlier in that jurisdiction. While the Tribunal did recognise the value of the foreign evidence, the Chilean Supreme Court overturned the ruling as the evidence was gathered abroad and its use was forbidden to sustain a similar behaviour in Chile.[84] Had a compulsory agreement between the Chilean and Argentinean Competition Authorities been in place, the recognition of the foreign evidence would have been upheld in the courts.

[82] Matsushita (1991: 189).
[83] Interview with Mehta, Kirtikumar (n 172).
[84] Horna, 'Regional Coordination in Cartel Investigations: The Liquid Oxygen Case' 298.

5.6. Summary

The discussions in this chapter assume that young competition authorities have a certain level of trust between each other, as was apparent from the interviews carried out with the heads of younger authorities at the latest ICN Annual Conference in May 2017. It seems that, rather than issues of trust, young competition authorities instead need to deal with more institutional, legal and procedural issues. These include the lack of a regional supranational authority, different legal standing as per the treatment of cartels, diversity in rules concerning powers of investigation and even, in some cases, diverse criteria in adjudication techniques.

The handling of these issues in young competition settings can be laid out in several stages: first, to look at the existence or not of a supranational authority that can effectively deal with regional issues. Second, and in the absence of that supranational entity, they would turn their attention to ways in which cartel cooperation can take place in direct institution-to-institution cooperation. In this regard, the first matter to deal with would be the diversity in terms of the legal standing of cartel offences, whether they are treated criminally, administratively or in a mixed system. Last but not least, other procedural issues would play a role in pivoting the cooperation to a more successful experience.

As will be clear from the exploration laid out in chapter five, regional competition law enforcement in younger competition authorities is still a considerable problem, even in the case of political and institutional willingness to cooperate, and legal hurdles play an important role in limiting the effect of any good-will attitudes among younger jurisdictions.

Further, the issues arising in export and import CBCs are directly related to how the political and economic considerations are negotiated in the relations between mature or large and young or small competition authorities. In other words, if a young but large competition authority such as Brazil or India wishes to investigate export CBCs impacting their own markets, the exporting jurisdictions' willingness to cooperate would depend on how much weight they place on the requesting competition authority. Based on reciprocity and beyond established legal boundaries can actually be a possible solution on how to deal with these types of CBCs. Even though this matter of reciprocity goes beyond the scope of the research, one could say that in this particular area, reciprocity, which is crucial in the international public law context, can actually be the basis for mutually accepted solutions for both jurisdictions involved in an export/import CBCs. In any event, as will be discussed in chapter nine, current solutions to export and import CBCs are relatively effective because of the nature of these practices that on many occasions will go well beyond the political willingness of the competition authority but rather diplomats at the ministry of foreign affairs or trade (anti-dumping) authorities.

Again, the question remains whether small or young competition authorities have a better chance to deal with these CBCs if the exogenous factors (as explained in chapter one) are positive and enable them to politically manoeuvre their counterparts in order to carry out informal consultations on the basis of reciprocity.

Table 5.1 below summarises the issues involved in regional, export and import CBC investigations for young and small competition authorities, assuming, as was indicated at the introduction of Part II, that international cooperation is needed. Therefore, it does not contemplate a situation where a young or small competition authority would wish to investigate on its own without the support of a foreign authority.

Table 5.1 Most common issues in regional, export and import cross-border cartel investigations amongst young competition authorities

Regional CBC investigations	**Export CBC investigations**	**Import CBC investigations**
Lack of a regional competition authority.	Lack of incentives and willingness to investigate export cartelists.	Lack of political interest to investigate import cartelists.
Different legal standing as per cartel offences.	Lack of compulsory agreements to gather information on behalf of the requesting young competition authority of the other party.	Limitations on the admissibility of foreign evidence resulting from the information exchanged with affected exporters.
Diverse set of rules concerning powers of investigation and level of fines.	N/A	N/A
Diverse criteria in adjudication techniques.	N/A	N/A

Source: own work.

6

Past Solutions to Combatting Cross-Border Cartels

If this research had been written 15 years ago (in 2003), it would have proposed the adoption of a Multilateral Agreement on Competition Policy within the framework of the World Trade Organization (WTO).[1] This binding document from the members of the WTO would have meant that CBCs were to be covered by the rule-based multilateral trade system, and one single institution would deal with multinational cartels affecting world trade.[2]

Notably, some have said that it was 'false hope' to conceive the idea of having competition policy under the auspices of the WTO.[3] This is because even if the WTO had the authority to tackle competition issues worldwide, the WTO dispute settlement regime would not have had a well-developed capacity to undertake economic analysis, despite ample opportunities for members of the panels and appellate body to exploit economic evidence in their own rulings.[4] The reasons behind the non-adoption of the WTO solution are beyond the scope of the present research because the main arguments discussed in the WTO Cancun Ministerial Conference in 2003 are no longer valid. The world has changed, and international cooperation has been identified as the main solution to fight CBCs across jurisdictions, as discussed in chapter three.

With the failure of the WTO as the single solution to the problem of CBCs, international cooperation mechanisms are the vehicle through which the additional legal instruments and solutions proposed or being used by major competition jurisdictions can counteract the harmful effects of CBCs in domestic and international markets. However, in the absence of international cooperation and coordination between competition authorities, there is uncertainty due to the lack of any global agreement as to the purpose of anti-cartel laws. This chapter therefore critically assesses the solutions which have been proposed in the past to address the issues involved in conducting CBC investigations described in chapters four and five. The assessment aims to identify the challenges in the

[1] See more in Taylor (2006).

[2] *Cf* the assessment provided by Lee when referring to the fact of incorporating binding strategies to regulate multinational cartels: Lee (2016).

[3] See more in Bradford (2007).

[4] Mavroidis and Neven (2016: 202).

implementation, the inherent limitations of, and the reasons why such proposed solutions have not been effective in helping younger competition agencies address the foregoing issues.

According to Stephan, anti-trust coordination problems have three possible solutions:

> First, states might adhere to a common standard of competition law. Second, states might accept a body of rules for allocating regulatory jurisdiction that ensures that one, and only one, state imposes its competition standards on any given transaction. Third, states might decline to cooperate.[5]

As a result, the competition of competition laws and forum-shopping might be an initial problem that young competition authorities could face. The so-called 'choice of law' and 'jurisdiction'[6] can trigger difficulties for young competition regimes which might be unfamiliar with these solutions. Other jurisdictions, such as mature ones, would find unilateral enforcement of competition rules to activities outside the territory of the affected jurisdiction (the extraterritorial application of competition rules) to be the only solution to address CBCs. Chapter nine discusses all these options and the variants proposed elsewhere.

6.1. Most Common Solutions to Improve Multijurisdictional Cooperation in Cross-Border Cartel Investigations

This section will discuss the common solutions which aim to improve cooperation in multinational and transnational CBC investigations, including the extraterritorial application of competition laws, leniency alignments proposals, joint investigation teams and information gateways, among others.

6.1.1. Extraterritorial Application of Competition Laws

The extraterritorial application of competition laws has been known to mitigate the effects of export CBCs by allowing the importing country limited jurisdiction to prosecute cartelists abroad.[7] However, it can also negatively impact cartel investigations by serving as a disincentive against cooperation, by enabling a

[5] Stephan (2004: 66).

[6] The conflict of laws or international private law considerations pinpoints three foreign elements when dealing with multinational aspects of a cartel investigation: jurisdiction, choice of law, and recognition and enforcement of foreign judgments. Clarkson, Jaffey and Hill (2006: 1–2).

[7] The principle is not applicable for import CBCs, as the cartel activity harms exporters' interest in an exporting country not having a direct impact in domestic markets.

competition authority to act unilaterally (even outside its jurisdiction), without the help of other competition authorities.

The principle of extraterritoriality involves two types of jurisdiction: legislative and enforcement. Legislative jurisdiction pertains to the establishment and application of laws while enforcement jurisdiction refers to implementation as condition of extraterritorial application of competition laws.[8] Since the landmark case *Aluminium Co of America (Alcoa)* of 1945, US anti-trust laws have reached foreign companies and individuals fixing prices abroad but with effects in US commerce and markets.[9]

The 'effects doctrine' emerged as a guiding principle to punish foreign cartelists even in cases where in the territory in which the price fixing took place cartels were lawful.[10] The effects doctrine basically means that 'competition laws can be applied extraterritorially only in cases where actions taken outside a country have a direct and substantial impact on competition in the domestic markets'.[11] It may be said that there is now international recognition of the effects doctrine as it has been adopted by two important international legal bodies: the International Law Association and *L'Institut de Droit International*.[12]

In any event, the effects doctrine is a matter of judicial forensics whereby the 'jurisdictional rule of reason' is applied in order to avoid having to select a jurisdiction to become the global forum of choice for cartel victims. In this connection, the *Empagran* case showed that the US courts cannot become the global jurisdiction for all cartel cases with global effect, as it held that the effects doctrine is not the only test to establish jurisdiction, but 'to develop a more subtle analysis that admits foreign plaintiffs where US interests are directly advanced, but turns away those claims where we should leave to regulation to others'.[13] By contrast, the European Court of Justice has refrained from a direct and clear adoption of the effects doctrine.

On this topic, two important cases in Europe and the US merit being mentioned.[14] The European wood pulp cartel case of 1988[15] (which established

[8] Ezrachi (2016: 627).

[9] 'In 1982, the U.S. Congress established a law on extraterritorial application (legislative jurisdiction) called the Foreign Trade Antitrust Improvements Act (FTAIA). However, the Department of Justice 1988 Antitrust Guidelines for International Operations focused only on anti-competitive actions that could be presumed to harm the competition in the U.S. market. The Guidelines did not address the subject of anti-competitive conduct that restricted U.S. exports to enforcement actions. In April 1992, however, the Department of Justice announced that it would begin enforcement of the U.S. antitrust laws extraterritorially with respect to foreign conduct restricting U.S. exports, regardless of whether the conduct harmed competition in the U.S. market. The new policy applies to anti-competitive conduct that could reasonably be expected to directly and substantially impact U.S. exports.' Japanese Ministry of Economy, Trade and Industry (2008: 480).

[10] Fox and Fox (2012: 177–78).

[11] Japanese Ministry of Economy, Trade and Industry (2008: 479).

[12] ibid: 478.

[13] Sprigman (2005: 279).

[14] For a comprehensive study of this principle, see Griffin (1999).

[15] *Ahlstrom v Commission* 5233 (ECR).

the 'implementation principle') and the American *Hartford Fire Ins Co v California* of 1993[16] (which established a more expansive approach of the effects doctrine).

The wood pulp case held that jurisdiction under EU competition law[17] 'exists over firms outside the Union if they implement a price-fixing agreement reached outside the EU by selling to purchasers within it'.[18] This implementation principle was later complemented by the EU Decision regarding the *Gencor* judgment by incorporating the 'immediate, foreseeable and substantial effects in the Union' requirement to the principle, so as to fully incorporate the so-called 'effects doctrine'.[19]

The *Hartford Fire* case, on the other hand, provided a rather aggressive stance on the extraterritorial application of US anti-trust laws by stating that a US court 'should not consider the interests of a foreign sovereign unless there is a true conflict between US Law and the Law of the foreign state'.[20] This judgment, which was considered a disturbance of the established trend of comity, made the extraterritoriality rule highly controversial as it swept away the notion of comity, which 'holds that a nation with lesser interests at stake should normally defer to a nation with greater interests at stake of conflict'.[21] As a result, many countries issued diplomatic protests and some even enacted blocking legislation, since they considered it an excessive application of US anti-trust laws.[22]

Thanks to the *Empagran* case, the negative trend has been gradually softened by the doctrine of comity.[23] US lower courts can adopt an approach based on both *Hartford* and *Empagran*, and introduce comity analysis into global cartel cases by developing their own comity-based limitations on jurisdiction. However, this could eventually lead to the expenditure of significant resources in determining whether there is a policy conflict[24] regarding the difference in the legal standing of cartel offences.

These frictions between jurisdictional and substantive law and policy caused by the US's unilateral extraterritorial application of its anti-trust legislation, without regard to the interests of foreign countries, has resulted in international conflicts. These foreign countries can be both mature and young competition regimes. In that particular situation, one could say that in CBC investigations whereby interactions with young or small competition regimes occur, they would have little to say about the conflicts amongst mature competition agencies (US and other

[16] *Hartford Fire Ins Co v California 509 US 764 (1993)* (US Court of Appeals for the Ninth Circuit).
[17] For a complete assesment of the reach of EU competition law in the area of cartels, see ch 4 in Ryngaert (2008).
[18] Ezrachi (2016: 628).
[19] *EU Case Gencor v Commission* (Court of First Instance).
[20] *Hartford Fire Ins Co v California* 509 US 764 (1993) (n 612) P 2919.
[21] Burr (1994: 223).
[22] Kojima (2002: 4).
[23] Fox and Fox (2012: 178).
[24] Sprigman (2005: 280–81).

mature authorities) on how the effects doctrine should be transposed to a lesser and objective approach of comity.

In relation to the collection of foreign evidence, the extraterritorial application of domestic rules on access to evidence or 'extraterritorial discovery' might be a solution to the failure of the Hague Convention. Extraterritorial discovery consists of the 'use of state power to coerce (compel under the threat of sanctions) conduct within foreign territory for the sake of securing evidence'.[25] This instrument has been exercised principally by the US in the application of anti-trust laws in criminal and civil cases, and was met with a very unfavourable response from foreign jurisdictions that have repeatedly enacted statutes hindering or blocking collection of and access to evidence.[26] In the EU, international law provisions limit the exercise of the EU Commission's competence within the EU's jurisdiction, as it would impinge upon the national sovereignty of the non-member country in whose territory it was purporting to act. Therefore, in the event of non-cooperation of foreign parties, the EU has no power to effectively sanction the foreign-based evidence request.[27] As a result of both jurisdictions' acts, there is no specific binding or appropriate solution wherein extraterritorial discovery can be applicable across jurisdictions; therefore, access to foreign evidence is still an issue, in particular when two competition authorities are engaged in formal investigations (at the investigation phase itself).

6.1.2. Addressing Differences in Leniency Applications Through 'One-Stop Shop' Models

Due to the growing number of countries initiating leniency programmes and the divergences between leniency and markers across jurisdictions, the Business and Industry Advisory Committee (BIAC), in 2013, proposed to the OECD member countries that they set up a 'one-stop shop' marker policy that could provide a uniform application on how markers are carried out in different jurisdictions.[28] In order to improve cooperation in multiple jurisdictions when it comes to leniency applications and markers, the experience of the International Patent System, established by the Patent Convention Treaty (PCT)[29] and administered by the World Intellectual Property Organisation (WIPO), can serve as inspiration.[30] The PCT

[25] Martyniszyn, 'Discovery and Evidence in Transnational Antitrust Cases' 18.

[26] Countries such as Australia, Canada, France, New Zealand, the Netherlands, the UK, Philippines, South Africa, among others have introduced legislation in reaction to the US jurisdiciton, although they were always framed in abstract terms. See Castel (1984).

[27] Martyniszyn, 'Discovery and Evidence in Transnational Antitrust Cases' 18 and 28.

[28] Business and Industry Advisory Committee to the OECD (BIAC) 3–4.

[29] The PCT is an international treaty with more than 145 contracting states. The PCT makes it possible to seek patent protection for an invention simultaneously in a large number of countries by filing a single 'international' patent application instead of filing several separate national or regional patent applications. See Patent Cooperation Treaty 1970, 52.

[30] Capobianco and Nagy (2016: 12).

allows a single application made by any of the WIPO member countries to have cross-border effects in the other member countries, that is to say, an automatic recognition in foreign jurisdictions, provided local conditions of the patent-granting local authority are met.[31]

One-stop shop models for leniency applications could increase administrative efficacy by avoiding duplication of effort and fragmentation of administrative costs and they would also ensure that pertinent and timely information is provided to the relevant competition authorities.[32] Calls for a 'one-stop European leniency shop' gained ground after the modernisation of European competition law in 2003.[33] This eventually led to the launch of a Model Leniency Programme by the European Competition Network (ECN) which aimed to improve the handling of parallel leniency applications in the ECN.[34]

This solution may be problematic for young competition authorities, since the actual enforcement of this option would require, first, that domestic leniency programmes are effective and that, for a number of reasons in younger competition regimes, is not the case. There are heavy burdens related to sharing information between competition authorities in order to implement an effective one-stop shop and take full advantage of its benefits.[35] However this information would be crucial for the success of the investigation as competition authorities need to obtain the necessary information in order to decide whether or not to open a formal investigation, and this is jeopardised by the divergence of procedures and requirements to open investigations among competition authorities, even within EU competition law, where procedural laws still have some differences among the 27 member states.

Another problem is that a one-stop shop solution does not necessarily ensure coherent outcomes, as the comprehensive receiving authority does not harmonise the substantive rules under different time schedules after the initial stage of notification or filings.[36] Of course, from the perspective of businesses, harmonising the substantive rules of leniency programmes would be the ideal option, but it requires considerable efforts on the part of the competition authorities. In that regard, the efforts made by the ICN in sharing the leniency materials and programmes of each of its members may be a valuable point of departure.[37]

[31] 'PCT FAQs'.

[32] Capobianco and Nagy (2016: 12).

[33] See Gauer and Jaspers (2006).

[34] The Model Programme responds to the call for a one-stop leniency shop and offers a set of rules on which all ECN programmes can align. It is therefore a first step towards a harmonised leniency policy throughout the EU. It sets out the main procedural and substantive rules which the ECN members believe should be common in all programmes. European Commission Press Release 'Competition: The European Competition Network Launches a Model Leniency Programme – Frequently Asked Questions'.

[35] Capobianco and Nagy (2016: 14).

[36] ibid.

[37] See more ICN, 'Leniency Materials. Country/Organization + Link(s) to Leniency Program Materials'.

6.1.3. Overcoming Legal Barriers Through Joint Investigative Teams and Cross-Appointments

A less ambitious and more realistic solution for young or small competition authorities is to engage in joint investigative activities and organise exchanges of staff with their counterparts. For this to work, there must be trust and mutual understanding at all times between the authorities.

The idea behind joint investigation teams is to set up a task force of two or more competition authorities wherein their lead investigation officers collect and share information in order to address a common infringement. An example of this in action is the joint investigation teams (JITS) in criminal cases in the EU, which operate through a convention-based scheme to fight against organised crime amongst EU member states.[38] The joint investigative activities and cross-appointments reflected in the Cooperation Agreement between New Zealand Commerce Commission and the Australian Competition and Consumer Commission in relation to the provision of compulsorily acquired information and investigative assistance is also linked to this idea.[39]

In both examples, the underlying motivation between the regional groupings in the EU and between Australia and New Zealand is the existence of a treaty with binding obligations on the parties to share information related to competition cases. However, the vast majority of young competition authorities' territories do not have the benefit of such a legal instrument. Therefore, this proposed solution would not be realistic for these competition jurisdictions around the world unless a framework with common grounds was put in place, such as in the case of the international fight against corruption at the level of the UN.[40]

To undertake such cooperative activity, young competition authorities need to develop trust. This is a process in which authorities must develop over time, and in order to achieve a successful working relationship between investigators across jurisdictions, young authorities would need to pass through three different phases within trust development: calculus-based, knowledge-based, and identification-based trust. Chapters 10 and 11 discuss this important solution for young or small competition authorities that are willing to develop trust and mutual understanding over time.

6.1.4. Addressing the Issue of Confidential Information Through Information Gateways and Appropriate Safeguards

The OECD has recommended that its member states promote 'the adoption of legal provisions allowing for the exchange of confidential information between

[38] See more in Tomescu (2014).

[39] Australia & New Zealand Governments, 'Cooperation Arrangement between the New Zealand Commerce Commission and the Australian Competition and Consumer Commission.'

[40] UN Office on Drugs and Crime, 'United Nations Convention Against Corruption.'

competition authorities without the need to obtain prior consent from the source of the information'.[41] 'Information gateways' refer to domestic legal provisions or international agreements that explicitly empower the enforcement agency to exchange confidential information with competition authorities in other jurisdictions under certain conditions.[42]

In 2013, the OECD reported that only four jurisdictions (UK, Australia, Canada and Germany) had provisions in their domestic legislation enabling them to exchange confidential information with other competition authorities without the consent of the parties.[43] In Latin America, only two competition authorities (Brazil in 2012[44] and Peru[45] in 2015) have adopted domestic legislation on the exchange of confidential information. At the regional level, provisions to exchange confidential information in the European Competition Network (ECN) exist.[46] These provisions are designed to considerably facilitate the exchange of confidential information amongst mature competition authorities. Of course, there are some costs that need to be borne by the adherent in terms of establishing sufficient safeguards in order to protect the confidential information that is exchanged.

The lack of information gateways between OECD members may be due to the fear that this will affect businesses' confidence in the treatment of confidential information. This concern may be more pronounced when it comes to young competition regimes which have yet to prove to international companies that they can protect confidential information by robust legislation[47] or by technical capacity. As a result, information gateways may not be the best solution to foster trust by international leniency applicants (see Section 8.2.2 for a more detailed discussion of trust and leniency programmes).

If, however, competition authorities' legislatures enable that possibility, this research proposes, in chapters 10 and 11, a modified version of the existing information gateway options, which can be used, subject to specific conditions being triggered. In this regard, in some cases this can avoid the counterfactual consequences of having information gateways for younger jurisdictions at the beginning of the trust development process, because the benefits of exchanging information through information gateways might undermine the positive development of trust that companies might have toward the young competition regime.

[41] OECD, 'Recommendation of the OECD Council Concerning International Co-Operation on Competition Investigations and Proceedings' 7.

[42] OECD, 'Contribution by OECD to the Roundtable on: "Modalities and Procedures for International Cooperation in Competition Cases Involving More than One Country"' 6.

[43] See for instance Pt 9 of the UK Enterprise Act 2002. OECD & ICN (2013: 132).

[44] See Brazilian Decree No 7.738/12 and CADE's resolution No 1/12; da Silveira and Tollini (2014: 178–79).

[45] See Peru Amendment of some Competition Act provisions 2015.

[46] OECD, 'Contribution by OECD to the Roundtable on: 'Modalities and Procedures for International Cooperation in Competition Cases Involving More than One Country" 6.

[47] Martyniszyn (2015:I 26).

6.1.5. Achieving More Comparable Sanctions and Remedies Through Cooperation at the Court Level

A complementary solution to the cooperation of competition authorities is that of the cooperation of the judiciary on cross-border competition cases. Rogatory letters[48] are the most common instrument of communication between courts, and are part of a wider concept of international judicial assistance that goes back to the times of ancient Greece, where the states of Calymna and Cos had a dispute over the repayment of a public loan.[49] Over the centuries, rogatory letters have become a customary international public law institution recognized by multilateral treaties such as the Hague Convention on Taking Evidence[50] and the Hague Convention on Service of Process in Civil and Commercial Matters.[51]

This instrument, however, has never been applied to competition cases and it is unclear if it can be used for such a purpose.[52] The following four reasons have been highlighted to explain why rogatory letters have not been used in competition cases:

1. complexity of drafting the rogatory letters;
2. inability to use it for investigatory purposes and the limitation that it may only be used in criminal investigations (as mentioned earlier, not all jurisdictions accord cartels a criminal legal standing);
3. divergent views between jurisdictions on pre-trial discovery and discovery of evidence; and
4. certain evidence may only be secured via a court order.[53]

Fostering private enforcement of competition rules in developing countries can trigger more court cooperation and civil litigation when it comes to claiming damages from cartel victims.[54]

[48] 'Letter rogatory requests generally are made through diplomatic channels and are a very lengthy process.' Capobianco and Nagy (2016: 17).

[49] Sutherland (1982:785).

[50] Hague Conference on Private International Law, 'Hague Convention on Taking of Evidence Abroad in Civil or Commercial Matters'.

[51] Hague Conference on Private International Law, 'Hague Convention on the Service Abroad of Judicial and Extrajudicial Documents in Civil or Commercial Matters'.

[52] Capobianco and Nagy (2016: 17).

[53] Citing OECD Competition Law Enforcement: International Cooperation in the Collection of Information 1984, Martyniszyn, 'Discovery and Evidence in Transnational Antitrust Cases' 8.

[54] 'In Europe, progress in promoting private enforcement has been slower owing to substantial legal and procedural impediments, but in recent years it has been concerted. As in the United States, advancement of private enforcement has been led largely by public institutions – the European Commission ('EC') and national competition authorities in particular. The EC has been active since at least 2005 in examining ways in which to promote private actions – primarily as a way of facilitating compensation for victims while also recognising, as a secondary benefit, the potential of such actions to complement the deterrence-driven strategy of the public authorities, thereby bolstering overall the effectiveness of the European competition rules.' Beaton-Wells (2015: 687).

6.1.6. Summary of the Previously Proposed Solutions

Table 6.1 summarises the solutions which have been previously proposed to improve cooperation in multinational and transnational CBC investigations, and the potential problems that may be encountered by younger competition authorities when availing themselves of such solutions in their own jurisdictions.

Table 6.1 Most common partial solutions proposed for multinational and transnational CBC investigations

Problem	Solutions proposed	Potential problems for young/small competition authorities
Lack of trust between mature and young competition authorities.	No cooperation – unilateral action: extraterritoriality principle of competition laws.	This unilateral enforcement of competition to foreign conduct requires a significant understanding of public international laws and their interface with competition law enforcement not only by courts but also adjudicative administrative competition authorities. Young competition regimes lack this high level of competition culture.
Differences in leniency programmes and lack of trust of leniency applicants in young competition authorities' leniency programmes.	Strengthening leniency programmes at the domestic level and 'one-stop shop' model.	While this system would be beneficial for businesses operating worldwide, it may be difficult to achieve due to the lack of a binding multilateral framework on competition that would have immediate effect in all jurisdictions that are part of this framework.
Differences in cultural legal barriers.	Joint investigative teams and cross appointments.	Trust and mutual understanding is a big concern amongst young or small competition agencies attempting to cooperate in open investigations.
Lack of international definition of confidential information.	Information gateways.	Difficult to achieve in younger jurisdictions where there is no sufficient legal provision allowing for the exchange of confidential information.
Difficulties in achieving comparable sanctions and remedies for cartel infringements.	Cooperation at court level.	May be challenging in jurisdictions where the notion of competition law is limited and the idea of cooperation between courts would rely on lengthy rogatory letters that would delay any effective cooperation scheme.

Source: own elaboration but based on two secondary sources: (1) Capobianco Survey 'Developments in International Enforcement Co-operation in the Competition Field'; (ii) Table 2 of the UNCTAD Secretariat Report 2017 entitled 'Enhancing international cooperation in the investigation of competition cross-border cases: tools and procedures' to be submitted to the Intergovernmental Group of Experts on Competition Law and Policy. Sixteenth session Geneva, 5–7 July 2017.

6.2. Most Common Partial Solutions to Improve Cooperation in Regional, Export and Import CBC Investigations

Solutions to improve cooperation in regional, export and import CBC investigations can be diverse, depending on the perspective of the competition authority and whether the authority is deemed to be mature, large, young or small, as per the classification provided in chapter one. This section deals with the solutions that young or small competition authorities can adopt when cooperation is the option to move forward.

6.2.1. Solutions Proposed for Regional CBC Investigations

The ideal solution for a regional CBC investigation would be the establishment of a regional competition authority such as the EU Commission for the EU member states. In the absence of the foregoing, some regions have resorted to a binding agreement that deals with regional matters on competition. Considering the infancy of the competition landscape in the jurisdictions where young competition authorities operate, it is likely that regional agreements and competition law enforcements are not available and not in their immediate horizon. Thus, there is a need to explore other solutions which could address the absence of these ideal instruments.

6.2.1.1. Addressing the Absence of Effective Regional Competition Authorities: The International Private Law Solution

Conflicts of competition jurisdictions and their divergent laws take place when parallel, related competition law proceedings arise, particularly in cases where similar intra-regional collusion practices take place within an economic regional grouping. The probability of this situation increases as young competition regimes proliferate across jurisdictions and as economic and trade ties intensify across countries within regional economic groupings.

An optimal solution to this problem would be to incorporate rules extracted from international private law discipline. The international private law solution emerges as an alternative to the principle of extraterritoriality of competition rules, discussed below. This alternative addresses the issue of having contrarily applicable competition laws in different countries. As a result, the conflict of mandatory competition laws could be settled if policy-makers are willing to provide an international private law solution to a cross-border context, such as the regional context, in which case 'a set of competition rules would not be applicable unless the dispute is sufficiently connected with the forum'.[55]

[55] Danov (2016: 92).

The resolution of jurisdictional issues in a cross-border cartel case where diverse legal traditions and competition cultures across the world are involved, particularly when young competition authorities are dealing with regional CBCs,[56] may be a worthwhile option. Private international law instruments, involving the selection of a jurisdiction and court which will take over the case, allow the coordination of the enforcement and adjudication efforts of several competition agencies. This suggests the active participation of courts through civil litigation and private enforcement of competition rules by creating the 'possibility for a national court to consider the compatibility of business activities with the laws applicable in cases where the infringers' conduct affects the process of competition and consumer welfare'.[57] The private international law solution would also preserve the inherent characteristics of the diverse competition law cultures, in accordance with the European model of integration and diversity.[58]

Consequently, a new 'mode of governance' may arise based on the level of substantive harmonisation of cartel laws (taking into account some of the differences of legal standing, of course) and bearing in mind the different procedural rules that differ across jurisdictions. Therefore, and despite criticism of the use of private international law,[59] the concept of a selected jurisdiction can be deployed to coordinate enforcement proceedings in competition cases.[60]

Take the example of *Nokia v AU Optronics Corporation et al*, where a mobile telephone manufacturer (Nokia) brought a case in one jurisdiction (the UK) against 25 international telecommunications companies which were not legally domiciled in the UK[61] for having fixed the prices and limiting the supply of LCDs in the global market. As a result, several competition rules could be applied, since the practice affected a number of jurisdictions. That situation did indeed arise when similar investigation proceedings in the US, EU, Japan, South Korea, Taiwan and Canada were opened, leading to inconsistent findings among the parallel proceedings worldwide. This was the obvious result of the fact that the laws of the available forums were markedly different, leading to inconsistent procedural

[56] ibid: 87–88.

[57] ibid: 90.

[58] See more inWatt, 'Integration and Diversity'.

[59] According to Andrew Guzman, choice of law cannot solve the issue of over or under regulation of cartels. Guzman (2004: 116–17).

[60] Danov (2016: 89).

[61] The companies were: (1)AU Optronics Corporation, (2) AU Optronics (Czech) SRO, (3) AU Optronics Europe BV, (4) Tatung Company, (5) Chungwha Picture Tubes Ltd, (6) LG Display Co Ltd, (7) LG Display Germany GmbH, (8) Samsung Electronics Co Ltd, (9) Samsung SDI Co Ltd, (10) Samsung SDI Germany GmbH, (11) Samsung Semiconductor Europe GmbH, (12) Samsung Semiconductor Europe Ltd, (13) Sharp Corporation, (14) Sharp Electronics (Europe) GmbH, (15) Toshiba Corporation, (16) Toshiba Electronics Europe GmbH, (17) Seiko Epson Corporation, (18) Epson Imaging Devices Corporation, (19) Epson Europe Electronics GmbH, (20) Hitachi Ltd, (21) Hitachi Displays Lt,d (22) Hitachi Europe Ltd, (23) Royal Philips Electronics BV, (24) Philips Components BV, (25) Philips Components International BV. *UK Nokia Corporation v Au Optronics Corporation & Others* [2012] Engligh High Court of Justice Case No HC09C04421/1.

rules applied at the pre-investigatory, investigatory and post-investigatory phases of the proceedings.[62] A private international solution would have avoided that by incorporating extra-legal factors in relation to a selected forum and avoiding 'forum shopping', which was perhaps the reason why Nokia brought this case in the UK in the first place.

The example above reflects an interesting solution but perhaps one which is only applicable to mature competition regimes, where courts have a more sophisticated understanding of competition laws not only at the domestic level, and where efforts to harmonise law at the international level have been more successful. Hence, the private international law solution will likewise not work if having courts decide a global competition case would be a challenge to the administrative jurisdiction of young competition authorities. Even if judicial adjudication is involved (such as the case of Panama and Chile in Latin America), there are still doubts as to whether the private international law solution would bring more problems than results, especially in relation to the execution and recognition of these judicial rulings across affected jurisdictions of the cartel. For these reasons, the option of private international law would not be efficient in cases where domestic intra-regional parallel investigations are taking place among young competition regimes unless a greater level of understanding for each other's' competition laws and procedures can take place. Chapter 10 covers this problem in more detail.

In sum, when targeted jurisdictions are chosen by international leniency applicants, the best method might be to apply the laws of the affected jurisdictions, while 'compromising [on] the differences on the basis of the relative strength of each legal order's claim to regulate'.[63] However, this option might not be feasible for young or small competition regimes, as they would encounter difficulty in situations where adjudication relies on administrative commissions or judges without a significant knowledge of competition law analysis. This situation becomes even more complicated if the forum is to be chosen by regional cartelists (companies) in one of these young jurisdictions with limited capacity to deal with complex cases, leading to a constrained ability to counteract the effects of the regional CBC. It is clear that the rule must first be further developed before it is applied to competition proceedings.[64]

In conclusion, the option of private international law solution is not realistically feasible for younger competition regimes wishing to address the harmful effects of regional CBCs in their domestic markets unless a more advanced level of trust is developed among the young competition authorities.

[62] Danov (2016: 89).

[63] Von Mehren (1974: 366).

[64] It has been claimed that the private international solution can be instrumental in dealing with export CBCs. The importing country receiving the cartelised exports has a stronger claim to regulate these types of cartel. Again, however, coordination and cooperation from the exporting country is necessary and, as claimed in ch 8, willingness to cooperate in these cases is not straightforward because it needs to be induced.

6.2.1.2. Addressing Different Legal Standings of Cartel Offences: Appointment of One or More Lead Jurisdiction(s) in Cross-Border Cases

The 'lead jurisdiction' concept involves assigning one jurisdiction to investigate an international case under its own laws and procedures. The lead jurisdiction, with the assistance of the other affected jurisdictions, decides the case, taking into account all the views and interests of the different jurisdictions. As a result, the problem of the legal standing of cartel offences may be addressed by selecting the most appropriate safeguards when it comes to due process, handling of evidence and the standard of proof in competition cases.

This model draws inspiration from the patent dispute resolution system developed by the Hague Conference on Private International Law, taking into account the asymmetric countries' development and the relationship of private parties involved in multijurisdictional litigation.[65]

There are indeed advantages to this model as it can avoid multiple and parallel proceedings. To this end, a community of interests among jurisdictions would need to be achieved so as to consider all individual interests of jurisdictions in one single case. As such, 'the lead jurisdiction model incentivizes relevant jurisdictions to consider not only their own country interests, but the interests of all affected interests'.[66]

Problems, however, may arise when two or more jurisdictions consider themselves better placed to investigate a particular CBC and to decide on behalf of all affected jurisdictions. Hence, objective and least-discretionary criteria must be adopted to avoid these potential shortcomings of the system.[67] Intrusiveness may be at stake here, in particular when the lead jurisdiction model is a mandatory one. Another challenge is when the lead jurisdiction cannot reconcile the interests of all affected jurisdictions because of distinctive rules and procedures as well as different business culture values.

Two different sub-regions of the world allow a pertinent comparison in this regard: the Nordic and Central American areas. In the former (Nordic Cartel Network), competition rules are well harmonised and cultural business values are well aligned, and trust between the competition authorities has also been well developed over time.[68] The latter (Central American) has been attempting to harmonise practices through the Network of Competition Authorities (RECAC) and even proposed a regional institutional framework based on the commonality

[65] See more in Municoy (2004) 4 Chicago-Kent Journal of Intellectual Property 342.

[66] Capobianco and Nagy (2016: 15).

[67] ibid.

[68] 'The Nordic Competition Authorities established in 2000 a model for cooperation between respective units for cartel investigation, the Nordic Cartel Network (NCN). The purpose of the cooperation was solely practical: Discussing cases and case collaboration, investigating techniques and other cartel and investigation issues of mutual interest.' Nordic Cartel Network (2012: 2).

of cultural business values within the Central American countries. However, trust between the competition authorities may need to be more developed in order to achieve what the Nordic authorities have achieved in terms of agreeing who could be the lead jurisdiction in certain regional CBCs.

Furthermore, the lead jurisdiction model could pose serious sovereignty problems to the different jurisdictions. This was the case when Costa Rica decided not to recognise the jurisdiction of the Central American Court of Justice, when the other Central American countries agreed that this regional court had jurisdiction to deal with regional CBCs in Central America.[69]

6.2.1.3. Addressing the Diverse Criteria in Adjudication Techniques: Recognition of Decisions Made by Agencies or Courts in other Jurisdictions

A less complicated approach than the one provided by the private international law solution is the recognition of administrative decisions made by foreign competition authorities, notably mature ones, in multinational and transnational CBCs.[70] The idea behind this solution is to reduce duplication and the overall costs associated with parallel international investigations of the same CBC, as well as saving the additional transaction costs of defining markets, establishing the duration of the cartel, and detecting the companies involved, among others.[71]

Clearly, this solution may be applicable at the adjudication phase after the two previous phases of the investigation are carried out (the pre-investigatory phase and the investigatory phase) and local elements of the cartel law in a given jurisdiction have been incorporated into the adjudication process, such as the 'identification of local customers [and] calculating the local turnover in the jurisdiction for fining purposes'.[72]

Although this solution has never been utilised as such, one could say that the Mexican and Brazilian prosecutions of the lysine and vitamin multinational CBCs in 1998 and 2007 (discussed in chapter two), may be a de facto demonstration that competition authorities may rely their findings on other jurisdictions' administrative rulings to support their decisions to impose locally a cartel fine to international cartelists. Unfortunately, as has been discussed earlier, not all attempts to rely on foreign judging have been successful.[73] This particular solution has the following limitations for young and small competition regimes:

[69] Ediciones El País, 'Costa Rica ignora una orden de la Corte Centroamericana de Justicia' (*EL PAÍS*, 18 January 2012), http://internacional.elpais.com/internacional/2012/01/18/actualidad/1326926845_688633.html, accessed 4 April 2017.

[70] Capobianco and Nagy (2016: 11).

[71] ibid: 12.

[72] ibid.

[73] *Cf* the case of Colombia with the Auto Parts Cartel Investigation in 2012. See at *Colombia Autoparts cartel – Closing the investigation.*

1. To have enforceable and mandatory mutual recognition of judgments requires the entry into force of a treaty between nations. As such, the experience provided by the Australia-New Zealand cooperation, agreement which allows the mutual recognition and enforcement of each jurisdiction's judgments, is an exception to the general rule of the lack of international treaties that support this solution.[74]
2. Even in the absence of international treaties, young competition authorities may rely de facto on foreign jurisdictions' rulings, as in the case of Brazil or Mexico. The differences in legal systems may hamper the extent of recognition of foreign court decisions and evidence admissibility. Once again the discussion between legal standing of cartel offence may arise, in particular the dichotomy between civil and criminal sanctions in multijurisdictional cartel investigations.

6.2.2. Proposed Solution for Export CBC Investigations

In 2007, Sweeney proposed an arrangement to curb the effects of export cartels, while suggesting the alignment of incentives for both exporting and importing countries.[75] This discussion becomes more critical when many developing countries are suffering from export cartels coming from developed nations[76] such as in the case of the American soda ash cases in India[77] and South Africa, whereby completely different outcomes were reached by the local jurisdictions attempting to apply the extraterritorially principle.[78]

Export cartels are often as a result of political motivations where national governments support their exporters' efforts to hit specific foreign markets. In the current times of political uncertainty and the rise of populism,[79] one could expect that international export cartels are likely to emerge, and also that there would be the imposition of tariffs on imports from imperfectly competitive foreign firms.[80]

[74] See 'Agreement between the Government of Australia and the Government of New Zealand on Trans Tasman Court Proceedings and Regulatory Enforcement'.

[75] Sweeney (2007).

[76] The author claims that while importing countries should evaluate foreign export cartels under a 'rule of reason', most of them will be constrained by a lack of technical expertise and limited enforcement capacity. A novel approach, based on parallels with anti-dumping procedures, would strengthen developing countries' efforts in dealing with export cartels. See Bhattacharjea (2004).

[77] Indeed, India's was the first competition authority to investigate and prosecute an international cartel, which was the soda ash export cartel in 2006. Connor, 'The Rise of Anti-Cartel Enforcement in Africa, Asia, and Latin America' 6.

[78] Martyniszyn, 'Export Cartels: Is It Legal to Target Your Neighbour? Analysis in Light of Recent Case Law' 17–26.

[79] See Inglehart and Norris (2016).

[80] See Brander and Spencer (1984).

For the reasons above, export CBCs could be effectively addressed by *amicus curiae*[81] submissions by foreign competition authorities or governments in domestic competition cases. Due to the political dimensions of this type of CBC and the specific trade and competition considerations involved, the resulting problems could be addressed jointly by a ministry of foreign affairs action representing the interests of both the competition authority and the trade authority of the importing country. Speaking with one voice might help the frictions between the different implications of trade and competition authorities' actions.

According to Martyniszyn, the use of foreign *amicus curiae* submissions serves a number of useful functions in international competition cases. First, the appreciation of foreign laws, procedures and policies by the foreign jurisdiction itself can be instrumental in understanding the full nature of the international case being heard by a domestic jurisdiction. Second, it provides an opportunity to reach out to foreign jurisdictions and ease unnecessary frictions and misunderstandings from the international relation viewpoint. Third, from a collaborative perspective, it allows concerns to be voiced and considered on an ad-hoc basis.[82]

Evidence shows that foreign *amicus curiae* submissions are situated at the intersection of competition and international law.[83] This intersection is explained when a mature or large competition authority tries to accommodate the interests of these briefs, where participation of foreign ministries through diplomatic channels and competition authorities is taking place. For example, the US government has taken part in 11 foreign private actions representing public interests[84] in line with US interests, and with a clear deference between the courts and executive branch, speaking with one voice; this suggests that the intergovernmental communication is critical.

The latter might be controversial and difficult to achieve in a young competition regime's setting as the adjudication in many new jurisdictions remains part of the executive branch, through independent commissions ruling on competition cases at the administrative level and where courts and competition authorities may have different views on how the principle of deference should be triggered.

Moreover, while *amicus curiae* submissions remain a 'versatile instrument, potentially serving various legal and political functions [as] they have the capacity to facilitate adjudication, influence development of international law … and serv[ing] domestic political ends without hampering foreign legal processes',[85]

[81] 'An amicus brief is a submission of a person who is not a party to a lawsuit but who petitions the court or is requested by the court to file a brief in action because that person has a strong interest in the subject matter'. Martyniszyn (2016: 612).

[82] ibid: 640.

[83] See Martyniszyn (2016).

[84] These cases were: *Pzifer v Gov. of India* (1978), *Matsushita v Zenith* (1986), *Hartford Fire v California* (1994), *US v Nippon Paper* (1997), *F Hoffmann La Roche v Empagran* (2004), *Intel Corp v Advanced Micro Devices* (2004), *US v Gosselin World* (2005), *Stolt Nielsen v US* (2006), *Spectrum Stores v Citgo Petroleum* (2011), *In re Flat Glass II Antitrust Litigation* (2012), *Motorola v Au Optronics* (2015); ibid: 638.

[85] ibid: 642.

it seems that the instrument has been used only between mature competition regimes, and there is still a long way to go in terms of passing that experience on to the vast majority of competition regimes in the world. In the last few decades, cases such as *Matushita*, *Hartford Fire* and *Empagran* have received *amicus curiae* submissions, but it is unclear how these submissions were treated by the courts and whether they were relevant to the subject matter before the court.[86]

6.2.3. Recognition of Foreign Evidence Provided by Affected Exporters in Import CBC Investigations

The discovery[87] and recognition of foreign evidence provided by affected exporters in an import CBC investigation can be found in the American civil litigation legal instrument called pre-trial discovery.[88] As a result of this legal figure, an affected exporter before a foreign tribunal can seek discovery within the US, or affected exporters litigating before a US tribunal can seek discovery abroad.[89]

However, the American approach, being common law in nature, clashes with civil law jurisdictions, and consequently civil law judges and competition authorities with adjudicatory functions may not be fully receptive and, in some instances, could feel 'antipathy to[wards] American-style civil litigation'.[90] Indeed, there are major differences between the two legal systems. First, the absence of the pre-trial in the majority of civil law adjudications across continents[91] as these jurisdictions' adjudicative system are not based on a jury trial.[92] Also, in civil law jurisdictions, eliciting general information or obtaining evidence from the opponent or from a third party against their will goes 'through a special and rigorous mechanism commonly known as "exhibition of documents" that has a difficult standard to meet and is largely controlled by judges'.[93] Panama is a notable exception in Latin America in relation to the issue of discovery.

With a judicial competition system, the Panamanian Competition System counts with the American common law instrument known as 'discovery',[94] This is

[86] ibid: 612.

[87] 'Gerber distinguishes two functions of the U.S. discovery system: (1) "to obtain reasonably identified evidence for use in proving contested facts (evidence gathering)", (2) "to search for information that may be used to identify such evidence (evidence seeking) [emphasis in original]". (3) He notes that while the first function is in line with the practise of other states, the second is generally not known outside the U.S. (4) Therefore, the U.S. rules on jurisdiction and discovery are at odds with customary international law and practise of most other states.' Martyniszyn (2016: 5).

[88] Hazard (1997: 1019).

[89] For a complete assesment of discovery in the US, see: Stucke (2012).

[90] Hazard (1997: 1017).

[91] The Philippines might be an exception to the rule, with two different legal traditions: civil law and common law.

[92] Hazard (1997: 1020).

[93] Hodges, Vogenauer and Tulibacka (2010: 392).

[94] Interview with Cardoze.

the case particularly in consumer protection law, maritime law, and labour law.[95] An approach given by Australia would rely on sharing information (not evidence) with foreign counterparts while preserving discretion in terms of putting in danger its own vital interests.[96] The latter can be considered a form of discovery.

Furthermore, claims for finding a broad, international view to effectively address the ill-effects of import cartels in domestic markets have been made.[97] For instance, the case of *Daishowa International v North Coast Export Co* illustrates how Japanese wood chip importers boycotted a US exporter and questioned the jurisdiction of a US judge over a Japanese import cartel.[98]

The question was unfortunately not raised in appeal in the US High Court, which would have been a unique opportunity to rule on a jurisdictional issue and would have also raised fundamental questions of public international law.[99] From the viewpoint of developing countries, the legalisation of import cartels by developed nations would harm their volume of exports massively and affect the price range paid to them for the imports permitted. Again, the rise of populism in major western economies would exacerbate this tendency.[100] In this connection, one could say that the financial constraints that many importing economies face has eventually led to them form import cartels where domestic governments had a tendency to turn a blind eye toward this fact.[101]

6.3. Summary

Except for the unilateral solution of extraterritoriality, all the solutions proposed in chapter six require a fundamental ingredient: cooperation. The private international law solution discussed relies on how countries and their respective competition authorities work together to decide the best adjudicative jurisdiction that would settle the international CBC case. Formal coordination through diplomatic channels would be another ingredient in some of the solutions proposed which may lead to lengthy procedures.

Even formal coordination between competition authorities requires the signature of cooperation agreements or MOUs, as discussed in chapter three. However,

[95] 'El 'Discovery' En El Derecho Marítimo Panameño'.

[96] Martyniszyn, 'Discovery and Evidence in Transnational Antitrust Cases' 1.

[97] Matsushita (1979).

[98] The question of reciprocity might have arisen when a US export cartel sued Japanese firms for allegedly conspiring to put a ceiling on the price they would pay the Webb-Pomerene Association. See the discussion in Stephan and Roin (2010).

[99] Zanettin (2002: 28).

[100] Inglehart and Norris (2016).

[101] Of course, the import reductions have frequently affected categories essential to investment and certain types of production. For example, many countries have reduced imports of machinery, equipment and industrial supplies. This, in turn, has led to lower levels of economic activity in most developing countries. Import compression after 1982 in several highly indebted developing countries, many of which, especially in Latin America, are major trading partners of the USA, accounted for a large part of the decline of exports from the USA after 1982. See more in Ocampo (2014).

several factors between young and mature competition authorities can substantially hamper cooperation if the investigation requires a number of jurisdictions with diverse legal standing on cartel offences.

Without binding agreements, formal coordination between authorities may not occur. In turn, informal cooperation has proved to be a success in certain phases of the investigation, when gathering intelligence and preliminary information on the markets affected in foreign territories.

The solutions proposed in this chapter may support this argument, through the example of successful informal cooperation agreements to jointly investigate certain CBC cases, such as the case of Lima Declaration in Latin America (discussed in chapter seven). Despite this achievement, the solutions proposed in this chapter have failed to decipher how to deal with trust, confidential information and differences of legal standing issues.

The complexity of international cooperation between competition authorities necessitates specific solutions to these problems, rather than institutionalising unilateral practices with international effects (ie the extraterritoriality principle) that have created reluctance and in some cases deadlocks that have significantly hampered cooperation in CBC investigations.

International cooperation is critical for young competition authorities because of the need to understand an international case and to get the necessary information to initiate proceedings. The information provided by a mature competition authority that has already dealt with the CBC is important for the young competition authority when starting to investigate the impact of the same CBC in its domestic markets. As such, a specific approach to develop a methodology for successfully prosecuting the CBC, as well as developing the most effective sanctions, should be the first objective of any solution for this problem.

In any case, if international cartelists know that competition authorities are working collectively and can make a concerted move against the cartel, the deterrent effects will be higher. In this regard, discussion on how international companies trigger leniency applications in selected key countries and not in other younger jurisdictions can be another problem. Consequently, cooperation will only take place between the authorities that received the applications because there were confidentiality considerations amongst these jurisdictions. Once again, affected younger jurisdictions are not part of this club and therefore even with leniency programmes in place, the information will not be disclosed to these jurisdictions. None of the solutions proposed in this chapter seem to address this problem.

Young and small competition agencies must carefully weigh whether the costs of international cooperation are not greater than the benefits arising from it. Young competition authorities have scarce resources and any additional cost in areas related to international cooperation should be carefully examined in the light of their prioritisation of enforcement activities, available resources, as well as the nature of the markets affected domestically. One cannot overestimate the expenses that mature competition authorities incur just to build up relationships over time with their partners.

In Latin America, as indicated in chapter seven, many competition authorities (young or small) have entered into cooperation agreements amongst each other and with mature agencies over the last 15 to 20 years. Those competition authorities that share common enforcement interests have been keener to cooperate than others while some of those that deem it important to cooperate, in some cases, have not been able to do so because of the costs of cooperation in a cartel case.

The solutions proposed in Chapter 6 imply additional costs for cooperation and coordination, including the assessment of foreign interests and legislation if a forum needs to apply both states' competition laws, as would be the case for the private international law solution. Besides the use of these legal instruments in other mature competition regimes, Latin America, even with its promising future in terms of competition law development, is not yet ready to incorporate these mechanisms that would require additional examination of how competition laws are being enforced in each jurisdiction.

In addition, the resulting exhaustion can deter countries from entering into this type of legal cooperation. Part III of the research attempts to provide realistic options for young competition authorities to participate in the investigations of the most relevant types of CBCs presented in chapter two, taking into account the problems presented in chapters four and five as well as the solutions discussed in chapter six. Table 6.2 provides a summary of the lessons learned from the solutions discussed in the present chapter.

Table 6.2 Solutions and measures that have partially addressed regional, export and import CBCs

Problem	Solutions proposed	Potential problems for young/small competition authorities
Lack of effective regional competition authorities.	Informal cooperation and private law solution.	Young or small competition authorities face a number of hurdles to implement this solution: structural legal problems such as cultural legal barriers to cooperate, lack of trust in the judicial system in developing countries by international companies, among other factors.
Different legal standing as per cartel offences.	Appointment of one or more lead jurisdiction(s) in cross-border cases.	This has only been possible in jurisdictions that share a great number of similarities in terms of culture, business and harmonised substantive and procedural rules, such as the Nordic Cooperation for Competition Law Enforcement. The identification of a lead jurisdiction might be a sensitive task where one jurisdiction creates problems through its perception of superiority towards the others. A negative reaction towards the unilateral extraterritorial application of laws has created unnecessary sovereignty problems as well.

(continued)

Table 6.2 ***(Continued)***

Problem	Solutions proposed	Potential problems for young/small competition authorities
Diverse criteria in adjudication techniques.	Recognition of decisions made by agencies or courts in other jurisdictions.	While reducing the investigative burden, the local element needed still requires a significant amount of resources and also the legal recognition of foreign evidence which is not necessary an easy task to overcome in countries which lack a developed competition culture.
Difficulties in achieving comparable sanctions and remedies to cartel infringements.	Cooperation at court level.	Difficult to achieve in courts where the notion of competition law is limited, and cooperation between courts would rely on lengthy rogatory letters that would delay any effective cooperation scheme.
Lack of incentives to provide evidence in export CBCs.	Foreign states' *amicus curiae* to domestic competition cases.	To undertake this activity, young competition regimes would first need to know where foreign jurisdictions are investigating their companies. With little interaction between mature and young competition authorities, flow of information is limited.
Lack of incentives to provide evidence in import CBCs.	Recognition of foreign evidence provided by affected exporters.	The issue of discovery is a problem in young competition authorities' jurisdiction. The alternative 'exhibition of documents' is difficult to implement in many countries.

Source: own elaboration based on two secondary sources: (1) Capobianco Survey 'Developments in International Enforcement Co-operation in the Competition Field'; (ii) Table 3 of the UNCTAD Secretariat Report 2017 entitled 'Enhancing international cooperation in the investigation of competition cross-border cases: tools and procedures' to be submitted to the Intergovernmental Group of Experts on Competition Law and Policy. Sixteenth session Geneva, 5–7 July 2017.

PART III

Novel Proposals to Target Selected Types of Cross-Border Cartels

Part III is divided into three chapters that examine specific solutions for several types of CBC investigation. The way forward is thus elucidated for two different scenarios: (1) the relations between mature or large and young or small competition authorities in dealing with transnational CBC investigations; and (2) the dynamics amongst young or small competition authorities in dealing with regional CBC investigations throughout different regional economic groupings around the world.

As the novel proposals suggested in chapters eight and nine needed to be triggered in some countries where young or small competition authorities can coexist with other young but large ones (in the case of Mexico or Brazil), the author chose the Latin American region to provide the basis for their analysis and formulation. In this regard, at the outset, **chapter seven** presents a case study of Latin America by addressing the legal, institutional and local circumstances as to how cartel laws in that region have developed over time. It then assesses the efforts made by the Latin American countries to counteract the harmful effects of CBCs.

Chapter eight addresses the relations between mature or large and young or small competition authorities in dealing with transnational CBC investigations. It puts forward three building blocks that aim to unleash the full potential of informal international cooperation and voluntary consultations: (1) trust development between mature and young competition authorities; (2) the utilisation of 'sharable' information or 'agency information' under the meaning provided by the ICN (see chapter three) at the pre-investigatory phase; and (3) the strengthening of already agreed international instruments such as the UN Set and the ICN schemes. As BRICS countries also support the idea of revitalising the available international instruments, it is anticipated that this solution will be put into practice in the years to come. Much of the cooperation that needs to be strengthened refers to the fact that many transnational CBCs are not being detected, investigated and sanctioned by the affected authorities. As such, chapter 10 puts forward suggestions to create a workable trust between distant competition authorities where the distributional conflict (as defined in chapter five) might be a disincentive for the mature agency to cooperate.

Chapter nine deals with regional CBCs amongst young competition. It outlines how to introduce the next level of trust development amongst similar competition authorities' regimes in regional economic groupings. Secondly, it elucidates the idea of introducing coordination game schemes to strengthen informal cooperation and networks in regional groupings such as Latin America. In this regard, focusing on Latin America, the various methods of dealing with regional CBCs and even sub-regional CBCs are reviewed, taking into account the current developments taking place in the region.

In considering novel proposals, one should be mindful about the following caveats that government officials from young or small competition authorities should follow when dealing with cooperation schemes that imply some type of intergovernmental deliberations and consensus-building. The following observations by the author are primarily based on the current work as lead coordinator of the UNCTAD Discussion Group on International Cooperation.

1. Cooperation with foreign peers sometimes requires the participation of ministries of foreign affairs (state-to-state cooperation vs. agency-to-agency cooperation). While some young and small competition regimes can ensure a working level of independency from the central government, in certain occasions, even independent competition authorities would require some type of 'clearance' from the Ministry of Foreign Affairs when dealing with other foreign peers. In some instances, independent competition authorities can represent the government in what is called *transgovernmental regulatory networks* as in the sense ascribed by AM Slaughter.[1] However, accountability issues can arise when transparency is diminished as decisions and documents are often available only to interested groups.[2]
2. Limits of intergovernmental deliberations and consensus-building. As international soft-instruments are typically the norm when agreeing on any sort of intergovernmental consensus-building, one can reckon up to what point domestic implementation is realistic given that the result of these deliberations is of non-binding nature. As advocated in this research, international cooperation has been found to solve the problem of CBCs and therefore the very nature of that cooperation is a recommendation for government agencies to consider.
3. Turfing and silos within domestic and cross-border levels. When two or more domestic institutions are in charge of enforcing competition rules in a given jurisdiction, turf and silos can become a challenge when representing the country before any *transgovernmental regulatory network* abroad. Dealing with and approaching civil servants in some jurisdictions can definitely represent a challenge if some of these internal matters are limiting the scope of the cooperation.

[1] See Slaughter and Hale (2010).

[2] See also the assessment of two Latin American networks through the benchmark of accountability and effectiveness. Horna (2012).

7

CBCs in Latin America

The local dynamics, historical, contextual and legal development of anti-cartel laws in Latin America are highlighted through the domestic anti-cartel enforcement of the different competition authorities in the region. As a result, the international activity in Latin America is also presented. This chapter discusses the major efforts carried out by Latin American countries in the fight against the five different types of CBCs, reviewing the experiences of these countries in signing bilateral competition agreements and competition provisions in regional trade agreements, and assessing how these agreements have been implemented so far. The chapter also discusses the revival of the regional competition law enforcement system in the Andean Community of Nations (CAN) in 2016, and the promising future of informal cooperation in the region for open cartel investigations.

The development of anti-cartel laws in Latin America, robust or otherwise, has undoubtedly brought about consequences as to whether Latin American competition authorities are better equipped to neutralise the effects of CBCs into their domestic markets. As such, small and young competition regimes would be able to 'free-ride' on what other competition authorities are doing to counter the effects of multinational CBCs. Of course, larger but still young jurisdictions such as Mexico and Brazil have demonstrated that they are ready to react effectively when a multinational cartel has domestic effects in their respective markets, such as in the cases of the lysine cartel in Mexico and the vitamins cartel in Brazil.

7.1. Competition Law and Policy Developments in Latin America

The latest developments in competition law and policy in Latin America have been a great step forward towards the internationalisation of competition laws in the region. As Commissioner Burnier from Brazil noted:

> Competition law and policy in Latin America has taken huge development steps in the last decade, which enables us to speak of a 'New Era' for competition enforcement in the region. Companies should be aware of this trend in order to increase efforts to comply with competition legislation, which are subject to modern investigation techniques and heavy fines.[3]

[3] Burnier da Silveira (2017: 24).

Argentina, Chile, Colombia and Mexico were some of the first Latin American countries to have competition laws. While Mexico's first competition-related legislation was in 1917, Argentina's first law[4] dates from 1923,[5] while Chile's[6] and Colombia's[7] laws were enacted in 1959. A common denominator of this legislation is that, with the exception of Chile,[8] none of it was enforced in practice until the enactment of subsequent laws, in the 1980s[9] in Argentina and 1990s in Colombia, in line with modern microeconomic theory.[10]

During the 1990s, the region saw the enactment of effective competition regimes and the revision of those historical laws enacted earlier by Argentina, Chile and Colombia thanks, partly, to the neoliberal policy reforms introduced in the 1980s and 1990s,[11] probably with the belief that less state intervention would improve the economic performance of Latin American economies.[12]

However, by 2009 the region was witnessing sparks of political populism and the reintroduction of government dirigisme.[13] Table 7.1 details three distinctive stages (developmental, neoliberal and institutionalist) in the development of competition laws in Latin America, each of which has faced specific shortcomings throughout its evolution over the last several decades.

The 'developmental' phase[14] was named due to the number of public policies geared toward the promotion of various economic sectors such as manufacturing during the first part of the last century.[15] It was believed that enactment of competition laws was a prerogative of government to intervene in the markets through provisions that could also be exempted if the stability of the economy

[4] Some have said that Argentina's competition laws are the oldest in the region, with a 1919 statute that was never enforced (Law No 11210/19). See De León (2009: 564).

[5] Argentina Competition Act 1923.

[6] Chilean Competition Act 1959.

[7] Colombia Competition Act 1959.

[8] Palacios (2017: 192).

[9] In 1980 Argentina introduced its first comprehensive modern antitrust regulation (Law No 22,262). Law No 22,262 took a less repressive approach and introduced new features, such as the creation of the Comisión Nacional de Defensa de la Competencia ('CNDC'), the rule of reason approach to anticompetitive conducts, and the concept of abuse of dominant position. See Burnier da Silveira (2017).

[10] Palacios (2017: 192).

[11] The laws enacted in the 1990s in Latin America established competition as a guiding principle for private and public actors. Their enforcement identified strucutral problems that prevented them from accomplishing their task effectively. The problems identified by Palacios were: (i) the political dependency of the enforcement agencies, (ii) the non-defferent effect of the punitive regimes, and (iii) the lack of adequate staff (especially economists) as well of other resources. Palacios has referred to the 'Institutionalist' stage because the amendments and the new regimes adopted displayed a particular concern for strengthening or providing for strong institutional foundations to the enforcement activities. See Palacios and Gutierrez (2016: 81).

[12] De León (2009: 585).

[13] ibid: 585.

[14] Named after the development of a 'regulatory developmental state' See Palacios and Gutierrez (2016: 78).

[15] Cardoso (1972).

Table 7.1 Development of Competition Law in Latin America

	Developmental (Few countries with basic laws and weak enforcement) [1910s–1990]	**Neoliberal (Modernisation of competition laws with a moderate enforcement) [1990–2000]**	**Institutionalist (Consolidation of existing regimes, enactment of new laws in Central America and international best practices) [2000–2016]**
Rationale	Social justice and national development.	Economic and consumer welfare.	Economic and consumer welfare and national competitiveness.
Scope	General prohibition and discretionary exemptions.	General and specific prohibitions, limited fines and some merger review provisions.	General/specific prohibitions, higher fines, leniency, powers of investigation, cooperation with other agencies, prosecution of international cartels.
Independence	Dependent agencies.	Semi-autonomous.	Autonomous agencies.
Composition, size and operation	Lawyerly staff & very limited resources.	Staff lawyers and economists & limited resources.	Staff increase and more resources.
Sources of resistance	Business Associations (BA).	BA and agricultural firms.	BA and agricultural firms and national champions.
Country specific cases	Argentina (1923, 1946) Brazil (1962) Mexico (1917, 1934), Chile (1959) and Colombia (1955, 1959).	Mexico (1992) Colombia (1991, 1992) Chile (1973, 1999), Venezuela (1992), Argentina (1999), Brazil (1994), Peru (1992), Costa Rica (1994), Andean Community (1991, 2005) and Mercosur (1996).	Mexico (2006, 2011, 2013, 2014), Chile (2002, 2003, 2009, 2015), Colombia (2009, 2014), Brazil (2011, 2012), El Salvador (2004, 2007), Peru (2008), Panama (2008), Ecuador (2011), Bolivia (2008), Paraguay (2011), Uruguay (2007), Nicaragua (2008) and Honduras (2006).

Source: based on Palacios & Gutierrez[16] and OECD-IADB Report.[17]

[16] Palacios and Gutierrez (2016: 77–78).
[17] OECD and IADB (2012).

was affected.[18] The 'neoliberal' phase refers to the ideology of open trade and market-oriented reforms which became dominant in the 1990s, following the demise of developmental ideas and models from the 1950s and 1960s.[19]

During the 1990s, key effective competition regimes in Latin America were developed so as to adopt systems that would consider, as final objectives, the consumer welfare approach as opposed to other non-economic goals. As a result, punishing cartels and unilateral conduct were part of the milestones of the Latin American competition authorities' enforcement priorities.[20] Yet, many of these competition authorities faced great difficulties due to the political interference and the lack of independence from central government administrations.[21] Consequently, limited resources were devoted to these regimes and the deterrent fines proved ineffectual as companies were not concerned about the harmful effects of their anti-competitive wrongdoing.

According to Palacios and Gutierrez, the last stage of Latin American competition law, the 'institutionalist' phase, arose because Latin American policymakers were particularly concerned about how to strengthen institutions and capacities in the area of competition law and policy in order to be more effective in their enforcement activities.[22] Consider, for example, the Chilean experience, whereby the law of 2003 strengthened the enforcement system of competition laws by separating the adjudicative and investigatory functions.[23] Despite the foregoing changes, by 2017, Latin American competition institutions were still considered to be 'receiving-end' jurisdictions rather than 'forefront' ones, as noted by Palacios: 'Latin America is at the *receiving end* of transnational networks [such as OECD or ICN] through which different theories circulate between law-producing jurisdictions [US, EU] and their peripheral counterparts'.[24] This quotation, albeit pessimistic, reflects the reality in many respects when assessing Latin American competition regimes.[25]

[18] Art 1 of the Colombian Act provides to the government the full discretion to exempt firms or sectors from the application of competition laws if such application affects 'their stability'. See Colombia Competition Act.

[19] Palacios and Gutierrez (2016: 79).

[20] ibid.

[21] Consider the case of Venezuela and Argentina. See De León (2009: 560), section 13.4.1 'Venezuela: From Show Case to a Basket Case'.

[22] Palacios (2017); Palacios and Gutierrez (2016).

[23] 'Enforcement has increased dramatically since legislative changes in 2003 strengthened sanctions and made enforcement an adversarial procedure. The most important change in enforcement was the creation of the Tribunal de Defensa de la Libre Competencia (TDLC). The TDLC, which performs both the decision-making and advocacy roles, has more independence, more qualified members, higher status, more power and a larger budget than the Commissions that it replaced, The structural changes made the system more transparent and more effective. The allocation of enforcement tasks between an independent investigative body, the Fiscalía Nacional Económica (FNE) and the separate, independent decision making authority, the TDLC, is working, so far. See OECD, 'Competition Law and Policy in Chile' (2010: 7).

[24] (Emphasis by author). Palacios (2017: 197).

[25] There is a so-called 'silent resistance' to the development of competition regimes in some Latin American countries. The case of Dominican Republic is a critical example whereby despite a

In the area of cartel enforcement in Latin America, the relatively good advances in cartel law means that 'successful cartel enforcement requires less analytical expertise and yields a potentially higher payoff in terms of successful enforcement actions'.[26] Indeed, through a number of key cartel cases in Latin America, notably from Brazil and Chile during the last 15 years, cartel enforcement has been prioritised and as a result has been where the 'action' is for the young and relatively small competition authorities wishing to gain legitimacy and experience in a relatively new environment.[27]

7.2. National Cartel Cases with Regional Cross-Border Dimensions

Latin American competition authorities have focused on detecting collusion as the most pernicious form of anticompetitive practice. Although there have been a number of cartel cases in major and advanced jurisdictions in Latin America (Argentina, Brazil, Colombia, Chile, Mexico and Peru), young competition authorities in Latin America, particularly in Central America (El Salvador, Nicaragua, Honduras, Dominican Republic) and Andean countries (Bolivia and Ecuador) still need to consolidate their national competition law enforcement to gather sufficient experience to deal with intra-regional collusion activity.

For instance, in Central America, one can find recurrent business alliances as a result of the existence of regional economic groups that have made significant intra-regional foreign direct investment. Sectors such as finance, communications, food, household products, air transport and commercial services and/or tourism are some of these cross-border sectors.

Of course, these economic groups have very diversified activities and often have family ties to the political sector, so there is no basis for them to collude or engage in other forms of anticompetitive agreements to exclude new entrants.

7.2.1. Four Central Aspects of Anti-Cartel Enforcement

Prior to the review of major domestic cartel landmark cases in Latin America, four central aspects of the cartel enforcement activities in Latin America will be reviewed in this subsection. First, the legal framework on fighting cartels; second, the main investigatory powers that competition authorities have; third, the leniency programmes in the region and their latest development and challenges; and

Competition Law being enacted in 2008, effective enforcement has not taken place so far. Palacios and Gutierrez (2016: 82).

[26] E Fox and Sokol (2009: 5).

[27] See for instance Burnier da Silveira and Sanchez (2017).

finally, the various settlement policies adopted by major competition authorities in the region.

7.2.1.1. The Legal Framework

Following the 'international trend'[28] of criminalisation[29] of anti-cartel laws[30] in Latin America, the legal apparatus to fight cartels at the domestic level is divided into criminal and administrative features, and Latin America clearly favours the administrative nature of anti-cartel laws. While Chilean,[31] Mexican and Brazilian[32] anti-cartel laws impose criminal sanctions on company executives in cartel investigations, they also have parallel administrative proceedings for the prosecution of cartels. While Colombia has introduced criminal sanctions against bid riggers only, the remaining Latin American countries only have administrative sanctions against cartelists, following the European tradition.

An important distinction needs to be made when it comes to the 'hybrid' anti-cartel enforcement systems in Latin America. While courts and competition authorities in Mexico,[33] Chile and Brazil impose criminal liability on individuals, the administrative liability for cartel offences remains at the jurisdictions of their competition authorities. In this case, two different and independent and sometimes parallel procedures are conducted to establish infringement of administrative and criminal sanctions. However, given the recent nature of the criminalisation of cartel offences and despite the fact that criminal enforcers are legally autonomous and not bound by the view of competition authorities, they tend to await the outcome of the administrative procedures before they commence their criminal ones.[34]

[28] The trend in favour of cartel criminalisation has developed asymmetrically across the globe. See Ezrachi and Kindl (2011: 421), 'The Heterogeneous Landscape of National Regimes'.

[29] In making the decision to criminalise and implement and enforce a criminal cartel regime, political support is essential. See the case of Australia in Beaton-Wells (2009).

[30] While the emerging legal landscape of anti-cartel activity is complex and varies significantly by jurisdiction, the clear trend is toward increased criminalisation, as well as more robust enforcement, including collaboration among national antitrust authorities through informal transgovernmental networks. See Shaffer, Nesbitt and Waller 'Criminalizing Cartels: A Global Trend?'.

[31] In 2016, the Chilean Congress amended the competition law to introduce criminal sanctions for cartel members. See 'Congreso Aprueba Reformas Al DL N° 211'.

[32] In Brazil, cartels are both an administrative as well as a criminal violation. Regarding the administrative prosecution of international cartels, the Brazilian Competition Law adopts the 'effects doctrine' and therefore applies it to any practice performed, in full or in part, on the national territory, or that produces or may produce effects thereon. It is also relevant to note that CADE considers cartels as a violation per se, and therefore it is not required to prove an actual effect. Ana Paula Martinez and Mariana Tavares de Araujo, 'Anti-Cartel Enforcement In Brazil: Status Quo & Trends'.

[33] 'For the first time, Mexico's Federal Commission for Economic Competition yesterday referred for prosecution individuals who allegedly violated the country's competition law, as part of the competition authority's investigation of collusion in public health tenders.' 'Mexico Pursues First Criminal Action against Cartelists'.

[34] For instance, in Russia, it is commonly understood that the Russian Competition Authoruty (FAS) will send materials on cartels revealed as a result of its investigations to criminal prosecutors

7.2.1.2. Investigatory Powers

In the area of cartel enforcement, Latin American competition laws have vested competition authorities with the necessary capacity to undertake investigations and inquiries, although some countries have experienced some difficulties in exercising these investigatory powers.[35]

The competition authorities have the power to request information from different sources and by different legal means, particularly the organisation of raids in companies being investigated.[36] Indeed, 'dawn raids' are critical for any competition investigation, as they collect evidence for the opening of the procedure and the determination of the competition infringement.[37]

However, problems in the implementation of such crucial power of investigation can be a drawback in some specific Latin American jurisdictions.[38]

only after the courts have supported the relevant FAS decisions if appealed. See more 'Russia: Cartel Investigations'.

[35] For instance, Art 15.3 of Legislative Decree 1034 (Peruvian Competition Act) states that the competition agency may require by subpoena the production of any documentary evidence. It establishes a special procedure regarding the gathering of private correspondence located in the undertaking's premises. According to this procedure, a criminal court judge must issue a judicial authorisation allowing the gathering of the aforementioned information. Provisions regarding the necessity of a judicial authorisation are found in most competition laws around the world. Yet the provisions set forth by the Peruvian law have caused much trouble when conducting dawn raids. Due to the difficulty of obtaining a judicial warrant (mainly because of lengthy judicial processes), the usual practice of the Peruvian authority has been to issue a search authorization itself, thus entering an undertaking's premises and exercising its investigative Ibid. and ICN, 'Anti-Cartel Enforcement Manual Chapter 1'.

[36] 'In developing countries most competition [authorities] cannot request information as easily as courts'. Since they are part of the executive branch, they cannot perform surprise raids without permission granted by a judge. In addition, a verification visit does not authorise the seizure of files or documents, only making copies … '(De León, 2009: 68').

[37] This is why it is important to determine from the outset the type of information and the objective should follow this inspection. Simple questions like what is needed and what one would expect to find, inform the role of the people in charge of the inspection which will collect relevant data, actors as managers, shareholders, staff, among others. Keep in mind that the parties reported must cooperate with the investigation, helping to install the inspectors and providing necessary facilities. The inspection should include a strategy with a team leader to identify the main points to investigate in order for it to be carried in an orderly manner with a fixed target. While in many cases there can be a strategy and objectives, it is vital to identify the regulatory framework from which emerge the scope and powers to allow action to the competent antitrust authorities. An example of this was the enactment of the Peruvian Competition Act in 2008, Legislative Decree 1034, and why the powers have been extended to the technical secretariat empowering it to require the production of all kinds of documents, including accounting and corporate books, payment vouchers, internal or external correspondence and magnetic records including, in this case, the programs that are necessary for reading them, as well as to request information regarding the organisation, business, market shares and ownership structure of the companies. Diario Oficial El Peruano, Peru Competition Act, Decreto Legislativo N° 1034, 2008.

[38] For example in Colombia, the practice of dawn raids, as read from the power contained in s 62 of Art 1 of Decree 4886 of 2011, it can be said that this faculty is contained in a provision of a general nature, which has no specifics in regard of the scope and limits that govern the SIC when making administrative visits. Therefore, conducting a dawn raid only referring to this faculty presents in many occasions complications, difficulties and discussion in respect of the powers of the SIC. 'Contribution from Colombia – Session III'.

7.2.1.3. Leniency Programmes

Leniency programmes are regarded as the most powerful tool to detect cartels in modern competition law.[39] Within Latin America, Brazil and Peru were among the first countries to introduce leniency programmes, in 2000 and 1996 respectively.[40] Brazil signed its first leniency agreement in 2003; by 2016, Brazil had 54 leniency agreements signed and monitored.[41]

The leniency system in Brazil has been an undoubted success, having effectively prosecuted a number of domestic, mixed and international cartels.[42] However, beyond Brazil's boundaries, the introduction of immunity and leniency programmes to fight hard-core cartels remains an important challenge in the region, as agencies would need to gain the 'necessary expertise to administer these programs, increasingly join and even cooperate with their international counterparts, and learn the nuances in their legal systems when implementing them and enforcing their competition legislation.'[43]

7.2.1.4. Sanctions, Remedies and Settlements

Anti-cartel laws will only produce the desired effects if they are effectively implemented. This means that sanctions, remedies and settlements appear to be crucial for encouraging competition law compliance.[44] Sanctions would need to have a sufficient deterrent effect for companies not to engage in conspiracies again.

Remedies would complement sanctions since they aim at safeguarding or restoring competition in cases where companies have distorted or are about to distort competition.[45] For instance, in the sugar import cartel in Colombia reviewed below, the Colombian Authority (*Superintendencia de Industria y Comercio*, or SIC) sanctioned sugar cartel importers with an exemplary fine, the highest ever imposed in that country. This helped the SIC to convey a straightforward message to the companies on the convenience and usefulness of the leniency programme.[46]

As for the level of fines in Latin America, since the assessment made by Connor in 2008, whereby he ascertained that the level of fines in the region was 'pitifully low relative to either affected sales (4.9 per cent on average) or to damages (less than 1 per cent)',[47] the level of fines has been considerably increased,

[39] UNCTAD, 'The Use of Leniency Programmes as a Tool for the Enforcement of Competition Law against Hardcore Cartels in Developing Countries'.

[40] OECD, 'Leniency Programmes in Latin America and the Caribbean: Recent Experiences and Lessons Learned'.

[41] Linhares Martins and Lin Fidelis (2016: 2).

[42] By 2016, Brazil had reported 70 cartel cases, which represents the highest number of cases in the region. Young Council Latin American Regional Forum (2016: 6).

[43] Mariscal and Mena-Labarthe (2010).

[44] UNCTAD, 'Appropriate Sanctions and Remedies' 3.

[45] ibid: 4.

[46] *Colombia Sugar Import Cartel* [2015] Superintendencia de Industria y Comercio (SIC) Resolution No. 103652.

[47] Connor, 'Latin America and the Control of International Cartels' 53.

culminating in the fine imposed by the Brazilian Competition Authority (CADE) in 2010 in the industrial medicine gas cartel.[48] Chapter 2 details this case.

7.2.2. Domestic Cartel Cases in the Region

Cartel activity in key markets and sectors has been investigated in Latin America. These sectors represent important household expenditures and thereby impact consumers' purchasing capacity markedly.[49] Recent statistics suggest that Brazil is by far the most active cartel enforcer in Latin America, followed by Mexico, Colombia, Chile and Argentina. The smaller competition authorities in Central America such as El Salvador, Costa Rica, Honduras and Nicaragua report few cartel cases.

Newer competition authorities, such as Ecuador, Bolivia, Paraguay and the Dominican Republic, have not yet reported any cartel cases. It is clear that cartel enforcement is highly diverse in Latin America, with some countries having more than 70 cartel cases in the same number of years during the 1990s, in contrast with other countries which had very few cases. As such, the enactment of modern competition rules in the 1990s was an important step for these jurisdictions. They began to catch up with others, but not enough to fully consolidate domestic cartel enforcement in the region. Table 7.2 provides further details of the statistics of the number of domestic cartel cases in the region.

From Table 7.2, one can note the active role of Brazil in the enforcement of anti-cartel laws. Connor suggested that in 2008, Brazil had 'the largest and most effective anti-cartel authority in Latin America',[50] and the trend up to 2017 was steady. While the use of indirect and circumstantial evidence in cartel enforcement is gradually becoming a trend in major and advanced competition regimes such as in Brazil,[51] simple and direct evidence can still be found in early cartel cases enforced in younger jurisdictions, as is the case for El Salvador.[52]

[48] 'Brazil's antitrust regulator … fined five companies and their executives three billion Brazilian reals ($1.7 billion) for forming a cartel to control the price of industrial and medical gases.' 'Brazil Fines Companies BRL3 Billion For Industrial, Medical Gas Cartel'.

[49] 'Milk, sugar, poultry, transport, energy and medicine make up between 15 percent and 20 percent of the expenditure of the average household in Latin America. For instance, by 2015 In Colombia, sugar mills, a trade association and trading companies coordinated to obstruct sugar imports from entering the market in order to keep domestic sugar prices artificially high. In Brazil, three firms appear to have agreed not to reduce the price of milk that is consumed by poorer households. In Honduras, the association of chemical pharmacists enforced minimum-distance rules between pharmacies, creating local monopolies. In Peru, five gas suppliers for domestic gas use allegedly raised prices simultaneously by $14 to $17 per metric tonne. In Mexico, bus companies agreed to fix prices and restrict their supply of services over four years. Licetti, 'Bad News for Cartels, Good News for the Poor in Latin America'.

[50] Connor, 'Latin America and the Control of International Cartels' 44.

[51] Burnier da Silveira and Reja Sanchez (2017: 235).

[52] The so-called 'ingenious' cartel as the economic agents published in a newspaper the collusive agreement. See Cader (2017: 231).

Table 7.2 Domestic cartel cases in major Latin American jurisdictions reported between 1995 and 2016[53]

Country	Number of Cartel Cases	Sectors/markets
Brazil	More than 50	Metro lines, hospitals, metal detector security donors, cement, LPG distribution, air freight, copyright collection, **industrial gases**, steel bars, security services, sand extractors, TFT-LCD, CDT, CPT, air freight forwarders, DRAM, ODD, underground cables, underwater cables, polymers, salt and silicate, and capacitors.[54]
Colombia	Around 32	Paper notebooks, security services, disposable baby diapers, **tissue paper**, cement, sugar, livestock, casting agencies, infrastructure (road paving), construction, natural gas, gasoline, health services, medicines, banking services, electric cables and conductors, airport services, and **oxygen supply**.
Argentina	25	Portland cement, **medical gases**, healthcare industry, oil and gas industry, brewing industry, sand (Parana City), transportation and telecommunications.
Mexico	24	Gas–liquid propane, chemicals, poultry, boiled corn and corn tortillas, corn mass and tortillas, health services (**medical gas**), consulting services (real estate) transport (tourist sector, maritime transport, cargo), entertainment (cable and cable products), food vouchers and salt.
Peru	17	**Poultry**, wheat flour, fast food, urban transport (two cases), freight transport insurance (two cases), healthcare (**oxygen distribution**), construction, public notaries, and **tissue paper**.
Chile	13	Petroleum products, **medical gases**, radio transmission, fridge compressors, **poultry**, transport and health care sectors, asphalt, maritime shipping, **tissue paper**, and laboratories.
Panama	12	The airline market, meat market, fuel distribution market, sugar market, laundry market, **liquid oxygen for hospitals**, and the poultry processing market.

(continued)

[53] Additional information from Ivaldi, Khimich and Jenny (2014), Appendix I: Major hard-core cartels prosecuted in selected developing countries (1995–2013).

[54] Martinez and de Araujo (2015: 261–62).

Table 7.2 *(Continued)*

Country	Number of Cartel Cases	Sectors/markets
El Salvador	7	Agricultural markets, flour, travel agencies, telecommunications, port and insurance.[55]
Costa Rica	5	Telecommunications and paper supply.
Uruguay	3	Maritime agency fees, waste disposal services and the tomato sauce market.
Venezuela	2	Banking services (credit cards).
Nicaragua[56]	1	Banking services (interest rates).
Bolivia/ Ecuador/ Paraguay	0	NA.

Source: Leniency: The Future for Cartel Enforcement in Latin America.[57] (Emphasis add by author to highlight regional signals.)

A remarkable development in the last few years has been that the enforcement record of the Colombian Competition Authority, or SIC, has surpassed Argentina and Chile not only in terms of the number of cartel cases investigated and sanctioned,[58] but also due to the choice of Colombia to investigate cartel cases in sensitive sectors such as the sugar market, private security services, and the notebook, baby nappies and toilet paper markets.[59] Chapter seven will review three cartels that the SIC sanctioned recently, all of which had a clear international dimension.

Three additional observations can be drawn from Table 7.2, particularly concerning the sectors highlighted in bold. First, similar or identical markets at the domestic level for the provision of liquid oxygen in seven jurisdictions saw prosecutions over the same period of time (2000–10), and three or four companies operating at the regional level in Latin America have been sanctioned. Second, in recent years (2015 and 2016), the market of tissue paper has been or is being sanctioned in three jurisdictions (Colombia, Chile and Peru).

Similar subsidiaries are being investigated not only at the domestic level but also at the sub-regional level in the Andean region. However, it is interesting to note the poultry market cartel cases in Chile and Peru, where similar patterns over different time periods led to a distorted vision of how opportunistic the effective enforcement of competition rules can be in both countries.[60]

[55] Burnier da Silveira and Reja Sanchez (2017: 231 and 232).
[56] Procompetencia (2016).
[57] Young Council Latin American Regional Forum (2016: 28).
[58] Young Council Latin American Regional Forum (2016: 28.).
[59] Carrillo (2016).
[60] Gomez (2016); Coronado (2014).

Taking into account similar regional patterns of these two markets, this chapter discusses these two markets in detail. A difference of competition systems between these two countries led to a gap of years between the five instances of the Peruvian competition system (two at the administrative level and three at the judicial system)[61] and the two instances of the Chilean system.[62]

7.3. Cross-Border Cartels in Latin America

Following the gradual but decisive setting up of competition authorities in the region in 1990s as discussed above, some of these Latin American competition authorities commenced their work to neutralise the impact of CBCs, in particular the multinational/global cartels, transnational, pockets of regional cartels and import cartels. The protagonists of this remarkable international work are Brazil,[63] Mexico and Chile.[64] Later in the 2010s, Colombia,[65] Peru and Honduras moved forward and rapidly caught up with their more advanced competition agency peers. Let us review the first international cartel cases handled by the Latin American countries since the prosecution of the lysine global cartel within the domestic boundaries of Mexico in 1998.

7.3.1. Mexico: The Lysine Cartel (1998)

The Mexican Competition Authority (*Comisión Federal de Competencia Económica – COFECE)* took action in 1997 following the public US source

[61] In Peru it took 12 years to confirm the ruling of the Peruvian agency in 1995–96 (being the first Peruvian cartel case) to 2010 whereby the Peruvian Supreme Court confirmed the decision. Agencia Andina (2010).

[62] Chile's system took only four years to confirm the final decision to rule the poultry cartel case: FNE Chile (2015).

[63] In fact, in Brazil around 2016, 26 international cartels were investigated, including the major global cartels addressed in chapter 1 (lysine, vitamins, marine hoses, air cargo, compressors, etc). See Young Council Latin American Regional Forum (2016: 29).

[64] Connor, 'The Rise of Anti-Cartel Enforcement in Africa, Asia, and Latin America' 1.

[65] Since 2012, the SIC has established the importance of investigating international cartels and not limiting investigations to domestic antitrust violations. The only case that the SIC is formally investigating, is the auto parts international cartel, which has already been filed by the Department of Justice of the United States, where the companies investigated pleaded guilty. The formal investigation of the cartel by the SIC started in October 2012 relying upon the plea agreements signed by the Antitrust Division of the US DOJ. In interviews with SIC case handlers, one has appreciated the legal and economic limitations that the SIC has in the international cartel investigation. The legal limitations transmitted were: (i) the restraint regarding Colombian international competition law enforcement, (ii) the absence of foreign companies participating in the investigation, (iii) the difficulties in evidence recollection and (iv) the legal requirements of the evidence to be considered legal proof. In addition, the only restriction involving economic limitations is Colombia as an emerging market economy. Foreign firms do not find the Colombian economy as important to defend themselves against from the charges pressed by the SIC. bogotapost, 'Crackdown on Business Cartels in Colombia'.

available, which was ADM's annual financial report.[66] The COFECE investigation found that, of the three companies present in the Mexican lysine market,[67] two of them (ADM and Fermex) had fixed the price and the amounts of lysine supplied in the domestic market, as a consequence of an agreement made by Archer Daniels and Kyowa Hakko. The agreement between the Mexican subsidiaries gave rise to substantial parallel price increases in the domestic market.[68] Although the fine imposed by COFECE on ADM was a modest one ($125,000), this case is remarkable since it was the first time that a Latin American competition agency took a pro-active role (via an ex officio investigation) to address the possible harmful effects of international price fixing arrangements in its domestic market.

7.3.2. Brazil: The Vitamins Cartel (2007)

Brazil investigated, prosecuted and sanctioned the multinational vitamins cartel thanks to the publication of proceedings by US courts in 1999.[69] The Brazilian Competition Tribunal (*Conselho Administrativo de Defesa Econômica*, CADE) decided to sanctioned BASF, F Hoffman-La Roche and Aventis for having for having taken part in a cartel that affected the Brazilian market,[70] in particular, for having exchanged critical information about prices and quantities of vitamins A, E and beta carotene which were exported to Brazilian markets.[71]

The global coverage of the vitamins cartel, which was already being investigated by the US, and sanctioned by the EU and other authorities worldwide, made a strong case for the Brazilian enforcers to prosecute the cartel in its domestic markets.[72] Notably, the extent and effects of this global cartel impacting Brazil was straightforward, as the demand for vitamins had always been met by heavily imported products; specifically during the second half of the 1990s the entry of Chinese vitamins, which would have meant cheaper prices of vitamins to Brazilian costumers, was prevented by this CBC.[73] At the end, on 11 April 2007,

[66] 'Amino-Acids Cartel – International Competition Law 2010–2011'.

[67] ADM Bioproductos, SA de CV (ADM) Fermentaciones Mexicanas, SA de CV (Fermex) (subsidiaries of Archer Daniels and Kyowa Hakko respectively), and Helm de Mexico, SA (Helm), of which Kyowa Hakko dominated lysine sales in the Mexican market. 'Cartel in the Lysine Market in Mexico'.

[68] ibid.

[69] Under the Administrative Proceeding N° 08012.004599/1999-18 when SDE (the Prosecutor office) brought the case before CADE Tribunal. See 'Contribution from Brazil'.

[70] Secretariat of Economic Law, Antitrust Division.

[71] The SEAE and SDE found that the managerial team of the firms responsible for the vitamin market in Latin America met in Sao Paulo two to four times a year to exchange information about prices and quantities sold of these products. These meetings had the purpose of monitoring the international cartel's activities within the Latin American and Brazilian markets, so that the sales and prices were kept in accordance with the international agreement among these firms 'Contribution from Brazil'4.

[72] In 2000, the Brazilian Secretariat for Economic Monitoring concluded that there was strong evidence that the international plot affected Brazilian markets, although the defendants pledged that no impact took place in Brazil. Burnier da Silveira and Tardelli Tollini (2014: 172).

[73] Secretariat of Economic Law, Antitrust Division (2009).

some defendants of the vitamins cartel were found not guilty while others were condemned to the payment of fines.[74]

7.3.3. Colombia: The Auto-Parts Cartel (2012)

In 2012 and 2013, the Colombian Competition Authority investigated the companies that had taken part in the international auto parts cartel, described above.[75] The investigation was established to investigate the same companies that had pleaded guilty in the US (Furukuwa Electric Co Ltd, Denso Corporation, Yazaki Corporation) and determine whether the international cartel had any effects in Colombian domestic markets.[76] Unfortunately, the Colombian enforcer committed a number of procedural errors in the investigations, such as not being able to localise the legal domicile of the investigated companies, in order to contact the relevant foreign competition authorities that dealt with the case earlier, and the authority ended up with non-official documents in a foreign language that could have led to violations of due process in the courts. For these reasons, the authority decided to close and archive the investigation without possibility to reopen the case.

7.3.4. Chile: The Shipping Cartel (2015)[77]

In 2015, the National Economic Prosecutor of Chile (FNE) requested the Tribunal for the Defence of Free Competition of Chile (*Tribunal de Defensa de la Libre Competencia*, TDLC) to sanction six vehicles shipping companies (Compañía Sudamericana de Vapores (CSAV) and Compañía Chilena de Navegación Interoceánica (CCNI); Korea's Eukor Car Carriers; Japanese lines K-Line, Mitsui OSK Lines (MOL) and NYK) for having colluded for a number of years over the shipping of almost 91 per cent of all cars entering Chile from Europe, America and Asia.[78] According to the FNE, the conspiracy was manifested through

[74] Burnier da Silveira and Tardelli Tollini (2014: 172).

[75] *Colombia Auto parts Cartel – Opening the investigation.*

[76] Since 2012, the Colombian Competition Authority Superintendencia de Industria y Comercio- SIC has established the importance of investigating international cartels and not limiting the investigations to domestic antitrust violations. In interviews with SIC case handlers, one has appreciated the legal and economic limitations that the SIC has in the international cartel investigation. The legal limitations transmitted were: (i) the restraint regarding Colombian international competition law enforcement, (ii) the absence of foreign companies participating in the investigation, (iii) the difficulties in evidence recollection and (iv) the legal requirements of the evidence to be considered legal proof. In addition, the only restriction involving economic limitations is Colombia as an emerging market economy. Foreign firms do not find the Colombian economy as important to defend themselves from the pressed charges by the SIC. See more bogotapost, 'Crackdown on Business Cartels in Colombia'.

[77] 'Chile Condemns International Shipping Cartel'.

[78] *Chile Shipping Cartel* (Fiscalia Nacional Economica (FNE)).

unlawful bid-rigging practices whereby the shipping companies would either bid with unrealistically high prices so as to be discarded for the benefit of other members of the cartel conspiracy, or would propose bids with conditions, making proposals unattractive or unworkable; or even would not enter into bids at all.[79] By February 2017, the case was pending final ruling by TDLC.[80]

7.3.5. Colombia: The Sugar Import Cartel (2015)

The sugar market in Colombia was the first ever import cartel market documented in Latin America. In December 2015, the Colombian Competition Authority (SIC) fined three sugar trade associations (ASOCAÑA, CIAMSA, DICSA), 12 sugar mills and 12 senior executives of the sector, for having participated in an import cartel (under the meaning given in chapter one above). In particular, the cartel involved the obstruction and restriction of sugar imports to Colombia from Bolivia, Guatemala, El Salvador and Costa Rica.[81] The investigation undertaken by the SIC revealed that the import sugar cartel members (trade associations) coordinated as a blocking mechanism to eliminate all real and potential import competition in the international sugar market.[82] The members of the sugar trade associations developed two main mechanisms through which the CBC operated in the Colombian market. First, they developed 'multiple consensus through common organisms (sugar trade associations), which exceeded their rights of association and free enterprise, and allowed the sugar mills to create opportunities to design, discuss and implement strategies related to their competitive performance',[83] and second, they set up a so-called 'Stabilisation Fund of Sugar Prices' (FEPA), whereby a steering committee distributed quotas of sugar production or supply in the Colombian market under the façade of a mechanism of state interventionism.[84]

7.3.6. Brazil: The Refrigeration Compressor Cartel (2016)

CADE, after a thorough seven-year investigation (2009–16), condemned Household Compressors Holding SpA (formerly ACC – Appliances Components Companies SpA), Danfoss A/S e Panasonic Electric Works Co Ltd (formerly Matsushita Electric Works, Ltd), as well as three individuals related to companies of the Tecumseh and Whirlpool/Embraco groups for having entered into a cartel

[79] 'Shipping Line Cartel Exposed in Chile Says FNE'.
[80] According to the website of the Chilean Tribunal for the Defence of Free Competition. See 'Rulings of the TDLC of Chile'.
[81] *Colombia Sugar Import Cartel.*
[82] Berryman (2015).
[83] Carrillo (2016).
[84] ibid.

in the international market of refrigerator hermetic compressors, consequently harming Brazilian and foreign consumers at least between 1996 and 2008.[85] According to the CADE judgment, the international cartelists through their local representatives in Brazil held a number of meetings to share commercially sensitive information on price readjustment rates and the control of compressors supply around the world.[86] As a result of hard evidence of the cartel behaviour, found in the raids of executive offices in 2009, the General Superintendence of CADE, acting as the responsible unit for investigations, stated that the violations occurred between 1996 and 2004 (extended to 2008 in the final judgment), initially forming in Brazil and then expanding worldwide.[87]

7.3.7. Colombia: The Nappy Cartel (2016)

2016 saw the highest fine ever imposed in the long history of Colombian competition law,[88] and the first ever case wherein a competition authority signed leniency agreements with cartelists in Colombia, granting full immunity for the first applicant and 50 per cent to the second applicant.[89] After a number of unsolicited raids in 2013 and thanks to the triggering of the Colombian whistle-blower programme, evidence collected led to the conclusion that a price-fixing cartel had formed to artificially raise the prices of baby nappies.[90] In June 2016, the Colombian Competition Authority sanctioned nappy manufacturers (some of them part of multinational companies Tecnoquímicas, Familia, Kimberly and 16 individuals (high-level employees), for having fixed prices of baby nappies in Colombia for more than a decade (2001–12).[91]

7.3.8. Peru: The Roll-On Roll-Off Cargo Cartel (2017)

On 9 May 2017, the Peruvian Competition Authority (INDECOPI) opened an ex-officio investigation of an alleged transnational CBC in the car carrier service within the international maritime market (roll on-roll off) to six international

[85] Assessoria de Comunicação CADE.

[86] See Vote of Commissioner Márcio de Oliveira Júnior; *Brazil – Refrigeration Compressor Cartel* (2016) Administrative Proceeding 08012.000820/2009-11 (Administrative Council for Economic Defense).

[87] 'Brazil: CADE Wants Execs Punished for Refrigeration Cartel'.

[88] Since 1955.

[89] 'Thanks to the leniency programme, Familia, in its condition of second applicant, received a reduction of 50 per cent of the fine imposed, and Kimberly, in its condition of first applicant, received total exoneration (100 per cent) of the fine imposed'. Carrillo (2016).

[90] Indeed, several companies and their respective directors and employees came to the SIC in order to recognise their participation in the price-fixing cartel and provide evidence to prove its existence and operation. This collaboration led to the subscription of two cooperation agreements under the leniency programme. See ibid.

[91] *Colombia Nappy Cartel* [2016] Superintendencia de Industria y Comercio (SIC) Resolution No 43218.

companies (Compañía Marítima Chilena SA, Compañía Sudamericana de Vapores SA, Eukor Car Carrier Inc, Kawasaki Kisen Kaisha Ltd, Mitsui OSK Lines Ltd and Nippon Yusen Kabushiki Kaisha) for having fixed prices during the period 2001 to 2012 in the international market for car carrier services.[92]

7.4. Existing Efforts of CBC Enforcement in Latin America

This section reviews the principal existing efforts to detect and tackle CBCs in Latin America. Efforts carried out by competition authorities worldwide to tackle the international nature of CBCs can involve a number of activities. These activities range from signing cooperation agreements to coordinating simultaneous searches, raids or inspections, exchanging information, conducting discussions on general orientations regarding investigations, or even gathering information and interviewing of witnesses on behalf of another agency;[93] this has been the case with authorities such as the European Competition Network (ECN) or the Nordic Cooperation. Increasingly, small or young competition authorities have been able to participate in some of these activities through informal arrangements, but not necessarily through formal cooperation framework agreements.

For these reasons, this section discusses the existing efforts that Latin American countries have made in the fight against CBCs. The section begins with an overall review of the bilateral agreements that have been signed by Latin American countries, then proceeds to review the main sub-regional platforms that have been set up to fight cross-border anticompetitive practices. It then looks at one case study of domestic cartel investigations that has drawn attention to the potential existence of a regional cartel (as per the meaning provided in chapter two). The final part of this section looks at the rise of informal cooperation arrangements between Latin American countries and examines ways to derive positive results from these arrangements. The status of these developments and the further challenges for the region are summarised at the end.

7.4.1. Bilateral and Regional Trade Agreements

Following the international trend of signing bilateral agreements discussed in chapter three, intra-Latin American agreements have been signed in recent years. The so-called 'spaghetti bowl'[94] of agreements being adopted by Latin American

[92] 'Indecopi Inicia Procedimiento Contra Seis Líneas Navieras Por Presuntas Prácticas Colusorias En El Servicio de Transporte Marítimo Internacional de Carga Rodante – Inicio – Indecopi'.

[93] ICN, *Co-Operation between Competition Agencies in Cartel Investigations* 7.

[94] For a definition of the term 'spaghetti bowl' see Kotera, 'RIETI – What Is the "Spaghetti Bowl Phenomenon" of FTAs?'.

countries demonstrate the willingness of competition authorities to cooperate or at least to declare their intentions to share information and work together towards a common objective: namely, the fight against anti-competitive practices taking place in the region.

In 1996, the Agreement between Chile and the MERCOSUR countries included competition and consumer protection-related provisions, which promoted measures to discipline anti-competitive practices[95] and the adoption of a most-favoured nation clause,[96] and established the path for the authorities to implement a certain level of cooperation and understanding.[97]

In 1999, the US and Brazil signed a landmark agreement on competition law and issues which included a number of provisions concerning cooperation in both the notification and enforcement of competition cases.[98] In the same year, Chile adopted a competition chapter with the Central American countries. This was more comprehensive than the one signed with MERCOSUR, as it included provisions on cooperation that adopted competition provisions that would nullify the effects of anticompetitive practices, thereby undermining the benefits of the free trade agreement,[99] as well as provisions on providing common definitions on monopolies and SOEs.[100] The Chile-Central America RTA led to the adoption in 2003 of a MOU specifically on competition matters between Chile and Costa Rica.[101] This was considered to be a pioneering measure, since at the time, only a few countries in the region had robust competition law enforcement records.[102] The competition provisions agreed were geared to set up general principles of the parties and to share tools and procedures to tackle anticompetitive practices in their respective territories.[103]

In 2004, Chile and Mexico entered into a comprehensive agreement which included positive comity provisions in the form of explicit notification procedures,[104] information-sharing provisions that observed domestic legal constraints,[105] coordinated action provisions,[106] and the crossing over of anticompetitive practices

[95] Chile & MERCOSUR, 'Chapter "Competition and Consumer Protection" of the Free Trade Agreement between Chile and MERCOSUR' (25 June 1996) Art 18.

[96] ibid Art 19.

[97] ibid Art 20.

[98] US & Brazilian Governments, 'Agreement between US and Brazil Regarding Cooperation between Their Competition Authorities in the Enforcement of Their Competition Laws'.

[99] Chile & Central American Countries, 'Chapter 15 'Competition Policy' of the Free Trade Agreement between Chile and Central America' (18 October 1999) Art 15.01.

[100] ibid Art 15.02.

[101] Costa Rica & Chilean governments, 'MoU on Competition Matters between the Ministry of Economy, Industry and Commerce of Costa Rica and the Fiscalia Nacional Economica of Chile' (6 August 2003).

[102] See more in Alvarez and Horna (2008).

[103] Costa Rica & Chilean governments, 'MoU on Competition Matters' Art II.

[104] Mexico & Chilean Governments, 'Agreement between the Competition Federal Commission of Mexico and the Fiscalia Nacional Economica of Chile' (14 June 2004) Art II.

[105] ibid Art III.

[106] ibid Art IV.

from one territory to the other.[107] The question remains, however, as to whether these provisions were implemented after the agreement came into force, as it appears that they were not triggered when Mexican enforcers were looking into the liquid oxygen cartel which had been sanctioned by Chile.[108]

Another active authority that has been signing bilateral agreements on both competition and consumer protection issues is the Panamanian Competition and Consumer Protection Authority. In 2007, Panama and Peru's competition authorities entered into an agreement to set up consultations between the two authorities.[109] In the same year, Panama and El Salvador signed the first intra-Central American competition agreement, which was very similar to the one signed by Panama and Peru.[110] In 2008, Panama and Costa Rica signed a cooperation agreement that went beyond simple notifications and provided positive comity actions, such as ways to address anti-competitive practices commissioned in one party's territory which affect the other,[111] similar to the Mexico-Chile Agreement. In 2009, Panama and Honduras also signed a cooperation agreement with detailed provisions on how to trigger cooperation when an anti-competitive practice taking place in one party's territory affects the other's territory.[112] El Salvador and Chile signed an agreement which incorporated technical assistance competition provisions as well as coordination actions where possible.

As we saw in chapter two, Brazil and Mexico show a strong record of enforcement of cartel cases and leniency applications in the region. Their cooperation with others in the region has likewise been exemplary. The Brazilian competition authority has inked cooperation agreements with Argentina,[113] Chile,[114] and Peru,[115] among others, while Mexico has signed cooperation agreements with Chile in 2004, El Salvador in 2007, Nicaragua in 2011 and Colombia,[116] the Dominican Republic and Ecuador in 2012.[117] These agreements allowed the

[107] ibid Art V.

[108] See below, section on the liquid oxygen cartels in Latin America.

[109] Peru & Panama Governments, 'Agreement in the Area of Competition and Consumer Protection between INDECOPI of Peru and ACODECO of Panama' (September 2007) Art III.

[110] Panama & El Salvador, 'Agreement between ACODECO of Panama and Superintendence of Competition of El Salvador in the Application of Competition Laws' (17 September 2007).

[111] See Costa Rica & Panama Governments, 'Agreement between COPROCOM of Costa Rica and ACODECO of Panama on Inter-Institutional Cooperation in the Area of Competition' (8 April 2008) Art V.

[112] Panama & Honduras, 'Agreement between ACODECO and the Comision Para La Defensa y Promoción de La Competencia of Honduras' (14 May 2009).

[113] For a comprehensive case study as to why the agreement between Brazil and Argentina did not work, see Botta (2009).

[114] Chile & Brazilian Governments, 'Cooperation Agreement between Fiscalia Nacional Economica of Chile and CADE of Brazil Regarding the Application of Their Competition Laws' (October 2008).

[115] Peru & Brazilian Governments, 'Cooperation Agreement between INDECOPI of Peru and CADE of Brazil' (29 July 2012).

[116] Colombia: the Superintendence of Industry and Commerce (SIC) has signed agreements with four of the seven jurisdictions under scrutiny: Ecuador, Panama, Peru and Mexico. Peru: INDECOPI has signed cooperation agreements with three of the seven jurisdictions under scrutiny: Chile, Colombia and Panama. Horna, 'Regional Coordination in Cartel Investigations: The Liquid Oxygen Case' 296.

[117] Peña (2014: 212).

possibility of notifications with respect to enforcement activities that may affect the other agency's interests, and also permitted consultations, technical cooperation, exchange of information (subject to the laws of each jurisdiction protecting confidential information), regular meetings and the granting of negative or positive comity considerations.[118] Whilst a number of bilateral agreements have been signed, the level of their implementation remains questionable:

> Even though many bilateral cooperation agreements have been signed among the different competition agencies throughout the region, actual utilization of these agreements remains low. Through some information informal cooperation has occurred, those cases are rare and did necessarily take place between with signed, formal cooperation agreements, but rather took place between official with good personal, informal ties.[119]

7.4.2. Sub-Regional Competition Regimes and Platforms

Three sub-regional competition platforms exist in Latin America: the Andean Community of Nations (*Comunidad Andina de Naciones,* or CAN), the Central American Network of Competition Authorities (*Red Centroamericana de Autoridades Nacionales encargadas del tema de Competencia*, or RECAC) and the Common Market of the Southern Cone (MERCOSUR). These organisations will be examined in the following section in order to assess the current state of sub-regional competition platforms in Latin America.

7.4.2.1. The CAN

Set up in the 1960s by Bolivia, Colombia, Ecuador, Peru and Venezuela[120] with the purpose of achieving a regional economic integration system amongst the signatory nations, the CAN is one of the oldest sub-regional organisations in Latin America.[121] In 1991, the CAN adopted competition provisions through Decision 285 that consisted more of an assessment of how to deal with trade barriers in the region rather than cross-border anticompetitive practices.[122] More progress was made in 2005, when Decision 608[123] provided a number of key powers for the Andean Community Secretariat (SG CAN)[124] to investigate cross-border anticompetitive practices through the setting up of the Andean Committee for the

[118] Horna, 'Regional Coordination in Cartel Investigations: The Liquid Oxygen Case' 295.
[119] Peña (2014: 212).
[120] Venezuela formally withdrew from the Andean Community of Nations due to the political reason that Colombia and Peru were about to start negotiations with the US on a regional trade agreement. Venezuela subsequently joined MERCOSUR. See Malamud, 'Venezuela's Withdrawal from the Andean Community of Nations and the Consequences for Regional Integration'.
[121] See Odello (2015).
[122] CAN Provision on Competition 1991 (Año VIII) 14.
[123] CAN Regional Competition Law 2005 (Año XXII) 1.
[124] Cortázar (2006).

Defence of Competition (CAN Committee),[125] which is composed of the national competition authorities of CAN member states. However, a 2012 assessment[126] reported under-enforcement of competition cases in CAN member states, with only one case in the palm-oil market, that was annulled by the Andean Tribunal in 2006/07.[127] During the first year of the implementation of Decision 608, the SG CAN and the CAN Committee mobilised an ambitious regional agenda in competition law enforcement[128] but it was limited due to the fact that two of the five members of the Community (Bolivia and Ecuador) had no competition law or authority in 2005. With the emergence of vigorous Bolivian and Ecuadorian

[125] The Andean Committee was created by virtue of Art 38 of the regional competition law decision 608, and is an essential part of the institutional mechanisms of the CAN. It institutionally interacts with the SG-CAN by virtue of assisting it in joint investigations. The Committee has two primary and formal functions: (i) to assist in the investigations carried out by the Andean Community Secretariat and (ii) to undertake advocacy activities. The latter shows the different underlying approaches and intentions under which the Andean Committee was created. Dealing with cross-border investigations and assisting the supranational authority in the investigations of cross-border anticompetitive behaviour are its main purpose. See Gaceta Oficial del Acuerdo de Cartagena.

[126] See Horna (2012).

[127] *Andean Community – Palm Oil Cartel* [2008] Tribunal de Justicia de la Comunidad Andina 01-AN-2006,02-AN-2006 y 01-AN-2007(Acumulados).

[128] During the second half of 2005, three ordinary meetings were held in September, October and November. As mentioned above, the Internal Regulations of the Committee were approved at the second meeting. Unfortunately, from 2006 to 2009, the Committee ceased operations as a result of several factors, including the change of political vision of the Bolivian government and the withdrawal of Venezuela as a member of the Andean Community, in 2006 and 2008, respectively. However, from September to December 2005, the Committee did address several issues, including a cross-border investigation. The latter was conducted under Decision 285 and discussed at the request of the Colombian delegation. In addition, the output of the Committee, as envisaged in accordance with the work plan approved at the second ordinary meeting of October 2005, consisted in issuing the following documents: (i) Procedural Regulations of Decision 608 to apply the community competition law provisions, (ii) Procedural Regulations of Decision 608 as national law for Bolivia and Ecuador, (iii) follow up on the consultancy work undergone to evaluate the feasibility of adopting a community law on mergers and acquisitions, (iv) proposal for a draft decision that will deal with unfair competition, (v) training workshops on recent regional legislation for Andean Community officials and Competition officials. In addition it was envisaged to sensitise judges from the Andean Court of Justice. Particular reference to Bolivian and Ecuadorian government officials and Academics, (vi) compilation of laws and jurisprudence on competition law in regulated sectors, and a compilation of law and jurisprudence on competition law in order to continue the work of the EU Competition Project. As can be seen from this ambitious work plan, the Committee's work was clearly going beyond mere policy coordination. Had all the output been completed under this framework, it would have had legally binding consequences under the meaning of the regional law and the Andean Community legal system. Unfortunately, none of this work was carried out during the subsequent ordinary meetings because they did not take place. Nonetheless, not only the institutional framework but also the legal provisions were converging for effective monitoring, compliance, and enforcement mechanisms. In addition, the role of domestic institutions is also envisaged in the enforcement of this internal regulation as the members of the Committee have their legal and domestic constraints which are sufficient to undertake the effective implementation of the internal regulations. Regrettably after the withdrawal of Venezuela from the Andean Community of Nations, the Committee went into a 'standstill situation' up to the present. However as regards the real-world change, cooperation did take place under the basis of regional technical assistance programmes that attempted to bring together the Member countries of the Committee through different initiatives at regional level. Andean Committee for the Defense of Competition, 'Minutes of the 2nd Ordinary Meeting of the Committee on 3 October 2005.' (Andean Community Secretariat 2005) Meeting report SG/R.CDC/II/ACTA 2.17.28.

competition authorities in 2010, there was more hope for the creation of a regional competition law.[129] In 2013, a Colombian company (ANGELCOM) invoked Decision 608, but unfortunately this action was dismissed at a preliminary stage of investigation due to insufficient evidence.[130]

In December 2015, another Colombian company (INTERNEXA) requested the opening of an investigation against an Ecuadorian telecoms company for an alleged abused of dominant position, which was endorsed by the SG CAN in early 2016.[131] In 2016, a Colombian citizen invoked Decision 608 to investigate an alleged regional cartel in the markets for nappies, notebook and toilet paper. Despite having unlawful allegations in the regional market, the investigation was closed due to the prescription of the action before the CAN.[132] Later in 2016 the SG CAN opened a new investigation in the regional market for tissue paper[133] and it was expected that during 2017 the case would be ruled by the Andean Tribunal.

7.4.2.2. The RECAC

Central America is a sub-region that has a decades-long tradition of regional and sub-regional economic integration.[134] With the furtherance of competition policy in the sub-region, particularly with the enactment of competition laws and the organisation of competition authorities, the Central American competition authorities formed a network in 2006 in order to maintain contact with each other, develop specific regional projects (such as market studies) and share some information about the cases that they handle.[135]

Despite the efforts made by RECAC, however, major challenges faced the region: first, the failure to enact a competition law in Guatemala despite efforts carried out by the government and the international community;[136] second, the absence of a regional competition legal framework; third, the lack of a workable definition of what is confidential; fourth, the lack of a competition culture that

[129] Horna (2012: 338).

[130] Roa, 'Evolución y Perspectivas Del Derecho de La Competencia Andino' Slide 19.

[131] *Andean Community – Opening of an investigation – Abuse of Dominant case in the Andean region* [2016].

[132] *Andean Community – Dismiss a Regional Cartel investigation in the markets of Nappies, Books and Toilet Paper for having prescripted the action* [2016].

[133] *Andean Community – Opening of a Cartel Investigation in the Tissue Paper Market against Kimberly Clark* [2016].

[134] CEPAL (2009). For a comprehensive history of the Central American Integration see Equipo Técnico Multidisciplinario (ETM) (1999).

[135] Odio-Rohrmoser (2016: 145).

[136] Pursuant to the EU-CA Association Agreement a Central American competition regulation and a competition authority shall be established according to Art 25 of the 'Protocol to the General Treaty on Central American Economic Integration' and Art 21 of the Framework Agreement for the Establishment of Central American Customs Union, within a period of seven years from the moment the Agreement comes into force 'EU-Central America Association Agreement – Trade – European Commission'.

could foster voluntary compliance in the private sector.[137] All the (then) heads of the Central American competition authorities agreed that political willingness was necessary to move forward, and identified their goals as the enactment of the competition law in Guatemala and the adoption of a regional competition law.[138]

It is worth noting that the work of RECAC is fully endorsed by the policymakers in charge of the sub-economic integration in Central America, represented by the Council of Ministers of Economy of Central America (COMIECO).[139] Despite the endorsement, it was recently reported that the members of COMIECO have failed to reach a consensus as to the scope and extent of the regional competition law proposed by RECAC.[140]

7.4.2.3. The MERCOSUR

In 1991, the governments of Argentina, Brazil, Paraguay, and Uruguay signed a treaty that gave rise to the Common Market of the South (MERCOSUR).[141] MERCOSUR became the largest economic bloc of South America, representing 72 per cent of South America's land area, 70 per cent of its population, and 80 per cent of its gross domestic product.[142] Competition provisions were included in a further protocol, known as the Fortaleza Protocol, which established a common competition statute to be implemented by a regional authority, the Committee for the Defence of Competition (CDC).[143]

The Fortaleza Protocol also provided for the distribution of competences between national and regional authorities, requiring the transfer of powers

[137] Odio-Rohrmoser (2016: 145).

[138] Escolán, former Superintendente de Competencia of El Salvador, points to three different challenges the countries face in implementing a regional competition law and policy: (a) the need to have a competition law and a competition authority in Guatemala, (b) asymmetries among countries, in terms of resources and experience, (c) the political issues and institutional arrangements, such as the resistance of some countries to accept jurisdiction of regional entities; the need to ensure a fair distribution of the costs and burden of maintaining a regional authority; and the need to ensure proper, effective coordination with local competition authorities, regulators and so on. According to Escolán, solving these issues will take long, so in the meantime joint enforcement may start by collaborating in the merger control. For instance, when the transaction has a regional dimension the review could be made by one agency. This would save time and resources for the authorities and the parties involved, as only one filing would be needed and one agency would do the review of the effects of the merger in the region as a whole. For Sittenfeld, information exchange is necessary but difficult to achieve. The gap in the level of resources and capacity of the authorities must be narrowed particularly in the way they interpret and apply, key concepts like confidential information, exemptions, efficiency, remedies and so on. There must be a strong political will to ensure all government agencies involved work in the same direction with the conviction that competition policy can have a real impact for the people. Ibid: 157–58.

[139] Horna (2016: 322).

[140] Interview with Lozano.

[141] Treaty of Asuncion establishing the Common Market between Argentina, Brazil, Paraguay and Uruguay 1991.

[142] Nilsen Ribeiro and Guimarães (2017: 315).

[143] The drafting of the Fortaleza Protocol is much closer to EU law rather than US antitrust provisions as the EU case law plays a 'non-negligible role' in the interpretation and application of national competition laws in Argentina and Brazil. Filho, Lixinski and Giupponi (2010: 301).

from the national competition authorities to the CDC.[144] As the Protocol was de facto unenforced,[145] one might have anticipated inactivity on the part of the MERCOSUR institutions; however, this changed when the member countries of MERCOSUR repealed the Fortaleza Protocol with a new 'Agreement for the Defence of Competition of MERCOSUR' under decision 43/10 of 2010 (the New Agreement[146]). The New Agreement removed the regional competition agenda from the negotiation table and focused on strengthening forms of cooperation among the national competition authorities through initiatives such as a new consultation mechanism.[147]

Some have credibly argued that external factors, such as the global crisis of 2007–10 (also known as the subprime mortgage crisis), triggered the creation of protectionist policies that led to the adoption of the New Agreement.[148] Arguably, the repeal of the Fortaleza Protocol represented the rejection of the ideas of a sub-regional supranational competition authority in MERCOSUR and a concomitant regional competition law for South America. The New Agreement opted for a less ambitious agenda that was perhaps more consistent with the socio-economic context of competition authorities at the national level across its member states.[149]

Argentina's competition law system has been problematic for a number of years, as observed by the chairman of Argentina's competition authority: 'the National Commission for Competition Defence had all sort of problems, from infrastructure to human resources, and a large back-log of files, some of them very old, that had to be dealt with … [and] competition law enforcement in Argentina has been erratic and subject to political considerations'.[150] Meanwhile, Paraguay is only just starting to develop a competition culture, having adopted its competition law in 2013 and possessing a fully operational competition authority by 2016.[151]

A fifth member joined MERCOSUR after leaving the CAN in 2006. In 2013, Venezuela enacted the Fair Price Law which created a new competition authority

[144] Nilsen Ribeiro and Guimarães (2017: 318).

[145] The Fortaleza Protocol was ratified only by Brazil and Paraguay. The fact that Paraguay is still in the process of adopting a national competition law, and that the second member of the Mercosur in terms of trade volume (Argentina) has not ratified the Fortaleza Protocol, made the Protocol de facto unenforced. A number of reasons may explain why Argentina has always refused to ratify the Fortaleza Protocol. In particular, according to Peña, Argentina was concerned by the consensus method followed in the Protocol, whereby a MS could block a CCM's Directive which would affect its industrial policy interests (Peña, 2001). In addition, even though the Protocol was intended to sanction cross-border anti-competitive practices like predatory pricing, the Mercosur MS never agreed to abolish the intra-block anti-dumping duties. Botta (2011: 10).

[146] Acuerdo de Defensa de la Competencia del MERCOSUR.

[147] Botta (2011: 11).

[148] Nilsen Ribeiro and Guimarães (2017: 319).

[149] Interview with Coloma.

[150] Competition Policy International.

[151] Paraguay – Appointment of the Investigation Director of the Competition Authority by the President of the Republic 2016.

called the Superintendence for the Defence of Socioeconomic Rights (the Venezuelan Competition Authority). The Venezuelan Competition Authority set reasonable profit margins as a benchmark to intervene or not in competition cases. That particular approach made enforcement weak and purely political. It has been asserted that enforcement of competition rules in Venezuela is 'highly selective and bribery-inviting, extortion in exchange for turning a blind eye',[152] a situation markedly different from that in 2007.[153]

7.4.3. Parallel Domestic Cartel Investigations

The purpose of this sub-section is to ascertain whether the domestic liquid oxygen cartels prosecuted in seven jurisdictions in Latin America amounted to a truly regional CBC, as in the meaning provided in chapter two, or were merely domestic cartels with some regional dimensions because the companies that were part of the investigations were almost the same.

Between 2000 and 2010, seven jurisdictions administratively, and in some cases judicially, sanctioned domestic cartels in the liquid oxygen market in Panama (2001), Argentina (2005), Chile (2007), Peru, Brazil and Colombia (2010).[154] In 2011, Mexico declined to sanction this anticompetitive practice due to weak evidence; nevertheless the cartel has been proved to have operated during the 1980s. With the exceptions of Colombia and Mexico, all cases concerned bid-rigging activities in the procurement of liquid oxygen for public hospitals or industrial activities. Below is a brief summary of the facts of these cases:

a. **Panama (2008):** the Panamanian Competition Authority at the time (CLICAC, now called ACODECO), established that the defendant firms colluded to organise the sales of industrial oxygen.[155] CLICAC presented statistical analysis as circumstantial evidence of the existence of the collusive practice, since there was a lack of direct evidence. The Court of First Instance, in 2004, and the Court of Second Instance (High Court), in 2008, awarded the decision to CLICAC. The court imposed a fine of $100,000 against each of the two economic agents involved in the

[152] Bertelsmaan Stiftung's Transformation Index (BTI) (2016: 17).
[153] *Cf* López-Galdos (2007).
[154] This section is based on Nilsen Ribeiro and Guimarães (2017).
[155] The collusive agreement consisted in distributing the rows (provinces) of the bid between two offer bidders. The row of the winning bidder showed a competitive offer of 0.01 USD in tanks of 12 and 14 cubic feet. In the rows of the losing bidder, a higher price offer was shown in tanks of 12 and 14 cubic feet. The rows were awarded by adding the prices of tanks of 12, 24 and 200 cubic feet. In tanks of 200 cubic feet the price offered was the real one. CLICAC based its statements on report tests made in the Social Security Administration, documents obtained in an exhibitory diligence and statistical expertise. In the statistical report, a probability (close to zero) that the two investigated companies had not agreed to submit a competitive proposal in any row of the bid, was calculated *Panama Oxigeno Medico* (Juzgado Noveno de Circuito de la Provincia de Panamá).

attempt to divide the national medical oxygen market, which was the maximum fine in 2008 under Act 29 of 1996.[156]

b. **Chile (2007):** after an investigation, the National Economic Prosecutor (FNE) brought a complaint against four oxygen providers (Aga SA, Air Liquid Chile SA, Indura SA and Praxair Chile Ltda), arguing that they had engaged in coordinated behaviour aimed at dividing the market, particularly in public hospitals. The Chilean Competition Tribunal (TDLC) accepted the application made by the FNE. The Tribunal found that the four enterprises had interfered with the procurement process conducted by the health procurement entity, CENABAST, to provide liquid oxygen to public hospitals in 2004.[157]

c. **Argentina (2005):** the *Comisión Nacional de Defensa de la Competencia* CNDC launched an investigation in 2001, when hospitals encountered issues in securing contracts for liquid oxygen from alternative suppliers. It was observed that the hospitals received bids only from their incumbent supplier. When competing bids were submitted, the incumbent was usually the lowest bidder. The hospitals' complaints led the Secretariat for Competition, Deregulation, and Consumers Defence (the predecessor to the Secretariat for Technical Coordination) to instruct CNDC to begin an investigation. The market for this product was highly concentrated, entry was difficult and there were effectively only four suppliers.[158] Following the investigation, CNDC fined the Argentine subsidiaries of Praxair, Air Liquide, AGA and Indura a total of $24.3 million in July 2005.

d. **Peru (2010):** the Peruvian Competition Authority, INDECOPI, imposed a fine of almost $8 million against the Peruvian subsidiaries of Praxair, AGA and Messer for having organised a market allocation cartel through the bid processes medical liquid oxygen between 1999 and 2004.[159]

e. **Brazil (2010):** CADE issued a landmark decision fining the medical and industrial gas producers Air Liquide, Air Products, IBG, Linde and White Martins more than $1.4 billion for price-fixing, customer allocation and bid-rigging. White Martins was fined approximately $1.1 billion as a repeat offender, the largest fine ever in the history of antitrust enforcement in Brazil, and the third largest in the

[156] This investigation began when a third player presented a claim in December 1997 asserting that the prospective bidding process had technical requirements that amounted to the imposition of anti-competitive barriers that favoured the other two companies that were finally sanctioned. It is important to mention as a particularity of the case, that officers of CLICAC were present at the opening of the bids, so a conclusion that could be drawn is that regardless of the close 'surveillance' of the authority of the bidding procedure, circumstantial evidence to support the existence of a concerted practice was detected. It has to be considered that CLICAC did not have powers to raid premises and Panama does not have an immunity and leniency programme for cartel detection. This kind of 'surveillance' when relevant bidding procedures are in course is seen also in other countries such as Chile (bidding process for TV transmission of soccer matches) but today is not a standard procedure in this country *Panama Oxigeno Medico* (Tercer Tribunal Superior de Justicia del Primer Distrito Judicial de Panamá).

[157] *Chile Oxigeno Liquido* [2006] Tribunal de Defensa de la Libre Competencia Sentencia No. 43/2006.

[158] *Argentina Oxigeno Liquido* [2005] Com Nac Def Competencia.

[159] *Peru Oxigeno Liquido* [2010] INDECOPI 051-2010/CLC-INDECOPI.

world at the time. CADE found that the cartel had been active since at least 1998 and that it had harmed the health-care industry and several other businesses. CADE also levied substantial fines on seven executives.[160]

f. **Colombia (2010):** following a five-year investigation of Fábrica Nacional de Oxigeno SA (Linde Colombia SA), Oxígenos de Colombia Ltda (Oxicol) and Gases Industriales de Colombia SA (Cryogas), SIC issued a ruling against the companies for having entered into concerted practices which were aimed at obstructing or impeding the entry of other firms into the Colombian market and trading channels for the distribution of liquid oxygen.[161]

g. **Mexico (2011)**: Mexico's CFC initiated formal proceedings in 2006, with the investigation covering practices that began in 1983. According to the testimony of former employees, the firms had an agreement that included cover denominations through different colours (red for AGA, blue for Infra Group, black for Praxair). The investigation also produced evidence of bid-rigging behaviour in detriment of the government petroleum producer, PEMEX. In 2009, a statement of objections was presented to the CFC. Although there were allegations of hard-core evidence obtained from testimonies during the hearings, requests for information and other economic evidence, CFC decided not to issue sanctions relating to any liquid oxygen cartel. All accusations were thereafter dismissed and the case was closed.[162]

Table 7.3 illustrates the investigated companies of the liquid oxygen cartel in Latin America.

It must be noted that, despite the recurrent and overlapping anti-competitive business patterns involved in the foregoing investigations and the informal contacts between the enforcers of the relevant Latin American competition authorities, no effective coordination of enforcement actions or sharing of non-confidential information occurred between these Latin American competition authorities. Had the Argentine authorities detected a problem in this market in 2001 and raided the premises of the companies involved, perhaps some of the actions of these multinational liquid oxygen companies would have been detected and prevented in other jurisdictions, well before the other competition authorities intervened.[163]

[160] The CADE decision led to a significant number of private actions for damages, including a collective action filed by more than 250 hospitals, in which a preliminary injunction was issued in order to displace the collusive price equilibrium. CADE´s investigation involved the production of relevant communications and documents seized after inspections and also obtained from telephone interceptions. CADE´s core analysis refers to the different rules implemented to stage the allocation of clients and markets by the defendants. The use of these powers resulted in extensive litigation due to the fact they were exercised in the context of parallel criminal proceedings against individuals implicated *Brazil – Industrial and Hospital Gases* [2010] Administrative Council for Economic Defense Case No. 08012.009888/2003-70.

[161] *Colombia Oxigeno Liquido* [2010] Superintendencia de Industria y Comercio Resolution No. 65477.

[162] *Mexico Oxigeno Líquido* [2011] Comisión Federal de Competencia DE-022-2006.

[163] 'In an ideal world, following the lead by Argentina and Panama, competition authorities in Peru, Chile, Colombia, Brazil could have launched an international investigation on a presumably domestic

Table 7.3 Companies involved in the Liquid Oxygen Cartels in Latin America

	Multinational companies involved				
Country	**Air Liquide**	**AGA**	**Praxair**	**Messer**	**Local companies**
Argentina	AL Argentina	✓	✓	✓	INDURA Argentina
Brazil	AL Brazil	✓	White Martins		Air Products Brasil, Industria Brasileria de Gases (IBG)
Chile	✓	✓	✓		INDURA Chile
Colombia			Oxigenos de Colombia (Praxair)		Fábrica Nacional de Oxigenos (LINDE) Colombia
Mexico	✓ (not relevant market share)	✓	✓ (Ahora Praxair absorbió a AGA)		INFRA Mexico
Panama			?		Aceti-Oxigento & Distribuidora de Gases Industriales
Peru		✓	✓	✓	

Source: Horna. See note 459 *supra*.

The original question raised at the outset is to ascertain whether or not Latin American competition authorities did face a truly regional CBC in the liquid oxygen cases. The answer is positive because of the following reasons: (1) as illustrated in the table, in the majority of cases, the companies were transnational, being Praxair and AGA in almost all domestic cartel investigations; and (2) the conduct was the same: bid-rigging activities in public procurement domestic activities. Had Latin America had a supranational regional authority, if the conduct had been taking place in more than two jurisdictions, the authority would have initiated a

cartel with regional dimensions. As the above experience shows, this type of cartel investigation has several advantages. Multinational companies have a physical presence, which allows authorities in affected countries to employ traditional investigative instruments, including dawn raids. There is no issue of the service of documents. Exchange of informal information may be enough to trigger follow-on investigations. These enforcement actions may in time be successfully coordinated in different countries and could lead to secure evidence that otherwise could be destroyed. Another great advantage, especially for developing countries, is that it allows them to build up reputation as active anti-cartel enforcers among multinational companies who are normally members of global cartels …' Horna (2016).

regional investigation and declared a regional CBC affecting all Latin American markets. In chapter 9, the research explores the case of the Airline sector and provides some solutions to this problem.

7.4.4. Informal Cooperation Arrangements

In March 2013, those who had handled the liquid oxygen cartel in their different jurisdictions discussed their experience at the International Bid-Rigging Workshop: Liquid Oxygen cases in Latin America.[164] Several months later, in June 2013, the Peruvian Competition Agency proposed to its South American peers the creation of a forum of competition authorities to deal with cross-border anti-competitive practices.[165]

In September 2013, during the OECD Latin American Forum, the competition authorities of Chile, Colombia and Peru signed the Lima Declaration, which aimed to establish a platform for the exchange of experiences and training among the participating competition agencies.[166] It has been reported that 'since the signing of the Lima Declaration, the three competition authorities and UNCTAD have met regularly to exchange views and strategies on the enforcement of competition law in cases of mutual interest and identify potential cross-border enforcement actions'.[167] Thanks to this informal exchange of experiences, cooperation in the investigation of cases and the sharing of intelligence as well as agency information became possible. As a result, two connected markets in these three jurisdictions have been investigated and sanctioned: the tissue and nappy cartels perpetrated by the multinational company Kimberly Clark.[168]

As discussed, Colombia sanctioned the nappy cartel in 2016, following a lengthy investigation that started in 2013. Thanks to informal cooperation consultations between Colombia, Chile and Peru, Chilean and Peruvian enforcers had access to specific information concerning market allocation in the region, where connected markets between tissue and nappies, two product markets of Kimberly Clark, were being manipulated.[169] This information also prompted the competition authority in Ecuador to open an investigation later in 2016.[170] It is clear from these developments that the unfortunate experience of the liquid oxygen cartel

[164] UNCTAD, 'International Bid-Rigging Workshop: Liquid Oxygen Cases in Latin America'.

[165] Tassano (2014: 5).

[166] Chile/Colombia/Peru Governments, 'Lima Declaration' (September 2013).

[167] UNCTAD, 'Informal Cooperation among Competition Agencies in Specific Cases' 15.

[168] 'El Cartel de Kimberly Clark (with Images) · Laradiodelsur' (*Storify*).

[169] Peruvian competition regulator INDECOPI confirmed the charges against Productos Tissue del Perú SA, local branch of Chilean paper giant CMPC, along with Kimberly Clark, over a far-reaching price-fixing agreement involving several tissue paper manufacturers, in what is known locally as the 'Comfort Cartel'. See 'Perú: Regulator Confirms Tissue Cartel Acting in Peru, Colombia and Chile | Competition Policy International'.

[170] NR consultants, 'They Investigate Cartel of Paper Tissue in Ecuador |'.

prosecution will not happen again, at least in that part of the world. The analysis and the implications of these interconnected markets will be further assessed in Chapter 9.

7.5. Summary

This chapter has looked at the particular dynamics of Latin America and examined how regional and sub-regional cooperation efforts may provide additional avenues to counteract the effects of CBCs in this context. The classification presented here sheds light on the specific issues encountered by young or small competition authorities for each type of CBC. As can be seen, with the exception of some successful examples (Mexico in the lysine cartel and Peru with the roll-off cargo cartel) Latin American competition authorities struggled to get the information needed from mature competition authorities to start the investigation of these cartels.

The chapter also provided an overview of the main efforts carried out by Latin American countries in the fight against the five different types of CBCs (as presented in chapter two). In the area of bilateral competition agreements and competition provisions in regional trade agreements, it is patent that there has been an extraordinary move towards competition authorities signing with their peer agencies a great number of cooperation agreements. Of course, the implementation of these agreements has been slow in some cases; a lack of implementation led to the unfortunate parallel proceedings of the liquid oxygen cartel cases in Latin America, examined in this chapter, where it is clear that conjoined action would have been much more efficient.

An interesting development in 2016 was the revival of the regional competition law enforcement system in the Andean Community of Nations (CAN) with the unexpected participation of the private sector (Internexa), in particular from Colombia. While this is the case for the Andean Community, the experience of MERCOSUR suffered a drawback when the idea of having a future supranational authority dealing with competition issues was completely lifted from the negotiation agenda. Similarly, Central American countries are still struggling to put together a regional competition law and an institutional framework that can bring together policymakers (COMIECO) and competition authorities.

It seems that all points to the promising future of informal cooperation. Already the signing of the Lima Declaration by Chile, Colombia and Peru has produced tangible results, in particular in information sharing in open cartel investigations. In this regard, it seems that this might be the road to take in future, particularly bodies such as MERCOSUR are suffering setbacks.

Finally, it is important to note the nature of multinational companies operating the region. As part of their core operations, these companies have their businesses in several countries, allowing them multi-market contact, and this frequent contact in turn facilitates the formation and operation of cartels across the region, thereby forming intra-regional cartels. The was the case in Latin America when multinational companies supplying medical liquid oxygen to hospitals formed bid-rigging domestic cartels in several jurisdictions, in which the subsidiaries of these multinational companies operated.

And so, multinational companies closely observe the developments and capabilities of cartel enforcement activity at the local level in different Latin American jurisdictions, and act in accordance with their limited abilities to counteract the effect of their illicit activities. This is also reflected in the way businesses comply or do not comply with the enforcement of competition laws. It is also clear that in some instances (e.g. the parallel liquid oxygen cases) multinational companies did not see progress or any serious effort to find new instruments for competition authorities to coordinate, cooperate and converge in its actions. That, of course, changed as of 2013 onwards in Latin America, thanks in part to the adoption of the Lima Declaration by three countries. However, the problem of coordination and cooperation in the region needs to be addressed because more and more regional trade agreements and bilateral agreements between Latin American countries will increase the trade flows, in particular within the process of regional integration taking place in Central America, where companies have a special motive to foster regional business alliances. A case study on the airline sector will be explored and discussed in chapter nine.

8

Strengthening Cooperation between Mature and Young Competition Authorities in Transnational Cross-Border Cartel Investigations

The dynamics for trust development between mature and young competition authorities differ from those between young competition authorities, particularly when dealing with transnational CBCs. In fact, in a transnational CBC investigation, mature and young competition authorities would normally need to interact due to the diversity of jurisdictions that the CBC affects.[1] In this case it is necessary to develop a special type of trust, where the mature competition authority is willing to cooperate with a younger one despite the costs of cooperation and the issue of distributional conflicts as detailed earlier in this research. In addition, there should be an incentive to share certain types of information at the investigatory phase despite the fact that the information might be protected under confidentiality rules. How the sharing of that information is to be conducted, and under which platform, is another important building block to be developed in any transnational cooperation scheme.

This chapter proposes a three-pronged approach. First, it introduces a type of experimental trust between mature and young competition authorities. Second, it develops a concept of sharable information whether the mature competition authority is at the pre-investigatory or investigatory phase. Third, it builds on the platform in which the cooperation should take place, whether through the ICN registration framework or through a complementary feature provided by the UN platform.

[1] Conversely, if a regional CBC is at stake, normally, it may include a handful of young competition authorities' jurisdictions that are part of the regional grouping with a regional trade agreement that could also have competition provisions. As a result, the dynamics for trust development may depend on how the intra-trade relations between the member countries are shaped and whether trade and competition authorities of that particular regional grouping have a workable level of cooperation. See chapter nine.

8.1. Introducing Calculus-Based Trust Activities

Chapter four outlined the main problems as to why competition authorities do not trust each other, and chapter six proposed solutions that unfortunately did not satisfactorily address the issue of trust between young competition authorities, as these solutions focused on issues that take place at the investigatory or post-investigatory phases, as assessed in chapter six. As competition authorities are public institutions organised in a certain structure and bound by certain public servant rules, there is a given role that trust can play in explaining business behaviour in interactions between competition. Hence, chapter eight outlines a solution driven by an interdisciplinary approach to improve the dynamics of trust development between institutions, based on the academic literature that has developed over the years on this subject matter.

The structure of the present sub-section is as follows: first, the conceptual framework of trust development is outlined, with reference to other disciplines such as management and organisation studies and related subjects. Second, how these concepts can apply to the world of authorities dealing with competition issues is explained. Third, specific examples of how trust has been developed in certain regional groupings in the world are detailed, in particular from instances of cooperation between mature competition authorities and young competition authorities.

8.1.1. Conceptual Framework for Trust Development

Chapter four introduced some concepts as to how trust can be developed so as to explain what is lacking in the international relations between competition authorities. Amongst them was the term 'knowledge-based trust'. The purpose of this sub-section is to explore the meaning of this term and to deepen the theoretical framework about the definitions, approaches, and types of trust in professional relationships and consequently to find ways to develop trust in organisations or institutions.

Trust is customarily regarded as 'the glue that holds a relationship together',[2] but indeed what the term 'trust' means exactly has received attention in several branches of social science such as psychology, sociology, political science, economics, anthropology, history and socio-biology, and each branch of social approaches the problem of trust through its own disciplinary lenses and filters.[3] Different definitions of trust therefore emerge from the above.

For instance, trust can be regarded as a manifestation of calculation and self-interest, or as a combination of relations dependent on the underlying social reality.

[2] Lewicki (2006: 92).
[3] ibid: 93.

Recent literature has included three approaches to trust: (1) trust as accumulated capital, where trust is seen as individualist interests to uphold one's reputation; (2) trust as risk, as all transactions boil down to a calculation of the costs versus the benefits to be derived from a relationship; and (3) trust as a relationship of delegation that will depend on the broader social network than the relationship itself.[4] As a result, trust can be developed in different ways if one is to reach institutional-based trust and interaction-based trust. As such, trusting someone builds on a decision which is based on an assessment of the other party's competence, integrity, and benevolence, including a quick and rough semi-conscious assessment of the unrecoverable costs that would occur if the other party turned out to be untrustworthy.

For these reasons, while there are several definitions and conceptualisations of trust between business relationships, a definition provided by sociologists and economists that focuses on trust as an institutional phenomenon describes it as a 'belief that future interactions will continue, based on explicit or implicit rules and norms'.[5] As such, trust becomes critical in building effective working relationships in organisational contexts. As noted by Bachmann and Inkpen:

> Trust has become a central concept in explaining business behaviour in organizational contexts. The ability to create trust has been widely recognized as hugely valuable because it can significantly reduce transaction costs and lead to the creation of new ideas, for example when knowledge is pooled in inter-organizational relationships.[6]

Organisational scholars have introduced the concept of 'institutional-based' trust in contrast to the concept of 'interaction-based' trust. While the latter would develop 'on the basis of personal face-to-face experience between two (or more) individuals without references made or being necessary to make institutional',[7] the former 'is a form of individual or collective action that is constitutively embedded in the institutional environment in which a relationship is placed'.[8] From an economic point of view, trust is related to confidence under the principal–agent relationship whereby the relations between them need to be 'sufficiently strong so that the agent will not cheat even though it may be rational economic behaviour to do so'.[9]

Within the concept of institutional-based trust, Shapiro et al suggested three types of trust in professional relationships: deterrence-based trust, knowledge-based trust and identification-based trust.[10] In what follows, each of these types of trust shall be examined.

[4] Reynaud (2017: 128).

[5] Citing Rousseau, Sitkin, Burt and Camerer, Lewicki conceptualised trust as a phenomenon within and among institutions. See Lewicki (2006: 93).

[6] Bachmann and Inkpen (2011: 281).

[7] ibid: 284.

[8] ibid.

[9] Reynaud (2017: 128).

[10] See Shapiro, Sheppard and Cheraskin (1992).

8.1.1.1. Deterrence-Based or Calculus-Based Trust (CBT)

Deterrence-based or calculus-based trust (CBT) is sustained by the threat of punishment if consistency is not maintained, whereby individuals would do what they promise because they fear the consequences of not doing what they say. Therefore, the significant motivator of this type of trust is the threat of punishment rather than the promise of reward. In economic terms, this type of trust is 'ongoing, market-oriented, a mere economic calculation whose value is determined by the outcomes resulting from creating and sustaining the relationship relative to the costs of maintaining or severing it'.[11]

An example of this type of trust can be seen in the MOU signed between a mature authority (US) and a young but large authority (China) in 2011,[12] as presented in chapter three. Both authorities assessed the costs and benefits in entering into an MOU, based on interdependence factors marked by geopolitical global dynamics between the US and China trade relations. Being the two most powerful economies in the world, there were associated costs if one of the parties destroyed trust by cheating or cozening the other; in this case the deterrence element was the more dominant motivator than the benefit-seeking elements. Thus, punishment for non-consistency was more likely to produce CBT than rewards or incentives derived from maintaining trust. Six years (2011–17) after the signature of the MOU, there is little likelihood of these countries signing a more comprehensive cooperation agreement, as CBT is the only trust that can be maintained giving the changing geopolitical dynamics and this type of trust is less conducive to fully fledged cooperation.[13]

8.1.1.2. Knowledge-Based Trust (KBT)

Unlike CBT, knowledge-based trust, or KBT, relies on information rather than deterrence. KBT is grounded in behavioural predictability, where one has enough information about others to understand them and to accurately predict their behaviour.[14] KBT is based on reciprocal information of the counterpart: 'the better we know the other individual, the more accurately we can predict what he or she will do'.[15] In this regard, KBT will remain as long as the other party remains predictable, that is they act consistently with our knowledge and thus confirm it.

There are three dimensions of KBT: information, predictability and accurate prediction.[16] An example of this KBT can be found in the signing of the informal cooperation agreement, the Lima Declaration, as discussed in chapter seven.

[11] Lewicki and Bunker (1995: 145).
[12] US & Chinese Governments, 'MoU on Antitrust and Antimonopoly Cooperation'.
[13] For a more detailed geopolitical analysis of the relations between US and China, see Lee (2012).
[14] Lewicki and Bunker (1995: 142).
[15] ibid: 42.
[16] Shapiro, Sheppard and Cheraskin (1992).

KBT was critical in the negotiation of this agreement between Colombia, Chile and Peru as peers to work together against CBCs and CAPs. UNCTAD was instrumental in facilitating the prior negotiations, together with the Peruvian Competition Authority (INDECOPI) when they organised a session with all South American counterparts in June 2013, months prior to the signing of the agreement in September 2013. Repeated interactions and regular communications between the three heads of the authorities enhanced their ability to understand the way how the others enforce competition rules domestically. Well before the regional model for cooperation between the cartel units of the Nordic competition authorities formed in 2000, the Nordic countries (Denmark, the Faroe Islands, Finland, Greenland, Iceland, Norway and Sweden) enjoyed a high level of mutual trust and were characterised by ethnic homogeneity, Protestant religious traditions, good government, wealth and income equality.[17]

8.1.1.3. *Identification-Based Trust (IBT)*

IBT involves the full internalisation of the other's desires and intentions take place as a result of a complete and mutual understanding of both parties or institutions to the extent that each can effectively act for the other without surveillance or monitoring of the trusted activities.[18] In fact, the 'acting for each other' in IBT relations would mean that the parties may come to know each other better and identify with the other in such a way that the parties would understand what they should do in order to sustain the others' trust in the long run.

A classic example of IBT in the competition world is the Nordic Competition Network (NCN), discussed in chapter three.[19] The NCN has developed as a result of these critical contextual factors.[20] Based on IBT, members of the NCN would meet to discuss common enforcement interests prior to making investigation into a business with possible links to other Nordic countries.

8.1.2. Applicability of the Framework to Competition Authorities

As discussed above, CBT, KBT and IBT are different types of trust that can be found in cross-border consultations that are held between competition authorities. If one looks closely at these types of trust, it becomes apparent that CBT governs

[17] For a detailed analysis of how national level of social trust can be achieved in different settings worlwide as opposed to the Nordic model, see Delhey and Newton (2005).

[18] Lewicki (2006: 96).

[19] For a detailed analysis of how national level of social trust can be achieved in different settings worldwide as opposed to the Nordic model, see Delhey and Newton (2005).

[20] Critical factors such as cultural similarities, harmonised competition legislations, among others. Nordic Cartel Network (2012: 222–23).

the relations between mature and young competition authorities based on the rationale that a scarce level of knowledge of each other is a constant factor between these institutions. According to the head of a relatively advanced but still young competition authority, Chile's, the best way to interact with mature competition authorities is to show them how case-interaction cooperation can be mutually beneficial to the two competition authorities, so that the mature competition authority would slowly understand the importance of engaging with younger authorities that can actually contribute to their own investigation at the domestic level.[21] In some situations, a younger competition authority wishing to enter cooperation with a mature one might like to incorporate a third party convener into the cooperation scheme so as to provide the credentials needed for the first-time encounters.[22]

Conversely, KBT can govern the relations between young competition authorities where they have more incentives to come forward with the information and to trust each other, as in the example of the Lima Declaration. In some instances, IBT can develop, but perhaps only between mature competition authorities due to a number of critical factors that are embedded in the institutional economics of these countries because of the way laws and institutions are set up.

Insofar as competition authorities are public institutions, institutional-based trust is the governing feature of cooperative relationships; insofar as they are composed of civil servants, however, attention must also be paid to personal interaction and the factors involved therein. However, in young competition authorities a high turnover of staff is common, and so there is the caveat that one cannot rely on personal trust dynamics and therefore the reputation of the young competition authority is the critical asset in its relations with mature authorities.

8.1.3. Building Trust Through Technical Assistance and Capacity-Building

At worldwide conferences such as the International Competition Network (ICN)[23] or UNCTAD's intergovernmental group of experts on competition law and policy,[24] mature and young competition authorities can meet and interact. For some young authorities, this interaction can be the first opportunity for two heads of authorities to introduce themselves.[25] That sort of interaction could be

[21] Interview at the ICN Annual Conference in Porto with Interview with Irrarazabal.
[22] Interview with Kovacic.
[23] See chapter three.
[24] See chapter three
[25] For instance, thanks to this preliminary interaction, competition authorities such as Panama and Taiwan can interact and that would be the basis for further interactions and exchange of experiences between these two authorities, as indeed happened when they met at the OECD Global Competition Forum and later ACODECO (Panama) sent its officers to participate in study tours to the Taiwan Competition Authority. Interview with Cardoze.

reflected at a later stage in capacity-building and technical assistance activities which could eventually form the necessary basis for future case-based cooperation. As a result, technical assistance and capacity building do have a role in fostering trust, in particular CBT as the younger competition authority would be interested in receiving assistance from the mature authority and in return, the mature authority can get specific information regarding an investigation whereby the younger competition authority may contribute leads and evidence.[26]

In some instances, it would be more important to develop CBT activities between two competition authorities, rather than trying to implement competition provisions already signed within regional trade agreements. An example of this was the relationship between the competition authorities of Panama and Taiwan. Trade relations between Taiwan and Panama were established in 2003 when they signed a free trade agreement which included a chapter on competition whereby cooperation was included as a provision.[27] However, it was not until the two heads of the authorities met in an international conference and exchanged staff that real cooperation took off, years after signature of the trade agreement. The latter proves that more important for specific cooperation between competition authorities than having competition provisions in free trade agreements is to have personal interaction. As such, this is an example whereby CBT reinforces cooperation, as both competition authorities had similar levels of development. Therefore, in a future transnational CBC investigation, Panama and Taiwan would be ready to cooperate and share agency information based on the CBT activities that they undertook prior to the case-based cooperation.

For competition authorities younger than Panama, a revealing testimony from a Central American competition authority established only in 2006 said that if they were to investigate a transnational CBC investigation, they would not request information from mature or larger authorities but rather they would probably request information from international organisations such as the World Bank or the Inter-American Development Bank, because, according to the authority, they have access to sensitive information at the international level.[28] Others would say that in a transnational CBC investigation, it would be best to first ask a third party, usually a mature competition authority, to introduce and provide credentials for the unknown competition authority which is seeking information or which wishes

[26] Indeed the latter has happened in different instances. For instance, when the US opened an investigation into the vitamins multinational CBC 12 years ago, a number of younger competition authorities worldwide were requested to ascertain what would be the effects of this multinational cartel in their own markets. Panama received an open and very specific request from US antitrust authorities on this particular case.

[27] Indeed the wording of Art 15.02 regarding cooperation stated: 'The Parties recognize the importance of the cooperation and coordination in the application of their enforcement mechanisms, including notification, consultations and mutual exchange of information regarding the enforcement of the competition laws and policies in the area of free trade as long as they do not contravene legal obligations regarding confidentiality'. Panama & Taiwan Governments, Panama – Taiwan Free Trade Agreement.

[28] Interview with Lozano.

to provide information.[29] In all of these cases, there is a component of technical assistance and capacity-building that either mature authorities or international organisations could undertake in order to engage with newer and younger authorities wishing to cooperate on the international stage. The first interaction between these authorities could be regarded as a CBT activity not only on the part of the mature authority wishing to engage with a younger one, but also the younger authority wishing to receive the assistance that they need in order to deal with complex competition cases affecting their domestic markets.

8.2. Towards an International Benchmark for the Definition of 'Sharable Information'

For private practitioners and mature competition authorities, having an international benchmark of the definition of confidential information would be a desirable solution to smooth information exchange flows with young competition authorities.[30]

This remains a challenging task, as there is little agreement on what constitutes confidential information in the competition realm. In international conventions and domestic legislation, confidential information typically refers to information that is 'not generally known' or 'not made publicly available'.[31] In this sense, if the information is legally accessible then it is no longer confidential. Hence, there is a common understanding among countries that it is information that would be 'difficult for anyone but the holder of confidential information to obtain legally and only through exerting certain effort such as by investing a certain amount of time, material and human resource can a non-owner of the information find and access it'.[32]

In chapter three, the type of information that competition authorities normally handle when investigating cartels was discussed. In this regard, reference was mentioned to the term 'agency information', which reflects the level of expertise and a priori knowledge possessed by the authority on a certain industry and the possible theories of harm that that would be necessary to answer enquiries on a certain product or market. In a transnational CBC investigation, mature competition authorities often would have already started their formal investigation and have enough information to share with their younger counterparts.

[29] In an interview with the head of the Chilean Competition Authority, he stated that if Chile needed to interact with an ASEAN younger competition authority such as the Philippines or Brunei Darussalam, he would ask the US authorities to make the proper introduction, as they handle worldwide technical assistance cooperation with all these authorities. The latter would facilitate the first-time interaction with a head of agency or officers in charge of cartel investigations. See Interview with Irrarazabal.

[30] Interview with Anderson.

[31] Shan (2008: 58).

[32] ibid: 59.

Therefore, sharing information overseas where technically there is no common ground for the concept of confidential information, would lead to the exchange of non-confidential information.

This section dissects the type of information that can be exchanged in the three different stages of any cartel investigation at the international level: the pre-investigatory, investigatory and post-investigatory phases. Normally, the 'information exchanged is determined by a procedural definition of confidential information, namely information obtained by investigative process'.[33] In this regard, if one could differentiate that this type of information can only be gathered when a formal investigation is opened, then public and agency information types will not be essentially protected under confidentiality restrictions. Therefore, the latter would be deemed 'sharable' information that can be exchanged by competition authorities only during the pre-investigatory phase. As a result of that, without having second-generation agreements such as the one signed between the EU and Switzerland,[34] competition authorities can only share information at the pre-investigatory phase when they have not formally opened an investigation.

Even at the pre-investigatory phase, when information handled by the authority does not strictly fall under the aegis of confidentiality rules, there are strategic reasons as to why many competition authorities would not feel comfortable in sharing their information overseas due to possible leaks from the companies operating in both jurisdictions and destruction of evidence prior to search warrants or dawn raids.[35] Unfortunately, this has happened in the past when a mature competition authority shared information with a younger one and the next day there was a press release in that country concerning the sensitive information.[36] A situation such as this can undoubtedly hamper the trust between the authorities in such a manner that cooperation would not take place in the future.

With the foregoing concerns in mind, it is necessary to disaggregate the types of information, confidential or not, that is needed to take on transnational CBCs. To this end, an investigation on how to implement specific measures for the design of information gateways in the absence of effective leniency programmes in younger jurisdictions will be undertaken below.

8.2.1. Information Needed for Transnational CBC Enforcement

In chapter five reference was made to the assessment of confidentiality by three Latin American competition authorities, Colombia, Chile and Peru, and how the

[33] Demedts (2014: 9).

[34] See EU & Swiss Governments, 'Agreement between the EU and the Swiss Confederation'.

[35] Several interviewed heads of agencies stated that a more likely scenario of sharing information with foreign counterparts would be once they open an investigation, and not before. See Interview with Cardoze; Interview with Irrarazabal; and Interview with Ratshisusu.

[36] Interview with Toh.

assessment might differ amongst these three young competition authorities. In what follows, an examination shall be made of the specific types of information that competition authorities normally receive in the course of the investigation and what should be deemed confidential and what should not.

8.2.1.1. Criteria Set by Young Competition Authorities

Some relatively advanced[37] but young competition authorities[38] have been establishing their own guidelines, for transparency purposes, as to what would be the most objective criteria to assess what is confidential and what is not, within the great amount of information that is gathered in the course of an investigation and which is often claimed by the parties involved as confidential per se.[39] Often, younger competition authorities extend confidential treatment for a number of reasons[40] to information provided by the parties that is relevant to the case.

Therefore, defining the term 'confidential business information' as 'information which concerns or relates to the operations, production, sales, shipments, purchases, transfers, identification of customers, inventories, or amount or source of any income, profits, losses, or expenditures'[41] should not be enough to deem it confidential. In fact, in some mature jurisdictions, such information is not considered confidential as long as it is concerning the past, and not current or future information.[42]

In the case of Peru, the administrative jurisprudence considers six criteria under which the information should be considered confidential or not. The six criteria are: (i) that the information should be relevant to the case; (ii) that the company should be precise in what type of information needs to be considered confidential; (iii) that the company needs to justify the grounds as to which the information should be considered confidential; (iv) that the company should also present a summary of the information that is non-confidential; (v) that the

[37] See the case of Chile in: FNE Chile (2013).

[38] Notably the case of the Peruvian Competition Authority issuing its guidelines for confidentiality based on its own practice and enforcement experience since 1992. See more in: Peru Lineamiento sobre Confidencialidad de la Comision de Defensa de la Libre Competencia 2013.

[39] Based on the author's observation and experience, some younger competition authorities such as the Philippines Competition Commission that was established in January 2016, are currently working on confidentiality rules that should be the basis for granting confidentiality to parties' claims based on specific and objective grounds for confidential treatment. By April 2017, a set of rules on confidentiality was being prepared by the authority in an effort to objectively incorporate transparency on how information provided by the parties can be proclaimed 'confidential' or not.

[40] The reasons can be connected to: (i) the harmfulness of the disclosure of such information to commercial interests; (ii) competitive advantage of the owner of the information; (iii) interests of a private individual to whom the information pertains; (iv) public interest; or (v) even to the nature of investigations conducted for the enforcement of the competition law.

[41] Philippine Government, Rules and Regulations to Implement the Provisions of Republic Act No 10667 (Philippine Competition Act) 2.

[42] Interview with Bezzi.

information is not known to the public; and (vi) that the information is a commercial secret whose disclosure would be harmful to the company itself.[43]

8.2.1.2. Criteria Used to Assess the Confidential Information by Young Competition Authorities in Latin America: Colombia, Chile and Peru

As there is no international definition of confidential information, competition authorities need to examine on a case-by-case basis whether the information received by the parties is confidential or not. The following section takes three Latin American competition authorities as an example of this confidentiality test.

As discussed in chapter seven, three Latin American competition authorities signed the Lima Declaration[44] in 2013 as an informal cooperation agreement on information-sharing between its members in relation to competition enforcement activities. Two rights are involved when competition agencies assess the confidentiality of the information received: the right to access to public information (democratic accountability)[45] and the right to protect sensitive information of the companies. This is critical for young competition agencies that wish to get domestic legitimacy from their constituencies, and at the same time, protect constitutional rights and principles such as the right to information by any citizen.

Young competition authorities in Latin America encounter difficulty getting information from companies, as the latter claim that the information is private or confidential and, therefore, should not be disclosed to a public authority that will not provide adequate protection.

In Chile[46] and Colombia,[47] the principle is to allow full access to all public information handled by government institutions unless exceptions are made in certain cases.[48] Peru, on the other hand, begins with a principle of reserving public information for all administrative proceedings handled by public institutions,[49] albeit with the overall principle of publicity of government information.[50]

[43] According to Peruvian practice, all six criteria need to be fulfilled. If there is failure to do so, the whole confidentiality claim would be denied by the Authority. See 'Indecopi Inicia Procedimiento Contra Seis Líneas Navieras Por Presuntas Prácticas Colusorias En El Servicio de Transporte Marítimo Internacional de Carga Rodante – Inicio – Indecopi'.

[44] See Chile/Colombia/Peru Governments, 'Lima Declaration'.

[45] 'The public's right to government-held information has been recognized by international human rights courts and implemented in national "sunshine" and freedom of information (FOI) laws.' Natural Resource Governance Institute, 'Chapter 3 : Commercially Sensitive Information and the Public Interest'.

[46] Biblioteca del Congreso Nacional, Chile – Transparencia de la Funcion Publica y de Accesso a la Informacion de la Administracion del Estado 2008 [Law 20.285].

[47] Colombia Código de Procedimiento Administrativo y de lo Contencioso Administrativo. 2011.

[48] See Art 21 of the Transparency Law in Chile whereby exceptions are made to the overall principle of access to information. See Biblioteca del Congreso Nacional.

[49] Peru Competition Act.

[50] Peru Ley de Transparencia y Accesso a la Informacion Publica 2002.

There is a difference between reserved and confidential information. In the above description, all administrative proceedings in Peru are reserved and may not be accessed by the public until the proceedings are finalised, unless the competition authority decides to grant access to legitimate third parties or authorised competition handlers. Confidential information, on the other hand, needs to be previously declared as such by the competition authority when the parties submit the information claimed to be considered as confidential in a formally opened cartel investigation. The legal effect of that declaration would mean that only the competition authority would have access to that information, and not the other parties to the proceedings.[51]

As for the test of confidentiality practiced by the competition authorities, in accordance to Article 39 bis of the Chilean Competition Act, information that contains formulas, strategies or commercial secrets or any other element whose disclosure may impact the competitive situation of the company should be declared confidential[52] unless that information needs to be transmitted to the other party so as to exercise its right to defence. In Peru, information provided by the party in a formal investigation can be declared confidential if that information is related to banking, tax, commercial, industrial, technological or stock exchange secrets as well as intimate family and personal information.[53]

Indeed, of the three countries under assessment, by 2017 only the Peruvian Competition Authority had issued specific guidelines regarding how to assess confidential information in competition cases,[54] including an annex whereby 'criteria to interpret the confidentiality requests' is provided for transparency purposes.[55] Its peer competition authorities can capitalise on this effort in order to harmonise their day-to-day practices. Unfortunately, there is still great diversity in how competition authorities treat confidentiality in their administrative proceedings, as the majority of young competition authorities are not as advanced as the three competition authorities presently under review. This uncertainty harms any attempt to move forward in cooperating against the harmful effects of CBCs.

In addition, within the framework of the sub-regional Andean competition law, Article 24 of Decision 608 sets forth the criteria for the confidentiality treatment under Andean Community competition law. There are four criteria that arise from this legal provision:[56] (1) the information is publicly available; (2) requested by the entity that provides the information; (3) the information needs to be justified,

[51] For example in Peru, the competition authority can negate the declaration of confidentiality if they believe that the other party needs that information to exercise its right for defence (due process considerations). See Diario Oficial El Peruano.

[52] See Art 39 Chile New Competition Act.

[53] Peru Lineamiento sobre Confidencialidad de la Comision de Defensa de la Libre Competencia 6.

[54] Chile has some information but not as detailed as the Guidelines provided by the Peruvian Authority, INDECOPI. See Chile – Tribunal de Defensa de la Libre Competencia – Auto Acordado sobre Reservan o Confidencialidad de la Informacion en los Procesos 2012.

[55] See Annex 1 Peru Lineamiento sobre Confidencialidad de la Comision de Defensa de la Libre Competencia.

[56] Interview with Van Brackel Barbosa.

ie industrial secrets on prices, and the like; (4) a summary of the non-confidential information must be provided.[57]

8.2.1.3. *Types of Information Handled by the Authority*

Following the common practice of young competition authorities, there are different types of information that could be gathered in the course of an investigation: information about the company, prices, sales, commercial or contractual, financial or accounting, output or production, and other information such as the identity of the sources. In all these cases, as long as the information is already public but not easily accessible, known by the suppliers or clients of the company and so forth, that information should be considered non-confidential. For instance, within the overall information of the company, the information that relates to the legal representatives of the company as well as their prerogatives is normally found in the public registry of commercial entities in a given jurisdiction and therefore should not be deemed confidential.[58] Similarly, when it comes to information on prices, only the information about the price listing that has been already disclosed elsewhere should not be declared confidential.

8.2.1.4. *Setting the Benchmark for Sharable Information*

Confidentiality is an essential element of trade secrets and has become the fundamental premise for their legal protection across jurisdictions because of the importance of having certain types of information 'hidden from competitors because of the information's commercial value and the likelihood that competitors would copy it'.[59] In this regard, the first benchmark that should be incorporated into the framework on sharable information should be that whatever is not confidential or declared as such, is potentially sharable.

As highlighted in chapter three, there are four types of information that a competition authority handles: public information, agency information, information from the parties already in possession of one agency, and information obtained from the parties at the request of another agency. Within these four types of information, there is always the possibility of sharing information with a foreign counterpart if the information has not been claimed as confidential.

A second benchmark should be the incorporation of an overall definition of sharable information for all stages of any cartel investigation. As such, already mature competition authorities such as the US have claimed that categories of sharable information should be (1) the existence of a formal and open investigation; (2) theories of harm, markets or remedies; and (3) industry background.[60]

[57] CAN Regional Competition Law 6.
[58] Peru Lineamiento sobre Confidencialidad de la Comision de Defensa de la Libre Competencia.
[59] Hill (1999).
[60] Damtoft (2014: slide 11).

A fourth category was proposed by a young enforcer in Central America: (4) the formation of the cartel.[61]

The problem with this second benchmark is that in some jurisdictions, such as South Africa, the existence of a formal and open investigation can be in itself privileged information because it was gathered from merger procedures cases where all the information gathered was confidential.[62]

In other jurisdictions such as Singapore, if the authority has not opened an investigation and there is a request by a foreign counterpart to disclose information about an industry, there is little that can be shared because the authority would not have collected any information about the industry.[63] In addition, younger but relatively advanced competition authorities such as Chile would claim that sharable information can only be exchanged when the authority has notified the parties or when the information gathered in a leniency application is not declared confidential.[64] As a result, in terms of the US's first criterion of the existence of a formal and open investigation, information can only be disclosed once the parties have been notified, that is to say, at the beginning of the investigatory phase.[65] On the second and third items suggested by the US, theories of harm and industry background, these could be shared with foreign counterparts in any stage of the investigation.

A third benchmark should be that the information is available on the internet, but it is not easily accessible by foreign counterparts due to a number of reasons such as language barriers or the fact that the public information is only disseminated in selected networks.

8.2.2. Establishing Conditional Information Gateways in the Absence of (Effective) Leniency Programmes

As indicated in chapter four, mature competition authorities and international leniency applicants will trust younger competition authorities only if there is a positive perception that the younger competition authority has developed a robust and effective leniency programme at home. An experimental way to solve this lack of trust is to foster CBT activities between mature and young authorities. Let us explain how this could come about.

First, the younger competition authority must have a clear picture as to the possible effects of a transnational CBC in its domestic markets and it would need

[61] Interview with Odio-Rohrmoser.

[62] See Interview with Harin; Interview with Ratshisusu.

[63] See Interview with Toh.

[64] See Interview with Irrarazabal.

[65] For example, in Panama, the Competition Authority (ACODECO) would communicate to the Ministry of Industry the occurrence of the dawn raid only one hour before the scheduled time. See Interview with Cardoze.

to engage with a mature competition authority where a leniency application has been submitted. The incentive from the young authority to enter into cooperation with a mature one is clear and the mature authority would be motivated by the need to get more information about the case from the perspective of the young competition authority's territory.

Second, beyond the legal loopholes of the leniency programme at the domestic level that may undermine the effectiveness of the programme, there is still a chance that the mature competition authority can provide the information needed. This can be done through conditional information gateways as proposed by OECD and discussed in chapter nine, with one underlying difference: the possibility to subscribe a multilateral memorandum of understanding concerning consultation and cooperation and the exchange of information. An example of this can be found at the International Organization of Securities Commissions (IOSCO)[66] whereby countries have been signing up to be part of it. Some have suggested that the ICN can provide the basis for this facilitation through the platform discussed in the next section.[67] CBT activities would be instrumental in this regard to incorporate key provisions that can first define the concept of sharable information as discussed earlier with a 'punishment clause' if the young competition authority does not comply with safeguarding the information, even if it is not confidential but sharable. Developing CBT on the basis of deterrence would mean that the technical assistance and capacity-building rendered to the young competition authority would be conditional if there is failure to safeguard the information exchanged in a transnational case. A first step towards common ground between them could be the adoption of general principles such as the ones adopted in the MOU of IOSCO under the section 'general principles regarding mutual assistance and the exchange of information'.[68]

Third, CBT activities in developing trust could lead to adopt an intermediary solution extracted from the experience of international cooperation among tax authorities. As the OECD discussed in 2012, it could be useful to explore other mechanisms to share information under OECD instruments such as the Model Tax Convention on Income and Capital of 2008, as well as the Model Agreement on Exchange of Information on Tax Matters of 2002.[69] The OECD Committee on Fiscal Affairs approved a Manual[70] to implement these instruments that will

[66] International Organization Of Securities Commissions (2010).

[67] The idea was proposed by Marcus Bezzi in an interview at the ICN Annual Conference in May 2017 in Porto. Basically, the ICN can provide the basis to incorporate a 'multilateral MOU' where ICN member authorities can just simply sign in. See Interview with Bezzi.

[68] 'This Memorandum of Understanding sets forth the Authorities' intent with regard to mutual assistance and the exchange of information for the purpose of enforcing and securing compliance with the respective Laws and Regulations of the jurisdictions of the Authorities. The provisions of this Memorandum of Understanding are not intended to create legally binding obligations or supersede domestic laws': International Organization Of Securities Commissions (2010: section 6).

[69] OECD, 'Improving International Co-operation in Cartel Investigations' 51.

[70] OECD Committee on Fiscal Affairs, 'Manual On The Implementation Of Exchange Of Information Provisions For Tax Purposes'.

ultimately provide practical assistance to tax officials wishing to exchange information by detailing the modes by which the information would be shared: exchange of information on request, spontaneous information exchange, automatic (or routine) exchange of information, and industry-wide exchange of information.[71]

8.3. Strengthening the ICN for Sharing Non-Confidential Information[72]

This sub-section does not aim to reinvent the wheel. Rather, it proposes to start moving the wagon with instruments that have already been adopted and proposed by young competition agencies as well as by international networks such as the ICN and UN. The objective is to facilitate flow of sharable information under the meaning provided in this chapter.

As presented in chapter three, the ICN framework was proposed by Japan in 2014 and has been operational since January 2016. However, as of April 2017, only 33 ICN member agencies have registered for it.[73] This suggests an underlying need to advocate the importance of this framework by raising awareness of the benefits for young competition authorities in particular when dealing with multinational CBCs as well as transnational CBCs. According to the primary sources consulted, some cooperation cases among younger and smaller agencies have taken place but not been made public under the ICN Framework.[74] Some other competition agencies have claimed to have little information about the ICN Framework.[75] The under-utilisation of the ICN Framework could be attributed to a host of issues, such as the differences between common and civil law jurisdictions when it comes to what public servants are permitted to do or disclose under the principles of administrative law, which could be an important legal barrier against cooperation as discussed in chapters three and four.[76] In addition, there are also difficulties associated with inter-agency evidence sharing in international competition cases,[77] an issue that has been successfully addressed by the European Competition Network[78] under Regulation 1/2003.[79] Finally, factors such as lack of inter-organisational trust and incentives to cooperate might also be considered

[71] OECD, 'Improving International Co-operation in Cartel Investigations' 52.
[72] This section is based on: Horna, 'David & Goliath: How Young Competition Agencies Can Succeed in Fighting Cross-Border Cartels'.
[73] Kasahara (2017: slide 20).
[74] Interview with anonymous referees carried out in January 2017.
[75] Interview with Guzman.
[76] Dyzenhaus, Hunt and Taggart (2001).
[77] See Martyniszyn (2015).
[78] See Capobianco (2004).
[79] Council Regulation (EC) No 1/2003 of 16 December 2002 on the implementation of the rules on competition laid down in Articles 81 and 82 of the Treaty.

in the issue at stake as discussed in chapter four. Other surrounding factors determine whether the ICN framework would be a success or not.[80]

Another limitation of the ICN Framework is that it limits cooperation between agencies that are members of the ICN and have been able to register onto that framework. Notably, one important economy of the several emerging and large competition agencies, representing economies that greatly influence the world economic and trading order, and which are nowadays shaping important developments in international competition law instruments,[81] is not a member of the ICN: China.[82] These agencies (ICN member states that have joined the ICN framework) have shown the intention to cooperate in investigation efforts. For instance, the Russian Federation, being one of the biggest competition authorities in the world (in terms of number of employees),[83] has recently proposed to the UN the possibility of strengthening international cooperation in the investigation of cases.[84]

As has been outlined in chapter three, the future work of the ICN Cartel Working Group is to improve the anti-cartel enforcement across the whole membership of the ICN.[85] The challenge is to go beyond the usual cooperation among friends and colleagues from the major competition regulators which founded the ICN back in 2002,[86] and expand the cooperation to all members of the network and beyond. In sum, it appears that the ICN framework could be an effective mechanism that can be expanded towards other younger and smaller jurisdictions seeking to cooperate and share non-confidential information when investigating cross-border cartels. However, to unleash the full potential of, and improve the trust and confidence in, the ICN Framework, further enhancement and dissemination in multilateral meetings and enhanced transparency between the members is essential.

8.3.1. Weaving the UN Mechanism into the ICN

The ICN's efforts in providing mechanisms for younger and smaller agencies are instrumental but need further reinforcements and incentives for the members to rely on this system. There are three main reasons why a UN mechanism could

[80] Information-sharing research relates to three main levels: (1) interpersonal, (2) intra-organisational; and (3) inter-organisational levels. For a review of the literature on information-sharing see Yang and Maxwell (2011).

[81] See the latest competition agreement in the BRICS countries at: BRICS Competition Authorities (2016).

[82] Hollman and Kovacic (2011: 275),.

[83] In 2004, it was reported to have 1827 employees throughout the country, with 75 regional offices. Presentation of the Federal Antimonopoly Service at the APEC Training Course in August 2005. See FAS (2005).

[84] FAS RFW (2017).

[85] ICN, 'Cartel Working Group 2015–2018 Work Plan'.

[86] For a complete survey on how international networks respond to international cooperation problems worldwide, see Marsden (2012).

strengthen the work of the ICN with the particularities and effectiveness of its framework.

(1) **Young and small agencies' trust and confidence in UNCTAD's work on competition law and policy:** taking into account 'UNCTAD's long tradition of representing the interests of developing countries, its legitimacy as part of the UN system, and its continued focus on the linkage between competition and development',[87] young and small competition agencies have appreciated the work of the UN in assisting them (through the government) in the enactment of their competition laws and capacity building efforts in strengthening their capacities and institutions to deal with competition law and policy implementation at large.

UNCTAD has largely supported the efforts of countries in their development for a number of historical, political and economic considerations.[88] Therefore, there is an underlying trust that countries, and the young and small agencies representing them, would put in UNCTAD and UN. Notably, UN instruments related to competition have long involved several jurisdictions, such as the establishment of Committee III on Restrictive Business Practices (RBPs) at the first session of the preparatory committee of the United Nations Conference on Trade and Employment (UNCTAE) in Church House, Dean's Yard, London, in February 1946.[89]

(2) **Wider membership in the UN:** ICN membership is an asset but not all major economies are part of this network.[90] In order to maximise the opportunities for cooperation, it would be important to look at UN's expanded network under the auspices of UNCTAD, which covers all of the ICN members as well as all major economies which are not affiliated with ICN.[91] UNCTAD's experience in addressing broad interest across regions with different development and priority needs might be an asset in the growing membership of the ICN so as to avoid fissures throughout the choice of ICN topics addressed in its regular meetings.[92]

[87] Lianos (2009: 42).

[88] Williams (1991).

[89] Horna, 'Seventy Years of Work on Competition Law and Policy in the United Nations (1946–2016)'.

[90] 'The most notable jurisdiction with a competition law and no representation in the ICN is China, which has three national competition agencies (MOFCOM, NDRC, and SAIC). China participates in the work of the OECD Competition Committee as an observer and is a member of UNCTAD. The Chinese agencies have not discussed their intentions concerning ICN membership'. Hollman and Kovacic (2011: 275) fn 3.

[91] At the latest UNCTAD meeting of October 2016, 22 delegates from China attended the meeting. See UNCTAD, 'List of Participants of the Intergovernmental Group of Experts on Competition Law and Policy Fifteenth Session Geneva, 19–21 October 2016'.

[92] 'Assembling a portfolio of projects that suits a network's members arises from expansions of membership. As a competition policy network grows, it may be difficult to pick topics that command broad interest across the network. Fissures may emerge on the basis of regional differences (e.g., competition agencies in the island economies of the Caribbean may have needs that are alien to the landlocked nations of Central Asia) or wide gaps in experience. In addition to, or as a substitute for their participation in the large, multinational networks, some countries might choose to focus resources competition initiatives undertaken in the context of regional networks such as ASEAN, CARICOM, and COMESA …' Hollman and Kovacic (2011: 275).

(3) **Additional advocacy activities in the multilateral arena:** the ICN Advocacy & Implementation Network Support Program (AISUP) does valuable work in encouraging ICN member agencies to greater implement ICN products and also by promoting more efficient and effective antitrust enforcement worldwide by enhancing convergence and cooperation.[93] AISUP's efforts can be further augmented by promoting ICN work products in wider audiences such as at the UNCTAD's annual sessions of the UNCTAD Intergovernmental Group of Experts on Competition Law and Policy, where competition agencies from the developing world are often present.

There has been extensive scholarship on the emergence of the UN Set, which was adopted by the United Nations General Assembly in 1980.[94] Among the different matters covered by the UN Set, Section F, related to international measures and voluntary consultations, has been the least explored.[95] Interestingly, recent expressions have called for Section F's potential to be unleashed for the benefit of the vast majority of young and small competition regimes worldwide,[96] particularly by an important UN member state.[97] Section F of the UN Set on Competition was originally conceived to address the harmful effects of a cross-border cartel impacting a company seeking to get enforcement actions with the competition agency in its own jurisdiction.[98] Section F.4 describes a voluntary consultation scheme, which bears similarities to the ones contained by the 1976 OECD Guidelines and the voluntary consultations in the old General Agreement on Tariffs and Trade (GATT):[99]

4. Consultations:

(a) Where a State, particularly of a developing country, believes that a consultation with another State or States is appropriate in regard to an issue concerning control of restrictive business practices, it may request a consultation with those States with a view to finding a mutually acceptable solution. When a consultation is to be held, the States involved may request the Secretary-General of UNCTAD to provide mutually agreed conference facilities for such a consultation;

[93] See ICN, 'Activity Report on ICN Advocacy and Implementation Network Support Program (AISUP) 2011–2012'.

[94] Davidow (1979); Davidow and Chiles (1978); Fikentscher (1982); Snell (1997); Timberg (1955).

[95] Initially, UNCTAD was supposed to play a role in dispute settlement, but after lively discussions during December 1979, delegations did not agree to have a binding resolution but instead a set of principles whereby affected countries would go on consultations with no prior commitment to binding arbitration or conciliation. Benson (1980: 452).

[96] In October 2016 at the 15th session of the IGE on Competition Law and Policy, the Russian Delegation to the United Nations submitted a key note speech delivered by the Head of the Federal Antimonopoly Service, FAS, mentioning the need to further enhance the usefulness of Section F of the UN Set when it comes to investigation of cross-border competition cases. UNCTAD, 'Report of the Intergovernmental Group of Experts on Competition Law and Policy on Its Fifteenth Session'.

[97] As a result of consultations, in May 2017, the Russian Federation proposed a toolkit to operationalise section F of the UN Set. See FAS (2017).

[98] The United Nations Set Of Principles And Rules On Competition.

[99] Oesterle (1981: 44).

(b) States should accord full consideration to requests for consultations and, upon agreement as to the subject of and the procedures for such a consultation, the consultation should take place at an appropriate time;

(c) If the States involved so agree, a joint report on the consultations and their results should be prepared by the States involved and, if they so wish, with the assistance of the UNCTAD secretariat, and be made available to the Secretary-General of UNCTAD for inclusion in the annual report on restrictive business practices.[100]

According to the above, there are the four key elements for the implementation of this provision, which shall be explored below.[101]

1. **An issue concerning the control of 'restrictive business practices'**: the content of the term restrictive business practice used in Section F4(a) can be found in Section B(i)1 of the UN Set. Restrictive business practices are deemed to include, inter alia, 'acts or behavior of enterprises which, through an abuse or acquisition and abuse of a dominant position of market power, limit access to markets or otherwise unduly restrain competition, having or being likely to have adverse effects on international trade'. Section D of the UN Set also elaborates on the meaning of 'restrictive business practices', particularly Sections D3 and D4, concerning horizontal coordinated conduct between enterprises and conduct abusive of market power, respectively. The list contained in Sections D3 and D4 are non-exhaustive, allowing for the addition of further anti-competitive practices.

2. **The nature of consultations**: two points can be made with regard to the nature of the consultations. First, it should be emphasised that Consultations under the UN Set are voluntary and States entering negotiations strive to find mutually agreed solutions.[102] Second, while Sections B and D address the actions of private enterprises, the Consultations are on a 'State-to-State' level. This is in line with the idea that consultations are cooperative in nature and do not directly seek the resolution of a case by a third party.[103]

3. **Full consideration to consultations:** the parties can request and agree upon the proceeding and substance. Indeed, while consultations are voluntary in nature, member states should be required to give full consideration to the request and should be encouraged to enter into the proceeding to explore, and if possible reach,

[100] The United Nations Set Of Principles And Rules On Competition.

[101] See Costa Rica's submission to the Sixth Review Conference of 2010 whereby it proposed specific modalities for the implementation of the voluntary consultations provided for in Section F(4) of the Set. The proposed modalities included a number of requirements for the application, the envisaged elements to be included in the response of the request and the possible extension of the UNCTAD secretariat's participation. See UNCTAD, 'Report of the Sixth United Nations Conference to Review All Aspects of the Set of Multilaterally Agreed Equitable Principles and Rules for the Control of Restrictive Business Practices'.

[102] Oesterle (1981: 43).

[103] See Brusick (1983).

mutually agreeable solutions. If a state declines to participate in the consultations it would be expected that a reasoned response would be filed to explain its decision. Responses so filed will help to improve future requests and make consultations more meaningful. Participation of the corresponding states in the proceedings will strengthen consultation as a valid and effective mechanism to address cross-border competition issues. If the states agree to enter into consultation, they have to agree on the subject and on the procedures of the consultation.[104] This makes the procedure more complex as it is one more thing the states have to discuss and agree on. This would also force the states to reinvent the wheel for every consultation. Even though the Sixth UN Conference of 2010 did not specifically instruct UNCTAD to design a procedure for the implementation of the Consultation despite the presentation of the modalities by a member state,[105] with the adoption of the GPPSF as described in chapter three, there is a prospect of adopting Guiding Principles and Procedures for the implementation of the Section F. of the UN Set for the Eighth during the UN Conference of 2020, based on the text adopted by the 18th Session of the IGE on Competition Law and Policy in July 2019.

4. **Joint report to be prepared by the states with the assistance of UNCTAD**: once the requesting state and the corresponding state(s) agree to enter into voluntary consultations, they may agree on specific mutually reciprocal solutions and this process could be crystallised in a joint report. Given the UNCTAD's expertise and knowledge, the states may also request UNCTAD's assistance in

[104] Proceedings should be optional to the states entering into consultations. In other words, the states may agree on different procedures. If the states decide to do so, they should still be able to get assistance from UNCTAD. Secondly, the proceeding should be as simple as possible with basic signals to light the path for the states to explore and reach mutually agreeable solutions. The proceeding must be respectful of local laws. States entering into consultations will try to find mutually agreeable solutions that are also consistent with their own local law. Thus, the proceeding should also be respectful of local laws. At the Sixth Review Conference of Nov 2010, UNCTAD member states of the 6th Review Conference in 2010 believed that there were benefits in having a 'default' set of procedural rules to implement the consultations pursuant to section F.4. The reasons referred to included (a) the consultations would offer the state another mechanism for cooperation, in addition to formal and informal networks and technical assistance; (b) having such rules would provide predictability for the state members; and (c) UNCTAD could have a role in providing conference facilities, technical assistance and monitoring the agreements, if requested by the parties. Several delegates said that the participation of UNCTAD as an impartial third party would add value to the mechanism and help to legitimise the participation of the states in the consultations before the stakeholders in their own country. While some states may be able to share confidential information, the proceedings must also guarantee such confidentiality. UNCTAD may assist the states in the definition of what information should or should not be shared or in ways to present information while preserving the confidential component, if the states request such assistance. Finally, the proceedings should be to implement consultations as a cooperation procedure, not as a conflict resolution forum. It also follows that UNCTAD may provide conference facilities and assistance if the states request so, but UNCTAD shall not act as a judge, nor as an arbitrator. See UNCTAD, 'Report of the Sixth United Nations Conference to Review All Aspects of the Set of Multilaterally Agreed Equitable Principles and Rules for the Control of Restrictive Business Practices'.

[105] See UNCTAD, 'Contribution from Costa Rica'.

seeking possible solutions and drafting the report. The conference may want to instruct UNCTAD to bring such assistance when requested by the states.

8.3.2. Towards a Voluntary Consultation Mechanism under Section F.4 of the UN Set of Competition

As discussed earlier, section F.4 of the UN Set provides key elements that could facilitate the signing-up of new members to this ICN Framework beyond the 33, and thereby add to the consequent sharing of non-confidential information. If the ICN framework is to have the key features of section F.4 of the UN Set successfully implemented, younger or smaller agencies would be willing to enter into voluntary consultations. The stages of cooperation of these consultations are detailed below.

Stage 1: In accordance with the ICN framework, participating agencies can register a liaison officer who would lead the communications with the other. The incentive for the mature agency's liaison officer to cooperate would be the possibility of having common enforcement interests with the small or young agency, which is seeking sharable information. To abbreviate bureaucracy and to avoid including too many people in the process, it is advisable that the liaison officer and the case team leader be one and the same person. Case team leaders who are fully involved in the case should also be at the forefront of communications with his/her foreign counterpart in order to prevent delays and errors in the communication of the critical information. This is important to ensure the efficiency and trust, as it has been said that: 'cooperation is more likely when the organisations involved are few in number and uncertainty can thereby be reduced'. This would also prevent having several officers in the agency possessing sensitive information, addressing concerns between international officers and case officers protecting their own turf.

Stage 2: When applying Section F of the UN Set, participating agencies would need to voluntarily agree on the subject and the specific procedures for each consultation. Since the subject matter and the procedures for the consultation is mutually arrived at, the participating competition agencies will have to have assurance of control over the mechanism. Previous agreement on the subject matter and the procedures would also prevent outright refusal to respond or provide information, as, absent any overwhelming concern, it would be unreasonable for an agency to suddenly change its mind as to what it wants to share or discuss. This is a critical stage, as the ICN framework might need this feature in order to bolster trust in the system based on reciprocity principles between the participating agencies.

While some participating agencies may be able to provide sharable information, the proceedings must also guarantee confidentiality. In the absence of an international definition of confidential information, it is important to set up the specific procedures for such consultation and eventually provide a definition of what information should or should not be shared or alternatively investigate how to present information while preserving the confidential component, in accordance with domestic laws. The goal should be to implement consultations as a cooperation procedure, not as a conflict resolution forum.

Stage 3: Once the subject matter and the procedures are established ad-hoc, the lead case team officers can provide information to each other in the following categories of agency sharable information: (1) information on the existence of an investigation; (2) theories about harm, markets, or remedies; and (3) industry background. These three categories do not constitute confidential information, as these were not provided by companies and are not protected by domestic laws. The ICN framework provides a detailed workflow that could be established at each competition agency for harmonised cooperation.

Stage 4: If the participating agencies agree, the process could be crystallised in a joint report that would track and record the consultations and the outcome of these communications. Even if the consultations do not result in the successful delivery of non-confidential sharable information, the fact that attempts to communicate were tracked and recorded could indicate to the ICN members that the system is progressing, and that it could eventually yield concrete results. In addition, the joint report could fuel more discussions about how international cooperation could be approved, by being presented at the annual conferences of the ICN. The joint report could also be submitted as an item to be discussed at the annual meetings of the UNCTAD Intergovernmental Group of Experts on Competition Law and Policy. Sharing the experience of the participating agencies could build trust and confidence in the system as a whole as the rest of the UN membership can appreciate these results. Figure 8.1 suggests the workflow of the four stages presented above and the key features of this tool for cooperation.

Figure 8.1: Reinforcing the ICN Framework to Foster International Cooperation in Case Investigations

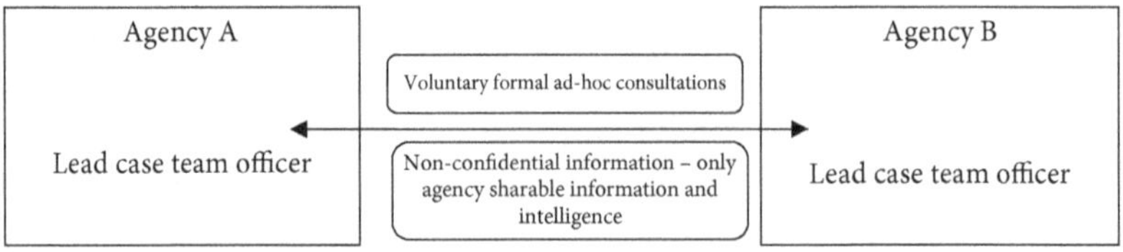

Source: Nambu T, 'Proposal for Establishing the ICN Framework for Promotion of Sharing Non-Confidential Information for Cartel Enforcement' (2014 ICN Cartel Workshop, Taipei, Taiwan, 2 October 2014) <http://www.ftc.gov.tw/icncartel2014/pdf/2014.10.02.%20Plenary%20III%20%20%20Toshiyuki%20Nambu%20JFTC.pdf>.

Figure 8.1 introduces the term 'voluntary formal ad-hoc consultations' as a result of considering the key features of Section F.4 of the UN Set. This system will build trust and confidence and allow ease in cooperation for competition authorities.

In sum, the application of the consultations contemplated in Section F.4 of the UN Set into the ICN Framework could help to achieve the cooperation required between competition agencies in different countries to fight international anticompetitive. Indeed, the mechanisms provided by the UN could provide additional methods to strengthen the existing ICN framework.

The two systems can nourish each other and the use of provisions from one need not cause friction. One should view it as an effort to use the best from both to create a greater and more efficient whole. Beyond this, however, there are some caveats that also need to be considered in the use of this tool:

(1) Entering into consultations with another state would eventually mean that the issue would move from 'a mere legal problem to a more political realm in which the outcome would depend on the relative bargaining power of the two states and the degree to which the two states wish to protect the respective interest of private companies doing business within their borders'. However, the world has changed since the adoption of the UN Set in 1980 and the specific elements of Section F.4 will eventually bring additional positive results of the ICN Framework, as it was proposed by Japan in 2015.

(2) Responses at the regional level to foster competition laws in different regional groupings also try to address the same problems that the UN Set was intended to solve in 1980, but they have been ineffective due to national difficulties in their implementations. As many young and small competition regimes are located in developing countries and economies in transition, conventional wisdom suggests that any international cartel regulation would interfere with their domestic economic policies, among other things, including industrial policy. Hence, there has been a historic resistance from the developing world to implement Section F of the UN Set. This has undermined the UN's efforts to implement effective international cartel regulation.

(3) Not having a pre-existing commitment for authorities in the respective jurisdictions to cooperate with each other or to jointly carry out the investigation of alleged anti-competitive conducts exacerbates the problem and leaves a large majority of small and young competition regimes with few options to address their problems. Worse, this may lead to them using mature competition laws to supplant their own laws in regulating their own markets.

8.4. Summary

In 2017, Peru launched an investigation into a transnational CBC that has already been investigated and in some cases sanctioned by mature and Latin American young competition authorities.[106] It remains to be seen how the transnational CBC investigation will conclude and how much cooperation the Peruvian authority

[106] 'Indecopi Inicia Procedimiento Contra Seis Líneas Navieras Por Presuntas Prácticas Colusorias En El Servicio de Transporte Marítimo Internacional de Carga Rodante – Inicio – Indecopi'.

can get from its counterparts and the parties involved.[107] In any event, Chapter 8 attempts to solve both the puzzle of trust and the possible legal constraints surrounding confidentiality with an international mechanism that could serve as a facilitator of transnational cooperation.

If the countries in question do not have a legal standing problem at the forefront of their legal concerns, then building trust should be a top priority. However, even where mature and young competition authorities are willing to cooperate there are costs to be borne, as chapter three indicated. As noted by the OECD:

> International co-operation involves resource (opportunity) costs. This can be seen at two levels. First, providing co-operation in a specific matter can be time and resource intensive. Second, at a more general level, co-operation is more likely where respective authorities have a relationship of trust and a good understanding of each other's legislation. Relationships of trust are important for both formal and informal co-operation. Achieving this trust is time consuming and resource intensive, particularly for smaller agencies. However, incurring these costs also brings benefits, both in terms of the specific enforcement activity and in building an ongoing relationship of trust with other agencies in which enforcers can assist each other over time and across multiple matters.[108]

A mature competition authority (the EU) once said that in deciding whether or not to cooperate, two factors must be taken into account: first, the perceived usefulness of that cooperation for both agencies; and second, the relationship between the agencies and the knowledge of each other's procedures.[109]

The three building blocks proposed in chapter eight intended to solve the problem of incentives and costs of cooperation by incorporating CBT activities as well as addressing the problem of sharing information at all stages of investigation by incorporating the term sharable information into the literature of international cooperation of competition authorities. The last building block proposes the joining of forces between the ICN and UN in order to answer the question as to where to cooperate in a transnational setting. This solution takes into account the concerns of a wide membership and the trust of developing countries for UN agencies such as UNCTAD.

[107] In an interview with the Head of the Peruvian Authority, the main issue that could be a restraint on cooperation with foreign authorities is not trust but rather legal specific issues surrounding confidentiality. See Gagliuffi (2017).

[108] OECD, 'International Cooperation in Competition Law Enforcement'.

[109] OECD, 'Improving International Co-Operation in Cartel Investigations' 313.

9

Strengthening Cooperation Among Young Competition Authorities in Regional Cross-Border Cartel Investigations

In 2014, Peña identified seven challenges in order to foster international cooperation in Latin America:

> (1) to have more Latin American countries going from receivers to givers of technical cooperation;[1] (2) to avoid having overlapping in the existing initiatives; (3) to avoid limiting the cooperation to the informal level; (4) to overcome the budget and geographic limitations; (5) to define what confidential information means; (6) legal limits to the recognition of evidence gathered abroad; and (7) to avoid copying models on a 'one-size fits all' basis without contemplating the local reality.[2]

To overcome these challenges, small and young Latin American competition authorities need to acquire more experience in dealing with CBCs and technical assistance from the larger authorities such as Brazil and Mexico, where appropriate. Recommendations were made to improve the level of coordination between the authorities in fighting CBCs in the region. Actions at the enforcing level may include the following:

> At the pre-investigatory phase: exchange public information not easily accessible and if trust is fostered, including some types of agency information. There should be mechanisms to be implemented by neighbouring agencies such as the creation of a notification system or databases. At the investigatory phase: If concurrent business practices are identified thanks to the successful transmission of public and agency information, agencies may be able to discuss and exchange strategies on how to approach the case and eventually coordinate dawn raids in order to avoid the destruction of evidence as such. The experience of EU-Swiss Cooperation Agreement could be the model for this cooperation. At the post-investigatory phase, all administrative rulings should be able to be publishable in a network database.[3]

[1] '... it is important to understand that the concept of international cooperation could be misleading when analysing the development of competition law in Latin America since it would be more appropriate in most cases to talk about technical assistance.' Peña (2014: 196).

[2] ibid: 213–14.

[3] Horna, 'Regional Coordination in Cartel Investigations: The Liquid Oxygen Case' 312–13.

For these challenges discussed above, many competition authorities cannot use the agreements they signed since they were only intended to cover the first and second types of information (public and agency information) but with the caveat of full protection of confidential information. As a result, only the information regarding the launch of enforcement activities may end up being exchanged. In practice, this scheme is not an effective form of cooperation.

Recently, Brazil stated that its cooperation initiatives are usually based on the exchange of non-confidential information and general views on the case.[4] In the majority of cases, information was obtained by the investigators through public vehicles, such as agencies' websites, which is regarded as information in the public domain and may serve as evidence in Brazilian proceedings. However, the issue of how foreign evidence should be treated in domestic cartel investigations remains. Finally, confidential information obtained from a defendant or foreign agency may serve as evidence within Brazilian proceedings but must be kept confidential within Brazil, which might cause a problem if the evidence is also needed in another jurisdiction in later enforcement activities. Confidential information is treated as such until a final decision is rendered or, depending on its content, may be kept confidential even after a final decision.

Another challenge is how the perception of the cartelists regarding the development of international cooperation of competition authorities can become a concern for regional and/or international effective enforcement responses. Depending on the seriousness of the efforts to cooperate and coordinate in enforcement actions, international companies tend to vertically integrate their operations at the regional level so as to act 'glocally' by adjusting their self-corporate governance rules to domestic competition rules, but act differently when it comes to cross-border business patterns (similar to international transfer pricing activities to avoid double taxation).[5]

This could be fostered by those companies that do not adopt policies and programs that amount to a 'race to the top', in the sense of considering the laws applied by the most active and sophisticated enforcement authorities as the basis for their corporate compliance policy, applied everywhere regardless of jurisdiction and cross-border effects. This results in a duality in business behaviour, depending on whether the firm operates only at a domestic or cross-border level, and incentives to collude may emerge between firms of the same industry, leading into the realm of international price fixing or export/import cartels and commission of offences that impact different local markets. Whether this is known to competition authorities remains uncertain. This will be further discussed below.

To provide solutions to these challenges, chapter nine suggests novel proposals that can strengthen the joint work of young competition authorities in the

[4] Interview with Ragazzo.

[5] Horna, 'Regional Coordination in Cartel Investigations: The Liquid Oxygen Case' 287.

fight against regional CBCs in Latin America. As discussed in chapter seven, Latin American countries have undertaken important actions in the fight against CBCs. In addition, sub-regional networks have played an important role in shaping regional competition law efforts in the region. To date, and as presented in chapter seven, only one sub-region grouping in Latin America (the Andean Community of Nations) has a regional competition authority that is currently investigating a regional CBC within the Andean member countries (Bolivia, Colombia, Ecuador and Peru). In what follows, two further building blocks are presented that will complement and augment the efforts made by Latin American competition authorities in the last years.

9.1. From Calculus-Based Trust (CBT) to Knowledge-Based Trust (KBT)

As noted in the conceptual framework in chapter eight, KBT activities are crucial in developing regional competition enforcement in Latin America. Sometimes, however, the value of these activities is underestimated, and their full potential is hampered due to political and institutional constraints in young competition regimes.

Chapter seven discussed the background of Latin American competition laws, and these developments have always been influenced by political willingness. That, of course, can easily undermine any prospect of KBT; Latin American peers know how challenging it is to implement competition laws and policies when the authority does not have full independence from the central government or when the public accountability of the authority is undermined by the way the head of authority or its representatives are appointed.

Trust has variously been either developed or destroyed in the main sub-regions in Latin America, but it has not been fully developed anywhere. CBT, in some instances, was never transformed into KBT let alone into IBT, which it would seem Latin American countries should have already achieved, given their cultural similarities, absence of language barriers and other unique concordances that even the Nordic countries might not rival.

9.1.1. Development of Trust in Selected Regional Groupings

To measure trust development in the three sub-regional groupings in Latin America, one should use the benchmark provided in chapter eight as to whether trust is CBT or KBT in nature. Overall, it seems that a workable level of trust has been achieved in Latin America; in other words, somewhere between CBT and KBT. In what follows, a detailed review of trust in the main sub-regional networks is presented.

9.1.1.1. The Andean Community

In a recent interview with a representative of the Andean Community Secretariat, it became plain that there remains an important problem of trust between the Andean Community national competition authorities. This is reflected in the following: (1) criticism between agencies about how their norms and procedures on competition should be applied; (2) different procedures as to how confidential information is treated, showing that information amongst them does not flow as it does when it comes to the regional competition authority. Trust will therefore be vertical, between national and regional authorities, rather than horizontal trust amongst the national competition authorities.[6]

Despite this, a working level of horizontal KBT activities can still be seen among the younger authorities (Bolivia and Ecuador[7]) vis-à-vis the relatively older ones (Colombia and Peru) beyond the work of the Andean Community of Nations. For example, through technical assistance programmes, members of these authorities have interacted in both personal and institutional manners, in the strengthening of their competition institutions and the capacities of their human resources in the area of competition law and policies.[8]

9.1.1.2. The Central American Network of Competition Authorities (RECAC)

According to recent interviews conducted to three heads of Central American competition authorities, a certain level of trust has been achieved thanks to the work carried out by the network of Central American competition authorities (RECAC), as discussed in chapter three.[9]

The trust achieved among Central American competition authorities rests on personal ties that the heads of the authorities have developed over time and transferred to the subsequent heads of authorities in recent years.[10] The question remains as to whether this level of trust refers to CBT, KBT or even IBT. The assessment carried out on the facts provided in the interviews suggest that KBT has developed so far in the central American sub-region, with the exception of

[6] Interview with Van Brackel Barbosa.

[7] 'The institutional and legal framework is 100% implemented in Bolivia or Ecuador whereby effective competition law enforcement (using substantive regional law provisions) is taking place in these markets, fostering the consolidated competition culture in the remaining Andean countries: Colombia and Peru': Horna (2012: 338).

[8] A positive experience of the interaction of Andean countries is the technical assistance of UNCTAD with the support of Switzerland. The COMPAL Programme was established in 2003 and has run for more than 15 years. In 2015, its third phase was launched in Lima. See 'La Cooperación Suiza En El Perú | Alianza Entre INDECOPI, UNCTAD y La Cooperación Suiza – SECO Continua Para El Lanzamiento Del Programa COMPAL III'.

[9] See the three interviews conducted at the ICN Annual Conference in Porto with Cardoze, Guzman and Lozano.

[10] Interview with Guzman.

Guatemala, which has no competition law or authority in place, despite obligations to third parties such as the EU. Informal cooperation based on KBT is facilitated by the RECAC with certain limitations, as much of the information exchanged is of general use and nothing sensitive is exchanged despite efforts to meet regularly amongst the heads of authorities.[11]

Unfortunately, KBT activities cannot lead to a full understanding of each other's laws and regulations and thus they cannot discuss case-specific regional cooperation because of the lack of independence of some Central American competition authorities to disclose information and speak on behalf of the authority at the international level.[12] Even if a central American competition authority is independent by law, there is always an influential way of intervening in some cases that are critical to the country and in some cases to the Central American sub-region.[13]

9.1.1.3. MERCOSUR

Similar to the Andean setting, in MERCUSOR there are two important and relatively advanced competition authorities (Argentina and Brazil) that traditionally compete with each other to be the leading competition authority in the sub-region. As discussed in chapter one, Brazil and Argentina's competition law systems date back several decades, but effective enforcement of competition rules only happened from the beginning of the 1990s. In contrast, Uruguay and Paraguay are two young and very small competition authorities that coexist with these two bigger authorities. These countries have little contestable markets, lack of sufficient human and financial resources to run competition authorities, and depend heavily on the bigger neighbouring authorities.

In fact, perhaps MERCOSUR competition authorities have gone through different stages of trust due to this spread in the levels of development of their competition authorities. For instance, despite Argentina and Brazil adopting a number of initiatives at regional and bilateral levels in order to increase coordination of their enforcement activities, little has been achieved, due to the asymmetric stages of development of these authorities and lack of confidence from the part

[11] According to the head of the Nicaraguan Competition Authority, Dr Luis Humberto Guzmán, under the Central American Integration scheme, confidential information is already exchanged in commercial matters. Hence, he does not see any problem if confidential information should also be exchanged in competition matters. Indeed, he refers to informal exchange of 'confidential' information among the head of agencies but has not led to any specific outcome. See Interview with Guzmán.

[12] For instance, the Costa Rican Competition Authority has a Commission (COPROCOM) that relies on its internal secretariat that is part of the Ministry of Economy. Clearly, the investigations carried out need to be endorsed first by the Minister of Economy and not necessarily by the Commissioners, which are not part of the Government. See OECD, 'Competition Law and Policy in Costa Rica'.

[13] Nicaragua is a good example where the authority is independent but political influence to the Head might lead to inconsistencies and interference in the way competition enforcement is handled. See Interview with Guzman.

of Brazil in the objectiveness of the functioning of the Argentine system.[14] In 2016, a change of government in Argentina brought a new head of the Argentine authority; if they can renew the ties with Brazil and other MERCOSUR countries, that would be a new beginning for trust development.[15]

9.1.2. Building Trust Among Young Competition Authorities for Regional CBC Investigations

Latin American cases as presented in chapter seven have the necessary elements to trigger the solutions proposed in the present chapter because competition authorities have already started the process of strengthening their trust and mutual understanding, particularly by signing an informal cooperation agreement called the Lima Declaration of 2013. This led, in April 2017, to the launch of a new strategic alliance between the more advanced competition authorities in the region (Argentina, Brazil, Chile and Mexico) to cooperate in the investigation of cartels and other forms of monopolisation and to advance a common enforcement agenda for the region.[16]

In particular, KBT activities in the Latin American region can be developed in the three different sub-regions through the overall frameworks that surround the member countries as well as the economic and commercial ties amongst them.[17] For instance, at the level of the RECAC in Central America, member countries need to ensure that a high-level understanding of each other's laws and regulations is achieved, particularly at the level of procedural laws and regulations. In the absence of a sub-regional competition authority such as the Andean Community, domestic competition authorities play a more important role in sharing regional competition law developments.

For these reasons, the following measures can be put into practice by young competition authorities at the three sub-regions geographically delimited throughout the region.

[14] Another reason which created obstacles to the development of the Argentina-Brazil partnership was the lack of personal contact between the officers and commissioners of the authorities, partly because of the limited number of commissioners participating in events organised by international fora. Botta (2009: 175).

[15] Esteban Greco, Head of the Argentinean Authority said recently: 'I am confident that we are starting a new chapter in the history of competition policy enforcement in Argentina. The new government that took office in December 2015 truly believes that competitive markets are a valid institution to efficiently allocate resources in the economy. In this context, therefore, competition law enforcement is a top priority to the government.' Competition Policy International (2016: 3).

[16] The alliance was announced by Mexico and they will invite Colombia and Peru to be part of this alliance. See 'Región: Surge Nueva Alianza de Cooperación Para La Competencia | Competition Policy International'.

[17] Interview with Guzman.

1. **For the Andean Community sub-region**: As KBT has been achieved in the Andean Community thanks partly to the sub-regional competition authority, there could be some specific actions to move forward towards IBT activities, in particular to develop a more horizontal trust among Andean competition authorities as explained above. In this regard, Andean competition authorities 'should engage in processes that permit them to share common group membership, common interests, common goals and objectives, similar reactions to common situations, and situations in which they stand for the same values and principles thereby demonstrating integrity'.[18]

2. **For the Central American sub-region**: Since there is a lack of a supranational and sub-regional competition authority in Central America[19] and chances are that this in the immediate run will not be changed (as discussed in chapter four), regional CBC investigations can instead be developed through the network of domestic competition authorities. This occurred when RECAC members held preliminary talks to investigate the agricultural markets in sub-region, in particular the fertiliser market, given the interlinked ties within Central American companies in this particular market.[20] In the same vein, Honduras' allegations of a regional CBC taking place in the sugar sector were only prosecuted and sanctioned at the domestic level in 2012. Therefore, KBT activities can foster not only through RECAC activities but also through technical assistance and capacity-building programmes.

3. **For the MERCOSUR sub-region**: Given the asymmetries discussed above that have hampered the development of trust among MERCOSUR members, including the latest member, Venezuela, which withdrew in 2006,[21] CBT activities would need to be re-established first in the MERCOSUR area before moving forward to the next stages of KBT and IBT.

Figure 9.1 summarises the stages in which the sub-regions are to be developed in the years to come.

[18] Lewicki (2006: 105).

[19] 'Escolán, former Superintendente de Competencia of El Salvador points to three different challenges the countries face to implement a regional competition law and policy: (a) the need to have a competition law and a competition authority in Guatemala, (b) asymmetries among countries, in terms of resources and experience, (c) the political issues and institutional arrangements, such as the resistance of some countries to accept jurisdiction of regional entities; the need to ensure a fair distribution of the costs and burden of maintaining a regional authority; and the need to ensure proper, effective coordination with local competition authorities, regulators and so on. According to Escolán, solving these issues will take a long time, so in the meantime joint enforcement may start by collaborating in the merger control. For instance, when the transaction has a regional dimension the review could be made by one agency. This would save time and resources for the authorities and the parties involved, as only one filing would be needed and one agency would do the review of the effects of the merger in the region as a whole.' Odio-Rohrmoser (2016: 158).

[20] Interview with Guzman.

[21] Malamud, 'Venezuela's Withdrawal from the Andean Community of Nations'.

Figure 9.1 The Stages of Trust Development in Latin America

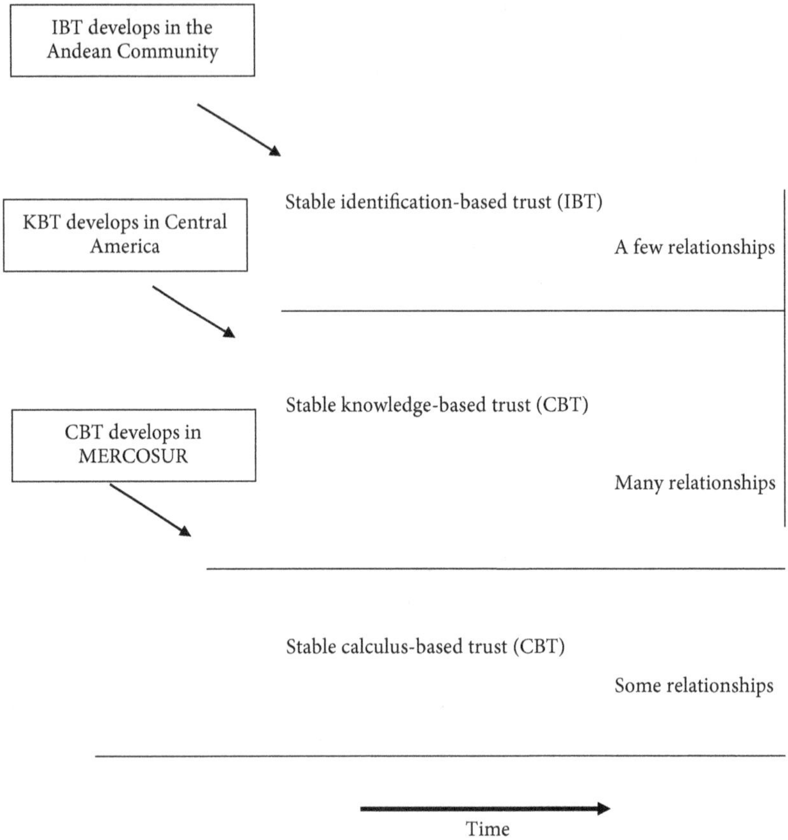

Source: adaptation from Lewicki 'Trust in Relationships', at p.156.

9.1.3. Introducing Ad-Hoc Information Gateways Among Young Competition Authorities

Due to failure in prompting effective leniency programmes in young competition authorities' jurisdictions[22] as well as the perception of regional leniency applicants as discussed in chapter eight, one way to strengthen the work of exchanging

[22] In developing countries the question would be to strike a balance between ex-officio investigations and leniency applications. As such, UNCTAD said 'A leniency programme is ineffective unless cartels are actively and significantly punished. If that precondition is not met, then it is rational to forgo a leniency programme.' UNCTAD, The Use of Leniency Programmes as a Tool for the Enforcement of Competition Law against Hardcore Cartels in Developing Countries' 14.

information amongst young competition authorities is to enable specific domestic legislations to safeguard sharable information exchanged at the cross-border level. The recent experience of Peru can prove to be useful to take into account in this regard by providing a sort of ad-hoc information gateway to the authority in case they need to share information with their foreign counterparts.

In December 2015, an amendment of the competition law was passed in Peru to allow the competition authority to exchange information (including confidential information) with other foreign competition authorities provided there are international agreements or agency-to-agency cooperation schemes, and provided the retention of information when it comes to leniency applications.[23] Peru is therefore a jurisdiction that has information gateways as in the meaning provided by the OECD.[24] In accordance with Ivo Gagliuffi, Head of the Peruvian competition authority (INDECOPI), the enabling statute of December 2015 provides the legal basis to exchange information with foreign competition authorities without having an international treaty between states, where a mere agreement between authorities would suffice. As a result, if reasonably good faith between the authorities is perceived by Peru then that would be sufficient to move forward in exchanging information, even if it is confidential. In this regard, no distinction between mature or young competition authorities can be deemed as a constraint.[25] Of course, it remains to be seen how this enabling legislation would be used in practice.[26]

9.2. Strengthening Information Cooperation Through Coordination Games

The benefits of coordination in competition cases can be appreciated from the following quotation which provides a practical dimension of why competition authorities (whether they are small, young, mature) need to cooperate:

> … it is possible that an agency may not be aware of a cartel affecting its jurisdiction, while another agency has cognisance of it. In the case of international cartels,

[23] See International Cooperation provision Peru Amendment of some Competition Act provisions P. 561987.

[24] '… when national legal provisions or international agreements explicitly empower the enforcement agency to exchange confidential information with other competition authorities in other jurisdictions, under certain conditions. These provisions allow the transmission of the confidential information even if the interested parties have not consented to the transmission. This paper will refer to these provisions as "information gateways" …' OECD, 'National And International Provisions For The Exchange Of Confidential Information Between Competition Agencies Without Waivers' 2.

[25] Interview with Gagliuffi.

[26] The survey by OECD and ICN in 2013 revealed that '… the gateway for disclosure to an overseas agency is quite heavily circumscribed by a number of considerations that the agency must make in relation to each disclosure. This means that the disclosure can be burdensome, in particular in balancing whether the disclosure of confidential information is necessary in the context of another agency's case …' OECD & ICN (2013: 131).

> coordination of investigatory measures may be necessary in order to avoid the risk of destruction of evidence if one agency moves before other agencies, on whose territory evidence may be located. Subsequently, agencies may well wish to gain access to evidence located outside their own jurisdiction. More general discussions and comparing of notes between investigators of the same cartel in different agencies may facilitate the smooth progression of the case, and better rebutting of the arguments of the parties. Information on turnover relevant for the calculation of sanctions may be exchanged.[27]

Therefore, as a way of finding an experimental solution to the problem of coordination, the possible use of coordination games to strengthen informal cooperation for cross-border investigations among young competition authorities should be considered. It presupposes one thing, though: an existing relationship of cooperation between the young competition authorities.

This subsection reviews the literature on the different coordination games, then discusses which coordination games could be applied by analogy to cross-border cooperation of young competition authorities, and provides specific proposals on how to strengthen informal cross-border coordination of young competition authorities to deal with regional CBCs, particularly in two of the three sub-regions (Central America and MERCUSOR).

9.2.1. The Problem of Cooperation vs The Problem of Coordination

At the outset, it is worth noting the difference between cooperation and coordination. Game theory provides useful insights that can underline the difference between these two concepts. In fact, game theory applied to competition is a method of analysis used to investigate problems of decision-making in situations involving competition, conflict, collusion and cooperation. As such, the game theorist wishes to understand the factual background in a situation of conflict or collusion.[28] It has been noted by Norman and Trachtman, however, that game theory models 'can never capture all real-world detail, including its highly nuanced decision making [nor can it] predict or prescribe behaviour, but to generate testable hypotheses that, once tested, are expected to tell us something useful about the world.'[29]

Having said the foregoing, coordination games refer 'to a game in which players have identical preferences over strategy combinations, with two or more

[27] ICN (2007: 7).

[28] Game theory is essentially 'the study of the basic elements of many person conscious conflict and cooperation. It deals, at a high level of abstraction, with the description and analysis of multiperson cross-purposes optimization.' Shubik (1991: 285).

[29] Norman and Trachtman (2005: 542).

(Nash equilibrium) combinations at which each player's strategy choice is a unique best reply if the other player correctly anticipates it, but not in general otherwise'.[30]

Following the concept above of game theory that is applicable to competition,[31] coordination games will be the conceptual framework that will be utilised in this sub-section to deal with problems of lack of coordination between young competition authorities in the Latin American region. Since the mid-1950s, the literature on game theory has been utilised in competition law analysis[32] and has provided useful insights in understanding adversarial posturing, managing conflict or cooperation among many parties with differing goals and varying strategic power.[33]

As far as coordination games are concerned, they could entail multiple equilibria payoffs[34] which could eventually offer a 'distributional choice between conflicting preferences of different individual, which must be made on the basis of some complex and contestable normative theory'.[35]

Often the problem of cooperation is represented by the prisoner's dilemma (PD) game wherein the puzzle is solved by changing the incentives to sanctions, that is to say, incorporating CBT activities that solve the problem of cooperation through deterrence between the parties that to failure to cooperate (neglect). In turn, the problem of coordination as represented by coordination games is solved by changing expectations rather than incentives. The solution to the problems of cooperation provided by the PD, however, represent a certain level of 'ineffectiveness and counter productivity of these sanctions in correcting the problem of defection or free riding in the [PD].'[36]

Coordination games provide an alternative to the problem of cooperation that has been traditionally exemplified by the PD in economics, politics and law. PD has been applied to explain topics such as contracts, property, international law,[37] and of course, competition law enforcement issues.[38]

The basic concept of PD refers to two parties pursuing 'their own individual interests and act in a rationally selfish manner, which results in both parties ending up in a worse position than if they had cooperated and pursued the group's interests instead of their own'.[39] As such, although PD is a brilliant way of illustrating the problem of cooperation, cooperation failures are not the only obstacles individuals

[30] The term 'coordination games' is from Crawford and Haller (1990: 571).
[31] Shubik (1956: 598).
[32] See Shubik (1991).
[33] Shubik (1991: 299).
[34] Opposite to single equilibrium games where it provides a tidy and definitive prediction of the behavioural outcome, multiple equilibria provides other factors such as culture and history because once factored into the payoffs, their influence is fully exhausted. McAdams (2008: 212).
[35] ibid: 212–13.
[36] Julia Y Lee (2012: 1138).
[37] See Norman and Trachtman (2005).
[38] For a complete analysis on how the prisoner's dilemma model destabilises cartels and the impact of leniency applications, see Leslie (2005).
[39] ibid: 455.

face in achieving their ends as society also needs mechanisms for coordination.[40] The problem of coordination arises when 'two or more individuals can reach some mutually desired outcome – or avoid some mutually undesired outcome – only by combining their actions in a certain way, but where more than one possible combination will suffice'.[41]

Legal scholars have been studying how legal rules impact strategic behaviour. Through assumptions such as the PD scheme as well as coordination games in its most common forms (assurance, battle of the sexes and chicken games), solutions as to how to solve the lack of coordination have been proposed.[42]

As indicated in chapter eight, building trust in its three forms (CBT, KBT and IBT) as well as increasing the perception that others are cooperating would be far more effective in solving the PD scheme, which is based on sanctions.

9.2.2. The Assurance or 'Stag Hunt' Game

The stag hunt (SH) or assurance game addresses the problem of coordination when 'one's actions with others in situations where everyone does best by cooperating, but otherwise should all defect'.[43] The standard graphic for this game can be best represented in a two-by-two matrix whereby there are two players (hunters) with two potential strategies (hunt a stag or a hare), each strategy having its potential payoff (Figure 9.2).

Figure 9.2 The 'Stag Hunt' or Assurance Game

Hunter 1

Hunter 2	Strategy 1: (Stag)	Strategy 2: (Hare)
Strategy 1 (Stag)	Bigger payoffs for both hunters: 4, 4	0, 3
Strategy 2 (Hare)	3, 0	Smaller payoffs for both hunters: 3, 3

Source: drawn from Lee 'Gaining Assurances' at p.1144.

As illustrated in Fugure 9.3, while hunting a stag needs the coordination of both hunters, a hare can be caught by only one hunter but with a lower payoff (3).

[40] The 'prisoners' (pure) coordination game' is mentioned in this analysis whereby the prisoners could eventually walk free out of prison if they previously agreed on the alibi that confirms their whereabouts at the time of the crime. Without previous coordination, it would be impossible to know that would be the consistent alibi that each prisoner would separately say and choose to match before the prosecutor. McAdams (2008: 218).

[41] ibid: 219.

[42] Lee, 'Gaining Assurances' (2012: 1138).

[43] ibid: 1143.

The ideal situation is to hunt a stag *together* with a superior nutritional value, and each of the hunters will have a payoff of 4 is attributed. The problem arises when hunter 1 cannot be reassured that its counterpart will hunt the same bait and as such hunting a stag alone will lead to starvation, that is, payoff of 0. As such, there are two different outcomes here: catching a stag would mean having a payoff of 4 for both hunters (optimal result) and by default, hunting a mere hare would mean a sub-optimal result of 3. According to conventional theory the solution to solve the coordination dilemma would be 'to get each of the players to expect that the other player will hunt stag [by incorporating] mechanisms that can assure that each [hunter] that the other will cooperate and hunt [the] stag'.[44]

9.2.3. The Battle of the Sexes Game

In the battle of the sexes game (BOS), there is a conflict because player 1 (husband) would prefer to go to A (prize fight) and player 2 (wife) prefers B (ballet), but neither wishes to attend the activity alone, and therefore they must negotiate to choose the most convenient one for both.[45] The key issue here is to avoid outcomes where each of them would be worse off than had an agreement been made. This situation is illustrated in Figure 9.3.

Figure 9.3 The battle of the sexes game (BOS)

		Wife	
		Option Prize fight	Option Ballet
Husband	Option Prize fight	Bigger payoff for husband: 3, 1	0, 0
	Option Ballet	0, 0	Bigger payoff for wife: 1, 3

Source: Derived from: Lee 'Gaining Assurances' at P. 1144.

As can be seen from the illustration, both players (husband and wife) should avoid mutual deference, as it would be the worst outcome (where husband and wife do prize fight and ballet on their own), and would in fact be worse than mutual non-cooperation. BOS is a useful model of bargaining and a typical example of the

[44] ibid: 1145.

[45] The BOS comes from the conventional name where the husband wants to go to the prize-fight while the wife wants to go to ballet, but neither wants to go alone and hence they negotiate in order to go to the less-favoured thing in order to be with the other, that is to say, they prefer togetherness rather than being alone heart their favoured event.

standard setting in company negotiations whereby different companies would need to agree to certain technical standards to allow their products to interact.[46]

9.2.4. Applying Coordination Games to CBC Enforcement Among Young Competition Authorities

Using the 'conversational game theory'[47] in analysing international cooperation, one can conclude that coordination would be more beneficial than cooperation when young competition authorities in Latin America already have reached some level of cooperation in certain cases, in particular when a sub-regional competition authority is already in place (eg, the Andean Community). When young competition authorities wish to coordinate their enforcement activities when fighting regional CBCs, key questions are raised as to how they can be aware of the existence of this regional unlawful activity and whether they can work together with neighbouring trading partners.

In an attempt to answer these questions, coordination games could play a role in this exercise because they would assist in laying out the specific strategies for young competition authorities to implement. For instance, in the liquid oxygen cases in Latin America discussed in chapter seven, none of the Latin American young competition authorities verified with their counterparts if the same liquid oxygen companies were undertaking the same actions in their respective territories. Neither did they discuss ways of approaching the same unlawful business practices, nor coordinate dawn raids at the regional level.[48] In this example, the introduction of coordination games would have meant efficiency of the resources allocated to investigate these cartels and ultimately better deterrence at the regional level.

What are the benefits of applying coordination games before the young competition authorities start an investigation? The first benefit would be the ability to receive tip-offs from other young but relatively advanced competition authorities that have already started investigating the company. Another benefit would be having intelligence information from other competition agencies that could help in analysing if the cartel has an impact in a particular jurisdiction.

Of course, at the pre-investigatory phase, young competition authorities would need to handle two different variables: strategy and risk. First, from the strategic viewpoint, young competition authorities face the important decision to either initiate a cartel investigation with regional dimension (a regional CBC) or to

[46] McAdams (2008: 222).

[47] Conversational game theory is mostly applicable to social sciences to illustrate new modes of thought and ways of viewing simple models that can be described verbally. Indeed, conversational game theory deals with the big picture, the basic concepts and principles at stake, not calculation or detail. Shubik (1991: 299–300).

[48] See more in: Horna, 'Regional Coordination in Cartel Investigations: The Liquid Oxygen Case'.

devote their efforts on domestic cartels with the same or even more harmful effects. During the latest ICN annual conference, one interviewee said that his competition authority had prioritised national over international cartels, in particular when the sector or market at stake was a key sector of the domestic economy.[49] Second, the risk of leaking agency information that could be sharable (under the meaning provided in chapter 10) may prevent the cooperation and the coordination of dawn raids where the authorities need to secure simultaneous search warrants in all the companies' premises.

Such strategy and risk present at the pre-investigatory phase may not be as relevant if one or two neighbouring competition authorities have already opened a formal investigation, as the information used to open an investigation is no longer confidential. Hence, relatively advanced but still young competition authorities would be in a better position to share information at the investigatory phase with its younger counterparts while respecting confidential information rules. Most probably they would only share summaries of the documentation received that could be deemed non-confidential or sharable. Benefits of cooperation at this stage would be three-fold: (1) ample knowledge of the approach of the case and the theory of harm so as to better scope the case and decide on the best pieces of evidence to seek at the domestic jurisdiction; (2) increased likelihood that cooperation would yield trust between companies and younger competition authorities as a result of the exchange of sharable information at the investigatory level, while respecting confidential information in the absence of waivers;[50] and (3) better possibility streamlining the investigation while keeping the costs down due to the more efficient ways of tracking information on the whereabouts of companies or individuals.

Coordination games can also help align strategies and information gathered from cartel enforcement cases and merger notifications. Indeed, when possible, agency and sharable information could be exchanged among young competition authorities when they receive merger notifications from regional companies operating in a regional relevant market.[51] This proposal assumes that an international merger transaction can be a way to legalise a regional CBC. As a result, incorporating the information gathered from merger notifications, whether they are hostile takeovers or any other kind, would deter cartels from taking that road and legalising a regional CBC.

[49] Interview with Toh.

[50] As discussed in chapter six, in particular section 6.1.2., young competition authorities may not develop the best leniency programmes that could develop trust to international applicants. Hence, the assumption here is that no waivers are granted by the leniency applicants or that a young competition authority has launched an ex-officio investigation whereby some intelligence information is demanded from its neighbouring trading partner (another young competition authority) and that would be the starting point for cooperation at this scenario.

[51] This information exchange can take place in two ways: internally within the agency or amongst competition peers. See more in: Cosnita-Langlais and Tropeano (2013).

9.2.5. Promoting Informal Coordination Through 'Coordination Games' in Latin America

The Lima Declaration signed between Colombia, Chile and Peru in 2013 is an important development that has led to the revival of the sub-regional competition law enforcement in the Andean community region with the investigation of regional cases.[52] This fact has facilitated the flow of information at the pre-investigatory phase within these three authorities and has created the incentives to the other Latin American competition authorities (Ecuador and Bolivia) to share information with the Andean Community Secretariat. However, there is still some way to go in terms of strengthening the coordination strategies of the young Latin American competition authorities, in particular when they are jointly fighting a regional CBC since there is no a pan-Latin American regional competition authority[53] that could deal with this type of regional CBC.

In what follows, this research proposes the application of the stag hunt game to address the problem of coordination among Latin American competition peers.

9.2.5.1. The Rationale of the Stag Hunt Game

As explained above, the SH game presupposes that both players would need to take the riskier strategy because it will provide the higher payoff. In this connection, both players would need to be reassured that both would follow the same strategy, which could be achieved by managing expectations through pre-play communication, learning about each other and other KBT activities (as indicated in chapter 10). Therefore, applying the SH or assurance game principle would allow younger competition authorities in Latin America to start coordinating their efforts against regional CBCs.

9.2.5.2. Solving the Coordination Problem

When applying the SH game, let us assume that the players would be the younger competition authorities in Latin America whereby strategy 1 would be: full coordination at the pre-investigatory phase, including simultaneous dawn raids and exchanging sharable; and strategy 2 would be: partial coordination once the investigation is opened because strategic information cannot be disclosed until the parties are notified. The payoffs would have four distinctive variables: '4' would mean full optimal deterrence of the regional CBC by prosecuting together the cartel at the domestic level; '3' would mean partial or sub-optimal

[52] See the opening of a regional investigation into the tissue paper cartel: *Andean Community – Opening of a Cartel Investigation in the Tissue Paper market against Kimberly Clark* (n 830).

[53] At the Andean sub-regional level, there is only one sub-regional competition authority in the region. See CAN Regional Competition Law.

deterrence of the regional CBC; '0' would mean the immunity of the regional CBC and proliferation of incentives to cartelise at the regional level. According to the SH standard graph applied to this problem, the simplest form would be as shown in Figure 9.4.

Figure 9.4 Coordination of Young Latin American Competition Authorities

		Young Competition Authority 2	
		Strategy 1	Strategy 2
Young Competition Authority 1	Strategy 1	4, 4	0, 3
	Strategy 2	3, 0	3, 3

Source: own elaboration based on the stag hunt game.

Figure 9.4 shows a multiple equilibrium (4,4 and 3,3) whereby the highest payoff for both authorities (4,4) would mean full deterrence of the regional CBC, seconded by the smaller but still significant payoff (3,3) for both younger competition authorities. The coordination problem could be solved if both younger competition authorities have repeated interaction at the level of heads of authorities and/or directors of cartel investigation units or even case lead officers. Those 'focal points', in the meaning provided by McAdams, can coordinate their behaviour and predict the likely behaviour of others.[54] In other words, IBT activities can be reached from the KBT assumptions that Latin American competition authorities already show.

9.2.5.3. A Hypothetical Case: The Airline Sector

A sector that has been gradually liberalised and deregulated in Latin America in recent years is the airline sector,[55] thanks to the multilateral agreement of open skies for the member states of the Latin American Commission of Civil Aviation.[56] The airline sector in Latin American markets has the following particularities:

[54] McAdams (2008).

[55] Historically the airline sector was a highly regulated market in the US until 1978 and the Airline Deregulation Act that allowed a progressive liberalisation and deregulation. In addition, the worldwide airline sector has been enlarged through a number of bilateral agreements that have allowed airline carriers to service different routes across continents. In the past, the prices were regulated by IATA as a market outside the scope of the WTO. As such, possibilities of international airline transport depended on the air freedom principles which are always subject to negotiation amongst states. 'Open skies' policies are therefore the rule in these particular agreements and at the domestic level, national regulations would govern the entry and operations of service providers (limits to capacity in the number of flights or seats available, routes designations, price approvals as well as other security concerns and environment protection). See more Lu (2002: ch 1).

[56] When the Fifth Worldwide Air Transport Conference met in 2003 there were 87 liberalised agreements involving 70 countries, 59 of which were US open-skies agreements. As of October 2012 there were over 400 liberalised agreements involving 145 states. Of these, over 100 were US open-skies

1. high entry barriers, as the 'freedoms of the skies' system limits the granting of freedom to foreign airlines to operate in domestic airports;[57]
2. the relevant markets are defined by 'city-pairs' rather than 'airport-pairs', as in the case of Europe;
3. there are no alternatives modes of transportations such as high-speed trains; and
4. an unprecedented number of mergers (takeovers) have been occurring, leading to high levels of aggregate concentration that can significantly impact regional competition in Latin America.

In fact, a 'duopoly' in the airline sector can be found between two main groups of companies, AVIANCA and LATAM. The former is part of 'Star Alliance' and the latter part of 'One World'.[58] The case of the airline sector can provide a good model for regional collusion between AVIANCA and LATAM, wherein they would divide the Latin American sub-regions by flight routes and airports as well as foreclose the entrance of new competitors.

Having provided the hypothetical scenario for the Latin American region, let us now review the preliminary questions that domestic competition authorities in the region have when trying to tackle the effects of a possible regional cartel AVIANCA-LATAM in their domestic jurisdictions.

Question 1: Whether there is a need for cooperation and coordination or whether the competition authorities can work on their own as long as the effects of this regional cartel are impacting their domestic markets.

Question 2: Whether there would be a handful of Latin American competition authorities that would need to start the investigation at the same time, such as simultaneous dawn raids (notably in the case of Chile and Brazil for LATAM and Colombia for AVIANCA) and how much information they would need to share at the pre-investigatory phase.

Question 3: Whether the participation of the other young competition authorities in the region, notably Central American countries and Andean countries, is beneficial in the regional CBC investigation.

agreements. In addition, the number of liberalising regional agreements has expanded since 2003; for example, Association of Southeast Asian Nations (ASEAN) members have concluded an agreement to achieve a single open-sky market by 2015, and other liberal agreements have been concluded by South Pacific island states, the Caribbean Community and members of the Latin American Civil Aviation Commission (LACAC) International Civil Aviation Organization, 'Liberalization of Market Access'.

[57] These restrictions preclude airlines from exploiting the benefits of operating as a network. Constraints on entry and foreign ownership have forced the major regional airlines, such as Avianca-TACA and LAN, to create subsidiary companies in different countries as a means to penetrate domestic markets. 'Sectoral Study on Competition on the Airline Passenger Transport in Latin America | Competition Policy International'.

[58] For instance, for decades, TACA absorbed the majority of national air carriers in Central America, and by 2009, TACA itself was absorbed by the Colombian conglomerate, the AVIANCA Group. In 2011, the LAN Group merged with the Brazilian TAM leading to the LATAM Group, being the biggest in the South American region.

Assuming that the answers to these three questions are positive, and then one could imagine the following strategies that the lead-investigating authorities would take in the regional CBC investigation.

Strategy 1 Exchange of information at the pre-investigatory phase: full cooperation and coordination between Brazil, Chile and Colombia in the exchange of intelligence information about the regional duopoly's business behaviour, possible theory of harm of the regional CBC and how the regional market has been divided over the flight routes and hub airports in the region. The coordination could also be helpful to organise simultaneous raids in the three jurisdictions at stake.

Strategy 2 Coordination at the investigatory phase: exchange of evidence gathered at the investigatory phase among the three jurisdictions provided no confidential information is exchanged unless there are information gateways between the three competition authorities.

The payoffs are organised as follows: '4' would mean full prosecution and deterrence of the regional CBC, ceasing of key documents and avoidance of evidence destruction in other jurisdictions, including other younger jurisdictions beyond Brazil, Chile and Colombia.

Payoff '3' would mean sub-optimal prosecution and deterrence of the regional CBC because some of the key competition authorities have problems in sharing information as there is no confidentiality waiver. But at least, at the investigatory phase, some information can be exchanged. Payoff '0' would mean no coordination, unilateral enforcement of competition rules and attempt to apply anti-cartel laws extraterritorially but with limited results. In addition, domestic key evidence was destroyed because the companies were notified that dawn raids were taking place in neighbouring countries.

Figure 9.5 demonstrates how the SH game can provide important insights as to the benefits of coordination in this particular regional CBC investigation.

Figure 9.5 Coordination of Young Latin American Competition Authorities in the Airline Sector

Young Competition Authority 1 \ Young Competition Authority 2	Strategy 1	Strategy 2
Strategy 1	4,4	0,3
Strategy 2	3,0	3,3

Source: own elaboration based on the stag hunt game.

The coordination game story provides clarity on the specific payoffs of each of the strategies at stake for the three competition authorities wishing to enter into a coordination scheme. Another benefit of the coordination game is to cross-share information gathered from the merger notifications when the air carriers provided information at the domestic level to seek domestic approval of their merger transactions, notably the case of Chile and Brazil at the LATAM merger operation of 2011.[59]

9.3. Summary and Outlook

Chapter nine presents the last proposal in this research to foster regional cooperation in young competition regimes, taking the example of Latin America as a case study. This novel proposal builds on specific foundations: trust, common ground and incentives. Chapter nine develops a theoretical approach on how trust can be boosted in Latin America. In addition, it incorporates ideas on how legal measures could be strengthened to facilitate cooperation through ad-hoc information gateways.

A contribution to the system of incentives provided by coordination games is to enable authorities to progress from CBT to KBT, and even in some cases to IBT where it can be incorporated in relatively advanced but still young jurisdictions such as Brazil, Chile and Mexico.

In sum, if young competition authorities in Latin America wish to strengthen their already significant cooperation efforts, heads of the authorities would need to invest more time and resources in international cooperation to tackle regional cartels in Latin America. It is not enough to have signed a great number of cooperation agreements between competition authorities or include competition provisions in regional trade agreements.

Regional competition enforcement is developed by case law and there is only one sub-region in Latin America that is currently advancing in this regard: the Andean Community. Still, only sub-regional cartels can be prosecuted in that grouping and therefore a need for a pan-regional competition law should be part of the agendas of the Latin American competition authorities.

Regional cartels do know the limitations of the domestic national competition authorities as in terms of prosecuting pan-Latin American regional cartels. In large jurisdictions such as Brazil and Mexico, one could say that extra-territorial application of competition rules might be the immediate solution. However, even there, no competition authority in Latin America is suitably self-sufficient to unilaterally apply competition rules to foreign companies and therefore there is still a need for international cooperation, over and above the need to further streamline the informal cooperation initiatives being proliferated in different sub-regions in Latin America.

[59] See Cosnita-Langlais and Tropeano (2013).

10

Conclusions

> By 2000 … [w]ith the encouragement from government officials, Whitacre applied for executive clemency from the President … His self-destructive history, driven by his psychological difficulties, had left him with a sentence that *took no account* of his unprecedented cooperation in exposing one of the largest corporate conspiracies in history.[1]

Unfortunately, Mr Whitacre's story, as presented in the Introduction, can be considered a disincentive to various top executives across jurisdictions wishing to cooperate with investigators, since he did not receive full immunity despite having cooperated for years with law enforcers in lysine cartel investigations.[2]

A lesson to the world, particularly to emerging competition regimes, is that if young or small competition regimes wish to effectively and successfully put in practice a leniency programme, it needs to provide full immunity to business applicants from all possible legal methods of being prosecuted for criminal, administrative and civil offences. This is the tip of the iceberg of international cooperation; this research takes the example as inspiration for other regions wishing to follow the incredible combination of business cooperation and successful deterrence by law enforcement in the lysine cartel.

As Latin America was the geographical focus of this research, the key chapters were drawn up to cover the latest work and best practices on international cooperation and how Latin American enforcers have addressed CBCs in their own jurisdictions.

Therefore, Part II of the research detailed the various hurdles and constraints that young competition authorities, large or small, can face when dealing with mature and large enforcers during two of the five types of CBCs presented in chapter two. Reasons were provided in the introduction to Part II as to why young and small competition authorities should not prosecute multinational CBCs as their top priority, but rather focus their resources on transnational or regional

[1] Emphasis added by author. Eichenwald (2009: 565).

[2] After all, Mr Whitacre is a proven voice for re-entry to business life after being an undercover agent for the FBI during the uncovering of the lysine cartel. As such, in December of 2006, he was the Chief Operating Officer (COO) and Chief Science Officer at Cypress Systems, Inc. Official Website of Mark Whitacre, PhD.

CBCs, whereby primarily younger or smaller jurisdictions may be impacted and may have a better chance of effectively deterring these practices.

10.1. Building Blocks for Effective Transnational CBC Investigations

The first hypothesis deals with transnational CBCs. Following the novel proposals suggested in chapter eight, on trust, sharable information and the platform through which the information would be exchanged, the following notes resulted from the interviews carried out at the 2017 ICN Annual Conference, whereby a sample of enforcers worldwide were asked about the experimental and novel proposals of this research.

10.1.1. On the Issue of Trust Development between Mature or Large and Young or Small Authorities

Several interviewees from mature authorities agreed that trust is an essential and unavoidable issue that needs to be secure in order to facilitate any type of cooperation that could happen between any authorities, in particular when dealing with transnational CBCs and the effectiveness of leniency programmes in developing countries. As such, measures to develop the first stage of trust (calculus-based trust, CBT) is to suggest activities that would close the gap between these authorities such as technical assistance and capacity-building in selected beneficiary jurisdictions.

The role of technical assistance and capacity-building would facilitate interaction between officials and provide the opportunity for the mature or large authority to slowly appreciate the domestic enforcement record, the seriousness of the authority and the recognition of the local constituencies in terms of being independent and accountable vis-à-vis central government.[3] One opinion was to incorporate third parties to provide the credentials of trustee between competition authorities that have not had any type of institutional interaction before.[4] In any case, the current deliberations among the 55 members of the UNCTAD Discussion Group on International Cooperation can provide additional avenues in this quest. Results can be tangible if members agree to consolidate a text that will foster international cooperation. This can happen in 2020 when UN member states meet for the Eighth Review Conference to Review All Aspects of the UN Set on Competition.

[3] Interview with Bezzi; Interview with Toh; Interview with Irrarazabal; and Interview with Ragazzo S.
[4] Interview with Kovacic.

10.1.2. On the Issue of Incorporating a New Concept of 'Sharable' Information

Key mature authorities say that the benchmark of what constitutes sharable information should be provided on the basis of trust, if they are to share intelligence information during the pre-investigatory phase and through informal cooperation mechanisms. Sharable information should be exchanged at the investigatory or post-investigatory phases, preferably when waivers are provided by the leniency applicants.

In the absence of these waivers, conditional information gateways (as proposed in chapter nine) could be the alternative only if enough institutional trust is in place, that is to say, if mature or large competition authorities had already achieved a workable CBT, as discussed in point 1 above. It would be very rare to share information without waivers, even when the information is declared non-confidential.[5]

10.1.3. On the Issue of the Platform Proposed

The maximisation of the available instruments provided by the ICN and the UN can be complementary, provided that they do not increase the costs of cooperation. International cooperation has become expensive, given the complexity of the international competition arena.

Hence, to maximise the efforts made by competition authorities, progress should be made by moving from bilateral to multilateral platforms, such as the adoption of the multilateral MOU at IOSCO discussed in chapter six, or the adoption of an ECN modified-structure.[6] Others have proposed the adoption of a convention on cartels[7] or an agreement at the UN to better implement Section F of the UN Set on Competition under the auspices of the Eighth Review Conference in 2020. In any of these proposals, there is a need to take into account the domestic dynamics over which each jurisdiction enforces its anti-cartel laws. As Maria Luisa Tierno Centella from the EU Commission said in 2016, 'there is *no single ideal system* which fits for all [as] anti-cartel enforcement regimes are incorporated in a certain culture and legal order'.[8]

[5] Interview with Toh.

[6] Interview with Capobianco.

[7] In October 2014, a proposal from the Russian Federation to further solve the problems of international cooperation in cartel investigations was made so as to address the five issues that need to be solved when investigating cartels internationally: (1) balance of global and national interests; (2) trust between agencies; (3) existence of appropriate legal frameworks; (4) differentiation in the levels of the information protection; (5) ensuring the appropriate level of protection for confidential information received during cooperation. The Russian proposal was based on an ICN/OECD Survey, the UNCTAD report of 2013 mentioned earlier and the OECD recommendation of 2014 regarding international cooperation. Khamukov (2014: slide 5).

[8] Tierno Centella (2016: 2).

In sum, the first hypothesis to the problem of cooperation in transnational cartel investigations can be improved if the three building-block proposal is triggered in a sequential manner so as to reduce the increasing costs of cooperation as well as the duplication of efforts to avoid parallel investigations of the same cartel practice in selected transnational jurisdictions.

This solution could be an alternative to the 'spaghetti bowl' of bilateral agreements as presented in chapter three. Some of the solutions provided in chapter eight could also be complementary, such as the lead agencies model to allocate investigatory powers to one authority allocating investigating powers, and even decision-making powers in the long term.

10.2. From Cooperation to Coordination in Regional CBC Investigations

Latin America is the most suitable model in which to consider the second hypothesis, which aims to solve the problem of addressing regional CBCs. Following the proposals in chapter nine, which covered in-depth trust at the sub-regional level as well as introducing coordination games to domestic competition authorities working together against regional CBCs, the following notes transpired from the interviews with Latin American enforcers.

10.2.1. On the Issue of Strengthening Trust in the Region

An important approach to develop trust in the region is through the three sub-regions that have developed a certain level of trust. To a certain extent, KBT activities are already happening in Latin America, with the adoption of a Latin American alliance in April 2017 by the largest jurisdictions of the region: Argentina, Brazil, Chile and Mexico.[9] Whether KBT activities can lead to more cooperation would also depend on how trust is applied when dealing with leniency applications and also assuming that the physical presence of cartelists are ensured in the regional economic grouping's jurisdictions.

10.2.2. On the Issue of Introducing Coordination Games

As an endorsement of the proposal to introduce coordination games to solve the problem of several Latin American competition authorities investigating a regional CBC together,[10] the system of payoffs that provide multiple equilibria

[9] 'Región: Surge Nueva Alianza de Cooperación Para La Competencia | Competition Policy International' (n 992).

[10] Interview with Coloma.

of the several strategies that the coordination game 'stag hunt' can serve as the basis for the maximisation of domestic resources for young and small competition authorities, while creating optimal deterrence of regional CBCs. The solution does not need legal reforms or the adoption of sub-regional competition authorities, but rather the political will of the heads of the authorities to trigger cooperation and more importantly coordination of their domestic enforcement actions. As a result, regional cartelists would face simultaneous investigations from different domestic young jurisdictions, including the prosecution of a sub-regional competition authority in the Andean Community covering the domestic concerns of four countries: Bolivia, Colombia, Ecuador and Peru.

10.3. Final Reflections

It is often argued that targeting transnational CBCs should *not* be a priority for younger or smaller competition authorities. However, more mature enforcers are now increasingly starting to appreciate the role that younger authorities can play, particularly in larger jurisdictions and emerging economies, such as the BRICS countries.[11] Moreover, this research demonstrates the merits of cross-border cartel enforcement even for smaller authorities, provided that they consider putting into practice the novel proposals set forth in this research.

In fact, referring back to the perceptions about CBCs outlined in the beginning of this research, it is fair to say that there is not only a growing scope of action for young or small authorities in cooperation with more mature and larger counterparts, but also important benefits that can be reaped from such cooperation.

The arguments can be summarised as follows.

Perception 1: Young or small competition authorities should prioritise going after domestic cartels before investigating complex CBCs. Chapter seven on the Latin American case study suggests that some younger jurisdictions would find it easier to prosecute a CBC compared to cracking domestic cartels, noting that the latter are often captured by local dynamics. This evidence suggests a window of opportunity to promote awareness among younger and small competition authorities about the urgency of targeting CBCs for the benefit of their respective economies. The analysis of the airline sector in Latin America as detailed in chapter nine supports this view.

Perception 2: Cross-border cartels are all the same, and there are one-size-fits-all solutions. It has been demonstrated that from the perspective of younger

[11] BRICS is an association of the largest emerging economies in the world: Brazil, Russia, India, China and South Africa. In 2016, the competition authorities of these countries signed a memorandum of understanding on competition matters to foster more cooperation among these authorities. In 2017, the Russian Competition Authority published a toolkit to facilitate international cooperation in competition matters.

and smaller competition authorities with fewer resources, it is very important for them whether a cartel is multinational, transnational, regional, or export, or import. Of course, for more mature and larger competition authorities, CBCs might be seen as all the same. A taxonomy that attempts to differentiate each type of CBC based on a set of clear criteria is presented in chapter two. In consequence, one cannot say that there is no difference between multinational and transnational CBCs. Once again, it is the perspective of younger or smaller competition regimes that is critical here. Therefore, a clear distinction is made between multinational and transnational CBCs, taking into account the perspective of the young and small competition authorities. With reference to the classification of CBCs in chapter two, and the distinction between multinational and transnational CBCs, it has been shown in this research that young or small competition authorities are well-positioned to counteract the latter. It was confirmed in numerous interviews that this is due to the greater ability of the concerned authorities to address the harmful effects of CBCs in their respective economies and stronger propensity for cooperation between mature or larger and young or smaller authorities.

Perception 3: Regional CBCs can be successfully targeted only by effective regional competition authorities. Although it goes without saying that the establishment of regional competition authorities (if they are as effective as in the European Union) significantly facilitates regional enforcement, particularly of CBCs, this may not be a feasible option in some parts of the world. As has been shown, the effective targeting of CBCs can also be achieved through cooperation and coordination among national competition authorities. As indicated in chapter nine, there is much potential to enhance and intensify existing cooperation efforts in Latin America or the ASEAN region. In fact, coordination can be effective even without the full-on harmonisation of substantive or procedural competition rules.

In this sense, informal cooperation settings should be expanded, such as the Lima Declaration adopted in 2013. Another example of informal cooperation is the recent declaration of Latin American criminal prosecutors against corruption, signed in Brasilia in February 2017, the Brasilia Declaration, on the basis of the UN Convention against corruption adopted in 2004, that formalised informal cooperation. Of course, the Declaration was as a response to a high-profile corruption scandal of a Brazilian company that created the 'world's biggest bribery ring', compromising high-level politicians, including presidents of the republic as well as top construction companies in several Latin American countries. The question that arises here is whether only such high-profile cases can act as triggers for promoting regional cooperation, and whether there are other ways to initiate and substantiate cooperation efforts.

Perception 4: Anti-cartel laws in emerging markets are still in their infancies. As seen with the example of Latin America, the perception that there is only limited cartel enforcement in emerging markets does not always hold true. As a matter of fact, the cases of Brazil and Mexico demonstrate how leniency programmes have become a critical instrument to effectively prosecute cartels. Institutional trust and mutual understanding between mature or large and young or small competition authorities can be developed through technical assistance and conditional information gateways for exchanging sharable information. Young but large competition authorities in the region (such as Brazil, Chile or Mexico) could support smaller counterparts in the region in linking up with regional discussions and good practices, thereby creating a level playing field for cooperation.

Perception 5: Trust is the first issue to look at when dealing with younger jurisdictions. Findings of the research suggest that while trust can be a major concern in some instances when dealing with international cooperation in CBC investigations, it is only a major concern when fealing with multinational or transnational CBCs, and if cooperation between more mature and younger competition authorities is required. As has been argued in chapter four, the level of trust and dynamics of its development hinges on the status of the competition authority, and specifically on the robustness of its enforcement regime and leniency programme.

Perception 6: In cartel enforcement, all information exchanged by competition authorities is confidential. Novel proposals in this research aimed at solving the issue of confidential information and attempted to suggest a way forward for those competition officials from older competition authorities which are (in some instances) extremely cautious when sharing information with their younger counterparts, typically based on the perception that everything they deal with should be confidential. To counter this, a new international benchmark for sharable information is provided in chapter eight.

BIBLIOGRAPHY

'18 U.S. Code § 1905 – Disclosure of Confidential Information Generally' (*LII/Legal Information Institute*), www.law.cornell.edu/uscode/text/18/1905, accessed 24 March 2017.

'ACCC in Cartel Case Contest' (15 November 2016), http://at.theaustralian.com.au/link/bfc8c848ee8a0bfd7a17e05e56ad1b12?domain=theaustralian.com.au, accessed 12 February 2017.

'Acting Assistant Attorney General Sharis A. Pozen Speaks at the Briefing on Department's Enforcement Action in Auto Parts Industry', www.justice.gov/opa/speech/acting-assistant-attorney-general-sharis-pozen-speaks-briefing-department-s-enforcement, accessed 10 February 2017.

Agencia Andina, 'Corte Suprema confirma decisión del Indecopi sobre concertación de precios del pollo en años 1995–1996 | Noticias |' (15 December 2010), www.andina.com.pe/agencia/noticia-corte-suprema-confirma-decision-del-indecopi-sobre-concertacion-precios-del-pollo-anos-19951996-333219.aspx, accessed 21 February 2017.

'Agreement between the Government of Australia and the Government of New Zealand on Trans Tasman Court Proceedings and Regulatory Enforcement (Christchurch 24 July 2008) – [2013] ATS 32' (11 October 2013), www.austlii.edu.au/au/other/dfat/treaties/ATS/2013/32.html, accessed 27 March 2017.

'Airbus Condemns Brexit, Trump as Double Protectionist Threat – Bloomberg', www.bloomberg.com/news/articles/2018-01-15/airbus-ceo-condemns-brexit-trump-as-double-protectionist-threat, accessed 26 February 2018.

Alvarez AM and Horna P, 'Implementing Competition Law and Policy in Latin America: The Role of Technical Assistance' (2008) 83 Chicago-Kent Law Review 91.

'Amino-Acids Cartel – International Competition Law 2010–2011', http://icl2010.wikidot.com/amino-acids-cartel, accessed 13 February 2017.

Ana Paula Martinez and Mariana Tavares de Araujo, 'ANTI-CARTEL ENFORCEMENT IN BRAZIL: STATUS QUO & TRENDS' [2015] *IBRAC* 257.

Andean Committee for the Defense of Competition, 'Minutes of the 2nd Ordinary Meeting of the Committee on 3 October 2005.' (Andean Community Secretariat 2005) Meeting report SG/R.CDC/II/ACTA 2.17.28.

Anderson K and Slaughter A-M, *Squaring the Circle? Reconciling Sovereignty and Global Governance through Global Government Networks* (JSTOR 2005), www.jstor.org/stable/4093380, accessed 26 January 2017.

Andrew, 'Asia Pacific to Continue Hold Dominance in Global L-Lysine Market – FrontResearch', www.frontresearch.com/news/asia-pacific-to-continue-hold-dominance-in-global-l-lysine-market/, accessed 9 February 2017.

Ankenbrandt B and Vormann T, 'Comparing U.S. and EU Trade Secret Laws' (Trans-Atlantic Business Council 2016), www.transatlanticbusiness.org/wp-content/uploads/2016/07/US-EU-Trade-Secret-Comparison-30-June-2016.pdf, accessed 24 March 2017.

'Argentina's Supreme Court Rejects Cartel Arguments', www.cemnet.com/News/story/152125/argentina-s-supreme-court-rejects-cartel-arguments.html, accessed 7 February 2017.

ASEAN Experts Group on Competition (AEGC), 'An ASEAN Competition Action Plan (2016–2025)' (2016), www.asean-competition.org/file/post_image/ACAP%20(Website)%2023%20December%202016.pdf, accessed 1 March 2017.

Australia & New Zealand Governments, 'Cooperation Arrangement between the New Zealand Commerce Commission and the Australian Competition and Consumer Commission.' (April 2013), www.accc.gov.au/system/files/Cooperation%20arrangement%20between%20the%20New%20

Zealand%20Commerce%20Commission%20and%20the%20Australian%20Competition%20and%20Consumer%20Commission.pdf, accessed 4 April 2017.

Australia Competition Law Org, 'ACCC v April International Marketing Services Australia Pty Ltd (No 8)' (25 February 2011), www.australiancompetitionlaw.org/cases/2011singapore.html, accessed 24 May 2017.

'Auto Parts Industry Executive Pleads Guilty to Obstruction of Justice', www.justice.gov/opa/pr/auto-parts-industry-executive-pleads-guilty-obstruction-justice, accessed 10 February 2017.

Bachmann R and Inkpen AC, 'Understanding Institutional-Based Trust Building Processes in Inter-Organizational Relationships' (2011) 32 *Organization Studies* 281.

Bajari P and Summers G, 'Detecting Collusion In Procurement Auctions' (2002) 70 *Antitrust Law Journal* 143.

Barboza D, 'China Passes Japan to Become No. 2 Economy' *The New York Times* (15 August 2010), www.nytimes.com/2010/08/16/business/global/16yuan.html, accessed 24 February 2017.

Barillas I, '¿Quién es la Red Centroamericana de Autoridades Nacionales Encargadas del Tema de Competencia?' (*Blogs de El Economista*, 30 January 2015), http://blogs.eleconomista.net/competencia/2015/01/quien-es-la-red-centroamericana-de-autoridades-nacionales-encargadas-del-tema-de-competencia/, accessed 10 April 2017.

Beaton-Wells C, 'The Politics of Cartel Criminalisation: A Pessimistic View from Australia' (Social Science Research Network 2009) SSRN Scholarly Paper ID 1406322, https://papers.ssrn.com/abstract=1406322, accessed 12 February 2017.

——, 'Private Enforcement of Competition Law in Australia-Inching Forwards' (2015) 39 *Melb UL Rev* 681.

Beaton-Wells C and Ezrachi A (eds), 'Criminal Sanctions for Cartels-the Jury Is Still Out', *Research handbook on international competition law* (Edward Elgar, 2012).

Benjamin Gomez, 'The Chain Reaction of the Poultry Cartel in Chile' (*Developing World Antitrust*, 18 January 2016), https://developingworldantitrust.com/2016/01/18/the-chain-reaction-of-the-poultry-cartel-in-chile/, accessed 21 February 2017.

Benson SE, 'UN Conference on Restrictive Business Practices' (1980) 74 *The American Journal of International Law* 451.

Bergman H and Sokol DD, 'The Air Cargo Cartel: Lessons for Compliance' (Social Science Research Network 2014) SSRN Scholarly Paper ID 2465012, https://papers.ssrn.com/abstract=2465012, accessed 6 February 2017.

Berryman F, 'Colombia's "sugar Cartel" Fined for Blocking Foreign Competition' (*Colombia News | Colombia Reports*, 10 October 2015), http://colombiareports.com/colombia-sugar-cartel-receives-record-fines-for-anti-competitive-conduct/, accessed 21 February 2017.

Bertelsmaan Stiftung's Transformation Index (BTI), 'BTI 2016 Venezuela Country Report' (Gütersloh: Bertelsmann Stiftung 2016), www.bti-project.org/fileadmin/files/BTI/Downloads/Reports/2016/pdf/BTI_2016_Venezuela.pdf, accessed 28 February 2017.

Bertilorenzi M, *The International Aluminium Cartel, 1886-1978: The Business and Politics of a Cooperative Industrial Institution* (Routledge, 2016).

Bezzi M, 'International Cooperation: Bearing Cartel Case Study' (ICN Cartel Workshop 2014, Taiwan, October 2014), www.ftc.gov.tw/icncartel2014/pdf/2014.10.02.%20Plenary%20II%20%20%20Marcus%20Bezzi%20slides.pdf, accessed 26 January 2017.

Bhattacharjea A, 'EXPORT CARTELS : A Developing Country Perspective' (Centre for Development Economics, Delhi School of Economics 2004) Working paper 120, https://ideas.repec.org/p/cde/cdewps/120.html, accessed 8 February 2017.

——, 'Predatory Pricing and Anti-Dumping Revisited' (2005) 40 Economic and Political Weekly 482.

Błachucki M and Jóźwiak S, 'Exchange of Information and Evidence between Competition Authorities and Entrepreneurs' Rights' (Social Science Research Network 2012) SSRN Scholarly Paper ID 2130849, https://papers.ssrn.com/abstract=2130849, accessed 26 January 2017.

Blair RD and Sokol DD, *The Oxford Handbook of International Antitrust Economics* (Oxford University Press, 2015).

'Blog' (*Mina Salib*), www.minasalib.com/blog/, accessed 29 May 2018.

bogotapost, 'Crackdown on Business Cartels in Colombia' (*The Bogotá Post*, 16 February 2016), http://thebogotapost.com/2016/02/16/crackdown-on-business-cartels-in-colombia/, accessed 5 February 2017.

Botta M, 'The Cooperation between the Competition Authorities of the Developing Countries: Why Does It Not Work? Case Study on Argentina and Brazil' (2009) 5 *The Competition Law Review* 153.

——, 'The Role of Competition Policy in the Latin American Regional Integration: A Comparative Analysis of Caricom, Andean Community and Mercosur', *IX Annual Conference of the Euro-Latin Study Network on Integration and Trade (ELSNIT): Revisiting Regionalism. Appenzel, Switzerland* (2011), www19.iadb.org/intal/intalcdi/pe/2012/09801a05.pdf, accessed 28 February 2017.

Bradford A, 'International Antitrust Negotiations and the False Hope of the WTO' (2007) 48 *Harvard International Law Journal* 383.

Brander JA and Spencer BJ, 'Trade Warfare: Tariffs and Cartels' (1984) 16 *Journal of International Economics* 227.

'Brazil: CADE Wants Execs Punished for Refrigeration Cartel | Competition Policy International', www.competitionpolicyinternational.com/CADE-wants-execs-punished-for-refrigeration-cartel/, accessed 21 February 2017.

'Brazil Fines Companies BRL3 Billion For Industrial, Medical Gas Cartel' (*ADVFN*), www.advfn.com/stock-market/EURONEXT/AI/stock-price, accessed 21 February 2017.

Breed HL-LM, Bernick JW and Emch A, 'Deferring to Chinese Government, US Court of Appeals Overturns Vitamin C Cartel Judgment | Lexology', www.lexology.com/library/detail.aspx?g=02c9bc3e-31f9-4824-adfd-d5c8cd9053d8, accessed 7 February 2017.

BRICS Competition Authorities, 'MoU between the BRICS Competition Authorities on Cooperation in the Field of Competition Law and Policy' (19 May 2016), http://en.fas.gov.ru/upload/other/Memorandum%20of%20understanding%20between%20the%20BRICS%20competition%20authorities%20on%20cooperation%20in%20the%20field%20of%20competition%20law%20and%20policy.pdf.

Bridgman B and others, 'The Economic Performance of Cartels: Evidence from the New Deal US Sugar Manufacturing Cartel, 1934–74' (Federal Reserve Bank of Minneapolis 2009), www.mpls.frb.org/research/sr/SR437.pdf, accessed 8 February 2017.

Brusick P, 'UN Control of Restrictive Business Practices – A Decisive First Step' (1983) 17 *Journal of World Trade Law* 337.

Budzinski O, 'The International Competition Network: Prospects and Limits on the Road towards International Competition Governance' (2004) 8 *Competition & Change* 223.

——, *The Governance of Global Competition: Competence Allocation in International Competition Policy* (Edward Elgar Publishing, 2008).

Bureau of International Narcotics and Law Enforcement Affairs, 'Treaties and Agreements' (*U.S. Department of State*), www.state.gov/j/inl/rls/nrcrpt/2012/vol2/184110.htm, accessed 28 March 2017.

Burnier da Silveira P and Reja Sanchez P, 'The Use of Indirect Evidences in the Fight Against Cartels in Brazil' in Paulo Burnier da Silveira (ed), *Competition Law and Policy in Latin America. Recent Developments* (Kluwer Law International, 2017).

Burnier da Silveira P and Tardelli Tollini P, 'International Cartels in Brazil : An Overview and a Look Forward' in Vinícius Marques de Carvalho, Carlos Emmanuel Joppert Ragazzo and Paulo Burnier da Silveira (eds), *International cooperation and competition enforcement: Brazilian and European experiences from the enforcers' perspective* (Kluwer Law International, 2014).

Burr S, 'The Application of US Antitrust Law to Foreign Conduct: Has Hartford Fire Extinguished Considerations of Comity?' (1994) 15 *University of Pennsylvania Journal of International Law*, http://heinonline.org/hol-cgi-bin/get_pdf.cgi?handle=hein.journals/tlr70&section=59, accessed 6 April 2017.

Business and Industry Advisory Committee to the OECD (BIAC), 'Discussion on International Co-Operation and the 1995 Recommendation: Next Steps' (BIAC: The voice of OECD Business, 2013), http://biac.org/wp-content/uploads/2014/05/11-120613_BIAC_Note_to_WP3_on_International_Cooperation.pdf, accessed 28 March 2017.

CADE, 'Superintendence Investigates International Cartel of Maritime Transportation of Automobiles –' (1 March 2016), http://en.cade.gov.br/press-releases/copy_of_superintendence-investigates-international-cartel-of-maritime-transportation-of-automobiles, accessed 26 May 2017.

CADE A de C, 'CADE Condemns Cartel in the International Market of Refrigerator Compressors –', http://en.cade.gov.br/press-releases/cade-condemns-cartel-in-the-international-market-of-refrigerator-compressors, accessed 21 February 2017.

Cader A, 'Ten Years Fighting Cartels: The Case of El Salvador' in Paulo Burnier da Silveira (ed), *Competition Law and Policy in Latin America. Recent Developments* (Kluwer Law International, 2017).

Capobianco A, 'Information Exchange under EC Competition Law' (2004) 41 *Common Market Law Review* 1247.

Capobianco A and Christiansen H, 'Competitive Neutrality and State-Owned Enterprises: CHALLENGES AND POLICY OPTIONS' (Organisation for Economic Cooperation and Development, 2011), http://search.proquest.com/docview/1351928539/abstract/17B9A40DD6E8498EPQ/1, accessed 6 February 2017.

Capobianco A and Nagy A, 'Survey: Developments in International Enforcement Co-Operation in the Competition Field' (2016) 7 *Journal of European Competition Law & Practice* 566.

Cardoso FH, 'Dependency and Development in Latin America' (1972), http://search.proquest.com/openview/030e4cd93efcc50458425c87fbaef59d/1?pq-origsite=gscholar&cbl=1819646, accessed 19 February 2017.

Carrillo P, 'Colombia: Superintendence of Industry and Commerce – The Antitrust Review of the Americas 2017 – GCR – Global Competition Review' (30 August 2016), http://globalcompetitionreview.com/insight/the-antitrust-review-of-the-americas-2017/1068708/colombia-superintendence-of-industry-and-commerce, accessed 21 February 2017.

'Cartel in the Lysine Market in Mexico', www.apeccp.org.tw/doc/Mexico/Case/mxcas08.html, accessed 13 February 2017.

'Cartels: EU Car Parts – "The Cartel of the Century"' (*Market Intelligence*) Volume 2 Issue 2, https://media2.mofo.com/documents/150501micartelsjapan.pdf, accessed 10 February 2017.

Castel J-G, *The extraterritorial effects of antitrust laws* (Martinus Nijhoff, 1984).

Cauffman C and Hao Q, *Procedural Rights in Competition Law in the EU and China* (Springer, 2016).

CEPAL, 'La Integración Económica Centroamericana y Sus Perspectivas Frente a La Crisis Internacional' (United Nations Commission for Latin America and Carribbean, 2009) LC/MEX/L.954, www.integracionycooperacion.org/wp-content/themes/enfold/documentos/cepal.pdf, accessed 27 February 2017.

Cernat L, 'Eager to Ink, but Ready to Act?' in Philippe Brusick, Ana Maria Alvarez and Lucian Cernat (eds), *Competition Provisions in Regional Trade Agreements: How to Assure Development Gains* (2005), http://unctad.org/en/docs/ditcclp20051_en.pdf#page=95, accessed 23 February 2017.

Chile & Brazilian Governments, 'Cooperation Agreement between Fiscalia Nacional Economica of Chile and CADE of Brazil Regarding the Application of Their Competition Laws' (October 2008), http://en.cade.gov.br/topics/bilateral_cooperation/bilateral-cooperation/understanding-of-cooperation-between-fiscalia-nacional-economica-of-chile-and-cade-sde-and-seae/ab-ingles.pdf/@@download/file/AB%20Ingl%C3%A9s.pdf.

Chile & Central American Countries, 'Chapter 15 "Competition Policy" of the Free Trade Agreement between Chile and Central America' (18 October 1999), www.fne.gob.cl/wp-content/uploads/2011/03/TLCC_centro.pdf, accessed 22 February 2017.

Chile & MERCOSUR, 'Chapter "Competition and Consumer Protection" of the Free Trade Agreement between Chile and MERCOSUR' (25 June 1996), www.fne.gob.cl/wp-content/uploads/2011/03/TLCC_mercosur.pdf, accessed 22 February 2017.

'Chile Condemns International Shipping Cartel' (*globalcompetitionreview.com*, 30 January 2015), http://globalcompetitionreview.com/article/1061499/chile-condemns-international-shipping-cartel, accessed 21 February 2017.

Chile/Colombia/Peru Governments, 'Lima Declaration' (September 2013), www.fne.gob.cl/wp-content/uploads/2013/09/dec_lima_2013.pdf, accessed 22 February 2017.

'China Fines 7 Shipping Companies $65 Million' (*Cartel Capers*, 28 December 2015), http://cartelcapers.com/blog/china-fines-7-shipping-companies-65-million/, accessed 12 February 2017.

China IPR SME Helpdesk, 'Intellectual Property Systems: China/Europe Comparison' (2015), www.china-iprhelpdesk.eu/sites/all/docs/publications/Intellectual_Property_Systems_China_Europe_Comparison.pdf, accessed 28 March 2017.

'China Vitamin C Price-Fixing Verdict Scrutinized by Court' *Bloomberg.com* (29 January 2015), www.bloomberg.com/news/articles/2015-01-29/china-vitamin-c-dispute-sets-up-clash-over-u-s-antitrust-law, accessed 7 February 2017.

Clark PB and Wilson JQ, 'Incentive Systems: A Theory of Organizations' (1961) 6 *Administrative Science Quarterly* 129.

Clarke JL and Evenett SJ, 'The Deterrent Effects of National Anticartel Laws: Evidence from the International Vitamins Cartel' (2003) 48 *The antitrust bulletin* 689.

Clarkson CMV, Jaffey AJE and Hill J, *The Conflict of Laws*, 3rd edn (Oxford University Press, 2006).

CNBC, 'Donald Trump Revealed His Plan for Squeezing OPEC in 2008' www.cnbc.com/id/104155641?view=story&$DEVICE$=native-android-mobile, accessed 3 June 2017.

Colgan JD, 'The Emperor Has No Clothes: The Limits of OPEC in the Global Oil Market' (2014) 68 *International Organization* 599.

'"Competition Law & Policy in Developing Countries: Explaining Variation" by Umut Aydin and Tim Büthe', https://scholarship.law.duke.edu/lcp/vol79/iss4/1/, accessed 20 May 2018.

Competition Policy International, 'Interview with Esteban Greco: Head of the Argentinian Competition Authority' (2016), www.competitionpolicyinternational.com/wp-content/uploads/2016/08/CPI-Talks-Greco-Interview.pdf, accessed 28 February 2017.

'Congreso Aprueba Reformas al DL N° 211', www.fne.gob.cl/2016/07/08/congreso-aprueba-reformas-al-dl-211/, accessed 13 February 2017.

Connor J, 'Is Auto Parts Evolving into a Supercartel?' (2013), www.antitrustinstitute.org/sites/default/files/AAI%20Working%20Paper%2013-06.pdf, accessed 10 February 2017.

——, 'Effectiveness of Antitrust Sanctions on Modern International Cartels', 6 *Journal of Industry, Competition and Trade* (2006) 195.

——, 'Optimal Deterrence and Private International Cartels', SSRN Scholarly Paper, ID 787927 (2007)

——, '"Our Customers Are Our Enemies": The Lysine Cartel of 1992–1995' (2001) 18 *Review of Industrial Organization* 5.

——, 'Private International Cartels: Effectiveness, Welfare, and Anticartel Enforcement' (Social Science Research Network 2003) SSRN Scholarly Paper ID 611909, https://papers.ssrn.com/abstract=611909, accessed 1 February 2017.

——, 'Global Antitrust Prosecutions of Modern International Cartels' (2004) 4 *Journal of Industry, Competition and Trade* 239.

——, *Global Price Fixing* (Springer Science & Business Media, 2007).

——, 'Latin America and the Control of International Cartels' (2008), www.researchgate.net/profile/John_Connor7/publication/269811374_Latin_America_and_the_Control_of_International_Cartels/links/549745cc0cf29b9448262277.pdf, accessed 20 February 2017.

——, 'The Great Global Vitamins Conspiracy', www.emmanuelcombe.org/great.pdf.

——, 'Price-Fixing Overcharges: Revised 3rd Edition' (Social Science Research Network, 2014) SSRN Scholarly Paper ID 2400780, https://papers.ssrn.com/abstract=2400780, accessed 11 February 2017.

——, 'Private International Cartels: A Concise Introduction' (Social Science Research Network 2014) SSRN Scholarly Paper ID 2523883, https://papers.ssrn.com/abstract=2523883, accessed 1 February 2017.

——, 'International Cartel Stats: A Look at the Last 26 Years' [2016] Browser Download This Paper, https://papers.ssrn.com/sol3/papers.cfm?abstract_id=2862135, accessed 26 January 2017.

——, 'The Rise of Anti-Cartel Enforcement in Africa, Asia, and Latin America', https://papers.ssrn.com/sol3/papers.cfm?abstract_id=2711972, accessed 26 January 2017.

——, 'Recidivism Revealed: Private International Cartels 1991–2009', SSRN Scholarly Paper, ID 1688508 (2010).

——, 'The Private International Cartels (CBC) Data Set: Guide and Summary Statistics, 1990–July 2016 (Revised 2nd Edition)', (2016).

——, 'The Rise of Anti-Cartel Enforcement in Africa, Asia, and Latin America', (2016).

Connor JM and Helmers CG, 'Statistics on Modern Private International Cartels, 1990–2005', SSRN Scholarly Paper, ID 1103610 (2007).

Connor JM and Lande RH, 'Cartels as Rational Business Strategy: Crime Pays', SSRN Scholarly Paper, ID 1917657 (2012).

'Contribution from Brazil – ROUNDTABLE ON CARTEL JURISDICTION ISSUES, INCLUDING THE EFFECTS DOCTRINE' (OECD Working Party No 3 on Co-operation and Enforcement 2008), www.oecd.org/officialdocuments/publicdisplaydocumentpdf/?cote=DAF/COMP/WP3/WD(2008)94&docLanguage=En, accessed 13 February 2017.

'Contribution from Colombia – Session III: Unannounced Inspections in Antitrust Investigations' (OECD LATIN AMERICAN COMPETITION FORUM 2013) DAF/COMP/LACF(2013)8, www.oecd.org/officialdocuments/publicdisplaydocumentpdf/?cote=DAF/COMP/LACF(2013)8&docLanguage=En, accessed 20 February 2017.

'Contribution from the European Union – Discussion on How to Define Confidential Information' (Working Party No 3 on Co-operation and Enforcement 2013) DAF/COMP/WP3/WD(2013)57, http://ec.europa.eu/competition/international/multilateral/2013_oct_confidential%20information_en.pdf, accessed 24 March 2017.

Capobianco A and Christiansen H, 'Competitive Neutrality and State-Owned Enterprises: challenges and policy options' (Organisation for Economic Cooperation and Development (OECD) 2011), http://search.proquest.com/docview/1351928539/abstract/17B9A40DD6E8498EPQ/1, accessed 6 February 2017.

Capobianco A and Nagy A, 'Survey: Developments in International Enforcement Co-Operation in the Competition Field' (2016) 7 *Journal of European Competition Law & Practice* 566.

Coronado J, 'Cartel Investigations and Poverty Reduction: A Taste Of Peru' (2014), www.competitionpolicyinternational.com/assets/Uploads/CartelFeb14.pdf, accessed 21 February 2017.

Cortázar J, 'Decisión 608 de la Comunidad Andina: un paso adelante para el Sistema Antimonopolio de la Región' (2006) 2 *Revista de Derecho Competencia* 123.

Cosnita-Langlais A and Tropeano J-P, 'Fight Cartels or Control Mergers? On the Optimal Allocation of Enforcement Efforts within Competition Policy' (2013) 34 *International Review of Law and Economics* 34.

Costa Rica & Chilean governments, 'MoU on Competition Matters between the Ministry of Economy, Industry and Commerce of Costa Rica and the Fiscalia Nacional Economica of Chile' (6 August 2003), www.fne.gob.cl/wp-content/uploads/2011/03/acoop_2003_CostaRica.pdf, accessed 22 February 2017.

Costa Rica & Panama Governments, 'Agreement between COPROCOM of Costa Rica and ACODECO of Panama on Inter-Institutional Cooperation in the Area of Competition' (8 April 2008), www.acodeco.gob.pa/acodeco/uploads/pdf/legislacion_normativas/ConvenioentreagenciaCostaRicayPanama_2011.09_09_2011_09_48_31_a.m.pdf.

Cowen T and Sutter D, 'The Costs of Cooperation' (1999) 12 *The Review of Austrian Economics* 161.

Crawford VP and Haller H, 'Learning How to Cooperate: Optimal Play in Repeated Coordination Games' (1990) 58 *Econometrica* 571.

Cseres KJ and others, *Criminalization of Competition Law Enforcement: Economic and Legal Implications for the EU Member States* (Edward Elgar Publishing, 2006).

Dabbah MM, *International and Comparative Competition Law* (Cambridge University Press, 2010).

Damro C, 'Transatlantic Competition Policy: Domestic and International Sources of EU-US Cooperation' (2006) 12 *European Journal of International Relations* 171.

Damtoft RW, 'Mechanisms for Cooperation: Informal Cooperation' (UNCTAD 14th Session of Intergovernmental Group of Experts, Geneva, Switzerland, 8 July 2014), http://unctad.org/meetings/en/Presentation/CCPB_IGE2014_RTPRESInfCoop_USFTC_en.pdf, accessed 23 February 2017.

Danov M, 'Global Competition Law Framework: A Private International Law Solution Needed' (2016) 12 *Journal of Private International Law* 77.

Davidow J, 'The UNCTAD Restrictive Business Practices Code' (1979) 13 *The International Lawyer* 587.

Davidow J and Chiles L, 'The United States and the Issue of the Binding or Voluntary Nature of International Codes of Conduct Regarding Restrictive Business Practices' (1978) 72 *The American Journal of International Law* 247.

De León I, *An Institutional Assessment of Antitrust Policy: The Latin American Experience* (Wolters Kluwer Law & Business/Aspen Publishers, 2009).

Decker C, *Economics and the Enforcement of European Competition Law* (Edward Elgar Publishing, 2009).

Delhey J and Newton K, 'Predicting Cross-National Levels of Social Trust: Global Pattern or Nordic Exceptionalism?' (2005) 21 *European Sociological Review* 311.

Demedts V, 'Confidential Information Exchange in Competition Cases: Perception versus Reality in the EU and US' (Centre for Antitrust and Regulatory Studies, University of Wars 2014), www.ascola-conference-2014.wz.uw.edu.pl/conference_papers/Demedts_Confidentional.pdf, accessed 23 March 2017.

Djelic M-L and Kleiner T, 'The International Competition Network: Moving towards Transnational Governance' [2006] *Transnational Governance: Institutional Dynamics of Regulation* 287.

Donnelly L, 'Competition Authorities' Cartel-Busting Pays off for SA' (*The M&G Online*), http://mg.co.za/article/2016-02-11-competition-authorities-cartel-busting-pays-off-for-sa/, accessed 7 February 2017.

Dyzenhaus D, Hunt M and Taggart M, 'The Principle of Legality in Administrative Law: Internationalisation as Constitutionalisation' (2001) 1 *Oxford University Commonwealth Law Journal* 5.

Economics Online, 'The European Chemical Cartel' (May 2006), www.economicsonline.co.uk/Business_economics/Soap_powder.html, accessed 24 May 2017.

Edwards CD, 'International Cartels as Obstacles to International Trade' (1944) 34 *The American Economic Review* 330.

Eichenwald K, *The Informant: A True Story* (Broadway Books, 2009).

'El Cartel de Kimberly Clark (with Images) · Laradiodelsur' (*Storify*), https://storify.com/laradiodelsur/el-cartel-de-kimberly-clark, accessed 5 February 2017.

'El "Discovery" En El Derecho Marítimo Panameño | El Financiero | Economía, Finanzas, Negocios, Tecnología', http://efpanama.com/el-discovery-en-el-derecho-maritimo-panameno/, accessed 26 May 2017.

Enright MJ, 'The Globalization of Competition and the Localization of Competitive Advantage: Policies towards Regional Clustering' in Neil Hood and Stephen Young (eds), *The Globalization of Multinational Enterprise Activity and Economic Development* (Palgrave Macmillan, 2000), http://link.springer.com/chapter/10.1057/9780230599161_13, accessed 23 February 2017.

Equipo Técnico Multidisciplinario (ETM), 'Marco Historico De La Integracion Centroamericana' (International Labor Organization (ILO) 1999), www.ilo.org/public/spanish/region/ampro/mdtsanjose/worker/integ_ca/final.htm, accessed 27 February 2017.

'Estructura Organizacional – Indecopi', www.indecopi.gob.pe/estructura-organizacional, accessed 5 June 2017.

EU & Russian Government, 'MoU on Cooperation between the Directorate-General for Competition of the EU Commission and the Russian Federal Antimonopoly Service' (10 March 2011), http://ec.europa.eu/competition/international/bilateral/mou_russia_en.pdf, accessed 22 February 2017.

EU & Swiss Government, 'Agreement between the EU and the Swiss Confederation concerning Cooperation on the Application of their Competition Laws', http://eur-lex.europa.eu/legal-content/EN/TXT/PDF/?uri=CELEX:22014A1203(01)&from=EN, accessed 22 February 2017.

EU Commission, 'Press Release – Antitrust: Commission Imposes € 8.9 Million Fine in Banana Cartel', http://europa.eu/rapid/press-release_IP-11-1186_en.htm, accessed 5 June 2017.

——, 'Press Release – Commission Imposes Fines on Vitamin Cartels', http://europa.eu/rapid/press-release_IP-01-1625_en.htm?locale=en, accessed 6 February 2017.

'EU-Central America Association Agreement – Trade – European Commission', http://trade.ec.europa.eu/doclib/press/index.cfm?id=689, accessed 28 February 2017.

European Commission Press Release, 'Antitrust: Commission Fines Four Consumer Electronics Manufacturers for Fixing Online Resale Prices', http://europa.eu/rapid/press-release_IP-18-4601_en.htm, accessed 25 October 2018.
European Commission Press Release, 'Competition: The European Competition Network Launches a Model Leniency Programme – Frequently Asked Questions', http://europa.eu/rapid/press-release_MEMO-06-356_en.htm, accessed 28 March 2017.
European Consumer Consultative Group, 'Policy Recommendations for a Safe and Secure Use of Artificial Intelligence, Automated Decision-Making, Robotics and Connected Devices in a Modern Consumer World' (2018), https://ec.europa.eu/info/sites/info/files/eccg-recommendation-on-ai_may2018_en.pdf, accessed 8 October 2018.
European Voice, 'EU Fines Banks €1.7bn for Libor Cartel' (*POLITICO*, 4 December 2013), www.politico.eu/article/eu-fines-banks-e1-7bn-for-libor-cartel/, accessed 11 February 2017.
Evenett S, Levenstein M and Suslow V, 'International Cartel Enforcement: Lessons from the 1990s' [2001] *World Economy*.
Ezrachi A, 'Cross Border Transfer of Wealth – Reflections on Competition Law and Developing Economies' (The University of Oxford Centre for Competition Law and Policy Working Paper CCLP (L) 32 2012) Working Paper ID 1988853, www.law.ox.ac.uk/sites/files/oxlaw/tw-ezrachi.pdf, accessed 1 February 2017.
——, *EU Competition Law: An Analytical Guide to the Leading Cases* (Bloomsbury Publishing, 2016).
——, 'Sponge' (2017) 5 *Journal of Antitrust Enforcement* 49.
Ezrachi A and Kindl J, 'Cartels as Criminal? The Long Road from Unilateral Enforcement to International Consensus' [2011] *Criminalising Cartels: Critical Studies of an International Regulatory Movement* 419.
Ezrachi A and Stucke M, *Virtual Competition* (Harvard University Press, 2016), www.hup.harvard.edu/catalog.php?isbn=9780674545472&content=bios, accessed 5 February 2017.
——, 'Algorithmic Collusion: Problems and Counter-Measures' (OECD Competition Committee, 2017) DAF/COMP/WD(2017)25, www.oecd.org/officialdocuments/publicdisplaydocumentpdf/?cote=DAF/COMP/WD%282017%2925&docLanguage=En.
FAS, 'Federal Antimonopoly Service of the Russian Federation (FAS Russia)' (APEC Training Course, Tokyo, Japan, August 2005), www.jftc.go.jp/eacpf/05/APECTrainingCourseAugust2005/Group2/Efimov_fas.pdf, accessed 22 February 2017.
FAS RFW, 'FAS Russia's Draft Toolkit on International Cooperation Is Now Available for Public Discussion | Федеральная Антимонопольная Служба – ФАС России' (5 May 2017), http://en.fas.gov.ru/press-center/news/detail.html?id=49965, accessed 8 May 2017.
Federal Trade Commission 'Competition & Consumer Protection Authorities Worldwide' (2019), www.ftc.gov/policy/international/competition-consumer-protection-authorities-worldwide, accessed 20 January 2019.
Fikentscher W, 'United Nations Codes of Conduct: New Paths in International Law' (1982) 30 *The American Journal of Comparative Law* 577.
Filho MTF, Lixinski L and Giupponi MBO, *The Law of MERCOSUR* (Bloomsbury Publishing, 2010).
Fink N and Frübing S, 'Legal and Illegal Cartels in the European Cement Industry', https://papers.ssrn.com/sol3/papers.cfm?abstract_id=2663474, accessed 8 February 2017.
First H, 'The Vitamins Case: Cartel Prosecutions and the Coming of International Competition Law' (2000) 68 *Antitrust Law Journal* 711.
——, 'Evolving toward What? The Development of International Antitrust' in Josef Drexl and Peter Behrens (eds), *The future of transnational antitrust – from comparative to common competition law* (Stæmpfli [u.a] 2003).
FNE Chile, 'Instructivo Interno Para El Desarrollo de Investigationes de La Fiscalia Nacional Económica' (May 2013), www.fne.gob.cl/wp-content/uploads/2013/05/Instr._investigaciones_2013.pdf, accessed 18 May 2017.
——, 'Chilean Supreme Court Upholds Fines for Collusion against Agrosuper, Ariztía and Don Pollo and Hardens Sanction against the Trade Association' (29 October 2015), www.fne.gob.cl/

english/2015/10/29/chilean-supreme-court-upholds-fines-for-collusion-against-agrosuper-ariztia-and-don-pollo-and-hardens-sanction-against-the-trade-association/, accessed 21 February 2017.

Foley and others, 'Trade Secret Protection in China: A Perspective from China and Hong Kong | Lexology', www.lexology.com/library/detail.aspx?g=bee3d833-06b9-4c01-861b-e49c3dadda6c, accessed 24 March 2017.

Folsom BW, *New Deal Or Raw Deal?: How FDR's Economic Legacy Has Damaged America* (Simon and Schuster, 2009).

Fonseca MA and Normann H-T, 'Explicit vs. Tacit Collusion – The Impact of Communication in Oligopoly Experiments' (2012) 56 *European Economic Review* 1759.

Fox EM, 'The Politics of Law and Economics in Judicial Decision Making: Antitrust as a Window' (1986) 61 *New York University Law Review* 554.

——, 'Competition Policy: The Comparative Advantage of Developing Countries' (2016) 79 *Law and Contemporary Problems* 69.

Fox EM and Fox EM, *Cases and Materials on U.S. Antitrust in Global Context*, 3rd edn (Thomson/West, 2012).

Fox EM and Sokol DD, *Competition Law and Policy in Latin America* (Bloomsbury Publishing, 2009).

Friedberg AL, 'The Future of U.S.-China Relations: Is Conflict Inevitable?' (2005) 30 *International Security* 7.

Gal M, 'Algorithmic Challenges to Autonomous Choice' (Social Science Research Network, 2017) SSRN Scholarly Paper ID 2971456, https://papers.ssrn.com/abstract=2971456, accessed 17 October 2018.

Gal MS and Fox EM, 'Drafting Competition Law for Developing Jurisdictions: Learning from Experience' 69.

Gauer C and Jaspers M, 'Designing a European Solution for a "One-Stop Leniency Shop"' (2006), www.biicl.org/files/2498_designing_a_european_solution_for_one_stop_leniency.pdf, accessed 28 March 2017.

Ghuman P, 'Analysis of Competition Cases Against Uber Across the Globe' (CUTS International 2017), www.cuts-ccier.org/pdf/Analysis_of_Competition_Cases_Against_Uber_Across_the_Globe.pdf, accessed 6 March 2018.

Gibson Dunn, '2016 Year End Criminal Antitrust and Competition Law Update' (2017), www.gibsondunn.com/publications/documents/2016-Year-End-Criminal-Antitrust-and-Competition-Law-Update.pdf, accessed 10 February 2017.

'Global Cartel Fines Reach New High in 2014 as Enforcers Continue to Focus on Auto Parts Sector – News – Allen & Overy', www.allenovery.com/news/en-gb/articles/Pages/Global-cartel-fines-reach-new-high-in-2014-as-enforcers-continue-to-focus-on-auto-parts-sector.aspx, accessed 10 February 2017.

Griffin J, 'Criminal Practice and Procedure Committee. Status Report: Criminal Fines, International Cartel Enforcement and Corporate Leniency Program' (US Department of Justice, 2001), www.justice.gov/atr/file/519036/download, accessed 9 February 2017.

——, 'Extraterritoriality in US and EU antitrust enforcement' (1999) 67 *Antitrust Law Journal* 159.

Guzman A, 'The Case for International Antitrust' (2004) 22 *Berkeley Journal of International Law* 355.

Guzmán AT, *Cooperation, Comity, and Competition Policy* (OUP, 2011).

Hafen JO, 'International Extradition: Issues Arising Under the Dual Criminality Requirement' [1992] *BYU L Rev* 191.

Hague Conference on Private International Law, 'Hague Convention on the Service Abroad of Judicial and Extrajudicial Documents in Civil or Commercial Matters' (15 November 1965), www.hcch.net/en/instruments/conventions/full-text/?cid=17, accessed 4 April 2017.

——, 'Hague Convention on Taking of Evidence Abroad in Civil or Commercial Matters' (18 March 1970), www.hcch.net/en/instruments/conventions/full-text/?cid=82, accessed 4 April 2017.

Ham AD, 'International Cooperation in the Anti-Trust Field and in Particular the Agreement between the United States of America and the Commission of the European Communities' (1993) 30 *Common Market Law Review* 571.

Hammond S, 'Dispelling The Myths Surrounding Information Sharing' (*The United States Department of Justice*, 20 November 2004), www.justice.gov/atr/speech/dispelling-myths-surrounding-information-sharing, accessed 23 February 2017.

Hansen M, Crocco L and Kennedy S, 'Challenges to International Cartel Enforcement and Multi-Jurisdictional Leniency Applications–Disclosure of Leniency Applicant Statements and Materials', *ABA International Cartel Workshop, Vancouver* (2012), www.lw.com/upload/pubContent/_pdf/pub4546_1.pdf, accessed 23 February 2017.

Harrington JE and others, 'The Discontent Cartel Member and Cartel Collapse: The Case of the German Cement Cartel' (2015) 42 *International Journal of Industrial Organization* 106.

Harrington JE and Skrzypacz A, 'Private Monitoring and Communication in Cartels: Explaining Recent Collusive Practices' (2011) 101 *The American Economic Review* 2425.

Hawk BE, *International Antitrust Law & Policy: Fordham Corporate Law 2004* (Juris Publishing, Inc 2005).

Hazard GCJr, 'Discovery and the Role of the Judge in Civil Law Jurisdictions' (1997) 73 *Notre Dame Law Review* 1017.

Henley A, 'Price Formation and Market Structure: The Case of the Inter-War Coal Industry' (1988) 50 *Oxford Bulletin of Economics and Statistics* 263.

Hill JW, 'Trade Secrets, Unjust Enrichment, and the Classification of Obligations' [1999] *Virginia Journal of Law and Technology*, www.vjolt.net/vol4/issue/home_art2.html, accessed 7 April 2017.

Hodges C, Vogenauer S and Tulibacka M, *The Costs and Funding of Civil Litigation: A Comparative Perspective* (Bloomsbury Publishing, 2010).

Hollman H and Kovacic W, 'The International Competition Network: Its Past, Current and Future Role' in Paul Lugard (ed), *The International competition network at Ten: origins, accomplishments and aspirations* (Intersentia, 2011).

Horna P, 'Can Accountability and Effectiveness Go Hand in Hand? Lessons from Two Latin American Competition Networks' in Ayelet Berman and others (eds), *Informal international lawmaking: case studies* (Torkel Opsahl Academic, 2012).

——, 'Seventy Years of Work on Competition Law and Policy in the United Nations (1946–2016)' [2016] *Sofia Competition Forum Newsletter* 23.

——, 'Regional Coordination in Cartel Investigations: The Liquid Oxygen Case' in Paulo Burnier da Silveira (ed), *Competition Law and Policy in Latin America. Recent Developments* (Kluwer Law International, 2017).

——, 'David & Goliath: How Young Competition Agencies Can Succeed in Fighting Cross-Border Cartels' [2017] The University of Oxford Centre for Competition Law and Policy, www.law.ox.ac.uk/sites/files/oxlaw/david_goliath_-_how_young_competition_agencies_can_succeed_in_fighting_cross-border_cartels_-_cclp_l_45.pdf, accessed 6 February 2017.

Horna P and Kayali BO, 'National Implementation of Competition-Related Provisions in Bilateral and Regional Trade Agreements', *Implementing Competition-Related Provisions in Regional Trade Agreements: is it possible to obtain development gains?* (United Nations Publications, 2007), http://unctad.org/en/docs/ditcclp20064_en.pdf, accessed 26 February 2017.

Huang Y, 'Pursuing the Second Best: The History, Momentum, and Remaining Issues of China's Anti-Monopoly Law' (2008) 75 *Antitrust Law Journal* 117.

——, 'Coordination of International Competition Policies – An Anatomy Based on Chinese Reality' in Andrew T Guzman (ed), *Cooperation, comity, and competition policy* (Oxford University Press, 2011).

ICN (ed), *Defining Hard Core Cartel Conduct: Effective Institutions, Effective Penalties* (Office for Official Publ of the European Communities, 2005).

——, 'Co-operation between Competition Agencies in Cartel Investigations' (2006), http://ec.europa.eu/competition/international/multilateral/2006.pdf, accessed 28 March 2017.

——, 'Co-operation between Competition Agencies in Cartel Investigations. Report to the ICN Annual Conference, Moscow, May 2007' (EUR-OP 2007).

——, 'Cartel Settlements. Report to the ICN Annual Conference Kyoto, Japan' (2008), www.internationalcompetitionnetwork.org/uploads/library/doc347.pdf, accessed 17 February 2017.

——, 'Anti-Cartel Enforcement Manual Chapter 1: Searches Raids and Inspections' (2009), www.internationalcompetitionnetwork.org/uploads/library/doc340.pdf, accessed 17 February 2017.

——, 'Anti-Cartel Enforcement Manual Chapter 2: Drafting and Implementing an Effective Leniency Policy' (2014), www.internationalcompetitionnetwork.org/uploads/library/doc1005.pdf, accessed 17 February 2017.

——, 'Anti-Cartel Enforcement Manual Chapter 3: Digital Evidence Gathering' (2014), www.internationalcompetitionnetwork.org/uploads/library/doc1006.pdf, accessed 17 February 2017.

——, 'Anti-Cartel Enforcement Manual Chapter 4: Cartel Case Initiation' (2010), www.internationalcompetitionnetwork.org/uploads/library/doc628.pdf, accessed 17 February 2017.

——, 'Anti-Cartel Enforcement Manual Chapter 5: Investigative Strategy and Interviewing' (2008), www.internationalcompetitionnetwork.org/uploads/library/doc344.pdf, accessed 17 February 2017.

——, 'Anti-Cartel Enforcement Manual Chapter 6: Interviewing Techniques' (2008), www.internationalcompetitionnetwork.org/uploads/library/doc345.pdf, accessed 17 February 2017.

——, 'Anti-Cartel Enforcement Manual Chapter 7: Case Resolution' (2011), http://internationalcompetitionnetwork.org/uploads/library/doc834.pdf, accessed 17 February 2017.

——, 'Anti-Cartel Enforcement Manual Chapter 8: Cartel Awareness, Outreach and Compliance' (2012), http://internationalcompetitionnetwork.org/uploads/library/doc835.pdf, accessed 17 February 2017.

——, 'Anti-Cartel Enforcement Manual Chapter 9: International Cooperation and Information Sharing' (2013), www.internationalcompetitionnetwork.org/uploads/cartel%20wg/icn_chapter_on_international_cooperation_and_information_sharing.pdf, accessed 17 February 2017.

——, 'Anti-Cartel Enforcement Manual Chapter 10: Relationships between Competition Agencies and Public Procurement Bodies' (2015), http://internationalcompetitionnetwork.org/uploads/library/doc1036.pdf, accessed 17 February 2017.

——, 'Trends and Developments in Cartel Enforcement' (9th Annual ICN Conference, Istanbul, Turkey, 29 April 2010), www.internationalcompetitionnetwork.org/uploads/library/doc613.pdf, accessed 17 February 2017.

——, 'Compilation of "Good Practices" from the Anti-Cartel Enforcement Manual of the ICN Cartel Working Group' (ICN Cartel Working Group Subgroup 2: Enforcement Techniques 2011), www.internationalcompetitionnetwork.org/uploads/library/doc756.pdf, accessed 17 February 2017.

——, 'Activity Report on ICN Advocacy and Implementation Network Support Program (AISUP) 2011–2012' (2012), www.internationalcompetitionnetwork.org/uploads/library/doc814.pdf, accessed 8 May 2017.

——, 'Investigative Tools Report' (ICN Agency Effectiveness Project on Investigative Process 2013), www.internationalcompetitionnetwork.org/uploads/library/doc893.pdf, accessed 5 April 2017.

——, 'Proposal for Establishing the ICN Framework for Promotion of Sharing Non-Confidential Information for Cartel Enforcement' (2015), www.internationalcompetitionnetwork.org/uploads/library/doc1043.pdf, accessed 17 February 2017.

——, 'Cartel Awareness & Outreach', www.internationalcompetitionnetwork.org/working-groups/current/cartel/awareness.aspx, accessed 17 February 2017.

——, 'Cartel Working Group 2015–2018 Work Plan', www.internationalcompetitionnetwork.org/uploads/library/doc1041.pdf, accessed 8 May 2017.

——, 'Leniency Materials. Country/Organization + Link(s) to Leniency Program Materials', www.internationalcompetitionnetwork.org/working-groups/current/cartel/awareness/leniency.aspx, accessed 17 February 2017.

——, 'Waivers of Confidentiality in Cartel Investigations – Explanatory Note', www.internationalcompetitionnetwork.org/uploads/library/doc1012.pdf, accessed 17 February 2017.

'ICN 2017 Annual Conference – Porto 10–12 May' (*ICN 2017 Annual Conference – Porto 10–12 May*), http://icn2017.concorrencia.pt/, accessed 16 May 2017.

Igami M and Sugaya T, 'Measuring the Incentive to Collude: The Vitamin Cartels, 1990–1999' (Social Science Research Network 2016) SSRN Scholarly Paper ID 2889837, https://papers.ssrn.com/abstract=2889837, accessed 10 February 2017.

IMDB.COM, 'The Informant! Trailer' (*IMDb*), www.imdb.com/video/imdb/vi2750218777/, accessed 4 June 2017.

'Import Cartels | World Problems & Global Issues | The Encyclopedia of World Problems', http://encyclopedia.uia.org/en/problem/164915, accessed 8 February 2017.

'Indecopi Inicia Procedimiento Contra Seis Líneas Navieras Por Presuntas Prácticas Colusorias En El Servicio de Transporte Marítimo Internacional de Carga Rodante – Inicio – Indecopi', www.indecopi.gob.pe/inicio/-/asset_publisher/ZxXrtRdgbv1r/content/indecopi-inicia-procedimiento-contra-seis-lineas-navieras-por-presuntas-practicas-colusorias-en-el-servicio-de-transporte-maritimo-internacional-de-ca?inheritRedirect=false, accessed 23 May 2017.

Inglehart R and Norris P, 'Trump, Brexit, and the Rise of Populism: Economic Have-Nots and Cultural Backlash' (Social Science Research Network 2016) SSRN Scholarly Paper ID 2818659, https://papers.ssrn.com/abstract=2818659, accessed 15 February 2017.

International Civil Aviation Organization, 'Liberalization of Market Access' (Worlwide Air Transport Conference (ATCONF) 2013) ATConf/6-WP/60, www.icao.int/Meetings/atconf6/Documents/WorkingPapers/ATConf6-wp060_en.pdf, accessed 21 May 2017.

International Organization of Securities Commissions, 'The IOSCO Multilateral Memorandum of Understanding (MMoU): An International Benchmark for Securities Enforcement' (*Univ. L. Rev.*, 2010), http://heinonline.org/hol-cgi-bin/get_pdf.cgi?handle=hein.journals/droit2010&section=45, accessed 15 May 2017.

Interview with Anderson, David, 'Interview at the ICN Annual Conference in Porto (10–12 May 2017) with a Brussels-Based Private Competition Practitioner' (11 May 2017).

Interview with Bacca, Germán, 'Interview with the Former Superintendent Delegate for Competition of the Colombian Competition Authority' (24 February 2017).

Interview with Bezzi, Marcus, 'Interview at the ICN Annual Conference in Porto (10–12 May 2017) with the General Manager of the Australian Competition and Consumer Protection Commission' (11 May 2017).

Interview with Capobianco, Antonio, 'Interview with a Senior Competition Officer of the Competition Division of the Organization for Economic Development and Cooperation (OECD)' (2 June 2017).

Interview with Cardoze, Oscar, 'Interview at the ICN Annual Conference in Porto (10–12 May 2017) with the Administrator of the Competition Authority of Panama (ACODECO)' (11 May 2017).

Interview with Coloma, Germán, 'Interview with the Director of Economic Studies of the Argentinean Competition Commission' (1 June 2017).

Interview with Damtoft, Russell W, 'Interview with the Associate Director of International Affairs, Federal Trade Commission of the United States of America' (January 2017).

Interview with Gagliuffi, Ivo, 'Interview at the ICN Annual Conference in Porto (10–12 May 2017) with the President of the Competition Authority of Peru (INDECOPI)' (12 May 2017).

Interview with Guzman, Luis Humberto, 'Interview at the ICN Annual Conference in Porto (10–12 May 2017) with the President of the Competition Auhtority of Nicaragua (PROCOMPETENCIA)' (11 May 2017).

Interview with Irrarazabal, Felipe, 'Interview at the ICN Annual Conference in Porto (10–12 May 2017) with the National Economic Prosecutor of Chile (FNE)' (10 May 2017).

Interview with Kovacic, William, 'Interview at the ICN Annual Conference in Porto (10–12 May 2017) with the Former Chairman of the Federal Trade Commission of the United States of America and Professor of Global Competition Law in GeorgeTown University' (12 May 2017).

Interview with Lozano, Alberto, 'Interview with the President of the Honduras Competition Commission and President Pro-tempore of RECAC 2017' (February 2017).

Interview with Lozano, Alberto, 'Interview at the ICN Annual Conference in Porto (10–12 May 2017) with the President of the Honduras Competition Commission' (11 May 2017).

Interview with Mehta, Kirtikumar, 'Interview with the Former Director of the Cartel Directorate, DG Competition of the EU Commission.' (1 June 2017).

Interview with Odio-Rohrmoser, Edgar, 'Interview with the ex-Commissioner of the Costa Rican Competition Authority (COPROCOM)' (30 May 2017).

Interview with Qaqaya, Hassan, 'Interview with the Former Head of the Competition and Consumer Policies Branch of the United Nations Conference on Trade and Development (UNCTAD)' (30 May 2017).

Interview with Ragazzo, Carlos Emmanuel Joppert, 'Interview at the ICN Annual Conference in Porto (10-12 May 2017) with the Former Superintendent of Investigation of the Brazilian Competition Authority (CADE) and Professor of Competition Law in Getulio Vargas Foundation, Sao Paulo (Brazil)' (11 May 2017).

Interview with Ratshisusu, Mulalo Hardin, 'Interview at the ICN Annual Conference in Porto (10–12 May 2017) with the Deputy Commissioner of the South African Competition Commission' (10 May 2017).

Interview with Toh, Han Li, 'Interview at the ICN Annual Conference in Porto (10–12 May 2017) with the Chief Executive of the Singapore Competition Commission' (12 May 2017).

Interview with Van Brackel Barbosa, Jean Paul, 'Interview at the ICN Annual Conference in Porto (10–12 May 2017) with a Staff Member of the Andean Community of Nations' (11 May 2017).

Ivaldi M, Khimich A and Jenny F, 'Measuring the Economic Effects of Cartels in Developing Countries' (2014), http://unctad.org/en/PublicationsLibrary/ditcclpmisc2014d2_en.pdf, accessed 21 February 2017.

Japanese Ministry of Economy, Trade and Industry, '"Excessive" Extraterritorial Application of Competition Laws' (2008), www.meti.go.jp/english/report/downloadfiles/2008WTO/2-14-2ExcessiveExtraterritorial.pdf, accessed 6 April 2017.

Jenny F, 'International Cooperation on Competition: Myth, Reality and Perspective' (2003) 48 The Antitrust Bulletin 973.

——, 'Export Cartels in Primary Products: The Potash Case in Perspective' (Social Science Research Network 2012) SSRN Scholarly Paper ID 2064686, https://papers.ssrn.com/abstract=2064686, accessed 8 February 2017.

Jensen MC, 'Self-Interest, Altruism, Incentives, and Agency Theory' (1994), https://papers.ssrn.com/sol3/papers.cfm?abstract_id=5566, accessed 17 January 2017.

Jensen-Eriksen N, 'Predators or Patriots? Export Cartels as a Source of Power for the Weak' (Working paper: Helsinki University 2007), www.gla.ac.uk/media/media_168473_en.pdf, accessed 8 February 2017.

Jones A and Sufrin B, *EU Competition Law: Text, Cases, and Materials* (Oxford University Press 2016).

Jr JEH, 'How Do Cartels Operate?' (2006) 2 *Foundations and Trends in Microeconomics* 1.

Kaira T, 'A Cartel in South Africa Is a Cartel in a Neighbouring Country: Why Has the Successful Cartel Leniency Policy in South Africa Not Resulted into Automatic Cartel Confessions in Economically Interdependent Neighbouring Countries?' [2015] Competition Authority of Botswana, www.competition.org.za/s/Thula-Kaira_Regional-cartels.pdf, accessed 8 February 2017.

Kaplow L, *Competition Policy and Price Fixing* (Princeton University Press, 2013).

Kasahara A, 'International Coordination to Increase the Efficiency of Cartel Investigations' (JFTC and KPPU Regional Training Course on Cross-border Competition Cases, Kuala Lumpur, Malaysia, 27 April 2017).

Khamukov M, 'International Cartel Investigations: New Levels of Cooperation' (ICN Cartel Workshop Annual Conference, Taiwan, October 2014).

King S, 'Agreements That Restrict Competition by Object under Article 101(1) TFEU: Past, Present and Future' (The London School of Economics and Political Science 2015), http://etheses.lse.ac.uk/3068/1/King_Agreements_that_restrict_competition_by_object_under_Article_101.pdf, accessed 2 February 2017.

Klein GJ, *Cartel Destabilization and Leniency Programs: Empirical Evidence* (ZEW, Zentrum für Europ Wirtschaftsforschung, 2010).

Kojima T, 'International Conflicts over the Extraterritorial Application of Competition Law in a Borderless Economy' [2002] Weatherhead Center for International Affairs, 2001.

Kotera A, 'RIETI – What Is the "Spaghetti Bowl Phenomenon" of FTAs?' (23 May 2006), www.rieti.go.jp/en/columns/a01_0193.html, accessed 6 June 2017.

Kovacic WE, 'An Integrated Competition Policy to Deter and Defeat Cartels' (2006) 51 *The Antitrust Bulletin* 813.
Kunene T, 'Challenges Faced by New Younger Competition Agencies in the Investigation of Cartels' 6.
Kwok T, 'Export Cartels: Analysing the Gap in International Competition Law and Trade' (2013) 2 *Edinburgh Student L. Rev.* 140.
'La Cooperación Suiza En El Perú | Alianza Entre INDECOPI, UNCTAD y La Cooperación Suiza – SECO Continua Para El Lanzamiento Del Programa COMPAL III', www.cooperacionsuizaenperu.org.pe/seco-proyectos-en-curso/gobernabilidad-economica-publica-efectiva-y-transparente/compal/proyecto-noticias/2291-06%20de%20marzo%20de%202015, accessed 23 May 2017.
Lande RH and Marvel HP, 'The Three Types of Collusion: Fixing Prices, Rivals, and Rules' (Social Science Research Network, 2000) SSRN Scholarly Paper ID 1134820, https://papers.ssrn.com/abstract=1134820, accessed 2 February 2017.
LeClair MS, *Cartelization, Antitrust and Globalization in the US and Europe* (Routledge, 2011).
Lee A, *What the U.S. Can Learn from China: An Open-Minded Guide to Treating Our Greatest Competitor as Our Greatest Teacher* (Berrett-Koehler Publishers, 2012).
Lee JS, *Strategies to Achieve a Binding International Agreement on Regulating Cartels: Overcoming Doha Standstill* (Springer, 2016), http://public.eblib.com/choice/publicfullrecord.aspx?p=4748055, accessed 19 March 2017.
Lee JY, 'Gaining Assurances' (2012) 2012 *Wisconsin Law Review* 1137.
Leslie CR, 'Antitrust Amnesty, Game Theory, and Cartel Stability' (2005) 31 *Journal of Corporation Law* 453.
Levenstein M and Suslow VY, 'Contemporary International Cartels and Developing Countries: Economic Effects and Implications for Competition Policy' (2003) 71 *Antitrust Law Journal* 801.
——, 'The Changing International Status of Export Cartel Exemptions' (2004) 20 *Am. U. Int'l L. Rev.* 785.
——, 'What Determines Cartel Success?' (2006) 44 *Journal of Economic Literature* 43.
Lewicki R, 'Trust, Trust Development, and Trust Repair' in Morton Deutsch, Peter Coleman and Eric Marcus (eds), *The handbook of conflict resolution: theory and practice*, 2nd edn (Jossey-Bass, 2006), http://profkaminskisreadings.yolasite.com/resources/Deutsch,%20Coleman,%20and%20Marcus.pdf#page=110.
Lewicki R and Bunker B, 'Trust in Relationships. A Model of Development and Decline' in Barbara Bunker and JZ Rubin (eds), *Conflict, Cooperation, and Justice: Essays Inspired by the Work of Morton Deutsch* (Jossey-Bass, 1995).
Li C, 'Assessing US-China Relations under the Obama Administration | Brookings Institution' (*Brookings*, 30 August 2016), www.brookings.edu/opinions/assessing-u-s-china-relations-under-the-obama-administration/, accessed 26 February 2017.
Lianos I, 'The Contribution of the United Nations to the Emergence of Global Antitrust Law' (Social Science Research Network 2009) SSRN Scholarly Paper ID 1398918, https://papers.ssrn.com/abstract=1398918, accessed 31 January 2017.
Licetti MM, 'Bad News for Cartels, Good News for the Poor in Latin America' (*Private Sector Development*, 23 October 2015), http://blogs.worldbank.org/psd/bad-news-cartels-good-news-poor-latin-america-0, accessed 20 February 2017.
Lieber JB, *Rats in the Grain: The Dirty Tricks and Trials of Archer Daniels Midland* (Four Walls Eight Windows, 2000).
Linhares Martins A and Lin Fidelis A, 'Nearly 16 years of the leniency program in Brazil: breakthroughs and challenges in cartel prosecution' (2016), www.competitionpolicyinternational.com/wp-content/uploads/2016/06/Amanda-Andressa.final2_.pdf, accessed 19 February 2017.
Linklaters, 'Pressure Points: Global Cartel Enforcement in 2018 | Insights |' (10 April 2018), /en/insights/publications/2018/april/global-cartel-enforcement-in-2018, accessed 24 January 2019.
Livesey F, *From Global to Local: The Making of Things and the End of Globalisation* (2017).
López-Galdos M, 'Noches De Boda Para El Derecho De La Competencia En Venezuela (Venezuela's Competition Law's Honeymoon)' [2007] *Gaceta Jurídica*, https://papers.ssrn.com/sol3/papers.cfm?abstract_id=2757893, accessed 28 February 2017.

Lu AC-J, *International Airline Alliances: EC Competition Law/US Antitrust Law and International Air Transport* (Kluwer Law International, 2002).

Malamud C, 'Venezuela's Withdrawal from the Andean Community of Nations and the Consequences for Regional Integration', www.files.ethz.ch/isn/31899/WP%2028,%202006.pdf, accessed 27 February 2017.

Malashevich B and Kobe K, 'The Use of Economics in Competition Law: What Works and What Doesn't Across National Jurisdictions?' in Theresa M Carpenter, Jansen Marion and Joost Pauwelyn (eds), *The use of economics in international trade and investment disputes* (Cambridge University Press, 2016).

Mariscal E and Mena-Labarthe C, 'Leniency Programs in Latin America: New Tools for Cartel Enforcement | Competition Policy International' (2010), www.competitionpolicyinternational.com/leniency-programs-in-latin-america-new-tools-for-cartel-enforcement/, accessed 19 February 2017.

Marsden P, 'Jaw-Jaw Not Law-Law – from Treaties to Meetings: The Increasing Informality and Effectiveness of International Cooperation' in Ariel Ezrachi (ed), *Research Handbook on International Competition Law* (Edward Elgar, 2012).

Marshall RC and Marx LM, *The Economics of Collusion: Cartels and Bidding Rings* (MIT Press, 2012).

Martyniszyn M, 'A Comparative Look on Foreign State Compulsion as a Defence in Antitrust Litigation' (2012) 8 *The Competition Law Review* 143.

——, 'Export Cartels: Is It Legal to Target Your Neighbour? Analysis in Light of Recent Case Law' (2012) 15 *Journal of International Economic Law* 181.

——, 'Discovery and Evidence in Transnational Antitrust Cases: Current Framework and the Way Forward' (Social Science Research Network 2012) SSRN Scholarly Paper ID 2142978, https://papers.ssrn.com/abstract=2142978, accessed 23 February 2017.

——, 'Inter-Agency Evidence Sharing in Competition Law Enforcement' (2015) 19 *The International Journal of Evidence & Proof* 11.

——, 'Foreign States Amicus Curiae Participation in U.S. Antitrust Cases' (2016) 61 *The Antitrust Bulletin* 611.

Mason ES, 'The Future of International Cartels' (1944) 22 *Foreign Affairs* 604.

Matsushita M, 'Export Control and Export Cartels in Japan' (1979) 20 *Harvard International Law Journal* 103.

——, 'The Role of Competition Law and Policy in Reducing Trade Barriers in Japan' (1991) 14 *World Economy* 181

Matsushita M, Schoenbaum TJ, Mavroidis PC and Hahn M, *The World Trade Organization: Law, Practice, and Policy* (Oxford University Press, 2015).

Mavroidis PC and Neven D, 'Land Rich and Cash Poor? The Reluctance of the WTO Dispute Settlement System to Entertain Economics Expertise: An Institutional Analysis' in Theresa M Carpenter, Jansen Marion and Joost Pauwelyn (eds), *The Use of Economics in International Trade and Investment Disputes* (Cambridge University Press, 2016).

McAdams RH, 'Beyond the Prisoners' Dilemma: Coordination, Game Theory, and Law' (2008) 82 *Southern California Law Review* 209.

McAllister DJ, 'Affect- and Cognition-Based Trust as Foundations for Interpersonal Cooperation in Organizations' (1995) 38 *Academy of Management Journal* 24.

Mehra SK, 'US v. Topkins: Can Price Fixing Be Based on Algorithms?' (2016) 7 *Journal of European Competition Law & Practice* 470.

Messerlin PA, 'Anti-Dumping Regulations or Pro-Cartel Law? The EC Chemical Cases' (1990) 13 *World Economy* 465.

Mexico & Chilean Governments, 'Agreement between the Competition Federal Commission of Mexico and the Fiscalia Nacional Economica of Chile' (14 June 2004), www.fne.gob.cl/wp-content/uploads/2011/03/acoop_2004_Mexico.pdf, accessed 22 February 2017.

'Mexico Pursues First Criminal Action against Cartelists' (*globalcompetitionreview.com*, 16 February 2017), http://globalcompetitionreview.com/article/1081445/mexico-pursues-first-criminal-action-against-cartelists, accessed 21 February 2017.

Michaels R, 'Supplanting Foreign Antitrust' (2016) 79 *Law and Contemporary Problems* 223.
Monti M and others (eds), *Fighting Cartels – Why and How?: The 3rd Nordic Competition Conference in Stockholm, September 2000* (Konkurrensverket, 2001).
Motta M, *Competition Policy: Theory and Practice* (Cambridge University Press, 2004).
Motta M and Polo M, *Leniency Programs and Cartel Prosecution* (European University Institute, 1999).
Muir Watt H, 'Integration and Diversity: The Conflict of Laws as a Regulatory Tool', http://cadmus.eui.eu//handle/1814/6657, accessed 11 April 2017.
Municoy M, 'Allocation of Jurisdiction on Patent Disputes in the Models Developed by the Hague Conference in Private International Law: Asymmetric Countries and the Relationship of Private Parties' (2004) 4 *Chicago-Kent Journal of Intellectual Property* 342.
Nambu T, 'Proposal for Establishing the ICN Framework for Promotion of Sharing Non-Confidential Information for Cartel Enforcement' (2014 ICN Cartel Workshop, Taipei, Taiwan, 2 October 2014), www.ftc.gov.tw/icncartel2014/pdf/2014.10.02.%20Plenary%20III%20%20%20Toshiyuki%20Nambu%20JFTC.pdf.
Natural Resource Governance Institute, 'Chapter 3 : Commercially Sensitive Information and the Public Interest' (Natural Resource Governance Institute) Contracts Confidential: ending secret deals in the extractive industries, www.resourcegovernance.org/sites/default/files/RWI_Contracts_Confidential_Chapter_3.pdf, accessed 7 April 2017.
Nelken D, 'Using the Concept of Legal Culture' (2004) 29 *Australian Journal of Legal Philosophy* 1.
Nilsen Ribeiro EC and Guimarães MC, 'The Defense of Competition in Mercosur' in Paulo Burnier da Silveira (ed), *Competition Law and Policy in Latin America. Recent Developments* (Kluwer Law International, 2017).
Noonan C, *The Emerging Principles of International Competition Law* (Oxford University Press, 2008).
Nordic Cartel Network, 'Joint Contribution by Denmark, the Faroe Islands, Finland, Greenland, Iceland, Norway and Sweden – Improving international co-operation in cartel investigations: the Nordic cartel network: a regional model for cooperation between cartel units of competition authorities' (Global Forum on Competition, 2012) DAF/COMP/GF/WD(2012)34.
Norman G and Trachtman JP, 'The Customary International Law Game' (2005) 99 *The American Journal of International Law* 541.
NR consultants, 'They Investigate Cartel of Paper Tissue in Ecuador |' (29 June 2016), http://nrconsultores.com/en/2016/06/29/they-investigate-cartel-of-paper-tissue-in-ecuador/, accessed 5 February 2017.
Ocampo JA, 'The Latin American Debt Crisis in Historical Perspective', *Life After Debt* (Springer 2014), http://link.springer.com/chapter/10.1057/9781137411488_4, accessed 15 February 2017.
Odello M, 'The Andean Community of Nations' in Marco Odello and Francesco Seatzu (eds), *Latin American and Caribbean International Institutional Law* (TMC Asser Press 2015), http://link.springer.com/chapter/10.1007/978-94-6265-069-5_5, accessed 27 February 2017.
Odio-Rohrmoser E, 'Competition Law in Central America and the Years to Come' in Julián Peña and Marcelo Calliari (eds), *Competition law in Latin America: A practical guide* (Kluwer Law International, 2016).
OECD, 'Competition Law and Policy in Chile' (2010), www.oecd.org/chile/47950954.pdf, accessed 19 February 2017.
——, 'Procedural Fairness and Transparency. Key Points' (2012), www.oecd.org/competition/mergers/50235955.pdf, accessed 23 March 2017.
——, 'National and international provisions for the exchange of confidential information between competition agencies without waivers' (2013) DAF/COMP/WP3(2013)4, www.oecd.org/officialdocuments/publicdisplaydocumentpdf/?cote=DAF/COMP/WP3(2013)4&doclanguage=en, accessed 17 February 2017.
——, 'Contribution by OECD to the Roundtable on: "Modalities and Procedures for International Cooperation in Competition Cases Involving More than One Country"' (Intergovernmental Group of Experts on Competition Law and Policy Geneva, 2013), http://unctad.org/meetings/en/Contribution/IGE2013_RT1_OECD_en.pdf, accessed 16 May 2017.

——, 'Challenges of International Co-operation in Competition Law Enforcement' (2014), www.oecd.org/daf/competition/Challenges-Competition-Internat-Coop-2014.pdf, accessed 6 February 2017.

——, 'Competition Law and Policy in Costa Rica.' (2014), www.oecd.org/daf/competition/CostaRica-PeerReview2014en.pdf, accessed 20 February 2017.

——, 'International Cooperation in Competition Law Enforcement' (Meeting of the OECD Council at Ministerial Level 2014) C/MIN (2014) 17, www.oecd.org/mcm/C-MIN(2014)17-ENG.pdf, accessed 10 April 2017.

——, 'Recommendation of the OECD Council Concerning International Co-operation on Competition Investigations and Proceedings' (2014), www.oecd.org/daf/competition/2014-rec-internat-coop-competition.pdf, accessed 17 February 2017.

——, 'Leniency Programmes in Latin America and the Caribbean: Recent Experiences and Lessons Learned' (Latin American and Caribbean Competition Forum 2016), https://one.oecd.org/document/DAF/COMP/LACF(2016)5/en/pdf, accessed 21 February 2017.

——, 'Algorithms and Collusion' (2017) DAF/COMP(2017)4, https://one.oecd.org/document/DAF/COMP(2017)4/en/pdf, accessed 6 March 2018.

——, 'Convention on the Organisation for Economic Co-operation and Development – OECD', www.oecd.org/general/conventionontheorganisationforeconomicco-operationanddevelopment.htm, accessed 25 February 2017.

——, 'History of the OECD', www.oecd.org/general/historyoftheoecd.htm, accessed 25 February 2017.

——, 'Improving International Co-operation in Cartel Investigations', www.fne.gob.cl/wp-content/uploads/2014/03/OECD_-2012-Improving-international-cooperation-in-cartel-investigations1.pdf, accessed 26 January 2017.

OECD and IADB, 'Competition in Latin America and the Caribbean 10 Years of the OECD-IDB Latin American Competition Forum' (2012), www.oecd.org/competition/latinamerica/LACF10thAnniversaryBrochureEN.pdf, accessed 19 February 2017.

OECD and ICN, 'Secretariat Report on the OECD/ICN Survey on International Enforcement Co-Operation' (2013) International Enforcement Co-operation, www.oecd.org/daf/competition/InternEnforcementCooperation2013.pdf, accessed 25 February 2017.

OECD Committee on Fiscal Affairs, 'Manual on the Implementation of Exchange of Information Provisions for Tax Purposes: Module on General and Legal Aspects of Exchange of Information' (23 January 2006), www.oecd.org/tax/exchange-of-tax-information/36647823.pdf, accessed 25 May 2017.

OECD Council, 'Recommendation of the Council Concerning Effective Action against Hard Core Cartels', https://legalinstruments.oecd.org/en/instruments/OECD-LEGAL-0452, accessed 15 August 2019.

OECD Directorate for Financial and Enterprise Affairs, 'Small and Developing Competition Agencies – UMANA – IDB – December 20 …' (16:03:24 UTC), www.slideshare.net/OECD-DAF/small-and-developing-competition-agencies-umana-idb-december-2017-oecd-discussion, accessed 28 May 2018.

'OECD Global Forum on Competition, "Challenges Faced by Young Competition Authorities"', www.oecd.org/daf/competition/GFC2009-Challenges-faced-by-young-competition-authorities.pdf, accessed 23 May 2018.

OECD Secretariat, 'Consumer Protection Enforcement in a Global Digital Marketplace' (2018) OECD Digital Economy Papers 266, www.oecd-ilibrary.org/science-and-technology/consumer-protection-enforcement-in-a-global-digital-marketplace_f041eead-en, accessed 19 October 2018.

——, 'Toolkit for Protecting Digital Consumers. A Resource for G20 Policy Makers' (2018), www.oecd.org/sti/consumer/toolkit-for-protecting-digital-consumers.pdf, accessed 8 October 2018.

Oesterle DA, 'United Nations Conference on Restrictive Business Practices' (1981) 14 *Cornell International Law Journal* 1.

Office of the United States Trade Representative, '2017 Trade Policy Agenda and 2016 Annual Report', /about-us/policy-offices/press-office/reports-and-publications/2017/2017-trade-policy-agenda-and-2016, accessed 26 February 2018.

Official Archive of the United Nations, 'Report of the 1st Session of the Preparatatory Committee of the UN Conference on Trade and Employment) 15 Oct to 26 Nov 1946' (United Nations Secretariat, 1946) E/PC/T/33.

——, 'Verbatim Report of the Second Meeting of Committee III' (1946) E/PC/T/C.III/PV/2, www.wto.org/gatt_docs/English/SULPDF/90220057.pdf, accessed 25 February 2017.

——, 'Proceedings of the UNCTAD, Fourth Session, Volume I, Report and Annexes' (United Nations Secretariat 1977) TD/218 (Vol I).

——, 'United Nations General Assembly Resolution 33/153' (1978), www.un.org.

Official Website of Mark Whitacre, PhD, 'Mark Whitacre', www.markwhitacre.com/index2.html, accessed 4 June 2017.

Oficina Económica y Comercial. Consulado General de España en China, 'El Sector de Equipos de Laboratorio En China' (Embajada de España 2002), www.exportapymes.com/documentos/productos/Ie1483_equip_laboratorio_china.pdf, accessed 8 February 2017.

País EE, 'Costa Rica ignora una orden de la Corte Centroamericana de Justicia' (*El País*, 18 January 2012), http://internacional.elpais.com/internacional/2012/01/18/actualidad/1326926845_688633.html, accessed 4 April 2017.

Palacios A, 'A Counterhistory of Anti-Trust in Latin America' in Pedro Rubim Borges Fortes and others (eds), *Law and Policy in Latin America: Transforming Courts, Institutions, and Rights* (Springer, 2017).

Palacios A and Gutierrez JD, 'Histories of Competition Law in Latin America' in Julián Peña and Marcelo Calliari (eds), *Competition Law in Latin America. A Practical Guide* (Wolters Kluwer 2016).

Panama & El Salvador, 'Agreement between ACODECO of Panama and Superintendence of Competition of El Salvador in the Application of Competition Laws' (17 September 2007), www.acodeco.gob.pa/acodeco/uploads/pdf/legislacion_normativas/AcuerdoElSalvador_17Sep2007.07 27_2016_10_18_31_a.m.pdf.

Panama & Honduras, 'Agreement between ACODECO and the Comision Para La Defensa y Promoción de La Competencia of Honduras' (14 May 2009), www.acodeco.gob.pa/acodeco/uploads/pdf/legislacion_normativas/AcuerdoHonduras_14Mayo2009.07_27_2016_10_22_04_a.m.pdf.

Panama & Taiwan Governments, 'Panama – Taiwan Free Trade Agreement' (21 August 2003), www.sice.oas.org/Trade/PanRC/PANRC_e.ASP, accessed 18 May 2017.

Paul JR, 'Comity in International Law' (1991) 32 *Harvard International Law Journal* 1.

Paulo Burnier Da Silveira Ed., *Competition Law and Policy in Latin America. Recent Developments* (Kluwer Law International, 2017).

PCL PP, 'Thailand & Neighbors Join Together on Rice' (http://www.bangkokpost.com), www.bangkokpost.com/learning/advanced/309007/thailand-neighbors-join-together-on-rice, accessed 7 February 2017.

'PCT FAQs', /pct/en/faqs/faqs.html, accessed 28 March 2017.

Peña J, 'The Role of International Cooperation in the Development of Competition Law in Latin America', *William E. Kovacic. An Antitrust Tribute-Liber Amicorum*, vol II (Institute of Competition Law, 2014).

Peru & Brazilian Governments, 'Cooperation Agreement between INDECOPI of Peru and CADE of Brazil' (29 July 2012), http://en.cade.gov.br/topics/bilateral_cooperation/bilateral-cooperation/technical-cooperation-agreement-between-the-administrative-council-for-economic-defense-cade-and-indecopi-of-peru/acordo-espanhol-peru.pdf/@@download/file/Acordo%20-%20Espanhol%20PERU.pdf.

Peru & Panama Governments, 'Agreement in the Area of Competition and Consumer Protection between INDECOPI of Peru and ACODECO of Panama' (September 2007), www.acodeco.gob.pa/acodeco/uploads/pdf/legislacion_normativas/ConvenioIndecopi_Septiembre2011.09_09_2011_09_47_25_a.m.pdf.

'Perú: Regulator Confirms Tissue Cartel Acting in Peru, Colombia and Chile | Competition Policy International', www.competitionpolicyinternational.com/peru-regulator-confirms-tissue-cartel-acting-in-peru-colombia-and-chile/, accessed 5 February 2017.

Pino M, 'The Marine Hoses Cartel' [2009] Competition Policy Newsletter, https://dialnet.unirioja.es/servlet/articulo?codigo=5488172, accessed 6 February 2017.

'Policing the Digital Cartels' (*Financial Times*, 8 January 2017), www.ft.com/content/9de9fb80-cd23-11e6-864f-20dcb35cede2, accessed 5 February 2017.

Post Publishing PCL, 'Thailand & Neighbors Join Together on Rice', www.bangkokpost.com/learning/advanced/309007/thailand-neighbors-join-together-on-rice, accessed 7 February 2017.

'Preparing for Our Future UK Trade Policy – GOV.UK', www.gov.uk/government/publications/preparing-for-our-future-uk-trade-policy/preparing-for-our-future-uk-trade-policy, accessed 26 February 2018.

'Price Signalling and Global Antitrust Enforcement: Practical Counselling Tips | Insight | Baker McKenzie', www.bakermckenzie.com/en/insight/publications/2017/01/price-signalling-and-global-antitrust-enforcement, accessed 25 October 2018.

Procompetencia, 'Cases followed by Nicaragua Pro-Competencia from 2009 to 2016' (2016), http://procompetencia.gob.ni/wp-content/uploads/2015/02/Casos-Tr%C3%A1mitados-2009-2016.pdf, accessed 21 February 2017.

Ramakrishnan RT and Thakor AV, 'Cooperation versus Competition in Agency' [1991] *Journal of Law, Economics, & Organization* 248.

'Región: Surge Nueva Alianza de Cooperación Para La Competencia | Competition Policy International', www.competitionpolicyinternational.com/region-surge-nueva-alianza-de-cooperacion-para-la-competencia/, accessed 10 April 2017.

'Report of the Discussion Group on International Cooperation' (Intergovernmental Group of Experts on Competition Law and Policy 17th Session 11–13 July 2018 2018) Agenda Item 3e of the IGE 2018, https://unctad.org/meetings/en/SessionalDocuments/ciclp17th_UNCTAD_rep_en.pdf, accessed 14 January 2019.

Reynaud B, 'Forms of Trust and Conditions for Their Stability' (2017) 41 *Cambridge Journal of Economics* 127.

Roa JC, 'Evolución y Perspectivas Del Derecho de La Competencia Andino', www.sela.org/media/2087816/juan-carlos-roa-can.pdf, accessed 27 February 2017.

Rodriguez AE and Coate MB, 'Competition Policy in Transition Economies: The Role of Competition Advocacy' (1997) 23 *Brook J Int'l L* 365, http://heinonline.org/hol-cgi-bin/get_pdf.cgi?handle=hein.journals/bjil23&section=23, accessed 1 March 2017.

Rosenberg B, 'National Implementation of Competition-Related Provisions in Bilateral and Regional Trade Agreements', *Implementing Competition-Related Provisions in Regional Trade Agreements: is it possible to obtain development gains?* (United Nations Publications 2007), http://unctad.org/en/docs/ditcclp20064_en.pdf, accessed 26 February 2017.

'Rulings of the TDLC of Chile', www.tdlc.cl/tdlc/sentencias/, accessed 21 February 2017.

'Russia: Cartel Investigations – Global Investigations Review – GIR', http://globalinvestigationsreview.com/insight/the-european-middle-eastern-and-african-investigations-review-2015/1024330/russia-cartel-investigations, accessed 13 February 2017.

Ryngaert C, *Jurisdiction over Antitrust Violations in International Law* (Intersentia, 2008).

Schoneveld FR, 'Cartel Sanctions and International Competition Policy: Cross-Border Cooperation and Appropriate Forums for Cooperation' (2003) 26 *World Competition* 433.

Scott A, 'The Evolution of Competition Law and Policy in the United Kingdom', https://papers.ssrn.com/sol3/papers.cfm?abstract_id=1344807, accessed 24 February 2017.

Secretariat of Economic Law, Antitrust Division, 'Fighting Cartels: Brazil's Leniency Program' (2009), www.cade.gov.br:8080/cade/acesso-a-informacao/publicacoes-institucionais/documentos-da-antiga-lei/brazil_leniencia_program_brochure.pdf, accessed 13 February 2017.

'Sectoral Study on Competition on the Airline Passenger Transport in Latin America | Competition Policy International', www.competitionpolicyinternational.com/sectoral-study-on-competition-on-the-airline-passenger-transport-in-latin-america/, accessed 21 May 2017.

Segovia A, *Integración Real y Grupos de Poder Económico En América Central: Implicaciones Para El Desarrollo y La Democracia En La Región* (Fundación Friedrich Ebert, 2005).

Setiawan C, 'Competition Law Enforcement' (Workshop on Best Practices on a Regional Cooperation Framework among ASEAN Competition Authorities, Manila, The Philippines, 3 November 2015).

Shaffer G, Nesbitt NH and Waller SW, 'Criminalizing Cartels: A Global Trend?' (Social Science Research Network 2013) SSRN Scholarly Paper ID 2288871, https://papers.ssrn.com/abstract=2288871, accessed 12 February 2017.

Shan H, *Protection of Trade Secrets in China* (Kluwer Law International/Aspen Publishers, 2008).

Shapiro DL, Sheppard BH and Cheraskin L, 'Business on a Handshake' (1992) 8 *Negotiation Journal* 365.

Shearman & Sterling LLP, 'Gas Insulated Switchgear. Cartel Digest | Cartel Detail', www.carteldigest.com/cartel-detail-page.cfm?itemID=8, accessed 24 May 2017.

Shepard G and Keyte J, 'Auto Parts and Antitrust: A Cautionary Tale' *New York Law Journal* (7 November 2014), www.skadden.com/sites/default/files/publications/07011141 2Skadden.pdf, accessed 10 February 2017.

'Shipping Line Cartel Exposed in Chile Says FNE' (*Automotive Logistics*, 3 February 2015), http://automotivelogistics.media/news/shipping-line-cartel-exposed-in-chile-says-fne, accessed 21 February 2017.

Shubik M, 'A Game Theorist Looks at the Antitrust Laws and the Automobile Industry' (1956) 8 *Stanford Law Review* 594.

——, 'Game Theory, Law, and the Concept of Competition Fourth Annual Corporate Symposium' (1991) 60 University of Cincinnati Law Review 285.

Slapper G and Kelly D, *English Legal System*, 4th edn (Cavendish, 1999).

Slaughter A-M, 'The Real New World Order' (1997) 76 *Foreign Affairs* 183.

Slaughter A-M and Hale T, 'Transgovernmental Networks' in Mark Bevir (ed), *The SAGE Handbook of Governance* (SAGE, 2010).

Slaughter and May, 'EU Competition & Regulatory. Legal and Policy Developments at the EU Level', www.slaughterandmay.com/media/2534641/eu-competition-and-regulatory-newsletter-16-oct-22-oct-2015.pdf, accessed 10 April 2017.

Snell SL, 'Controlling Restrictive Business Practices in Global Markets: Reflections on the Concepts of Sovereignty, Fairness, and Comity' (1997) 33 *Stan J Int'l L* 215.

Sofia Competition Forum, 'Comparative Overview of the Balkan Competition Regimes in the Field of INSPECTIONS ON SPOT' (Sofia Competition Forum 2015), http://scf.cpc.bg/uploads/data/2015/report%20SCF%20inspections.pdf, accessed 5 April 2017.

Sokol DD, 'What Do We Really Know About Export Cartels and What Is the Appropriate Solution?' (2008) 4 *Journal of Competition Law and Economics* 967.

Spagnolo G, *Self-Defeating Antitrust Laws: How Leniency Programs Solve Bertrand's Paradox and Enforce Collusion in Auctions* (Fondazione Eni Enrico Mattei, 2000).

Sprigman C, 'Fix Prices Globally, Get Sued Locally? U.S. Jurisdiction over International Cartels' (2005) 72 *The University of Chicago Law Review* 265.

Stephan PB, 'Against International Cooperation' in Michael S Greve and Richard Allen Epstein (eds), *Competition laws in conflict: antitrust jurisdiction in the global economy* (AEI Press, 2004).

Stephan PB and Roin JA, *International Business and Economics: Law and Policy* (LexisNexis, 2010).

Stucke ME, 'Discovery in a Global Economy' in Jürgen Basedow, Stéphanie Francq and Laurence Idot (eds), *International antitrust litigation: conflict of laws and coordination* (Hart, 2012).

Stucke ME and Ezrachi A, 'How Pricing Bots Could Form Cartels and Make Things More Expensive' (*Harvard Business Review*, 27 October 2016), https://hbr.org/2016/10/how-pricing-bots-could-form-cartels-and-make-things-more-expensive, accessed 6 March 2018.

Sutherland PF, 'The use of the letter of request (or letter rogatory) for the purpose of obtaining evidence for proceedings in England and abroad' (1982) 31 *International and Comparative Law Quarterly* 784.

Sweeney B, 'Export Cartels: Is There a Need for Global Rules?' (2007) 10 *Journal of International Economic Law* 87.

Sweeney BJ, *The Internationalisation of Competition Rules* (Routledge, 2009).

Synced, 'Jürgen Schmidhuber: True Artificial Intelligence Will Change Everything' (*Medium*, 10 July 2017), https://medium.com/syncedreview/j%C3%BCrgen-schmidhuber-true-artificial-intelligence-will-change-everything-dc6b36bb6146, accessed 11 October 2018.

Tassano HT, 'La Declaración de Lima: Una acción concreta para el fortalecimiento de la cooperación entre agencias en la fiscalización de actividades anticompetitivas transfronterizas' (2014) 2 *Revista de Defesa da Concorrência* 4.

Taylor MD, *International Competition Law: A New Dimension for the WTO?* (Cambridge University Press, 2006).

Terhechte JP, *International Competition Enforcement Law Between Cooperation and Convergence* (Springer Science & Business Media, 2011).

——, 'International Competition Enforcement Law Between Cooperation and Convergence – Mapping a New Field for Global Administrative Law' Working Paper CCLP (L) 26 The University of Oxford Centre for Competition Law and Policy, www.law.ox.ac.uk/sites/files/oxlaw/cclp_l._26.pdf, accessed 15 March 2017.

'Thailand Abandons Plan for Southeast Asian Rice Cartel' (CBC News), www.cbc.ca/news/world/thailand-abandons-plan-for-southeast-asian-rice-cartel-1.718617, accessed 5 June 2017.

'The Curious Case of the Cement Cartel' (*India Corporate Law*, 14 November 2016), http://corporate.cyrilamarchandblogs.com/2016/11/curious-case-cement-cartel/, accessed 7 February 2017.

'The Global Citric Acid Conspiracy: Legal-Economic Lessons' (PDF Download Available) ResearchGate, www.researchgate.net/publication/227645450_The_global_citric_acid_conspiracy_Legal-economic_lessons, accessed 9 February 2017.

'The International Cartel Movement' (*CQ Researcher by CQ Press*), http://library.cqpress.com/cqresearcher/cqresrre1928060400, accessed 8 February 2017.

'The Marine Hose Cartel: A New Era In International Co-Operation – Criminal Law – UK', www.mondaq.com/x/57462/Corporate+Crime/The+Marine+Hose+Cartel+A+New+Era+In+International+CoOperation, accessed 10 February 2017.

'The United States Officially Withdraws from the Trans-Pacific Partnership', /about-us/policy-offices/press-office/press-releases/2017/january/US-Withdraws-From-TPP, accessed 26 February 2018.

Thiel P, 'Competition Is for Losers' *Wall Street Journal* (12 September 2014), www.wsj.com/articles/peter-thiel-competition-is-for-losers-1410535536, accessed 5 March 2018.

Thomas C and De Stefano G, 'Extradition & Antitrust: Cautionary Tales for Global Cartel Compliance' (Mlex Ab Extra, 2016), www.hoganlovells.com/~/media/hogan-lovells/pdf/publication/hogan_lovells_ab_extra_30_09_16.ashx, accessed 28 March 2017.

Tierno Centella ML, 'EU Cartel Enforcement in the International Context' (16 June 2016), http://ec.europa.eu/competition/speeches/text/sp2016_07_en.pdf, accessed 4 June 2017.

Timberg S, 'Restrictive Business Practices as an Appropriate Subject for United Nations Action' (1955) 1 Antitrust Bulletin 409.

Tomescu IR, 'The Joint Investigation Teams – A European Instrument of Fight against Terrorism' [2014] Annals of the „Constantin Brâncuşi" University of Târgu Jiu, Letter and Social Science Series, https://papers.ssrn.com/sol3/papers.cfm?abstract_id=2802441, accessed 4 April 2017.

Tourk KA, 'Opec Cartel: A Revival of the Dominant-Firm Theory' 2:2 J. Energy Dev.; (United States), www.osti.gov/scitech/biblio/7209487, accessed 6 February 2017.

Tyhurst JS, 'The Adjudication of Competition Law Issues in Theory and Practice : An Assessment of the Reviewable Matters Jurisdiction of the Restrictive Trade Practices Commission', http://digitool.library.mcgill.ca/R/?func=dbin-jump-full&object_id=64728&local_base=GEN01-MCG02, accessed 28 February 2017.

UN Office on Drugs and Crime, 'United Nations Convention Against Corruption' (2004), www.unodc.org/documents/brussels/UN_Convention_Against_Corruption.pdf, accessed 4 June 2017.

UNCTAD, 'The Use of Leniency Programmes as a Tool for the Enforcement of Competition Law against Hardcore Cartels in Developing Countries' (2010) TD/RBP/CONF.7/4, http://unctad.org/en/Docs/tdrbpconf7d4_en.pdf, accessed 17 February 2017.

——, 'Appropriate Sanctions and Remedies' (2010) TD/RBP/CONF.7/5, http://unctad.org/en/Docs/tdrbpconf7d5_en.pdf, accessed 21 February 2017.
——, 'Model Law on Competition (2010) – Chapter IX' (2010) TD/RBP/CONF.7/L.9, http://unctad.org/en/Docs/ciclpL2_en.pdf, accessed 15 March 2017.
——, 'Report of the Sixth United Nations Conference to Review All Aspects of the Set of Multilaterally Agreed Equitable Principles and Rules for the Control of Restrictive Business Practices' (2011) TD/RBP/CONF.7/11, http://unctad.org/en/Docs/tdrbpconf7d11_en.pdf, accessed 17 February 2017.
——, 'Cross-Border Anticompetitive Practices: The Challenges for Developing Countries and Economies in Transition' (2012) TD/B/C.I/CLP/16.
——, 'International Bid-Rigging Workshop: Liquid Oxygen Cases in Latin America' (12 March 2013), http://unctad.org/en/pages/MeetingDetails.aspx?meetingid=272, accessed 27 February 2017.
——, 'Modalities and Procedures for International Cooperation in Competition Cases Involving More than One Country' (2013) TD/B/C.I/CLP/21.
——, 'The Impact of Cartels on the Poor' (2013) TD/B/C.I/CLP/24/Rev.1, http://unctad.org/meetings/en/SessionalDocuments/ciclpd24rev1_en.pdf, accessed 25 February 2017.
——, 'Informal Cooperation among Competition Agencies in Specific Cases' (2014) TD/B/C.I/CLP/29.
——, 'Model Law on Competition (2015) – Revised Chapter I' (2015) TD/RBP/CONF.8/L.1, http://unctad.org/meetings/en/SessionalDocuments/tdrbpconf8l1_en.pdf, accessed 15 March 2017.
——, 'Report of the Intergovernmental Group of Experts on Competition Law and Policy on Its Fifteenth Session' (2016) TD/B/C.I/CLP/40, http://unctad.org/meetings/en/SessionalDocuments/ciclpd40_en.pdf, accessed 17 February 2017.
——, 'List of Participants of the Intergovernmental Group of Experts on Competition Law and Policy Fifteenth Session Geneva, 19–21 October 2016' (2016) TD/B/C.I/CLP/INF.6, http://unctad.org/meetings/en/SessionalDocuments/ciclpinf6_en.pdf, accessed 17 February 2017.
——, 'Enhancing International Cooperation in the Investigation of Cross-Border Competition Cases: Tools and Procedures' (2017) TD/B/C.I/CLP/44, http://unctad.org/meetings/en/SessionalDocuments/ciclpd44_en.pdf, accessed 16 May 2017.
——, 'Report of the Intergovernmental Group of Experts on Competition Law and Policy on Its Sixteenth Session' (2017) TD/B/C.I/CLP/47, http://unctad.org/meetings/en/SessionalDocuments/ciclpd47_en.pdf, accessed 3 March 2018.
——, 'Contribution from Costa Rica – Compilation of the contributions submitted for the conference' (Sixth UN Conference to review the UN Set on Competition Policy Geneva, 8 – 12 November 2010), http://unctad.org/en/Docs/tdrbpconf7contributions_en.pdf, accessed 17 February 2017.
——, 'Unctad.Org | History', http://unctad.org/en/Pages/About%20UNCTAD/A-Brief-History-of-UNCTAD.aspx, accessed 25 February 2017.
UNCTAD Drafting Committee, 'Guiding Policies and Procedures under Section F of the UN Set on Competition' (13 June 2019), https://unctad.org/meetings/en/SessionalDocuments/ccpb_comp1_%20Guiding_Policies_Procedures.pdf, accessed 29 July 2019.
UNCTAD Secretariat, 'Report of the Intergovernmental Group of Experts on Competition Law and Policy on Its Seventeenth Session' (2018) TD/B/C.I/CLP/52, https://unctad.org/meetings/en/SessionalDocuments/ciclpd52_en.pdf, accessed 15 January 2019.
——, 'Report of the Meeting of the UNCTAD Ad Hoc Expert Meeting on Competition International Cooperation' (8 April 2019), https://unctad.org/meetings/en/SessionalDocuments/Report%20of%20the%20UNCTAD%20Ad%20hoc%20Expert%20meeting%20on%20Competition%20%2010%20May%202019.pdf, accessed 15 April 2019.
——, 'Unctad.Org | Ad Hoc Expert Group Meeting on Competition Law and Policy' (8 April 2019), https://unctad.org/en/pages/MeetingDetails.aspx?meetingid=2075, accessed 29 July 2019.
US & Autralian Governments, 'Agreement between the Government of the United States of America and the Government of Australia on mutual antitrust enforcement assistance' (27 April 1999), www.justice.gov/sites/default/files/atr/legacy/2015/01/15/311076.pdf, accessed 11 April 2017.
US & Brazilian Governments, 'Agreement between US and Brazil Regarding Cooperation between Their Competition Authorities in the Enforcement of Their Competition Laws' (26 October 1999), www.justice.gov/sites/default/files/atr/legacy/2006/08/10/3776.pdf, accessed 22 February 2017.

US & Chinese Governments, 'MoU on Antitrust and Antimonopoly Cooperation between US Department of Justice/US Federal Trade Commission; and the People's Republic of China National Development and Reform Commission (NDRC), Ministry of Commerce (MOFCOM), and the State Administration for Industry and Commerce (SAIC)' (27 July 2011), www.justice.gov/sites/default/files/atr/legacy/2011/08/03/273310a.pdf, accessed 18 February 2017.

US & EU Governments, 'Agreement between US and EU on the Application of Their Competition Laws' (23 September 1991), www.jstor.org/stable/20693634, accessed 22 February 2017.

——, 'Agreement between US and EU on the Application of Positive Comity Principles in the Enforcement of Their Competition Laws' (4 June 1998), www.jstor.org/stable/20698829, accessed 22 February 2017.

US & Mexican Governments, 'Agreement between US and Mexico Regarding the Application of Their Competition Laws' (11 July 2000), www.justice.gov/sites/default/files/atr/legacy/2006/04/27/5145.pdf, accessed 22 February 2017.

US Department of Justice, 'Auto Parts Investigation 2015 | ATR | Department of Justice', www.justice.gov/atr/division-update/2015/auto-parts-investigation-2015, accessed 10 February 2017.

US Department of Justice and Federal Trade Commission, 'Antitrust Guidelines for International Enforcement and Cooperation', www.justice.gov/atr/guidelines-and-policy-statements-0/antitrust-guidelines-international-enforcement-and-cooperation-2017, accessed 14 January 2017.

'[USC07] 15 USC Ch. 88: International antitrust enforcement assistance', http://uscode.house.gov/view.xhtml?req=granuleid%3AUSC-prelim-title15-chapter88&edition=prelim, accessed 28 March 2017.

Verdier P-H, 'Transnational Regulatory Networks and Their Limits' (2009) 34 *Yale Journal of International Law* 113.

Victor AP, 'Export Cartels: An Idea Whose Time Has Passed' (1991) 60 *Antitrust Law Journal* 571.

Vilakazi T, 'Regional Cartels and a Review of Developments in the Cement Industry', www.competition.org.za/s/Thando-Vilakazi_Regional-cartels-and-a-review-of-developments-in-the-regional-cement-industry.pdf, accessed 6 February 2017.

Voice E, 'EU Fines Banks €1.7bn for Libor Cartel' (*POLITICO*, 4 December 2013), www.politico.eu/article/eu-fines-banks-e1-7bn-for-libor-cartel/, accessed 12 February 2017.

von Mehren AT, 'Special Substantive Rules for Multistate Problems: Their Role and Significance in Contemporary Choice of Law Methodology' (1974) 88 *Harvard Law Review* 347.

Watt HM, 'Integration and Diversity: The Conflict of Laws as a Regulatory Tool', http://cadmus.eui.eu//handle/1814/6657, accessed 11 April 2017.

Whish R and Bailey D, *Competition Law* (Oxford University Press, 2015).

Williams M, 'Third World Cooperation: The Group of 77 in UNCTAD' (Burns & Oates, 1991).

Williams SA, 'The Double Criminality Rule and Extradition: A Comparative Analysis' (1991) 15 *Nova L Rev* 581.

Wils WPJ, 'Is Criminalization of EU Competition Law the Answer?' (Social Science Research Network 2005) SSRN Scholarly Paper ID 684921, https://papers.ssrn.com/abstract=684921, accessed 19 March 2017.

Winston & Strawn LLP, 'U.S., China Sign Memorandum of Understanding on Antitrust Cooperation | Lexology', www.lexology.com/library/detail.aspx?g=c227b49b-ea66-4ce2-8f74-e18ce1151d6b, accessed 25 February 2017.

Woodward R, 'The Organisation for Economic Cooperation and Development' (2004) 9 *New Political Economy* 113.

WTO, 'Provisions on Hardcore Cartels' (2002) Working Group on the Interaction between Trade and Competition Policy WT/WGTCP/W/191, http://docsonline.wto.org/imrd/directdoc.asp?DDFDocuments/t/WT/WGTCP/W191.doc, accessed 10 April 2017.

WTO official database, 'WTO | Regional Trade Agreements' (December 2016), http://rtais.wto.org/UI/PublicAllRTAList.aspx, accessed 25 February 2017.

Yang T-M and Maxwell TA, 'Information-Sharing in Public Organizations: A Literature Review of Interpersonal, Intra-Organizational and Inter-Organizational Success Factors' (2011) 28 *Government Information Quarterly* 164.

Yeh BT, 'Protection of Trade Secrets: Overview of Current Law and Legislation' (Congressional Research Service Informing the legislative debate since 1914 2016) CRS Report prepared for Members and Committees of Congress, https://fas.org/sgp/crs/secrecy/R43714.pdf, accessed 28 March 2017.
Young Council Latin American Regional Forum, 'Leniency: The Future for Cartel Enforcement in Latin America' (International Bar Association, 2016).
Yu Y, 'The Impact of Private International Cartels on Developing Countries' (2003), https://pdfs.semanticscholar.org/6d71/34ef780b0574706a66437eba056fbb94a938.pdf, accessed 8 February 2017.
Zander M, 'The Act of State Doctrine' (1959) 53 *The American Journal of International Law* 826.
Zanettin B, *Cooperation Between Antitrust Agencies at the International Level* (Hart, 2002).
Zimmerman JE and Connor JM, 'Determinants of Cartel Duration: A Cross-Sectional Study of Modern Private International Cartels', SSRN Scholarly Paper, ID 1158577 (2005).

Cases

16–1220 Animal Science Products, Inc v Hebei Welcome Pharmaceutical Co (06/14/2018) 15.
Ahlstrom v Commission 5233 (ECR).
Andean Community – Dismiss a Regional Cartel investigation in the markets of Nappies, Books and Toilet Paper for having prescripted the action [2016].
Andean Community – Opening of a Cartel Investigation in the Tissue Paper market against Kimberly Clark [2016].
Andean Community – Opening of an investigation – Abuse of Dominant case in the Andean region [2016].
Andean Community – Palm Oil Cartel [2008] Tribunal de Justicia de la Comunidad Andina 01-AN-2006,02-AN-2006 y 01-AN-2007(Acumulados).
Argentina Oxigeno Liquido [2005] Com Nac Def Competencia.
Brazil – Industrial and Hospital gases [2010] Administrative Council for Economic Defense Case No. 08012.009888/2003-70.
Brazil – Refrigeration Compressor Cartel (2016) Administrative Proceeding 08012.000820/2009-11 (Administrative Council for Economic Defense).
Chile Oxigeno Liquido [2006] Tribunal de Defensa de la Libre Competencia Sentencia No. 43/2006.
Chile Shipping Cartel (Fiscalia Nacional Economica (FNE)).
Colombia Auto parts Cartel – Opening the investigation [2013] Superintendencia de Industria y Comercio Resolution No. 6398.
Colombia Autoparts cartel – Closing the investigation [2015] Superintendencia de Industria y Comercio Resolution No. 37523.
Colombia Nappy Cartel [2016] Superintendencia de Industria y Comercio (SIC) Resolution No. 43218.
Colombia Oxigeno Liquido [2010] Superintendencia de Industria y Comercio Resolution No. 65477.
Colombia Sugar Import Cartel [2015] Superintendencia de Industria y Comercio (SIC) Resolution No. 103652.
EU Case Bearing Automative Cartel [2014].
EU Case COMP/36545/F3 – Amino Acids 2001/418/EC EUR-Lex-32001D0418-EN-EUR-Lex.
EU Case COMP/F/38899 Gas Insultated Switchgear [2007].
EU Case Gencor v Commission (Court of First Instance).
GlaxoSmithKline Services v Commission 2969 (ECR II).
Hartford Fire Ins Co v California 509 US 764 (1993) (US Court of Appeals for the Ninth Circuit).
Mexico Oxigeno Líquido [2011] Comisión Federal de Competencia DE-022-2006.
Panama Oxigeno Medico (Juzgado Noveno de Circuito de la Provincia de Panamá).
Panama Oxigeno Medico (Tercer Tribunal Superior de Justicia del Primer Distrito Judicial de Panamá).
Peru Oxigeno Liquido [2010] INDECOPI 051-2010/CLC-INDECOPI.
UK Nokia Corporation v Au Optronics Corporation & Others [2012] Engligh High Court of Justice Case No. HC09C04421.

US Societe Nationale Industrielle Aerospatiale And Societe De Construction D'avions De Tourisme, Petitioners v United States District Court For The Southern District Of Iowa, Etc (United States District Court For The Southern District Of Iowa).
US Vitamin C Export Cartel [2011] US District Court New York Case 1:06-md-01738-BMC-JO Document 440.

National Legislation

Biblioteca del Congreso Nacional, Chile – Transparencia de la Funcion Publica y de Accesso a la Informacion de la Administracion del Estado 2008 [Law 20.285].
Acuerdo de Defensa de la Competencia del MERCOSUR.
Argentina Competition Act 1923.
CAN Provision on Competition 1991 (Año VIII) 14.
CAN Regional Competition Law 2005 (Año XXII) 1.
Canadian Competition Act 1985.
Chile New Competition Act 1973.
Chile- Tribunal de Defensa de la Libre Competencia – Auto Acordado sobre Reservan o Confidencialidad de la Informacion en los Procesos 2012.
Chilean Competition Act 1959.
Colombia Código de Procedimiento Administrativo y de lo Contencioso Administrativo. 2011.
Colombia Competition Act 1959.
Costa Rica _ Ley 7472 1995.pdf.
Council Regulation (EC) No 1/2003 of 16 December 2002 on the implementation of the rules on competition laid down in Articles 81 and 82 of the Treaty 2003.
Paraguay – Appointment of the Investigation Director of the Competition Authority by the President of the Republic 2016.
Patent Cooperation Treaty 1970 52.
Peru Amendment of some Competition Act provisions 2015.
Peru Competition Act 2008.
Peru Ley de Transparencia y Accesso a la Informacion Publica 2002.
Peru Lineamiento sobre Confidencialidad de la Comision de Defensa de la Libre Competencia 2013.
Rules and Regulations to Implement the Provisions of Republic Act No. 10667 (Philippine Competition Act).
The United Nations Set of Principles and Rules on Competition.
Treaty of Asuncion establishing the Common Market between Argentina, Brazil, Paraguay and Uruguay 1991.
US Sherman Antitrust Act 1890.

INDEX

abbreviations used in the index
AISUP (ICN Advocacy & Implementation Network Support Program)
BIAC (Business and Industry Advisory Committee)
BRICS (association comprising Brazil, Russia, India, China and South Africa)
CADE (Brazilian Competition Authority)
CAN (Andean Community of Nations)
CAPs (crossborder anti-competitive practices)
CARICOM (Caribbean Community)
CBC (cross-border cartel)
CBT (deterrence-based/calculus-based trust)
CIS (Commonwealth of Independent States)
COMESA (Common Market for Eastern and Southern Africa)
COMIECO (Council of Ministers of Economy of Central America)
Discussion Group (UNCTAD, Discussion Group on International Cooperation) (UN Set, Section F)
ECN (European Competition Network)
ECOSOC (Economic and Social Council)
FTAIA (Foreign Trade Antitrust Improvements Act)
GPPSF (Guiding Policies and Procedures under Section F of the UN Set on Competition)
IAEAA (International Antitrust Enforcement Assistance Act 1994)
IBT (identification-based trust)
ICN Framework (ICN Framework for Promotion of Sharing Non-Confidential Information for Cartel Enforcement)
ICN (International Competition Network)
ICN Manual (ICN 'Anti-Cartel Enforcement Manual')
IGE (UNCTAD Intergovernmental Group of Experts on Competition Policy)
IOSCO (International Organization of Securities Commissions)
JFTC (Japan Fair Trade Commission)
KBT (knowledge-based trust)
MERCOSUR (Mercado Comun del Sur)
MLATS (mutual legal assistance treaties)
MOFCOM (Ministry of Commerce of the People's Republic of China)
NAFTA (North American Free Trade Agreement)
NCN (Nordic Cartel Network)
OPEC (Organisation of Petroleum Exporting Countries)
PCT (Patent Convention Treaty (1970))
RECAC (Central American regional network)
RTA (regional trade agreement)
SACU (Southern African Customs Union)
SADC (Southern African Development Community)
Section F (UN Set, Section F (international cooperation))
SIC (Colombian Competition Authority)
UN Set (UN Set of Multilaterally Agreed Equitable Principles and Rules for the Control of Restrictive Business Practices/UN Set of Principles and Rules on Competition)
UNCRBP (UN Conference on Restrictive Business Practices)
UNCTAD (UN Conference on Trade and Development)
UNCTAE (UN Conference on Trade and Employment)
WAEMU (West Africa Economic and Monetary Union)
WIPO (World Intellectual Property Organisation)
WTO (World Trade Organisation)
YSA (young and/or small competition authority), 195
adjudication techniques
diversity, 113–14
impact on exchange of information, 114
air cargo cartel, 46, 55, 89, 158
algorithms, pros and cons, 25–9